M000111216

EXCELLENCE IN PRACTICE Series
Katharine G. Butler, Editor

Hispanic Children and Adults with Communication Disorders

Assessment and Intervention

EXCELLENCE IN PRACTICE Series
Katharine G. Butler, Editor

Conversational Management with Language-Impaired Children
Bonnie Brinton and Martin Fujiki

Successful Interactive Skills for Speech-Language
Pathologists and Audiologists
Dorothy Molyneaux and Vera W. Lane

Communicating for Learning: Classroom Observation
and Collaboration
Elaine R. Silliman and Louise Cherry Wilkinson

EXCELLENCE IN PRACTICE Series
Katharine G. Butler, Editor

Hispanic Children and Adults with Communication Disorders

Assessment and Intervention

Henriette W. Langdon, EdD, CCC–SP
Bilingual Speech and Language Specialist
Private Practice
Cupertino, California

with

Li–Rong Lilly Cheng, PhD
Assistant Dean of Student Affairs
College of Health and Human Services
Assistant Professor
Department of Communicative Disorders
San Diego State University
San Diego, California

AN ASPEN PUBLICATION®
Aspen Publishers, Inc.
Gaithersburg, Maryland
1992

Library of Congress Cataloging-in-Publication Data

Langdon, Henriette W.
Hispanic children and adults with communication disorders "
assessment and intervention / Henriette W. Langdon with Li-Rong
Lilly Cheng.
p.   cm. — (Excellence in practice series)
Includes bibliographical references and index.
ISBN: 0-8342-0288-3

1. Speech therapy. 2. Hispanic Americans—Diseases. 3. Hispanic
Americans—Communication. 4. Communicative disorders. I. Cheng.
Li-Rong Lilly. II. Title. III. Series
RC429.L36   1992
616.85'5'008968073—dc20
91-42491
CIP

Copyright © 1992 by Aspen Publishers, Inc.
All rights reserved.

Aspen Publishers, Inc., grants permission for photocopying for limited personal or
internal use. This consent does not extend to other kinds of copying, such as copying
for general distribution, for advertising or promotional purposes, for creating new
collective works, or for resale. For information, address Aspen Publishers, Inc.,
Permissions Department, 200 Orchard Ridge Drive, Suite 200,
Gaithersburg, Maryland 20878

Editorial Services: Ruth Bloom

Library of Congress Catalog Card Number: 91-42491
ISBN: 0-8342-0288-3

Printed in the United States of America

1   2   3   4   5

Con todo cariño and love
to Carl and Maxine

Table of Contents

Contributors

Gustavo Arámbula, MA
Bilingual Speech and Language
  Pathologist
Meadowbrook Neurologic Care
  Center
Santa Clara, California

Carol Beaumont, MA
Bilingual Speech and Language
  Pathologist
Doctoral Candidate—Bilingual
  Education Program
Stanford University
Stanford, California

Barbara J. Merino, PhD
Associate Professor
School of Education
University of California at Davis
Davis, California

Series Foreword

The *Excellence in Practice* series has a number of concurrent themes that constitute a skein of intertwined interests on the part of speech-language pathologists and other language specialists. One of those themes is a strand that carries our professions forward in our quest to become multiculturally adept. The first book in the series was *Assessing Asian Language Performance* by Li-Rong Lilly Cheng. Published in 1987, it was a seminal work directed toward the monolingual English-speaker whose task is made more difficult when faced with providing services to individuals who may have Limited English Proficiency. Cheng's contribution was the first in-depth attempt to deal with this knotty problem on behalf of those who benefit from speech and language services when appropriately provided. Five years later, Dr. Henriette Langdon has undertaken a similar challenge with a similar focus and has also produced a seminal work. It, too, is the first time in which tremendous amounts of information related to communication disorders among Hispanic bilingual or monolingual individuals has been brought together. While there is much more available to language specialists written in English regarding Spanish as a language and a literature, there is surprisingly little available that ties theory to practice and research to service regarding speech-language disorders and their treatment.

Langdon has provided all who work with the communicatively disabled individual whose primary language is, or was, Spanish, with a much expanded armamentarium for providing speech, language, and hearing assessment and intervention. As she notes, there are 23 million Hispanics in the United States and a distressingly small pool of bilingual Spanish-speaking clinicians. While that pool has been growing slowly, the need remains great for non-Hispanic clinicians to increase their contributions. Services to Hispanic children and adults must rest upon a greater appreciation of the contributions of culture, perhaps a truism in today's world, but one which remains a truth. For those who would bulwark their efforts by finding the answers in child development studies, they may be disconcerted to find that child development researchers have failed to pay sufficient attention to the cultural and environmental conditions in which Hispanic children grow up (Adler, 1991). It is highly doubtful whether studies reported that fail to identify the cultural background or ethnicity of their sample can be applied to all children. A recent review of infant studies in major child development journals reported that almost half of the 102 articles did not include such information, nor did they provide data on socioeconomic status (Adler, 1991). Those engaged in research may be well aware of such deficits but find that such information is difficult to ascertain given the constraints placed upon their access to information. Nevertheless, it is critical that children's social, economic, and cultural backgrounds be taken into account. As readers of research know, poverty as a single factor tends to outweigh all other factors as a predicter of how children develop. *Hispanic Children and Adults with Communication Disorders: Assessment and Intervention* addresses the concerns of Hispanic populations and of the language specialists who attempt to meet their needs. There are indications in the press, in policy statements, and in ethnographic literature that the needs of Hispanic bilingual students are being more carefully addressed (Cummins & Miramontes, 1989; Corchardo, 1990; Rogler, Cortes, & Malgady, 1991; Stevenson, Chen, & Uttal, 1990; Westby, 1990).

While much has been written about the acquisition of English, its phonology, grammar, syntax, semantics and pragmatics, and is thus available to readers dealing with nonminority children and who must simply differentiate a disorder, a delay, or some other aspect of language acquisition, there is much less available to the monolingual clinician working with Hispanic/Latino or others whose first language is not English. The authors and contributors, therefore, have attempted to gather together what is known about the acquisition of syntactic and phonological features in Spanish as well as communicative patterns in Hispanic families. Each provides new insights on the acquisition and development of not only Spanish but English in Spanish speakers. In addition, the authors provide specific recommendations for speech-language clinicians, noting that

> Given the ethnic, cultural, and linguistic diversity of the United States, it is difficult for clinicians to develop an in-depth knowledge of each student's language, cultural history, and social background. . . . Excellence in the delivery of speech, language, and hearing services requires a culturally heterogeneous cadre of professionals who are knowledgeable and understanding of related social, linguistic, cultural, educational and economic factors (p. 192).

The chapters following the recommendations noted above provide a plethora of suggestions for those who would assess the speech and language of bilingual Hispanic students and, concomitantly, provide language intervention. Teaching strategies are not neglected and stem from practice as well as research. All of those who contributed to this volume have had extensive experience in providing services to Hispanic individuals. As professionals, as speakers of both Spanish and English, and as contributors to the literature, the authors provide readers a glimpse of what it might be like if we all had access to their knowledge and skills. They portray for us how educational and clinical services will be modified as the ranks of professionals become more culturally heterogeneous. Until that day arrives, this text will serve as a significant resource.

Katharine G. Butler, PhD
Director, Center for Research
and
Chair, Department of Communication
Sciences and Disorders
Syracuse University
Syracuse, New York

REFERENCES

Adler, T. (1990). Culture, race too often ignored in child studies. *APA Monitor, 22*(9), 14–15.

Cummins, N.L., & Miramontes, O.B. (1989). Perceived and actual linguistics competence: A descriptive study of four low-achieving Hispanic bilingual students. *American Educational Research Journal, 26*(4), 443–472.

Corchado, A. (Dec. 17, 1990). Losing battle. Schools fail Hispanics, whose dropout rates exceed other groups. *The Wall Street Journal, CCXVI*(118), A1, A5.

Rogler, L.H., Cortes, D.E., & Malgady, R.G. (1991). Acculturation and mental health status among Hispanics: Convergence and new directions for research. *American Psychologist, 46*(6), 585–597.

Stevenson, H.W., Chen, C., & Uttal, D.H. (1990). Beliefs and achievement: A study of Black, White, and Hispanic Children. *Child Development, 61*(2), 508–523.

Westby, C. (1990). There's no such thing as culture-free testing. *Tejas, XVI*(1), 4–5.

Preface

There is no question that a common language facilitates communication and contact between speech-language clinicians and their clients. It is even more important, however, that clinicians understand the linguistic/cultural characteristics and needs of the population with which they are working. Furthermore, understanding the nature of communication disorders as they relate to language and learning constitutes a beginning toward solving some of the questions that are increasingly appearing in the daily practice of speech-language clinicians and audiologists. This is the main topic of this book.

Designed primarily to assist non–Spanish-speaking speech-language clinicians work with preschoolers, school-aged children, and adolescents—as well as adults—whose first or dominant language is Spanish, this book focuses on assessment and intervention strategies, as well as on related issues such as communication patterns in Hispanic families and the process of second-language acquisition. In Chapter 1, Beaumont and Langdon provide a theoretical framework for assessment and intervention strategies for language/learning-disabled (LLD) Hispanic students. In Chapter 2, Langdon describes the various Hispanic subgroups and presents statistics on characteristics such as median age, level of education, and number of LLD students. Merino describes trends in Spanish language acquisition and development in Chapter 3, while Langdon describes various sociocultural and communication patterns in Hispanic families in Chapter 4. Second-language acquisition and development are discussed by Langdon and Merino in Chapter 5. The controversy surrounding bilingual education is discussed by Langdon and Cheng in Chapter 6. The discussion of applications begins with Chapter 7, in which Langdon describes the speech-language assessment of the Hispanic student, and continues with Chapters 8 and 9, in which Beaumont delineates intervention strategies, issues, and implementation. Arámbula addresses the

management of the Hispanic adult with acquired neurological disabilities resulting from stroke, head trauma, or degenerative disease in Chapter 10.

We hope that *Hispanic Children and Adults with Communication Disorders:
Assessment and Intervention* will be helpful to practicing speech-language pathologists and audiologists, educators, and other health-related professionals who
come in contact with individuals whose primary or dominant language is Spanish.

Henriette W. Langdon

Acknowledgments

A book of this nature could not be completed without the help of a number of persons. We thank Dr. Nadeen Ruíz for her input of early versions of Chapters 8 and 9, and Dr. Belinda Reyes for her review of Chapter 10. We also appreciate the personal contacts that we have had with several other practicing clinicians and university professors who have provided additional helpful information and input: Dr. Rhoda Agin, Donna Jackson-Maldonado, Dr. Vicki Jax, Ana Hernández-Grein, Dr. Hortencia Kayser, Dr. Janna Lang, and Dr. Carol Westby. Last, but not least, we thank the students in the Department of Communication Disorders of San Diego State University, who took extra time in reviewing some of the chapters and were able to provide us with many constructive suggestions.

This book could not have been written without the leadership, editorial advice, and support of my friend and colleague, Dr. Lilly Cheng. I thank her with all my heart for her continual support, care, and selfless dedication to this project. I also thank Dr. Katharine Butler, who encouraged me all the way along and offered her precious time for comments and editorial advice. I thank my contributors, who endured my constant demands for changes, revisions, and deadlines. My great thanks to Dr. Barbara Merino, Carol Beaumont, and Gustavo Arámbula—without their valuable information this book could not have been completed. Finally, I thank the reviewers whose input was very helpful; the staff at Aspen, in particular Loretta Stock and Ruth Bloom; former Aspen development editor, Nancy Weisgerber; and copyeditor, Gail Martin.

I am very grateful to the children and the families with whom I have worked over the years, because they have helped me learn what I don't know. Dr. Paula Menyuk's teaching has provided me with a lasting inspiration to pursue further knowledge in our emerging field. Many friends and colleagues have heard me talk about writing this book in the last couple of years and have patiently listened to my tales of the progress and frustration that go along with such a task. I want to thank them all, particularly Dr. Pat Sheffer, for always boosting my morale. Finally, two persons have been very patient with me and have felt that they did not have a wife or a mother for a while. Thank you, Carl and Maxine!

Chapter 1

Speech-Language Services for Hispanics with Communication Disorders: A Framework

Carol Beaumont and Henriette W. Langdon

Distinguishing a language difference from a language disorder continues to be a challenge for clinicians who work with any bilingual population. Despite numerous books, articles, workshops, and symposia on nonbiased assessment (Cummins, 1984; Erickson & Omark, 1981; Hamayan & Damico, 1991; Mattes & Omark, 1984), recent reports indicate that limited-English–proficient (LEP) Hispanic and other language minority students continue to be misplaced (Figueroa, Fradd, & Correa, 1989). In some cases, these students have been overrepresented or underrepresented in special education classes. In still other cases, the labeling of these students has shifted, for example, from mildly retarded to language- or learning-disabled (Ortíz & Yates, 1987). Furthermore, assessment and intervention issues pertaining to adults from diverse cultural or linguistic backgrounds with acquired neurological disabilities have been neglected (Wallace & Freeman, 1991).

THEORIES OF LANGUAGE DEVELOPMENT

The process of language development has fascinated theorists and researchers for decades. Cambourne (1987) discussed the paradoxes, which help explain this fascination.

> On the surface, learning to talk the language of the culture into which one has been born is one of the "simplest" achievements known to the human race; it's usually painless, almost unconsciously done, nearly always successful, and seems to "just occur" when the conditions for learning have been established. At a more macroscopic level this simplicity is, of course, illusory. It conceals a complexity of interacting and transacting factors which are excruciatingly complicated and detailed. (p. 33)

1

There are several different views on the major theories of language acquisition. As Lahey (1988) pointed out, "normal developmental sequences provide the best hypotheses about the sequence in which the language-disordered child will learn language" (p. vii). The framework of form, content, and use described by Bloom and Lahey (1978) provides a helpful lens for viewing the shifts in theoretical viewpoints that have occurred over the last 40 years. The dimension of *form* includes phonology, morphology, and syntax; the concept of *content* pertains to the semantic system or the system that helps convey the intent and meaning of words and sentences; and the term *use* involves pragmatics, referring to the function of language in communication and including both verbal and nonverbal expression.

Behavioristic Viewpoint

Behaviorists believe that language is learned primarily by imitation and is shaped by feedback and reinforcement. It gradually develops into the complex chains of behavior that make up adult language through a process of differential reinforcement. From this perspective, language is similar to other human behaviors. There is limited emphasis on the relationship of language to cognition or to other aspects of a child's development or environment. Communication patterns are studied by observing and recording discrete units of language behaviors. This construct is the foundation for most discrete-point language tests. These tests measure discrete items such as vocabulary or use of specific grammatical features. Intervention based on this theoretical viewpoint emphasizes form and is characterized by (1) stimulus-response interactions, (2) the breakdown of language into small component parts, (3) adult selection of form and content, (4) differential reinforcement of responses to shape them toward accuracy and increased complexity, and (5) imitation and extensive practice as primary tools for establishing and strengthening behaviors (Engelmann & Osborn, 1976; Skinner, 1957; Staats, 1969).

Nativist Viewpoint

Like the behaviorists, nativists (also known as innatists) emphasize form and, to some extent, content. In contrast to the behaviorists, however, they argue that language develops because of innate structures present in all neurologically normal individuals; children are said to be "wired" for language. Nativists believe that the environment plays an important role in triggering these innate structures and in providing children with opportunities to discover the particular details of their own language (Chomsky, 1965, 1968; McNeill, 1970). As the theory has evolved, more emphasis has been placed on the interaction of these innate structures with general cognitive and processing abilities (Cromer, 1974). Authorities such as

Nelson (1974) and Halliday (1978) have expanded the theory that the environment triggers the child's innate "language acquisition device," noting that children also learn language through interaction with the world. The intervention focus based on this theory is also on form, however, particularly syntax—the language structures that children use to code their understanding of the world.

Interactionist Viewpoint

The interactionist position developed as a response to research findings that language development overlaps and interacts with other aspects of a child's development. For example, assistance and social interaction with more expert peers and adults may enhance language development. The difference between the child's present and potential language attainment is referred to as the "zone of proximal development" (Vygotsky, 1962), and this zone is considered the basis for cognitive growth. Following these premises, the emphasis of research in language began to shift from form to use—the ways in which children construct meaning and the context in which they acquire language (Cazden, 1987; Wells, 1981). Then, language becomes a tool not only for making sense of the world, but also for communicating meaning to others.

The interactionist viewpoint is the model currently used in describing language learning (Table 1-1). In the assessment process and intervention, more emphasis is placed on language use. Thus, an attempt is made to re-create the conditions that occur naturally in a child's communication environment during intervention. Many opportunities are created for (1) a wide range of language uses, (2) communication with responsive peers and adults, and (3) development of an internal model of the world. Integration of form, content, and use is a primary goal.

The shift in emphasis from form and content to use in theories of language development raises questions about the optimal conditions for language learning. Although there is evidence of universal language mechanisms and processes that facilitate language acquisition (Menyuk, 1988), there is now a growing awareness of individual and cultural differences (Heath, 1983, 1986a, 1986b). In their review of research on cross-cultural differences in language acquisition, Bates, Bretherton, and Snyder (1988) concluded that a variety of environments and interaction patterns foster language development. The availability of input and the responsiveness of caregivers, peers, teachers, and other adults to the child's attempt to interact communicatively appear to be consistent across a variety of contexts. Cambourne (1987) described eight conditions that are universally present as children acquire language.

1. *immersion.* Children are surrounded by meaningful language from the moment that they are born.

Table 1-1 Overview of Language Development Theories

Theory	Basic Beliefs	Primary Theorists/ Researchers (Partial List)	Assessment/ Intervention Focus
Behaviorist	Children learn language by imitation. Language is shaped by feedback and reinforcement. Complex language develops through differential reinforcement. Verbal behavior is like any other behavior (e.g., discussion of relationship to cognition is unnecessary). There is not an innate human ability for language.	Skinner (1957) Staats (1969) Engelmann & Osborn (1976)	Language broken down into components Adult selection of form and function Imitation primary way of eliciting language Responses differentially reinforced
Nativist	Children have innate knowledge of language structure. Innate component includes cognitive abilities adapted for processing language.	Chomsky (1965, 1968) McNeill (1970)	Development of syntactical structures Patterned sentences used as models
Interactionist	Children learn language as a result of an interactive process in a responsive environment. Language is a tool for making sense of the world. Children acquire language "incidentally" while in process of communicating.	Wells (1981) Cazden (1987)	Creation of communicative environment Development of language as a tool for organizing the world Child's interests and purposes focus of intervention All structures necessary elicited by purposeful communication

2. *expectation*. Adult members of the community naturally expect that children will learn to talk.
3. *demonstration*. Competent speakers of the language demonstrate effective language use constantly in natural daily interactions.
4. *engagement*. Children are involved in purposeful, meaningful communication daily.
5. *practice*. In a community of speakers, children are given constant practice in communicating.
6. *approximation*. Children's approximations of adult language are accepted, welcomed, and praised as normal steps on the way to well developed communicative competence.
7. *response*. There is mutual exchange between experts and novices so that children's attempts at constructing meaning are always received.
8. *responsibility*. Children are given more and more responsibility for communicating as they mature.

A result of this shifting perspective is the emphasis on communicative competence as an inclusive measure of language ability. Communicative competence can be defined as the ability to participate in social, cognitive, cultural, and linguistic interactions (Gumperz, 1981; Hymes, 1974).

As von Tetzchner, Siegel, and Smith (1989) pointed out, a theory of language development is useful only if it accounts for atypical development as well. They suggested that, within an interactionist model, atypical development should not be defined as a function of an inborn inability to respond appropriately. Rather, it should be considered a function of some continuous malfunction in the organism-environment transaction that prevents children from organizing and adapting to their world. The transaction of many complex factors accounts for effective or ineffective language (Cambourne, 1987; von Tetzchner et al., 1989).

Therefore, it is very important that the clinician assessing and working with a student from a different linguistic and cultural background be familiar with the "linguistic and social conventions of the particular language and culture in which the communication occurs" (Cheng, 1987, p. 51). Once a language-learning problem has been identified, intervention approaches should focus on modifying the environment and encouraging the learners to examine new ways of interacting within that environment in order to improve the quality of the transaction.

IDENTIFICATION AND ASSESSMENT ISSUES

The process of identifying Hispanic children who may have a communication disorder is complicated by several factors that are often intertwined and are difficult to separate. Some factors are related to the identification and assessment process itself: (1) limited research on the best assessment techniques to use in determining if indeed a Hispanic child has a communication disorder; (2) reliance on test instruments that are inadequately normed and have questionable validity and reliability; (3) federal and state mandates requiring that the student's language performance be translated into percentiles and standard deviations that are difficult to derive, given the great variability in language ability of children who are bilingual or LEP; (4) difficulty of access to test instruments due to their discontinued publication; (5) incomplete research on Spanish language development and on the performance of Spanish-speaking students learning English over time; and (6) inconsistent definition of the term *learning disabilities*.

Traditional definitions of learning disabilities have included neurological impairments, processing difficulties, language disorders, specific reading disabilities, and social deficits. Current definitions distinguish learning disabilities from learning problems that stem from sensory impairment, mental retardation, emotional disturbance, or environmental influences (Dudley-Marling & Rhodes, 1987; Kamhi & Catts, 1989). Wallach and Liebergott (1984) pointed out the difficulty of arriving at one definition that adequately describes the wide variety of behaviors displayed by these students, however. Most important, they questioned the wisdom of distinguishing language disorders from learning disabilities. As more and more emphasis is placed on the reciprocal relationships of the four language processes—listening, speaking, reading, and writing—it becomes clear that learning is dependent on language and that language continues to develop as new learning takes place. "All language processes are dependent on some superordinate cognitive abilities. The relationships between oral and written language are fundamental and reciprocal, reading and writing are initially dependent on oral language and eventually extend oral language abilities" (Kamhi & Catts, 1989, p. 199).

Traditional Approaches

The debate over definitions, labels, and approaches has obscured the importance of two traditional underlying assumptions: (1) the learning difficulty is intrinsic to the child, which reflects a deficit orientation, and (2) learning is a process of combining small pieces of behavior into a whole, which reflects a reductionistic perspective.

The deficit model and reductionistic view of learning have had devastating effects on Hispanics, as well as on other minority students. As indicated by Ruíz and Figueroa (1988), these students are especially susceptible to misplacement in special education. These researchers cautioned that "each and every Hispanic student with a low academic achievement profile is 'at risk' of being diagnosed as learning handicapped" (p. 1). Although language/learning disorders do occur in Hispanic students, their overrepresentation in special education has been a concern for more than a decade (Figueroa, 1989; Ortíz & Yates, 1983, 1987; Rueda, 1989). There is no evidence, however, that these children as a group learn any differently from others or have particularly severe processing problems. A number of researchers have attempted to determine the reason for their inappropriate referral and program placements.

Misunderstanding of second-language acquisition patterns and the difficulty of distinguishing language differences from language disorders have also affected Hispanic students' success in school settings. Some patterns of language behavior that may be misconstrued as language disorders are really typical of the second-language acquisition process (Mercer, 1987). Such patterns include discrepancy between verbal and performance measure on intelligence tests, academic learning difficulty, attention and memory problems, and others (Table 1-2; Fradd, Barona, & Santos de Barona, 1989). The combination of these misunderstandings often leads to curricular fragmentation, as students are pulled out for instruction in English as a second language or remedial academic work. Trueba (1987) identified curricular fragmentation as a primary cause of the deteriorating academic performance of bilingual students who had been receiving special education services. Cazden (1987) also blamed a disjointed curriculum for the academic failure of language minority students.

Deficit Model of Learning

A deficit orientation in schools mirrors the stratification that occurs in the larger society. Cummins (1989) noted that "school failure on the part of minority students was generally attributed to some inherent deficiency within the child which served to deflect attention away from the inferior educational programs the children were receiving" (p. 15). Many studies have documented the low expectations and inadequate teaching methods used in instructing minority students (e.g., drill and practice, rote memorization), in marked contrast to the more enriched experiences available to others (Cazden, 1987; Díaz, Moll, & Mehan, 1986; Trueba, 1987).

In assessing a student's difficulty, the goal of those with a deficit orientation is to determine the cause of the problem and the best way to remediate, repair, or compensate for the apparent disability (Launer & Lahey, 1981). More recent studies (Bogdan & Knoll, 1988; Coles, 1987; Mehan, Hertweck, & Meihls, 1986) have challenged this assumption, however. They indicate that categories of learning disabilities represent social constructs rather than fixed, stable child characteristics. As with theories of normal language development, the role of the context or

Table 1-2 Indicators of Learning Disabilities That Are Also Behavior Characteristics of Students in the Process of Learning English

Indicator	Cultural or Linguistic Explanation
Discrepancy between verbal and performance measures on intelligence tests	This discrepancy is predictable because those who are not proficient in the language of the test are often able to complete many of the nonverbal tasks correctly (Cummins, 1984).
Academic learning difficulty	Students in the process of learning a new language often experience difficulty with academic concepts and language because these terms and ideas are more abstract, less easily understood and experienced than ideas and terms that communicate social interactions and intents (Cummins, 1984).
Language disorders	When second-language learners enter into meaningful communication, language disorders often appear because of disfluencies that are a natural part of second-language development (Oller, 1983).
Perceptual disorders	Even the ability to perceive and organize information can be distorted when students begin to learn a new language (DeBlassie, 1983).
Social and emotional problems	Students in the process of learning how to function successfully in a new language and culture predictably experience social trauma and emotional problems (DeBlassie and Franco, 1983).
Attention and memory problems	When students have few prior experiences on which to relate new information, they may find it difficult to pay attention and to remember (DeBlassie, 1983).
Hyperactivity or hypoactivity; impulsivity	When students have little prior knowledge or experiences on which to base present information, they frequently become restless and inattentive (DeBlassie, 1983).

Source: From *Meeting the Needs of Culturally and Linguistically Different Students* (p. 78) by S.H. Fradd and M.J. Weismantel (eds.), 1989, Austin, TX: PRO-ED, Inc. Copyright 1989 by PRO-ED, Inc. Reprinted by permission. Adapted from *Students with Learning Disabilities,* 3rd ed., by C.D. Mercer, 1987, Columbus, OH: Charles E. Merrill Publishing Company.

the setting is taking a more prominent place; these researchers believe that the assessment of learning disabilities is inseparable from the context in which they are observed and measured.

After reviewing a number of studies evaluating the interaction between behavior and context, Ruíz and Figueroa (1988) noted that Mercer's (1973) identification of the "six hour retarded child" should have alerted those in the special education field that contextual features may yield very different views of some children. For example, school personnel may perceive a child as "retarded"; family members may consider the same child a competent member of the community.

Reductionistic Perspective of Learning

The concept that learning can be segmented into small parts has been the foundation for much of education for many years. Shuy (1984) pointed out that the general education curriculum was built on these basically reductionistic principles, reflecting the earlier emphasis among linguists on the forms of language, which "fit nicely into the general form-oriented approach to teaching" (p. 168). This emphasis has been particularly marked in the field of learning disabilities. Poplin (1984) also characterized the compartmentalization of learning as reductionistic, adding that, "by breaking the learning process into sequential instructional objects, we strip from the activity the student's own interpretation from which she/he makes sense of the new information, making learning not less difficult, but more so" (p. 291). Dudley-Marling and Rhodes (1987) indicated that, while segmentation is appropriate for some forms of learning, there are significant difficulties in applying this model to higher forms of human learning.

Cazden (1987) identified reductionism as one of the "barriers to excellence" for language minority students. "The danger of reductionism, fractionating complex tasks into component parts that, no matter how well practiced can never reconstitute the complex whole, applies to all education today. But it must be of special concern where language learning is a significant educational goal" (p. 11).

Clay (1985) observed that, while creative, integrated approaches to language learning are now more frequently offered to "normal" students, schools still generally rely on the teaching of specific, sequential skills for those who have learning difficulties. Like Poplin (1984, 1988a, 1988b) and Cazden (1987), Clay noted that fragmented approaches actually construct barriers to learning. She advised educators to take advantage of the reciprocal nature of language processes and help children work with the interrelationships across all forms of language activities from the beginning, rather than to implement interventions that focus on identifying, testing, and teaching small pieces of language—oral or written—in isolation.

These two traditional approaches to learning disabilities—a deficit model and a reductionistic perspective—have formed the framework for assessment and intervention for many years. There are many serious problems with these approaches, however. They are unsupported by research in language acquisition and development, which emphasizes the importance of contextual and sociocultural factors. They neglect to take into account the interaction patterns available in the child's learning environment. They support a medical model in which one member of a pair intends to "fix" another, a model that often prevents the development of an authentic, meaning-centered environment. They inhibit children's ability to demonstrate the upper range of their abilities (since isolated skills chosen by the adult are presented for practice). Finally, they prevent the integration of old and new information, which is so important in developing an internal model of the world.

Successful Teaching Approaches for Second-Language Learners

Delgado-Gaitán (1983, 1990a, 1990b) referred to differences in home and school language and learning patterns as "continuities" and "discontinuities." These differences occur in interactional styles between adults and children, in the ways that children organize themselves for play and work, and in language used for communication. The concepts of continuities and discontinuities, which apply to all children as they begin their school careers, are not inherently positive or negative. Delgado-Gaitán (1983) indicated that, for example, the continuity of adult authority in the home and classroom "places children in a submissive status in the classroom and inhibits their opportunity to ask questions and challenge the process" (p. 219). On the other hand, discontinuities that are bridged carefully can offer children opportunities for growth and development. Both researchers and practitioners have discovered that children make more rapid academic and social gains if their language and culture are perceived as rich sources of experience and learning for themselves, their teachers, and their peers (Olson, 1987; Tharp & Gallimore, 1988; Wong Fillmore, 1990, 1991). Two factors should be considered in bridging the gaps between home and school: use of the primary language and incorporation of communication events typical of the child's family and community.

Primary-language instruction may be one of the most efficient ways to ensure academic success for bilingual children (Cummins, 1989; García, 1988; Krashen & Biber, 1988; Wong Fillmore, 1985). Not only do skills learned in the primary home language transfer more quickly and completely, but the affective benefits to children of having their language respected and used as a tool for learning are significant. The implementation of bilingual education was originally intended to help students become bilingual, biliterate, and bicultural. With bilingual education assistance, these students' language proficiency could eventually be equally high in both languages; furthermore, such assistance would facilitate their acculturation process and preserve their ethnicity. Even when primary-language instruction is not possible, schools can convey the message that their students' language is valued by incorporating some of the ideas of the New Zealand Department of Education (1988).

- encouraging students to use their native language among themselves while in school and to produce written materials in their language

- promoting a multicultural environment in the school by posting signs in the different languages, displaying pictures of the different countries, and providing books written in the different languages
- recruiting tutors for the students who speak the different languages and/or inviting members of the community to interact both formally and informally with students who speak those languages.

Although the students would not receive formal instruction in their primary language, they would feel that their language and cultural backgrounds are respected.

Incorporating a variety of relevant communication events in the classroom gives students an opportunity to function at the upper range of their abilities. The use of structures that are familiar allows both teachers and students to use language in authentic, meaningful ways that provide bridges between home and school. Enright (1985) noted that, "instead of waiting for students to adapt themselves to the new linguistic and cultural environment, teachers must adapt their communication patterns and environment to permit the bridging of the two worlds" (p. 441). A well-known example of this incorporation of communication events took place in the Kamehameha Early Childhood Education Project (KEEP) for Creole-speaking Hawaiian children (Au, 1984; Au & Jordan, 1981). The reading lessons were based on the "talk story," which is an important nonschool communication event in the Hawaiian culture. Talk story consists of a "rambling personal experience narrative mixed with folk materials" (Watson, 1975, p. 54). The event involves the joint narration of two or more participants. The achievement of students who were exposed to this strategy was higher than that of students from similar cultural backgrounds who were exposed to more traditional reading techniques (Au, 1984). Techniques that incorporated the children's cultural and communication patterns produced similar results with language/learning-disabled students (Ruíz, 1988, 1989; Westby & Rouse, 1985).

INTERVENTION ISSUES

The focus of speech-language assessments has shifted from diagnosing the cause of a problem to delineating strategies to help students cope more efficiently with classroom demands and become better communicators (Nelson, 1989). This shift in orientation results from increasing research that suggests a very close link between oral and written language (Hoskins, 1990; Wallach & Miller, 1988; Westby, 1985). Furthermore, lack of academic progress may be a manifestation of earlier oral language difficulties that have become more apparent (Bashir, Kuban, Kleinman & Scavuzzo, 1983; Maxwell & Wallach, 1984; Spreen & Haaf, 1986). More and more researchers are recognizing the importance of the relationship between assessment and intervention. It is not sufficient to state that a person has a problem; it is also necessary to delineate strategies to remediate the problem. As Miller (1990) noted, "Traditional tests were administered to describe people's limitations and disabilities." She proposed that, instead, it would be more constructive to describe "what" and "how" people know what they know rather than describe what they do not know or cannot do" (p. 4). In order to achieve this purpose, it is necessary to use a dynamic approach in describing their communication patterns. Damico (1991) summarized this point very succinctly by stating that "language and communication must not be treated as static, divisible and autonomous. Rather, these complex human behaviors should be treated as dynamic, synergetic, and integrative with both intrinsic cognitive factors and extrinsic contextual features" (p. 177). Thus, the clinician should supplement the assessment information data with observations of the student's educational performance and communication needs. One of the great difficulties is that assessment instruments are constructed according to a reductionistic model. The clinician must make the connection between what the student can do or has difficulty doing, and determine which situations seem to improve the student's performance.

Planning intervention strategies based on assessment data is always a challenge. Miller (1990) and Wallach and Miller (1988) have provided helpful insights on ways to bridge assessment and intervention. Yet, this information is still emerging. A recent survey conducted by the American Speech-Language-Hearing Association indicated that the need for more extensive "treatment efficacy studies/utilization review data" is a primary area of concern (Spahr, 1989). In contrast to those with a deficit-oriented, reductionistic approach, constructivists consider the learner part of a larger context that gives meaning to the interaction. Shuy (1984) summarized the constructivist perspective by stating, "It is felt that the best way to find out how things work is to start with an entire context, the relevant whole, and to help children actively construct the focus of their world with as many of the clues available to them as possible" (p. 168). There is an interaction between a context and what the child brings to a given situation. Language learning depends on background knowledge, purpose, and desire to create meaning (Douglass, 1989).

Poplin (1988a, 1988b) suggested that the paradigm of holistic constructivism is an essential approach to learning disabilities, given the negative effects of a reductionistic approach. Some authorities have incorporated not only this basic constructivist view but also Vygotsky's (1962) emphasis on the importance of community and assisted learning in the process of the child's acquisition of knowledge. Ruíz (1989), for example, commented that effective instruction from these combined perspectives encourages students to construct meaning by integrating their new knowledge with the previous knowledge that they learned from trusted and experienced teachers. This, in turn, fosters interaction in high-interest activities and allows students to develop their abilities and to take new risks.

Cummins (1989) in his "interactive/experiential" model, and Tharp and Gallimore (1988) in their "contextualized/interactionist" model have offered similar paradigms.

The major implications for instruction consistent with these approaches include

- emphasis on authentic, purposeful use of language
- construction of meaning through reflection, personal interpretation, and acceptance of divergent responses
- learning through interaction with competent members of the community
- interactive group structures as an alternative to teacher-directed lessons
- incorporation of student experiences (e.g., linguistic, cultural, background knowledge) into classroom learning
- curricular content determined by student interest
- instruction geared toward higher levels of thinking (e.g., frequent use of metalinguistic and metacognitive strategies)
- student use of the four language processes (i.e., speaking, listening, reading, and writing) interactively for a wide range of purposes in all academic tasks
- perception of "errors" as appropriate developmental markers and opportunities for further learning in all language processes

These program characteristics reflect the current trend in emphasizing whole language teaching. According to Schory (1990), such a program "is based on a developmental perspective and parallels the acquisition of oral language. Learning activities derive from the child's strengths. No predetermined curriculum is prescribed and the teacher functions as facilitator rather than instructor" (p. 206). In this manner, students become active participants in the learning process.

Although there is great value in this constructive process of learning, Chaney (1990) noted that it is still worthwhile to integrate some "more traditional" approaches into reading instruction for some young children. Specifically, direct instruction of reading increases metalinguistic awareness. Therefore, some students may need a balance between the two approaches. Both regular and special education programs that have incorporated these features of holism with language minority students have shown promising results. Moll (1988) and García (1988) observed that elementary school teachers who used this approach with both bilingual and English-only students maintained high expectations for student learning and rejected the notion that at-risk students are unable to learn difficult material.

In their study of Hispanic students, Díaz, Moll, and Mehan (1986) found a dramatic contrast in the students' performance when instruction shifted from a focus on mastery of discrete units to an emphasis on comprehension of high-level texts by constructing meaning through personal experience. In her study of Chinese and

Hispanic elementary school children, Wong Fillmore (1985) found that Hispanic children were much more successful when instruction was characterized by careful language use and curriculum goals were defined to meet the students' instructional needs. "When they were given an education which was rich in content, and when teachers emphasized comprehension and student participation, the Hispanic children blossomed" (p. 479).

Ruíz (1989) summarized the effective instructional variables as (1) incorporating students' personal experiences into oral language and literacy lessons, (2) using informal cooperative structures, and (3) promoting activities that encourage the upper range of student abilities. Although research on Hispanic students with language-learning disabilities is scarce, the few studies that have been conducted indicate that Hispanic children in special education classrooms improve as a result of implementing some of these instructional components (Ruíz, 1988; Willig & Swedo, 1987).

Several challenges remain in working with Hispanic persons who have language-learning disabilities. In order to meet these challenges, clinicians must broaden their perspective; they must be aware of

- Spanish language development in monolingual speakers
- communication patterns and sociocultural characteristics of Hispanic families residing in the United States
- English language development in persons from Spanish language/culture backgrounds
- best practices in identifying and assessing a possible language-learning difficulty in Hispanic students
- best practices in working with Hispanic students/families with language-learning difficulties
- best practices in assessing and working with Hispanic adults with acquired neurological disabilities

There is limited core research on the best practices to assess communication disorders in Hispanic students or on specific strategies to work with Hispanic students needing special assistance in language and academic learning. In order to resolve the remaining dilemmas, it is necessary to determine how to assess students with the traditional norm-referenced tests without falling into a reductionistic paradigm (while conforming to federal and state regulations demanding "scores") and how to implement effective programs when appropriate materials and Spanish-speaking personnel are not readily available. A clinician who is knowledgeable of the issues involved in the area of assessment and intervention for communication disorders in language/culture minority groups and who is willing to take risks can be successful in working with the Hispanic population, however.

REFERENCES

Au, K.H. (1984). Vygotskian perspectives on discussion processes in small group reading lessons. In P. Peterson, L. Wilkinson, & M. Hallinan (Eds.), *The social context of instruction.* New York: Academic Press.

Au, K.H., & Jordan, C. (1981). Teaching reading to Hawaiian children: Finding a culturally appropriate solution. In H.T. Trueba, G.P. Gurthrie, & K.H. Au (Eds.), *Culture and the bilingual classroom: Studies in classroom ethnography* (pp. 139–152). Rowley, MA: Newbury House.

Bashir, A., Kuban, K., Kleinman, S., & Scavuzzo, S. (1983). Issues in language disorders: Considerations of cause, maintenance, and change. In J. Miller, D. Yoder, & R. Schiefelbush (Eds.), *Contemporary issues in language intervention: Report No. 12* (pp. 92–106). Rockville, MD: American Speech-Language-Hearing Association.

Bates, E., Bretherton, I., & Snyder, L. (Eds.). (1988). *From first words to grammar.* New York: Cambridge University Press.

Bloom, L., & Lahey, M. (1978). *Language development and language disorders.* New York: John Wiley.

Bogdan, R., & Knoll, J. (1988). The sociology of disability. In E.L. Meyen & T.M. Skirtic (Eds.), *Exceptional children and youth: An introduction* (3rd ed.) (pp. 449–478). Denver: Love.

Cambourne, B. (1987). *Coping with chaos.* Portsmouth, NH: Heinemann.

Cazden, C. (1987). Teachers as language advocates for children. In R. Rigg & D.S. Enright (Eds.), *Children and ESL: Integrating perspectives.* Washington, DC: TESOL.

Chaney, C. (1990). Evaluating the whole language approach to language arts: The pros and cons. *Language, Speech, and Hearing Services in Schools, 21,* 244–249.

Cheng, L.L. (1987). English communicative competence of language minority children: Assessment and treatment of language "impaired" preschoolers. In H.T. Trueba (Ed.), *Success or failure? Learning & the language minority student* (pp. 49–68). New York: Newbury House.

Chomsky, N. (1965). *Aspects of the theory of syntax.* Cambridge, MA: MIT Press.

Chomsky, N. (1968). *Language and the mind.* New York: Harcourt Brace Jovanovich.

Clay, M. (1985). *The early detection of reading difficulties* (3rd ed.). Portsmouth, NH: Heinemann.

Coles, G.S. (1987). *The learning mystique: A critical look at learning disabilities.* New York: Pantheon.

Cromer, R.F. (1974). The development of language and cognition: The cognition hypothesis. In B. Foos (Ed.), *New perspectives in child development* (pp. 184–252). Baltimore, MD: Penguin Books.

Cummins, J. (1984). *Bilingualism and special education: Issues in assessment and pedagogy.* Clevedon, England: Multilingual Matters.

Cummins, J. (1989). *Empowering minority students.* San Francisco: California Association for Bilingual Education.

Damico, J.S. (1991). Descriptive assessment of communicative ability in limited English proficient students. In E.V. Hamayan & J.S. Damico (Eds.), *Limiting bias in the assessment of bilingual students* (pp. 157–217). Austin, TX: PRO-ED.

DeBlassie, R.R. (1983). Emotional and behavioral disorders in bilingual children. In D.R. Omark & J.G. Erickson (Eds.), *The bilingual exceptional child* (pp. 255–268). San Diego, CA: College Hill Press.

DeBlassie, R.R., & Franco, J.N. (1983). Psychological and educational assessment of bilingual children. In D.R. Omark & J.G. Erickson (Eds.), *The bilingual exceptional child* (pp. 55–68). San Diego, CA: College Hill Press.

Delgado-Gaitán, C. (1983). *Learning how: Rules for knowing and doing for Mexican children at home, play, and school.* Unpublished doctoral dissertation, Stanford University.

Delgado-Gaitán, C. (1990a). *From home to school.* New York: Praeger.

Delgado-Gaitán, C. (1990b). *Literacy for empowerment: The role of parents in children's education.* London: Falmer Press.

Díaz, S., Moll, L., & Mehan, H. (1986). Sociocultural resources in instruction: A context-specific approach. In California State Department of Education, Bilingual Education Office (Ed.), *Beyond language: Social & cultural factors in schooling language minority students* (pp. 187–230). Los Angeles: California State University, Evaluation, Dissemination and Assessment Center.

Douglass, M. (1989). *Learning to read.* New York: Teacher College Press, Columbia University.

Dudley-Marling, C., & Rhodes, L.K. (1987). Pragmatics and literacy. *Language, Speech, and Hearing Services in Schools, 13,* 41–52.

Engelmann, S., & Osborn, J. (1976). *Distar Language I* (2nd ed.). Chicago: Science Research Associates.

Enright, S. (1985). Yes! Talking: Organizing the classroom to promote second language instruction. *TESOL Quarterly, 19,* 431–453.

Erickson, J.G., & Omark, D.R. (Eds.). (1981). *Communication assessment of the bilingual bicultural child.* Baltimore: University Park Press.

Figueroa, R. (1989). Psychological testing of linguistic-minority students: Knowledge gaps and regulations. *Exceptional Children, 56,* 145–152.

Figueroa, R., Fradd, S.H., & Correa, V.I. (1989). Bilingual special education and this issue. *Exceptional Children, 56,* 174–178.

Fradd, S.H., Barona, A., & Santos de Barona, M. (1989). Implementing change and monitoring progress. In S.H. Fradd & M.J. Weismantel (Eds.), *Meeting the needs of culturally and linguistically different students* (pp. 34–62). Austin, TX: PRO-ED.

García, E. (1988). Effective schooling for language minority students. *Focus, 1,* 1–10.

Gumperz, J. (1981). Conversational inference and classroom learning. In J.L. Green & C. Wallat (Eds.), *Ethnography and language in educational settings* (pp. 3–23). Norwood, NJ: Ablex.

Halliday, M.A. (1978). *Language as a social semiotic: The social interpretation of language and meaning.* Baltimore: University Park Press.

Hamayan, E.V., & Damico, J.S. (1991). *Limiting bias in the assessment of bilingual students.* Austin, TX: PRO-ED.

Heath, S.B. (1983). *Ways with words.* New York: Cambridge University Press.

Heath, S.B. (1986a). Sociocultural contexts of language development. In California State Department of Education, Bilingual Education Office (Ed.), *Beyond language: Social & cultural factors in schooling language minority students* (pp. 143–186). Los Angeles: Evaluation, Dissemination and Assessment Center, California State University.

Heath, S.B. (1986b). Taking a cross-cultural look at narratives. *Topics in Language Disorders, 7*(1), 84–94.

Hoskins, B. (1990). Language and literacy: Participating in the conversation. *Topics in Language Disorders, 10*(2), 46–62.

Hymes, D. (1974). *Foundations in sociolinguistics.* Philadelphia: University of Pennsylvania Press.

Kamhi, A.G., & Catts, H.W. (Eds.). (1989). *Reading disabilities: A developmental language perspective.* Austin, TX: PRO-ED.

Krashen, S.D., & Biber, D. (1988). *On course: Bilingual education success in California.* Sacramento: California Association for Bilingual Education.

Lahey, M. (1988). *Language disorders and language development.* New York: Macmillan.

Launer, P., & Lahey, M. (1981). Passages: From the fifties to the eighties in language assessment. *Topics in Language Disorders, 1*(3), 1–30.

Mattes, L.J., & Omark, D.R. (1984). *Speech and language assessment for the bilingual handicapped.* San Diego, CA: College Hill Press.

Maxwell, S., & Wallach, G. (1984). The language-learning disabilities connection: Symptoms of early language disability change over time. In G.P. Wallach & K.G. Butler (Eds.), *Language learning disabilities in school age children* (pp. 35–59). Baltimore: Williams & Wilkins.

McNeill, D. (1970). *The acquisition of language.* New York: Harper & Row.

Miller, I. (1990). The roles of language and learning in the development of literacy. *Topics in Language Disorders, 10*(2), 1–24.

Mehan, H., Hertweck, A., & Meihls, J.D. (1986). *Handicapping the handicapped.* Stanford, CA: Stanford University Press.

Menyuk, P. (1988). *Language development.* Glenview, IL: Scott, Foresman & Co.

Mercer, C.D. (1987). *Students with learning disabilities* (3rd ed.). Columbus, OH: Charles E. Merrill.

Mercer, J.R. (1973). *Labeling the mentally retarded.* Berkeley: University of California Press.

Moll, L. (1988). Some key issues in teaching latino students. *Language Arts, 65,* 465–472.

Nelson, K. (1974). Concept, word, and sentence: Interrelations in acquisition and development. *Psychological Review, 81,* 267–285.

Nelson, N.W. (1989). Curriculum based language assessment and intervention. *Language, Speech and Hearing in the Schools, 20,* 170–184.

New Zealand Department of Education. (1988). *New voices: Second language learning and teaching: A handbook for primary teachers.* Wellington: Department of Education.

Oller, J.W. (1983). Testing proficiencies and diagnosing language disorders in bilingual children. In D.R. Omark & J.G. Erickson (Eds.), *The bilingual exceptional child* (pp. 69–88). San Diego, CA: College Hill Press.

Olson, L. (1987). *Crossing the schoolhouse border.* San Francisco: California Tomorrow.

Ortíz, A., & Yates, J.R. (1983). Incidence of exceptionality among Hispanics: Implications for manpower planning. *NABE Journal, 7,* 41–54.

Ortíz, A., & Yates, J.R. (1987). *Characteristics of learning disabled, mentally retarded, and speech-language handicapped Hispanic students at initial evaluation and reevaluation.* (Unpublished report, University of Texas at Austin, Department of Special Education, Handicapped Minority Research Institute.

Poplin, M. (1984). Toward a holistic view of persons with learning disabilities. *Learning Disabilities Quarterly, 7,* 290–294.

Poplin, M. (1988a). Holistic/constructivist principles of the teaching learning process: Implications for the field of learning disabilities. *Journal of Learning Disabilities, 21,* 401–416.

Poplin, M. (1988b). The reductionistic fallacy in learning disabilities. Replicating the past by reducing the present. *Journal of Learning Disabilities, 21,* 389–400.

Rueda, R. (1989). Defining mild disabilities with language-minority students. *Exceptional Children, 56,* 121–128.

Ruíz, N. (1988). *Language for learning in a bilingual special education classroom.* Unpublished dissertation, Stanford University.

Ruíz, N. (1989). An optimal learning environment for Rosemary. *Exceptional Children, 56,* 130–144.

Ruíz, N., & Figueroa, R. (1988). *Special education research project on Hispanic pupils.* Unpublished manuscript, University of California, Division of Education, Davis, CA.

Schory, M.E. (1990). Whole language and the speech-language pathologist, *Language, Speech, and Hearing Services in Schools, 21,* 206–211.

Shuy, R. (1984). Language as a foundation for education: The school context. *Theory into Practice, 23,* 167–174.

Skinner, B.F. (1957). *Verbal behavior.* Englewood Cliffs, NJ: Prentice-Hall.

Spahr, F. (1989). *Results of grantseeking questionnaire (Memo).* Rockville, MD: American Speech-Language-Hearing Association.

Spreen, O., & Haaf, R.G. (1986). Empirically derived LD subtypes: A replication attempt and longitudinal patterns over fifteen years. *Journal of Reading, 19,* 170–180.

Staats, A. (1969). *Learning, language, and cognition.* New York: Holt, Rinehart & Winston.

Tharp, R., & Gallimore, R. (1988). *Rousing minds to life: Teaching, learning, and schooling in social context.* New York: Cambridge University Press.

Trueba, H. (1987). Cultural differences or learning handicaps? Towards an understanding of adjustment process. In S. Goldman & H. Trueba (Eds.), *Schooling language minority youth: Proceedings of the University of California linguistic minority research project conference, Vol. II* (pp. 45–79). Los Angeles: University of California.

von Tetzchner, S., Siegel, L., & Smith, L. (Eds.). (1989). *Social and cognitive aspects of normal and atypical language development.* New York: Springer-Verlag.

Vygotsky, L. (1962). *Thought and language.* Cambridge, MA: MIT Press.

Wallace, G.L., & Freeman, S.B. (1991). Adults with neurological impairments from multicultural populations. *ASHA, 33,* 58–60.

Wallach, G.P., & Liebergott, J.W. (1984). Who shall be called learning disabled: Some new directions. In G.P. Wallach & K.G. Butler (Eds.), *Language learning, disabilities in school-age children* (pp. 1–14). Baltimore: Williams & Wilkins.

Wallach, G.P., & Miller, L. (1988). *Language intervention and academic success.* Austin, TX: PRO-ED.

Watson, K. (1975). Transferable communicative routines: Strategies and group identity in two speech events. *Language and Society, 5,* 53–72.

Wells, G. (1981). *Language through interaction.* New York: Cambridge University Press.

Westby, C. (1985). Learning to talk—Talking to learn: Oral-literate language differences. In C.S. Simon (Ed.), *Communication skills and classroom success: Therapy methodologies for language-learning disabled students* (pp. 181–213). San Diego, CA: College Hill Press.

Westby, C., & Rouse, G. (1985). Culture in education and the instruction of language-learning disabled students. *Topics in Language Disorders, 5*(4), 15–28.

Willig, A., & Swedo, J. (1987, April). *Improving teaching strategies for exceptional Hispanic limited English proficient students: An exploratory study of task engagement and teaching strategies.*

Paper presented at the annual meeting of the American Education Research Association, Washington, DC.

Wong Fillmore, L. (1985). Research current: Equity or excellence? *Language Arts, 89,* 474–481.

Wong Fillmore, L. (1990, May). Latino families and the schools. Remarks prepared for the seminar on California's change in face of race relations: New ethics in the 1990's. Sponsored by the Senate Office of Research in cooperation with the University of California Policy Seminar, Sacramento, CA. (To appear in a *California Tomorrow* anthology.)

Wong Fillmore, L. (1991). Language and cultural issues in early education. In S.L. Kagan (Ed.), *The care and education of America's young children: Obstacles and opportunities* (pp. 30–49). The 90th Yearbook of the National Society for the Study of Education. Chicago: University of Chicago Press.

Chapter 2

The Hispanic Population: Facts and Figures

Henriette W. Langdon

The United States is a relatively new nation, only 200 years old, and immigrants have come from all corners of the world, representing a multitude of racial, ethnic, and linguistic groups. Symbolically, the United States may be viewed as a large quilt that has been assembled with different pieces, each portraying a unique group of people. These people share some linguistic and cultural ties, yet the pieces of the quilt are made of different patterns. Some are of older fabric, while others are of newer fabric. A binding thread that signifies for most the land of better life opportunities holds the pieces together. One of the larger pieces represents the Hispanics. As a matter of fact, the United States has the seventh largest number of Hispanics in the world; the U.S. Hispanic population is exceeded only by those in Mexico, Spain, Argentina, Colombia, Peru, and Venezuela.

During the last decade, the number of Americans of Asian or Pacific Island background has more than doubled, increasing from 3.5 million to 7.3 million. During the same period, the number of Hispanic Americans also grew by more than half; it rose from 14.6 to 23.4 million, exceeding the predicted total of 20.8 million (Current Population Reports, 1990). After African-Americans, Hispanics constitute the largest minority group in the United States. Assuming an annual increase of 1 million, the total Hispanic population will be more than 30 million by the year 2000. The percentage of Hispanics in the U.S. population is projected to equal that of African-Americans by the year 2020—approximately 14% for each group. The percentage of the White non-Hispanic population will decrease from 72% in the year 2000 to 65% in the year 2020. In contrast, the Asian and other racial minorities will increase only slightly during those years: from 4.3% in 2000 to 6.4% in 2020 (Davis, Haub, & Willette, 1983). There is no question that the nation will experience an important racial/ethnic composition shift in the next 30 years (Figure 2-1).

20

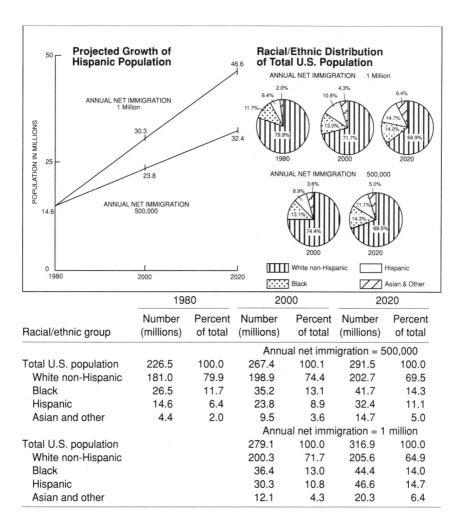

	1980		2000		2020	
Racial/ethnic group	Number (millions)	Percent of total	Number (millions)	Percent of total	Number (millions)	Percent of total
			Annual net immigration = 500,000			
Total U.S. population	226.5	100.0	267.4	100.1	291.5	100.0
White non-Hispanic	181.0	79.9	198.9	74.4	202.7	69.5
Black	26.5	11.7	35.2	13.1	41.7	14.3
Hispanic	14.6	6.4	23.8	8.9	32.4	11.1
Asian and other	4.4	2.0	9.5	3.6	14.7	5.0
			Annual net immigration = 1 million			
Total U.S. population			279.1	100.0	316.9	100.0
White non-Hispanic			200.3	71.7	205.6	64.9
Black			36.4	13.0	44.4	14.0
Hispanic			30.3	10.8	46.6	14.7
Asian and other			12.1	4.3	20.3	6.4

Figure 2-1 Population 1980 and as Projected for 2000 and 2020: Hispanics, Total U.S. Population and Four Main Racial/Ethnic Groups. *Source:* From "U.S. Hispanics: Changing the Face of America" by C. Davis, C. Haub, and J. Willette, 1983, *Population Bulletin, 38,* p. 39. Copyright 1983 by Population Reference Bureau. Reprinted by permission. Data from *The Future Racial Composition of the United States* by L. Bouvier and C. Davis, 1982, Washington, D.C.: Demographic Information Services Center of the Population Reference Bureau.

It is commonly believed that earlier immigrants acquired English and entered the mainstream culture faster than the more recent immigrants from Latin America are doing. The constant influx of Mexicans to the Southwest, of Central and South Americans to California and to large metropolitan areas (e.g., New York, Boston, and Washington, D.C.), of Puerto Ricans to the Northeast, and of Cubans to Florida may be responsible for the lack of integration. All these immigrants have kept the Spanish language and culture alive in the United States. As Valdivieso and Davis (1988) noted, "As long as immigration continues, bilingualism may persist longer among Hispanics than it did among other immigrant groups" (p. 9). Yet, Veltman (1988) found that Hispanic immigrant families have almost totally lost their Spanish by the third generation, just as other immigrants have lost their native languages. He commented that, by the time they have been in the United States for 15 years, some 75% of all Hispanic immigrants are speaking English on a regular daily basis. He also indicated that 7 of 10 children of Hispanic immigrant parents become English speakers for all practical purposes, and their third-generation children have English as their mother tongue. (Naturally, there are individual exceptions to this language shift.) Furthermore, the loss of their native language does not imply that the people feel part of the American society. Often, even those immigrants who may have lost their native language have more in common with the "low-income mainstream poor than their counterparts in the host country or mother country" (Trueba, 1989, p. 12). Nevertheless, most immigrants assimilate eventually, although perhaps at different rates and degrees.

In his theory of assimilation, Sandberg (1986) suggested that ethnic identity decreases with length of time in the United States. Assimilation, which can be defined as the process of becoming "Americanized," includes the process of acculturation. In contrast, ethnic identity or ethnicity involves the retention of customs, attitudes, and beliefs of the culture of origin (Kitano, 1989). Culture is a difficult term to define because it encompasses so many elements. Cheng (1987) defined the term by saying that "culture is the total way of life of people in a society" (p. 4). Assimilation and ethnic identity can be represented along vertical and horizontal lines that intersect, resulting in four quadrants. Each quadrant represents one of four types of individuals. Figure 2-2 illustrates the continuum of assimilation, ethnic identity, and language use, according to Kitano's (1989) model.

Type A individuals are high in assimilation and low in ethnic identity; these individuals are "Americanized." They may continue to have friends from the same ethnic group and to identify with the group, however. Type B individuals are high in assimilation and high in ethnic identity; essentially, they are bicultural. Intellectuals and business persons who have constant contact with two cultures, for example, fit into this category (Kitano, 1989). Type C individuals are high in ethnic identity and low in assimilation; in this category are recently arrived immigrants and older people who have spent most of their lives in ethnic communities. Finally, Type D individuals are low in assimilation and low in ethnic identity. They have difficulty accepting both the role of the dominant society and their ethnic

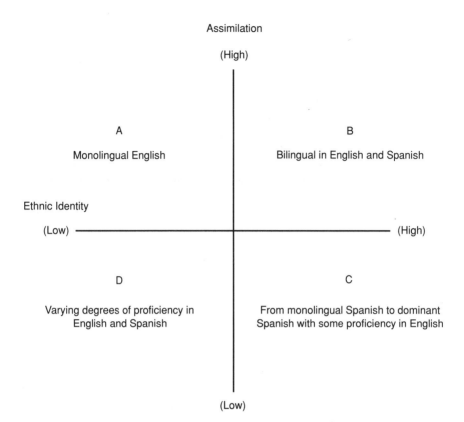

Figure 2-2 Relationship of Assimilation, Ethnic Identity, and Proficiency in Spanish and English. *Source:* From *Counseling Across Cultures* (p. 143) by P.B. Pedersen et al., 1989, Honolulu, HI: University of Hawaii Press. Copyright 1989 by University of Hawaii Press. Adapted by permission.

role. Kitano (1989) included the mentally ill and "drop-out" individuals in this category. No individual fits neatly into any of these categories, and there may be differences from generation to generation within one family. Although Kitano (1989) does not address the use of the native language directly, it is possible to hypothesize that it varies from category to category. Type A persons seem likely to be essentially monolingual in English. Type C and D persons may have varying proficiencies in each language, but Type C persons are likely to use the native language primarily. Type B persons are probably bilingual, with equivalent proficiency in both languages.

HISPANICS: A DIVERSE GROUP

The Spanish influence in the United States dates from the 1500s, when Columbus arrived on the North American continent. Today, the Hispanic population is as diverse in the United States as it is in Latin American countries. Some Hispanics are descendants of Native Indians who settled in the Americas long before the Spanish conquest. The Mayans, for example, lived in what is today Guatemala, Mexico, Honduras, and El Salvador. The Aztecs settled primarily in Mexico; the Incas, in Peru, southern Colombia, Ecuador, Bolivia, and northern Chile. Some Hispanics are direct descendants of Spanish and European settlers, but the great majority are Mestizo, having both Indian and European heritage. Still other Hispanics have African-American ancestors, and a few have Asian ancestry as well. Those who have primarily African-American and White heritage are referred to as Mulattoes. Still others are referred to as Creoles, denoting those born on the American continent whose direct ancestors are of European or Spanish descent. Discrimination based on racial heritage may occur among the different subgroups and even within a given subgroup.

Hispanics also vary in the status of their U.S. residency. Some are citizens by birth; others are naturalized citizens, refugees, owners of permanent "green cards," or illegal aliens (Melville, 1987; Treviño, 1987). For example, it is estimated that approximately 2 million Mexicans have entered the United States illegally (Paul, 1987). Consequently, when referring to a Hispanic individual, it is best to avoid generalizations; it is necessary to consider the person's origin, reason for migration, and length of residence in the United States.

Definition of Hispanic

Prior to the 1970s, Hispanics were referred to either as Latinos or, more specifically, as Cubans, Puerto Ricans, or Mexicans, or they were identified by their racial background. The term *Hispanic* was seldom used before the 1970s to designate persons from as close to the United States as Mexico and as far as Chile, Argentina, or Spain (Davis, Haub, & Willette, 1983). Because the influx of Hispanics had become so great by 1970, the government decided to identify this group in the 1970 census. Prior to the census, a sample was taken in those states where the concentration of Hispanics was the greatest (e.g., Arizona, California, Colorado, Texas) to identify characteristics of the Hispanic population. These characteristics included having a Spanish surname or birthplace, or fluency in the language. Varying numbers of Hispanics were identified by means of these categories. For example, identifiers such as place of birth or parentage appeared to yield fewer Hispanics nationwide than did identifiers such as Spanish language fluency or heritage. However, none of these characteristics is sufficiently accurate in identifying Hispanics.

In the 1970 census, individuals were asked to specify if their origin was Mexican, Puerto Rican, Cuban, Central or South American; if they were of a different Spanish extraction; or if they had any association with that origin or descent. The question directly probed the persons' Hispanic identity and was subsequently clarified in the 1980 census and the 1990 census to include a definition of Spanish origin. "A person is of Spanish/Hispanic origin or descent if the person identifies his or her ancestry with one of the listed groups, that is, Mexican, Puerto Rican, etc. Origin or descent (ancestry) may be viewed as the nationality group, the lineage, or country in which the person or the person's parents or ancestors were born" (Davis, Haub, & Willette, 1983, p. 6). However, caution is necessary when attempting to determine the language proficiency of a child or any person who is of Hispanic origin. A Hispanic name does not provide any clues to the individual's proficiency in either Spanish or English.

In 1968, New Mexico's Senator Joseph A. Montoya and the other Spanish origin congressmen proposed that the word *Hispanic* be used to denote those of Spanish origin and that the week beginning September 15 and 16 be recognized as National Hispanic Week. Subsequently, in the late 1970s, the Congressional Hispanic Caucus, which had been formed in the early 1960s, created an organization to promote projects and programs to benefit Hispanics (Melville, 1987).

Different Subgroups

As shown in Figure 2-3 (Current Population Reports, 1990), the largest portion of the Hispanic population in the United States is Mexican (58%), followed by Central and South American (14%), Puerto Rican (13%), other Hispanics (9%), and Cuban (6%). In the "other" group are those who report that their geographical or familial origins are in Spain or that they are descendants of families who have been in the United States for one or several generations. According to the 1980 census, 80% of this "other" group were born in the United States.

Although all these subgroups speak the same language, there are phonological and lexical variations in the Spanish spoken in their countries of origin. A diversity of Indian and European languages may be spoken in these various countries as well. Each country of origin has its own history, celebrates different patriotic holidays, and has its own music and dances. The majority of Hispanics are Roman Catholic, but religious symbols, such as the Virgin Mary, are represented differently based on the specific ethnicity of the particular population. For example, the Virgen de Guadalupe has Mexican Indian features, whereas the Virgen del Cobre is Black. Also, each Hispanic immigrant group has its unique immigration history. Most of the Hispanic immigrants to the United States in the 1950s were Puerto Ricans, whereas the Cubans and Central Americans were the largest groups to immigrate in the 1960s and 1970s. The trend for the 1980s continued to be greater

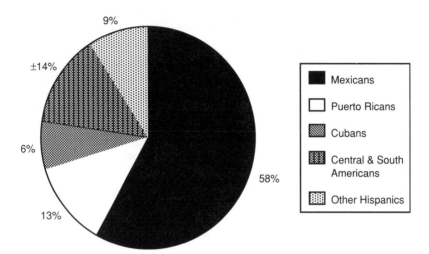

Figure 2-3 Percentage of Each Hispanic Subgroup. (Note that percentages are rounded up.) *Source:* From *The Hispanic Population in the United States,* Current Population Reports, 1990, Washington, D.C.: Bureau of the Census.

immigration of Central Americans, a trend forecasted to last until the end of the 20th century (Davis, Haub, & Willette, 1983). In comparison, Mexican immigration was stable throughout this period. The greater visibility of Hispanics is also attributable to a higher birth rate; it is estimated that the birth rate for all Hispanics is 25.5/1,000, compared to 14.7/1,000 for non-Hispanics (Davis, Haub, & Willette, 1983).

Distribution of Hispanics in the United States

The largest percentage of Hispanics in the United States reside in the states that border Mexico (Figure 2-4). California and Texas have the largest proportions in the nation, 34% and 21% of the U.S. Hispanics, respectively. This represents more than 13 million persons, approximately 55% of the Hispanic population. Other states with a significant number of Hispanics are, in decreasing order, New York, Florida, Illinois, Arizona, New Jersey, New Mexico, and Colorado.

Table 2-1 shows the distribution of bilingual Spanish-speaking clinicians who rate themselves as proficient in the language and whose names appear in the 1990–1991 *Directory of Bilingual Speech-Language Pathologists and Audiologists* (American Speech-Language-Hearing Association, 1990). Only 0.05% or 258 members indicate that they are proficient in Spanish. As can be noted, the

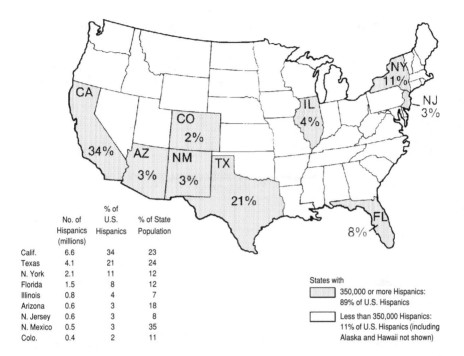

	No. of Hispanics (millions)	% of U.S. Hispanics	% of State Population
Calif.	6.6	34	23
Texas	4.1	21	24
N. York	2.1	11	12
Florida	1.5	8	12
Illinois	0.8	4	7
Arizona	0.6	3	18
N. Jersey	0.6	3	8
N. Mexico	0.5	3	35
Colo.	0.4	2	11

States with
- 350,000 or more Hispanics: 89% of U.S. Hispanics
- Less than 350,000 Hispanics: 11% of U.S. Hispanics (including Alaska and Hawaii not shown)

Figure 2-4 Distribution of Hispanics in the United States. *Source:* From "U.S. Hispanics: Challenging Issues for the 1990's" by R. Valdivieso and C. Davis, 1988, *Population Trends and Public Policy, 17.* Copyright 1988 by Population Reference Bureau. Reprinted by permission.

distribution of bilingual professionals does not always correspond to the number of Hispanics in a given state. California, with 34% of Hispanics, has close to 33% of the Spanish-speaking clinicians; Texas, with 21% of Hispanics has less than 15% of the bilingual clinicians, however. The percentages are more equivalent for New York, Illinois, and Arizona. In contrast, Florida with only 8% of the Hispanic population has 14.3% of the bilingual clinicians listed in the *Directory*.

Group and Subgroup Characteristics

Not only do characteristics such as age, family size, income, education, occupation, and health care utilization often differ between the Hispanic group as a whole and the rest of the U.S. non-Hispanic population, but also they may differ among the various Hispanic subgroups.

Table 2-1 Distribution of Speech-Language Pathologists and Audiologists (Bilingual in English and Spanish)

State	Number	Percentage	U.S. Hispanic Population (millions)
California	85	32.9%	6.6
Texas	38	14.7%	4.1
New York	27	10.4%	2.1
Florida	37	14.3%	1.5
Illinois	9	3.4%	0.8
Arizona	6	1.5%	0.6

Source: Data from *Directory of Bilingual Speech-Language Pathologists and Audiologists* by American Speech-Language-Hearing Association, 1990.

Age

The Hispanic population in the United States is particularly young. The mean age is 26 years, whereas the median age for the non-Hispanic population is 33 years (Figure 2-5). Specifically, the Mexican subgroup has the youngest mean age (24 years), while the Cuban subgroup has the oldest (39 years).

On the other end of the age continuum, approximately 13% of the non-Hispanic population is 65 years old and over, compared with only 5% of the Hispanic population (Figure 2-6). The Cubans have the largest proportion of older Hispanic citizens (14%). The Mexicans and the Central and South Americans have the smallest proportions (approximately 3% to 4% each).

Today, the proportion of the population aged 5 to 19 years, school-aged youngsters, is somewhat the same for both the Hispanic and the non-Hispanic group: 30% and 21%, respectively (Figure 2-7). The school-aged group makes up the largest percentage, 30%, among the Mexicans and Puerto Ricans; it makes up only 16% of the Cuban subgroup. In the years to come, however, the number of children of Hispanic origin who are attending schools in the United States will increase. This shift is already noticeable today. Projections of the number of school-aged children in California suggest that, by the year 2020, the percentage of 6- to 12-year-old children who are Hispanic will be greater than the percentage of those who are Anglo (Figure 2-8). Approximately 43% will be Hispanic, while nearly 35% will be Anglo (Bouvier & Martin, 1987). The projected figures are similar for those in the 13- to 17-year-old age group.

Family Size and Income

Hispanic families are generally larger than are non-Hispanic families, but there are variations among the Hispanic subgroups. The average size of Hispanic fami-

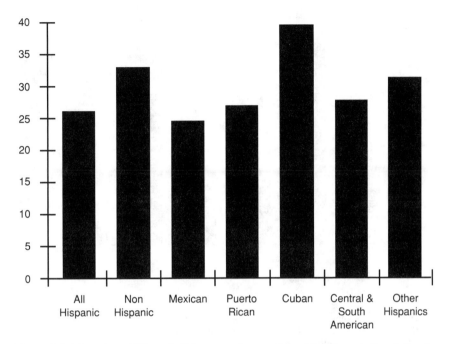

Figure 2-5 Mean Age of Hispanic Subgroups. *Source:* From *The Hispanic Population in the United States,* Current Population Reports, 1990, Washington, D.C.: Bureau of the Census.

lies is 3.8 members, compared to 3.1 members for non-Hispanic families. The average for the Mexican subgroup is 4.1 members (Valdivieso & Davis, 1988).

A greater proportion of Hispanics live below the poverty level compared to non-Hispanics—26% as opposed to 12%. The lack of opportunity for education, low-status occupations, and high unemployment contribute to the decreased income of many Hispanics. As of 1990, for example, 33% of Puerto Ricans and 28% of Mexicans in the United States were living below the poverty level, compared to approximately 15% of Cubans (Figure 2-9).

Another variable that affects the income level of Hispanic families is the family composition. The number of traditional married-couple families has steadily decreased over the years, and the mother is often the main source of financial support for the family. Recent figures indicate that 16% of households are headed by women in the non-Hispanic group, while 23% of households are headed by women in the Hispanic group (Current Population Reports, 1990).

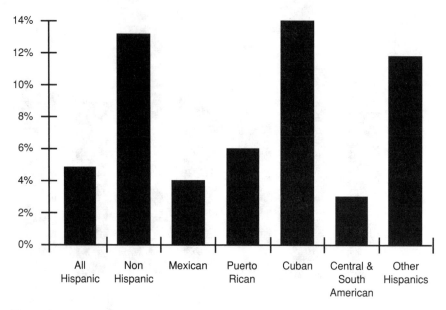

Figure 2-6 Percentage of Hispanics Aged 65 and Over in 1990. *Source:* From *The Hispanic Population in the United States,* Current Population Reports, 1990, Washington, D.C.: Bureau of the Census.

Education

Current Population Reports (1990) indicated that only 58% of Hispanics in the United States, compared to 89% of non-Hispanics, have at least a high-school education by age 25 to 34 years (Figure 2-10). The Cuban and other Hispanic subgroups approximate the non-Hispanic average of 89%. Only 54% of the Mexican subgroup complete their high-school education, however. In addition, only 10% of Hispanics complete 4 years of college or more, in contrast to 22% of the non-Hispanic group (Figure 2-11). The Cuban and other Hispanic subgroups are those with the highest number of college graduates (20%). These statistics document the alarmingly low proportion of Hispanics who have a high-school and higher education.

In addition to the dilemma of determining the effectiveness of certain programs for second-language learners, such as bilingual education programs, educators must confront (1) fluctuating local, state, and federal funding for different programs designed to assist second-language learners; (2) the need to educate students whose school attendance may have been irregular in their country of origin or in the United States because their families have had to move from location to

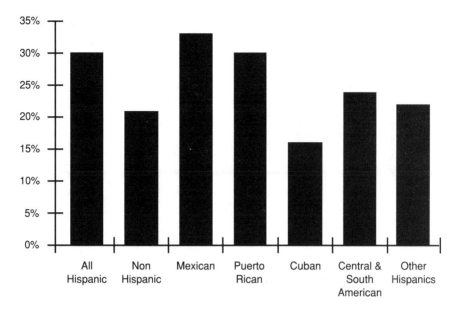

Figure 2-7 Percentage of Hispanic Children Aged 5 to 19 in 1990. *Source:* From *The Hispanic Population in the United States,* Current Population Reports, 1990, Washington, D.C.: Bureau of the Census.

location in pursuit of seasonal jobs; and (3) the students' culture shock and clash in expectations. Many immigrants have fled from economic and political oppression and are ill-prepared to cope with a new, technologically oriented culture. Thus, the expectations of U.S. teachers and schools may be completely new experiences for many incoming children and their parents.

Occupations

Those in the different Hispanic subgroups hold a variety of jobs. Among the subgroups, Mexican men are least likely to hold managerial or professional jobs; only 8% hold such jobs (Current Population Reports, 1990). In contrast, they hold more jobs in farming, forestry, and fishing (11%) than do any other Hispanic subgroup. Cubans tend to be employed in greater proportions in managerial and professional areas (25%), as well as in technical, sales, and administrative support services (28%). Very few Cubans or Puerto Ricans work in farming, forestry, or fishing (not quite 2%). The discrepancies among the different subgroups are much less in other occupations, such as production crafts and repair.

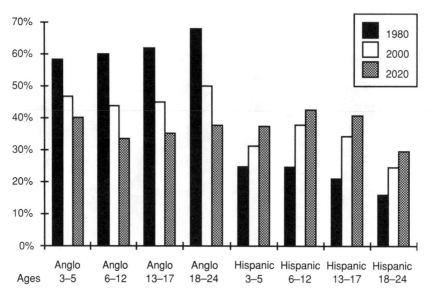

Figure 2-8 Projections for the School-Aged Population in California. *Source:* Data from *Population Change and California's Education System* by L.F. Bouvier and P.L. Martin, 1987, Washington, D.C.: Population Reference Bureau.

Health Care Utilization

Most of the data on the utilization of medical and health-related services pertain to the Hispanic group as a whole rather than specific subgroups. There are some exceptions, however. Pérez-Stable (1987) and Andersen, Giachello, and Aday (1986) reported that Mexicans are three times more likely to be without health insurance than are other Hispanic subgroups and, therefore, are least likely to visit a physician; only about 66% do so regularly. The Mexican subgroup also visits dentists the least frequently. Mexicans and Cubans visit a physician's office as their source of care more frequently than do Puerto Ricans, who use the emergency room more regularly (Schur, Bernstein, & Berk, 1987). Puerto Ricans are twice as likely to be without health insurance than is the non-Hispanic population. On the other hand, consistent with their overall socioeconomic, educational, and occupational attainments, Cubans have the highest proportion of private health insurance and pay the most for medical services out of pocket (Schur et al., 1987). Data on health services utilization by Central and South Americans or other Hispanics are difficult to find. The 1990 census should provide more reliable information on each Hispanic subgroup's access and utilization of health care services.

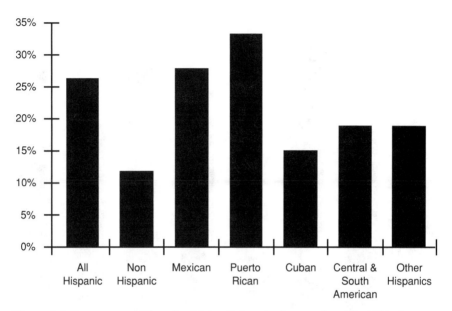

Figure 2-9 Percentage of Hispanics Living Below the Poverty Level in 1990. *Source:* From *The Hispanic Population in the United States,* Current Population Reports, 1990, Washington, D.C.: Bureau of the Census.

IDENTIFYING THE MEXICAN SUBGROUP

Various names, such as Mexican-Americans, Chicanos, and Mexicans, have been used with no apparent consistency for the Mexican population in the United States. Lampe (1984) proposed three different labels for Mexicans residing in the United States: (1) Mexican-Americans for those who were born and raised in the United States, (2) Mexicans for those who go back and forth to Mexico, and (3) American-Mexicans for those who have U.S. citizenship and reside in the country. Although the term *Chicanos* has been used to refer to some Mexican-Americans, Chicanos have very specific characteristics. Both Mexican-Americans and Anglos, as well as African-Americans, have described the Chicanos as less well assimilated into the mainstream and prouder of their Indian and Spanish ancestry than other Mexicans (Lampe, 1982).

In the assimilation–ethnic identity paradigm (Kitano, 1989; see Figure 2-2), the first group identified by Lampe (1984), the Mexican-Americans, could be placed anywhere in Quadrant A or B, depending on the length of residence and contact with the Spanish language and Mexican culture (Figure 2-12). Those referred to as

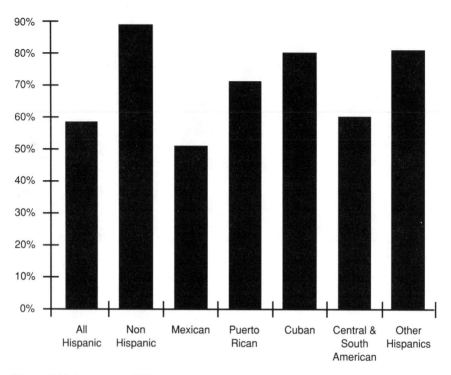

Figure 2-10 Percentage of Hispanics Who Complete High School. *Source:* From *The Hispanic Population in the United States,* Current Population Reports, 1990, Washington, D.C.: Bureau of the Census.

Mexicans would belong in Quadrant C. American-Mexicans would most likely be in Quadrant A or B, again depending on their contact with the Spanish language and Mexican culture. Chicanos, on the other hand, would be placed in Quadrant C or D, also depending on their Spanish-English proficiency and degree of assimilation to each one of the two cultures.

Geography and History

Mexico's border to the north is the United States, while Guatemala and Belize are to the south. Mexico has an area of 767,919 square miles and an estimated population of 84 million. Its capital, Mexico City, is one of the largest cities in the world, with more than 20 million inhabitants. The ethnic composition of Mexico is 60% Mestizo, 30% Indian, and 10% Caucasian (Dostert, 1989). The greatest number of Indian groups live in the southwest—in the states of Chiapas and

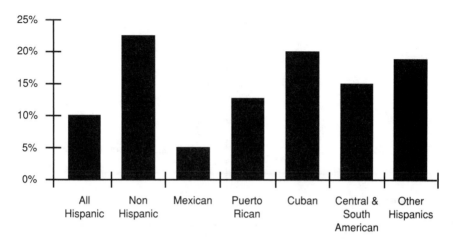

Figure 2-11 Percentage of Hispanics with 4+ Years of College. *Source:* From *The Hispanic Population in the United States,* Current Population Reports, 1990, Washington, D.C.: Bureau of the Census.

Oaxaca—and the center and Mideast regions—in the states of Guanajuato, Querétaro, Veracruz, and Puebla, and the state of Mexico. A map of Mexico and the main Indian groups, as well as their locations, is provided in Figure 2-13, A and B.

Spanish is the principal language, but at least 52 different Indian languages are spoken by specific groups. These languages are often unintelligible to the other linguistic groups. Some 4 million of the Mexican Indians speak only Indian languages, and their participation in the mainstream society is almost nonexistent (S. Wyszewiañski, personal communication, September 1990). Despite their minimal proficiency in Spanish, some have traveled to Mexico City in pursuit of better economic opportunities, and a few have even emigrated to California.

Conquered by Spain in 1521, Mexico gained its independence in 1821. In the first part of the 19th century, Mexico's territory was vast. It included not only the territory that is Mexico today, but also several U.S. states: Texas, California, Nevada, Utah, New Mexico, and most of Arizona, as well as parts of Wyoming and Colorado. Mexico lost all of its U.S. land as a result of the Mexican-American War of 1846–1848. Following the annexation of this land to the United States, the inhabitants of these territories automatically became U.S. citizens. Many Mexicans continued to cross the border between Mexico and the United States freely until 1930, however, when border controls were established between the two countries.

Figure 2-12 Relationship between Assimilation and Ethnic Identity According to Lampe (Adapted from Kitano) for the Mexican Subgroup. *Source:* From *Counseling Across Cultures* (p. 143) by P.B. Pedersen et al. (eds.), 1989, Honolulu, HI: University of Hawaii Press. Copyright 1989 by University of Hawaii Press. Adapted by permission.

Today, the border stretches along the Río Grande more than 1,400 miles. Despite immigration restrictions, illegal entries into the United States are common because of Mexico's severe economic crisis. At the same time, Mexico is burdened by an increasing number of Central Americans, mostly Guatemalan Indians, who fled to Mexico in 1982 to escape army massacres. Approximately 400,000 Central Americans have remained in Mexico illegally (Paul, 1987).

It has been estimated that 10% of Mexico's population owns 40% of the national wealth; conversely, the poorest 40% owns 10% of the wealth. Approximately 30% of the population has no access to safe water, and 40% are undernourished. Literacy for those who have access to education is estimated to be 88%, up

Figure 2-13A Map of Central America. *Source:* From *The Children's Atlas* (p. 73) by D. Wright and J. Wright, 1989, London: George Philip Ltd. Copyright 1989 by George Philip Ltd. Reprinted by permission.

SONORA
1. Seris
2. Yaquis
CHIHUAHUA
3. Tarahumaras
NAYARIT
4. Coras

JALISCO-NAYARIT
5. Huichols
MICHOACAN
6. Purepechas
GUANAJUATO
7. Chichimecs
QUERÉTARO
8. Otomis

VERACRUZ
11. Totonacs

CHIAPAS
15. Lacandons
16. Choles
17. Tzotzilos
18. Tzeltalos
19. Tojolabalos
20. Mames

STATE OF MEXICO
8. Otomis
9. Mazahuas

HIDALGO
8. Otomis

PUEBLA
8. Otomis
10. Nahuas
11. Totonacs
12. Tepehuas

SAN LUIS POTOSI
13. Huaxtecs

YUCATAN
14. Mayans

OAXACA
21. Mixtecs
22. Mazatecs
23. Cuicatecs
24. Chinantecs
25. Mixes
26. Zapotecs
27. Huaves
28. Triques
29. Chatinos
30. Amuzgos

Figure 2-13B Locations of Principal Indian Groups in Mexico. *Source:* From *Musée National d'Anthropologie: Guides Panorama,* Col. Anzures, Mexico: Panorama Editorial, S.A., 1988.

from 20% in 1910 (Dostert, 1989), but many of the poor do not have access to education and remain illiterate. Yet, the National University of Mexico is the oldest Latin American university and is recognized as one of the leading learning institutions of the southern hemisphere. Furthermore, Mexico has universities in 17 of its 28 states. Even so, only 1 in 1,000 Mexicans completes the equivalent of a U.S. college education.

Many of the Mexican immigrants to the United States come from the lower socioeconomic brackets. Although some Mexicans migrate from rural to urban areas within Mexico, many choose to leave Mexico for the United States for economic reasons. U.S. employers hire these immigrants because they are willing to work for lower pay or to take jobs that are unattractive to other Americans. Presently, there are approximately 14 million Mexicans in the United States. It is estimated that 1.5 to 3 million live in the United States illegally, despite the Immigration Reform and Control Act that Congress passed in 1986 to establish sanctions against the employers of illegal aliens.

A large proportion of Mexican immigrants are migrant workers who move from state to state in pursuit of seasonal jobs, mostly related to agriculture. Several U.S. school districts have instituted special school schedules to accommodate the educational needs of these children. The programs operate during the months that the children's parents are working instead of the regular academic year. When the children identified as "migrant" move from place to place, their files with all the necessary medical and educational information go with them. In some California and Texas districts, these children may qualify for certain programs, such as summer school, that are not open to children whose parents are not migrant workers.

Personal Accounts

A second-generation Mexican-American woman reports.

> As I tell you my story, I rather use English than Spanish because my vocabulary is better. I was born in northern California, but my parents met in Arizona before they settled in my place of birth. My mother was born in the U.S. from parents who had both moved from Sonora, Mexico. My father met my mother in the 1950s as he came to work in the "bracero" program [Migrant-occupation implying the use of one's arms "brazo"]. He came originally from Michoacán, Mexico, and his family was very poor. With the money he made here in the U.S., he could support his mother and six siblings. After my parents met, they decided to come up to California. Neither of my parents were able to complete grade school. However, my mother was proficient in the two languages, and my father has learned enough English to communicate

with his fellow workers. He started as a farm worker, but then became a truck driver. My parents sent us kids to Catholic school. The nuns were tough, but I am proud of having completed high school and 2 years of business college. My own husband comes from Michoacán, too, and has been in this country for 10 years. He had difficulty completing his own education beyond the fifth grade in Mexico. He, too, came to work in the fields as a young man, and then my father helped him get into the trucking business. My husband has some learning problems, and his English is poor. We speak Spanish at home, but I am happy to be bilingual because I can go to school to talk to the teachers and help my own kids with their homework.

I believe in education. I am not able to work now because I am raising my family, but, eventually, I want to get into a computer training program and take a job as a secretary in an office.

A first-generation Mexican women tells her story.

My husband and I are from the same state of Durango, Mexico, but we met in this area through mutual friends. We both have been here 12 years. Neither of us went beyond the sixth grade in Mexico. Our parents came along with us to join some relatives. One of my brothers was born here; he is 11. I am 28 years old. When I came here, I tried to study English at school, but I had a hard time and I dropped out. Now that we are separated, I have had to take on a housekeeping job in a motel to help support my two preschool-aged children. At home, I speak Spanish to my kids, but they are learning English in their Head Start program. I want them to be bilingual. Sometimes I miss Mexico; I have only been back one time since we came here for good. But I know the economy is bad there and we are lucky to be here. I hope my kids like school and do well so they can choose a job—not like me.

The words of these two women express the feelings and background of some families of Mexican origin, as well as their goals and hopes as they become part of their new country. These two stories also emphasize the desire of the mothers for their children to be bilingual; eventually, their children may be truly bilingual-bicultural and fit into Quadrant B of the paradigm in Figure 2-12.

IDENTIFYING THE PUERTO RICAN SUBGROUP

Puerto Ricans are also referred to as Neoyoricans because so many of them originally migrated to New York.

Geography and History

Puerto Rico is an island situated at the northeastern area of the Caribbean Sea. Roughly rectangular in form, it is 100 miles long and 35 miles wide. The population is estimated at 3.5 million (Dostert, 1989). The capital, San Juan, is a port on the northeastern coast of the island (Figure 2-14).

Christopher Columbus reached Puerto Rico in 1493. At that time, the island was inhabited by three native Indian tribes of Arawak origin. When the island was taken under Spanish rule, Ponce de León was its first governor. Because of its strategic location, the island was a military target from the very beginning. The Spanish built massive fortifications to repel the French, British, and Dutch. Puerto Rico attempted an unsuccessful revolution against Spain in 1868. Following the Spanish-American War of 1898, Spain ceded Puerto Rico, along with Guam and the Philippines, to the United States.

Initially, Puerto Rico was an unincorporated territory, but it has been a self-governing commonwealth since 1952. The people elect a governor and legislative assembly to serve for 4-year terms. In addition, they elect a resident commissioner to the U.S. House of Representatives. This official can introduce legislation, but

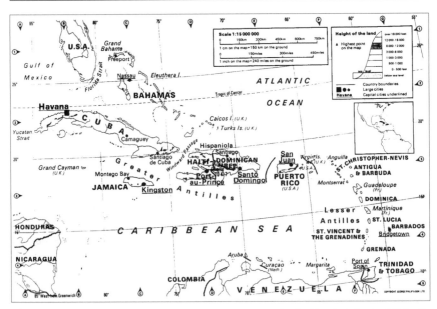

Figure 2-14 Map of the Caribbean Area. *Source:* From *The Children's Atlas* (p. 74) by D. Wright and J. Wright, 1989, London: George Philip Ltd. Copyright 1989 by George Philip Ltd. Reprinted by permission.

cannot vote. At the end of World War I, Congress granted all Puerto Ricans U.S. citizenship; however, they do not vote in national elections and do not have to pay income tax. The people have divided opinions regarding whether Puerto Rico should become a state, seek independence, or remain a commonwealth. Referendums held in 1967 and 1981 indicated that the majority wish to remain a commonwealth, although this opinion may change (Skabelund & Sims, 1990).

As a result of increased job opportunities on the mainland and more regular, less expensive air service between San Juan and New York in the 1950s, a vast migration to the mainland took place at that time. Nearly one in every six Puerto Ricans migrated during that decade. Since the 1950s, however, migration has decreased (Davis, Haub, & Willette, 1983; Dostert, 1989).

It is difficult to determine the exact number of Puerto Ricans who reside on the mainland because of their continual migration between the United States and the island. The number is estimated to be approximately 2 million. According to the 1980 census, half of the Puerto Rican residents were born on the mainland and settled mostly in New York, New Jersey, and Massachusetts. For many newcomers, adjusting to the colder climates of the northeastern states has been difficult. Many have reported missing the sunshine of the island. It is interesting that Puerto Rican settlement has been primarily in the northeast rather than the southeast (e.g., Florida). It is possible that New York, which has always been the initial port of entry for newcomers, attracted the first Puerto Ricans. Once these people were established, others found it easier to begin their new lives in the same place. Unlike Mexicans and Central or South Americans, Puerto Ricans do not have to work on the mainland under illegal conditions, although many have found it necessary to change their occupation from agriculture to factory, manufacturing, or service professions.

Personal Account

A young Puerto Rican man tells his story.

> My parents immigrated to Boston when I was 4 years old. Their move was prompted by a severe economic change in the island. My father had been a fairly successful farmer in the city of Ponce. In the 50s, as the economy began to change, my father's property lost its value. We had some relatives on the East Coast, and that's why we decided to move to the mainland. I remember the first winter we spent in the city. My parents were very depressed. For one, the weather was so cold; we were not used to the long and cold winters. My father knew very little English. While we were receiving welfare (my parents were very ashamed of this), my father was being trained as an electrician. As he was completing his training, his English also began improving.

After finishing his program, he got a paying job. We were able to move from the apartment complex where we were living to a house we shared with some of our relatives. Although we were a bit crowded, we were happy to have our own place.

I began attending the Boston schools and really enjoyed it. There was a great deal of support for bilingual education and, although I felt a bit of discrimination from some of the Anglo and Black kids, I had very supportive teachers. I graduated from high school and then was able to enter a state college. Now I am completing my bachelor's in computer science and, because I have bilingual skills, I hope to find a job easier than the person who only speaks English. I wish all persons could be bilingual; the society would be so much better off. We have been back and forth to Puerto Rico for some visits. It is nice to go see the place where you were born, but I don't want to live there. We are happier here.

Very likely, the migration of Puerto Ricans to the mainland will continue to slow down in the years to come. The Puerto Rican government has initiated a program to enhance the island's trade with its Caribbean neighbors, and U.S. investments have increased. Even though the number of Puerto Ricans in the United States is relatively small, they constitute a specific Hispanic subgroup with special needs and characteristics that should be familiar to any professional who works with this subgroup (Dostert, 1989). In the paradigm of assimilation–ethnic identity (see Figure 2-2), the clinician may encounter Puerto Ricans who fit into Quadrants A, B, or C, depending on their contact with each language and culture. Second- and third-generation Puerto Ricans tend to fit into Quadrant A, although some may fit best into Quadrant B.

IDENTIFYING THE CUBAN SUBGROUP

Today's Cuban population in the United States is approximately 1 million (Valdivieso & Davis, 1988). Most of these Cubans reside in Florida, and in the New York and Washington, D.C., areas. Cuba has experienced considerable upheaval in its efforts to become independent and to preserve its political stability. The two major emigration waves from Cuba into the United States are both attributable to the political changes in that country.

Geography and History

Cuba is the largest and most westerly island of the Caribbean Sea (see Figure 2-14. It lies only 90 miles south of Florida and has 44,217 square miles, making it 11 times larger than Puerto Rico. The population is approximately 11.5 million and is 51% Mulatto, 37% White, and 11% Black (Dostert, 1989).

Christopher Columbus landed in Cuba in 1492, and Spain ruled the island for almost 400 years afterward. A decade long independence war broke out in the 1860s, with limited success. In 1890, José Martí, a Cuban who believed in independence, rekindled the war. It lasted 3 years, ending only when the United States intervened. Cuba gained its independence in 1898, but the United States occupied its territory until 1902. The Platt Amendment gave the United States rights to intervene in the case of any revolt, but this right was abrogated in 1934 (Dostert, 1989).

Until the 1930s, a series of governments characterized by political corruption and economic instability ruled Cuba. In 1933, Juan Batista took over the government on a provisional basis. Supported by several existing parties, including the Communists, he became Cuba's president in 1940. Although the country prospered initially, opposition soon arose. His government was overthrown in 1958, and Fidel Castro became Cuba's leader. During Castro's tenure, Communist influence increased. By 1960, the pro-Communist government had created great discontent among many Cubans, and the first wave of Cubans emigrated to the United States. An estimated 1 million fled their country at that time. According to the 1980 U.S. census, the first Cuban arrivals were generally well educated and came from the upper class, which may well be the reason that, as reported earlier, they tended to obtain better jobs and earn higher incomes than did other Hispanic subgroups in the United States. Those who learned English then fit the description of persons belonging in Quadrant B (bilingual-bicultural) in the assimilation–ethnic identity paradigm (see Figure 2-2).

Following the victory of the Bay of Pigs in 1961, Castro declared Cuba a socialist country. The Soviet Union continued to send military equipment to the island. Almost simultaneously, leftist revolutionary propaganda was aimed at other Latin American countries, including Mexico and Argentina. Diplomatic ties between Cuba and the United States were severed and were not reestablished until 1977. A second wave of immigrants entered the United States after 1980. Many of the persons who left Cuba at that time (approximately 125,000) were prisoners and mentally ill patients. Castro's anger toward Peru, which had offered asylum to future Cuban refugees, prompted him to permit this new wave of immigration. In 1984, the United States and Cuba reached an agreement under which 2,700 new refugees who were not allowed entry into the United States because of their criminal past or mental status would be deported back to Cuba. In return, better relations were to be established between the two countries. The agreement was canceled, however, following broadcasts by Radio Martí's, a U.S.–based radio station, that brought a non-Communist view to the Cubans.

Today, Cuba continues to spend large sums of money on military weapons and an army of approximately 200,000, even though its economy is suffering. Recent mold and sugar rust fungus infestations have curtailed the growth of two of its main products, tobacco and sugar. Also, consumer goods are poorly manufactured and distributed. As of 1989, relations with the Soviet Union have deteriorated because of the Cuban government's unwillingness to accept "glasnost" (openness) and perestroika (reform). The future of the country is difficult to predict (Dostert, 1989).

Personal Account

The following is a recounting by a young Cuban man.

> My ancestors were Spaniards. For all intents and purposes, I am what you call a Creole. When I was born in 1950 in La Havana, my father worked as an engineer for the Public Works Department. My mother had to quit her grade-school teaching to take care of me. I have a younger sister who was born 3 years later. When my father realized that the political climate was unstable, we decided to pack and join some distant relatives who lived in the Washington, D.C., area. By then, the revolution had already started. We were lucky to be able to take our belongings with us. Only a few years later, everyone who left the country had to leave their possessions behind. As a matter of fact, my grandfather, who had a successful business, lost it all and came to live with us in 1962.
>
> To make a living, my father worked in a factory, repairing equipment. Slowly, he began taking classes to get his accreditation and, after 5 years, got his bachelor's. My parents were somewhat fluent in English when they emigrated to the U.S., so there was not such a large language barrier. My father eventually was hired as an engineer for Shell Oil. He worked there from 1960 until his retirement 2 years ago. My mother pursued her teaching credentials after we kids went to school, and she worked as a bilingual teacher until 2 years ago as well. My parents are retired. I finished college and met my wife, who is an American-born Hispanic. We have a 5-year-old who is perfectly bilingual. I work as a businessman for a manufacturing company. We do a lot of business in many countries in Central and South America. I am still very proud of being Hispanic and regret I had to leave the country where I was born.

IDENTIFYING THE CENTRAL AND SOUTH AMERICAN SUBGROUPS

Castro's Cuba has had a substantial influence on other Latin American countries, such as El Salvador and Nicaragua, that have also had long civil wars. Indeed, more and more immigrants from those Central American countries have been settling in the United States since the beginning of the 1990s. Most of the recent immigrants from Central and South America are from Guatemala, Nicaragua, El Salvador, the Dominican Republic, Panama, Chile, or Argentina. It is not uncommon, however, to come in contact with immigrants from other Hispanic countries.

Immigration Information

Hispanics from Central and South America are classified in one category for census data, making it more difficult to differentiate the various subgroups. It is estimated that 14%, or approximately 3.5 million persons in the United States, are from one of several Central or South American countries (Figure 2-13A; see Figure 2-15). In many cases, the United States does not recognize their refugee status, and some persons have had to return to their country of origin or settle in other countries, such as Mexico. There is no particular area within the United States where Central and South Americans live; they tend to settle where there are jobs and economic opportunities, as well as where they may have a network of relatives or friends. They tend to reside in the great metropolitan areas of the Midwest, West, and East, such as Chicago, Los Angeles, and New York.

Subgroups' Background

Although immigrants from Central and South American countries share many aspects of geography, history, culture, and society, there may be exceptions and individual differences. For example, the majority of Argentineans are of European descent, and Spanish is the principal language. English, German, and Italian are also spoken in Argentina, however. On the other hand, Chile has a different ethnic composition; the majority of people are Mestizos. Thus, Spanish, German, and two Indian languages (i.e., Quechua and Araucanian) are spoken.

The ease with which these immigrants adapt to the United States varies from group to group and from individual to individual. For example, Suárez-Orozco (1987) reported that Central American children adapt to U.S. schools better than do children from Mexico and some of the other Hispanic countries. The particular group that he studied was greatly motivated by their parents to succeed. Also, it is not unusual for children from some of the Central American countries to reside with relatives or friends while their parents and siblings are still in the country of origin. In many cases, parents send children alone to spare them from the devastation of civil war. Pérez-Stable (1987) reported that, because of trauma caused by war, Salvadorans, for example, evidence stress comparable to that of U.S. soldiers returning from Vietnam.

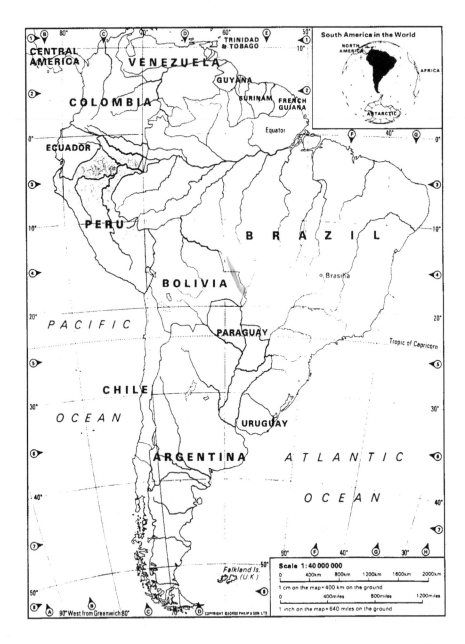

Figure 2-15 Map of South America. *Source:* From *The Children's Atlas* (p. 77) by D. Wright and J. Wright, 1989, London: George Philip Ltd. Copyright 1989 by George Philip Ltd. Reprinted by permission.

Personal Account

Political unrest and economic hardship are the two main reasons that individuals leave their countries. A Nicaraguan woman who recently immigrated to the United States tells her story.

> My husband, daughter, and I are recent immigrants from Nicaragua. The economy was so bad—due to the political situation—that my husband and I decided to leave. We did not want to go to Mexico because of its own devastating economy. In Nicaragua, we had a fairly successful clothing store, but, the last few years, we could not break even. People were in debt and we could just not keep up. We decided to sell and join some distant relatives here in New York, and they were able to sponsor us.
>
> I come from a family of four children. We lived in a small rural area of Nicaragua near Managua. My parents are farmers and had very limited education themselves, but they believed in us going to school. They sent us to a Catholic boarding school. We all graduated from high school. All my three brothers have a college degree, and perhaps some day they will be able to come here, too.
>
> The first 2 years in the U.S. were very difficult for us. We spoke some English, but really experienced what you call "cultural shock." To support ourselves, we worked as nurse's aides; my husband took the night shift, and I did the day shift so that our daughter would be taken care of. We also attended classes. Both of us have finished 2 years of college and hope to continue. I want to become a nurse, and my husband is thinking about going into business school and pursuing a career in retailing. We are very happy here, but I miss our family and friends.

As with any group, there are individual differences. For example, Nicaraguans who have immigrated to the United States have had varied occupational and educational experiences in their own country. Furthermore, some may have lived in Mexico a few years before they entered the United States.

IDENTIFYING THE OTHER HISPANICS SUBGROUP

Recent immigrants from Spain and others whose families may have immigrated many centuries ago are included in the other Hispanics subgroup. Some do not identify themselves as coming from Spain, for example, but feel that they are of "Hispanic origin." There are approximately 1.5 million persons in this category. They are settled in all states where there are large percentages of Hispanics. Many of these persons reside in New Mexico and Arizona. A map of Spain appears in Figure 2-16.

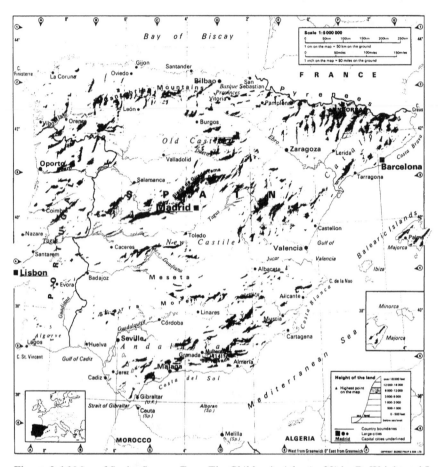

Figure 2-16 Map of Spain. *Source:* From *The Children's Atlas* (p. 30) by D. Wright and J. Wright, 1989, London: George Philip Ltd. Copyright 1989 by George Philip Ltd. Reprinted by permission.

In the next few decades, the number of Hispanics in the United States will increase as a result of population growth and migration from many Central and South American countries. It seems that, 500 years after the Spaniards first arrived on the center of the American continent and began their journey into the South, the Hispanic influence will soon penetrate the northern part of the continent. Thus, increasingly, the Hispanic presence will be felt in the United States and Canada throughout the economic, political, and educational fields.

SPEECH AND LANGUAGE-LEARNING DISABILITIES IN HISPANICS

Assuming that 10% of the Hispanic population may have various speech- and language-related problems, approximately 2.3 million persons of Hispanic origin need speech, language, and hearing services. The identification of these individuals is often difficult, however. The number of Hispanic children and adolescents who may have various speech and language problems fluctuates, depending on the methodology and criteria used to collect such information. This often results in over- or underidentification of that segment of the population and may have adverse repercussions for the individual and family. There are no data on Hispanic adults who have different speech and language impairments; data are available on Whites and Blacks only. Thus, the incidence of different speech and language impairments in the adult Hispanic population can only be estimated.

Children and Adolescents

Determining the number of Hispanic children and adolescents with various speech/language disorders or learning disabilities is difficult because of four principal factors (Dew, 1984). First, some students receive services from different special programs, yet they are "categorized" under one main label. For example, a student who is considered "learning-disabled" may also have a speech and language problem. This piece of information may not be directly logged for counting or statistical purposes.

Second, the percentage of students served under one category may vary from district to district, county to county, region to region, and even school to school, depending on the availability of programs. Fewer students seem to be referred for special education when bilingual programs are available within the regular classroom to meet their needs (Finn, 1982). The data may be misleading, however, because some students may not be adequately served in the regular bilingual programs.

Third, national surveys come primarily from two sources in the federal government: the Office of Civil Rights, which conducts biannual surveys, and the Office of Special Education Programs Child Count, which takes place annually. Thus, proportions of handicapped students reported under different categories and across ethnic groups vary because of the methods and timing of data collection. It may be that it will always be difficult to obtain accurate numbers.

Finally, a sizable number of Hispanic students are migrant or limited-English–proficient (LEP), but their numbers cannot be accurately determined due to their frequent moves and their spotty school attendance. The language dominance/proficiency of Hispanic students is often assessed inaccurately because of language and cultural barriers related to the different assessment methodologies and interpretations of the results. For instance, the group of speech and language clinicians in California interviewed by Carpenter (1983) reported that 20% of their caseloads involved LEP students, but the district reported only 1%. Another study by Cegelka, Rodríguez, Lewis, Pacheco, and Santa Cruz (1984) indicated that the proportion of LEP students receiving special education services was higher than was the proportion of the state's population at large, that is, 11% as opposed to 7%. Despite discrepancies between the data obtained by federal and state agencies, data obtained by the Office of Civil Rights appear to be the most comprehensive on the incidence of ethnic minorities in special education (Chinn & Hughes, 1987).

Table 2-2 shows the percentages of Hispanics and Whites identified in each category of exceptionality for the years 1978 through 1986 at 2-year intervals. As noted from these data, the percentage of Hispanics in the educable mentally retarded category is underrepresented for each year, as is the percentage of those in the speech-impaired category. The proportion of learning-disabled students has been closest to the actual proportion of Hispanics in this category (using the 10% criterion). Possibly, some students who would otherwise have been classified as educable mentally retarded or speech-impaired have been classified in the broader category of learning-disabled. For Whites, the proportions in the learning-disabled and speech-impaired categories have been close to their representation in the schools. There is also a significant discrepancy between the two groups in the gifted/talented category. More Whites are represented in this category proportionately to their enrollment in the schools as compared to Hispanics.

The percentages of all children identified in the speech-impaired and learning-disabled categories shift dramatically between the Head Start and the school-aged population (Figure 2-17). For example, 62.9% of Head Start children were identified as speech-impaired and only 5.6% as learning-disabled during the 1985–1986 school year (United States Department of Health and Human Services, Administration for Children, Youth, and Families, 1987). During the 1986–1987 school year the percentages of children identified in the K–12 grades were 25.8% for speech-impaired and 43.6% for learning-disabled (Tenth Annual Report to Congress on the Implementation of the Education of the Handicapped Act, 1988). These percentages are illustrated in Figure 2-17. This change in labeling reflects the fact that speech and language problems are more readily identified in the early years, but later on language difficulties are often observed in conjunction with academic learning, including learning disabilities (Wallach & Butler, 1984). Data on Hispanic or other minorities are not available for preschool age children.

The proportion of children served in either the speech-impaired or learning-disabled categories is slightly lower for Hispanics than for Whites, compared to their representation in the schools. There are wider discrepancies in other categories, such as gifted and talented. Naturally, these conclusions are tentative, given

Table 2-2 Percentage of Hispanics and Whites Enrolled in Each Category of Exceptionality

Category	1978	1980	1982	1984	1986
			(Percentage)		
Hispanic					
EMR	4.61	4.84	3.73	10.11	6.30
TMR	6.95	8.53	7.70	11.90	10.70
SED	6.14	7.24	5.01	7.63	6.20
LD	7.54	8.53	8.81	13.38	11.90
SI	6.02	7.30	6.53	10.17	9.40
G/T	5.12	5.43	4.00	7.17	6.50
Percentage in total					
school population	6.75	9.03	8.64	13.22	12.50
White					
EMR	56.07	48.50	41.21	39.92	47.40
TMR	64.19	58.80	53.05	51.79	54.80
SED	68.26	63.09	61.69	60.23	65.60
LD	75.41	69.76	62.08	58.61	63.30
SI	77.2	71.60	65.85	63.26	65.90
G/T	80.90	78.77	80.01	72.78	74.80
Percentage in total					
school population	75.32	67.96	62.48	57.86	61.80

Note: EMR, educable mentally retarded; TMR, trainable mentally retarded; SED, seriously emotionally disturbed; LD, learning-disabled; SI, speech-impaired; GT, gifted/talented.

OCR reports. *Source:* Data from "Representation of Minority Students in Special Education Classes" by P.C. Chinn and S. Hughes, 1987, *Remedial and Special Education, 8,* pp. 41–46, PRO-ED, and from the Council for Exceptional Children. The 1986 OCR data provided by B.A. Ramirez (Council for Exceptional Children).

the variations from one district to another in the identification process and availability of programs. Furthermore, there are no national statistics on how many LEP students have Spanish as their first language. It appears that eligibility for special education depends on whether appropriate school programs are available rather than on whether a student indeed has a language/learning disability. The lack of statistics presents a very serious problem.

The labeling process can have a profound emotional impact on students and their families. In his review of eligibility criteria for special education, Rueda (1989) discussed issues of misidentification that are applicable to all students, and especially LEP students. These issues include primarily the inadequacy of assessment instruments, controversy over definitions of learning disability, and diffi-

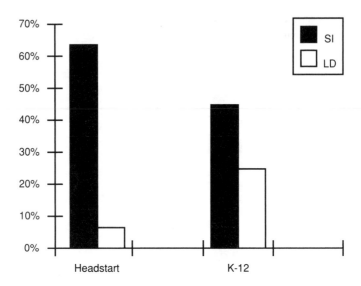

Figure 2-17 Speech-Impaired and Learning-Disabled Children in Head Start and Grades K–12 (Total Population): 1985–1986 and 1986–1987. *Source:* U.S. Department of Health and Human Services, Administration for Children, Youth, and Families (Fourteenth Annual Report on Services Provided to Handicapped Children in Project Head Start, 1987). K–12 (Tenth Annual Report to Congress on the Implementation of the Education of the Handicapped Act, 1988).

culty in translating assessment data into practical suggestions for educational intervention. The idea of utilizing special education as a substitute for needed school programs that are nonexistent is a well-documented phenomenon. Professionals agree that it is time to structure regular programs so that they can accommodate a broad range of students who can succeed when offered alternative ways to learn. Conversely, special programs should be left for those who have not been able to progress, despite repeated attempts to modify the regular curriculum.

Discrete-point tests (tests that measure discrete language items such as vocabulary or use of specific grammatical features) or proficiency tests, which are often used as sole measures in labeling and classifying students' language proficiency in any given language, should be interpreted with care. Other data, such as those drawn from observations and modifications of the regular program, need to be considered. Obviously, the process is more complex and time-consuming when the student comes from a non-mainstream background. Nevertheless, the process should be carried out so that second-language students may receive a fair and equitable education.

Adults

Statistics on adults with communication disorders are important in planning needed services for this particular population. Although there are no data available on the prevalence of speech/language impairments in Hispanics, there are data available for Whites and Blacks (Table 2-3). Proportionately more Black adults than White adults have a tendency to be affected by a speech or language impairment. The prevalence of speech and language impairments for both groups is higher for those in the 65 to 74 years category, for example, but higher for Blacks (44/1,000) than for Whites (9/1,000).

The number of aphasic adults is difficult to estimate. Approximately one fifth of adult stroke patients have aphasia (National Institute of Neurological and Communicative Disorders and Stroke [NINCDS], 1985). Part of the National Institutes of Health, the NINCDS estimates that roughly 500,000 cases of acquired neurological disabilities result from stroke; 200,000 from head wounds; and 300,000 from infections, exposure to toxic materials, lead poisoning, and other causes. Stroke is most likely to occur in those who are 55 years old or older (Table 2-4).

The prognosis for stroke survivors varies: 10% will return to their past activities and work, 40% will have a mild residual disability, 40% will require moderate assistance, and 10% will need long-term residential care ("Psychological and Social Adjustment," 1988). Statistics for Hispanics are not readily available. Based on a population of 23 million Hispanics, however, there are likely to be approximately 32,000 to 35,000 cases of stroke and 16,000 cases of head trauma among that population each year.

Table 2-3 Speech Impairment Conditions per 1,000 Persons by Race and Age in the United States (1987)

	Different Age Groups				
Race	*Under age 45*	*45–64*	*Under 45–64 TOTAL*	*65–74*	*Over 74*
White	10.4	4.0	7.8	9.3	5.5*
Black	18.8	15.4*	41.2*	43.7*	37.0*

*An estimate for which the numerator has a relative standard error of more than 30 percent.

Source: From *Current Estimates from the National Health Interview Survey, United States, 1987,* by C.A. Schoenborn and M. Marano, Vital and Health Statistics Series 10, No. 166, U.S.D.H.H.S. Pub. No. 88-1594, Washington, D.C.: National Center for Health Statistics.

Table 2-4 Percentage of Total Persons in Each Age Group Relative to Stroke Patients

U.S.	All Ages	Under 35	35–44	45–54	55–64	65–74	75–84	85+
Population	100.0	58.3	10.4	11.4	9.5	6.6	3.3	1.0
Stroke patients	100.0	1.2	2.0	6.8	15.6	28.3	33.4	12.7

Source: From *National Survey of Stroke,* 1980, Rockville, MD: Office of Biometry and Field Studies, National Institute of Neurological and Communicative Disorders and Stroke.

CONCLUSION

In order to obtain more accurate information on speech and language disorders in the Hispanic population, investigators should

1. gather data on the Hispanic group at large and the different subgroups to identify the numbers of handicapped children enrolled in Head Start programs. In gathering such information, it would be possible to obtain incidence data that could be used to determine prevalence more accurately.
2. determine the proportion of LEP Hispanic children and adolescents who have speech or language impairments.
3. document the number of adults affected by different neurological problems, such as stroke, head trauma, and progressive neurological diseases.
4. determine the proportions of both Hispanic and non-Hispanic adults who have had chronic speech and language problems since childhood and those who have sustained a problem as a result of stroke, brain trauma, head injury, or a progressive neurological disease.

With an estimated 2.3 million Hispanic speech-, language-, and hearing-handicapped individuals and a very small pool of bilingual Spanish-speaking clinicians, it is imperative to determine how clinicians can best identify and work with this population.

REFERENCES

American Speech-Language-Hearing Association. (1990). *Directory of bilingual speech-language pathologists and audiologists (1990–1991).* Rockville, MD: ASHA.

Andersen, R.M., Giachello, A.L., & Aday, L.A. (1986). Access of Hispanics to health care and cuts in services: A state of the art overview. *Public Health Reports, 101,* 238–251.

Bouvier, L.F., & Martin, P.L. (1987). *Population change and California's education system*. Washington, DC: Population Reference Bureau.

Carpenter, L. (1983). *Communication disorders in limited- and non-English proficient children*. Los Alamitos, CA: National Center for Bilingual Research.

Cegelka, P.Y., Rodriguez, A., Lewis, R.B., Pacheco, R., & Santa Cruz, R. (1984). *Special education services for LEP handicapped students: State of the art and future directions. Specially prepared annotation of project findings.* San Diego, CA: San Diego State University.

Cheng, L.L. (1987). *Assessing Asian language performance*. Gaithersburg, MD: Aspen Publishers.

Chinn, P.C., & Hughes, S. (1987). Representation of minority students in special education classes. *Remedial and Special Education, 8,* 41–46.

Current Population Reports. (1990). *The Hispanic population in the United States: March 1990*. Washington, DC: Bureau of the Census.

Davis, C., Haub, C., & Willette, J. (1983). U.S. Hispanics: Changing the face of America. *Population Bulletin, 38,* 1–44.

Dew, N. (1984). The exceptional bilingual child: Demography. In P.C. Chinn (Ed.), *Education of culturally and linguistically different exceptional children*. Reston, VA: Council for Exceptional Children.

Dostert, P.E. (1989). *Latin America*. Washington, DC: Stryker-Post Publications.

Finn, J.D. (1982). Patterns in special education placement as revealed by OCR survey. In K.A. Heller, W. Holtzman, & C.S. Messick (Eds.), *Placement of children in special education: A strategy for equity* (pp. 322–381). Washington, DC: National Academy Press.

Kitano, H.H. (1989). A model for counseling Asian Americans. In P.B. Pedersen, J.G. Draguns, W.J. Lonner, & J.E. Trimble (Eds.), *Counseling across cultures* (pp. 139–151). Honolulu: University of Hawaii Press.

Lampe, P.E. (1982). Ethnic labels: Naming or name calling. *Ethnic and Racial Studies, 5,* 512–518.

Lampe, P.E. (1984). Mexican Americans: Labeling and mislabeling. *Hispanic Journal of Behavioral Sciences, 6,* 77–85.

Melville, M.R. (1987). Hispanics: Race, class or ethnicity? *The Journal of Ethnic Studies, 16,* 67–83.

National Institute of Neurological and Communicative Disorders and Stroke. (1980). *National Survey of Stroke*. Rockville, MD: U.S. Department of Health and Human Services, NINCDS.

Paul, N. (1987). Mexico's population: A profile. *Population Education Interchange, 16,* 2.

Pérez-Stable, E. (1987). Issues in Latino health care. *Western Journal of Medicine, 146,* 213–218.

"Psychological and social adjustment after stroke." (1988). *Federal Register,* February 17, 1988, p. 4823.

Rueda, R. (1989). Defining mild disabilities with language-minority students. *Exceptional Children, 56,* 121–128.

Sandberg, N. (1986). *Jewish life in Los Angeles*. Lanham, MD: University Press of America.

Schur, C.L., Bernstein, A.B., & Berk, M.L. (1987). The importance of distinguishing Hispanic sub-populations in the use of medical care. *Medical Care, 25,* 627–641.

Skabelund, G.P., & Sims, S.M. (1990). *Culturgram for the '90's.* Provo, UT: Brigham Young University, David M. Kennedy Center for International Studies Publications Services.

Suárez-Orozco, M.M. (1987). Towards a psychosocial understanding of Hispanic adaptation to American schooling. In H.T. Trueba (Ed.), *Success or Failure* (pp. 156–168). New York: Newbury House.

Tenth Annual report to Congress on the implementation of the Education of the Handicapped Act. (1988). Washington, DC: U.S. Department of Education.

Treviño, F.M. (1987). Standardized terminology for Hispanic populations. *American Journal of Public Health, 77,* 69–72.

Trueba, H.T. (1989). *Raising silent voices: Educating the linguistic minorities for the 21st century.* New York: Newbury House.

U.S. Department of Health and Human Services, Administration for Children, Youth and Families. (1987). *Fourteenth annual report to Congress on the status of handicapped children in Head Start Programs.* Washington, DC: U.S. Department of Health and Human Services.

Valdivieso, R., & Davis, C. (1988). *U.S. Hispanics: Challenging issues for the 1990's.* Washington, DC: Population Reference Bureau.

Veltman, C.J. (1988). *The future of the Spanish language in the United States.* Washington, DC: Hispanic Policy Development Project.

Wallach, G.P., & Butler, K.G. (Eds.). (1984). *Language learning disabilities in school age children.* Baltimore: Williams & Wilkins.

Chapter 3

Acquisition of Syntactic and Phonological Features in Spanish

Barbara J. Merino

As it has to some extent with English, research into the acquisition of Spanish as the first language has focused largely on syntax and to a lesser degree on phonology (Anderson & Smith, 1986; Clark, 1985; González, 1978a, 1978b; Merino, 1982; Ortíz, 1980; Van Naerssen, 1980). More recently, the development of pragmatic skills has received more attention from linguists and sociolinguists, and an evaluation of these skills has become an important part of the assessment of children's language competence in English (Brinton & Fujiki, 1989; Ripich & Spinelli, 1985). Less of this type of research has been conducted with monolingual speakers of languages other than English or bilingual individuals, however.

The traditional research trends reflect early definitions of language proficiency (Cohen, 1975). The principal areas of interest were the form of language, its syntax and morphology, phonology and semantics, and comparison of receptive and expressive language skills. These early constructs of language proficiency were influenced by N. Chomsky (1968), who noted that "to have command of a language is to be able, in principle, to understand what is said and to produce a signal with an intended semantic interpretation" (p. 115).

There are two reasons for the interest in the study of Spanish syntax. First, because syntax has been the most researched area of language acquisition in English and other languages, comparisons of progress in the acquisition of language can be made most easily in this area. Second, syntax is least likely to be affected by dialectal and stylistic variation (Dulay, Hernández-Chávez, & Burt, 1978). Some researchers have challenged this view to some degree in response to new constructs of language proficiency (Damico & Oller, 1980). More recent definitions of language proficiency have focused on incorporating notions of language in use in a variety of different contexts.

OVERVIEW OF THE SPANISH LANGUAGE

Historical Origins

Spanish, like English, is an Indo-European language. It is a member of the Italic group (i.e., Oscan, Umbrian, Latin) and, as a direct descendant of Latin, is usually labeled a Romance language, along with Italian, French, Provençal, Catalan, Portuguese, Rhaeto-Romanic, and Rumanian. All were spoken in former enclaves of the Roman empire (Spaulding, 1975). The framework of Spanish and the majority of its vocabulary come from Latin, particularly Vulgar Latin (spoken Latin). Many Spanish words are derived from contact with languages of Germanic tribes before the rise and after the fall of the Roman Empire, however, and from contact with Arabic during the Moorish invasion of Spain in the 8th century.

The rise of Castile as a military power in the 10th century, the popularity of the mid-12th century epic poem *El Cid* (written in Castilian), and the influence of Alfonso X (1252–1284) as one of the founders of Castilian prose culminated in the unification of Aragon and Castile when Ferdinand of Aragon married Isabella of Castile in 1469 (Lockwood, 1972; Spaulding, 1975). Under the rule of Ferdinand and Isabella, the political and military power of the provinces (territories) began to rise. Many administrative reforms, as well as the conquest of the remaining Moorish possessions, reinforced this power. Thus, Castilian evolved as the language of political and literary prestige, overshadowing other languages in the Spanish peninsula (Menéndez Pidál, 1926). (See Figure 2-16 for a map of Spain.) Nonetheless, three dialects of Castilian (Andalusian, Leonese, and Aragonese) continued to be used within their own spheres of influence.

Many of the features found in the Spanish of the New World came from the Andalusian spoken by soldiers sent to Latin America. Seville, the principal city of Andalusia, was the center for colonial trade. At that time, many Spaniards thought that Andalusian was a slovenly articulated Castilian. In Andalusia, vowels are pronounced in a more open manner than in Castile. Also, /s/ is substituted for /θ/ and is frequently reduced to aspiration at the end of a syllable. Thus, *usted* (formal form of *you*) becomes *uhte*. In Murcia, especially, /r/ at the end of a syllable is replaced by /l/; *entender*, for example, becomes *entendel*. One prominent feature of Andalusian semantics is the substitution of *ustedes* for *vosotros* (Navarro Espinosa, & Rodríguez Castellano, 1933). Many of these features occur in varying degrees in the Spanish spoken in the New World.

Spanish and English in Contrast

Spanish differs significantly from English in its phonological, syntactical, semantic, and pragmatic systems. Contrastive analysis, the study of differences and similarities between languages, was for a time a very fruitful area of research. It was considered essential for an understanding of the second-language acquisition process, as many authorities hypothesized that a contrastive analysis of their first and second languages would explain most errors produced by second-language speakers. When actual empirical data were collected on second-language acquisition in speakers from a variety of first languages, however, it was discovered that considerably fewer errors than expected could be ascribed to the first language's interference with the learning of the second language (Dulay, Burt, & Krashen, 1982). Nonetheless, in the early stages of acquisition, particularly in pronunciation, the first language can play a significant role. Thus, it is still useful for clinicians to consider the contrast between the two systems.

Phonology

Spanish has 18 consonants, including 4 semivowels, and English has 24, with 3 semivowels as well (Table 3-1). Spanish has 5 vowels, whereas English has 12 to 14. The labiodental voiced fricative /v/ appears only in English. Spanish speakers tend to replace it with a /b/ or its allophone /ß/. The occurrence of a sound as an allophone in the first language does not necessarily facilitate its acquisition in the second language. For example, Spanish speakers often experience difficulty with the /z/ phoneme, even though this sound occurs in Spanish as a variant of /s/ pronounced before voiced consonants, as in *desde*. Thus, *roses* may be pronounced as /rosəs/. Some sounds may be difficult for Spanish speakers because a contrast preserved in some positions may be absent in others. For example, they may differentiate /m/, /n/, and /ŋ/ in most positions, when they appear at the beginning of a word and between vowels. Yet, the distinction among these sounds is lost before a consonant; only /m/ appears before a labial, and /n/ before a dental or before a velar. A Spanish speaker, thus, may pronounce *sometimes* as /səntaim/ (omitting the final /s/). Mastering vowels in English may be particularly challenging for Spanish speakers. Whereas in English there is a distinction between the long and short vowels, in Spanish there are equivalents only of short vowels (see Table 3-1).

Syntax

One major difference between English and Spanish is the importance that English gives to word order to communicate grammatical meaning, while Spanish relies more frequently on inflection. For example, a question is formed from an affirmative statement in Spanish by raising the intonation. For example, *tú tienes una manzana*, meaning 'you have an apple', means 'do you have an apple?' when the intonation is raised.

The noun phrase has the same paradigm in both English and Spanish.

Noun phrase = Determiner + Noun
[NP = D + N]

Table 3-1 Consonants and Vowels of English and Spanish

Consonants

Manner of Articulation	Bilabial E	Bilabial S	Labio-dental E	Labio-dental S	Dental E	Dental S	Alveolar E	Alveolar S	Retroflex E	Retroflex S	Alveo-palatal E	Alveo-palatal S	Velar E	Velar S	Glottal E	Glottal S
Stop Consonant	p b	p b			t d	t• d•							k g	k g		
Affricate							s z	s •			tʃ dʒ	tʃ •				
Fricative			f v	f •	θ ð	(θ) •					ʃ ʒ	• •		•	x	h	•
Nasal/Lateral	m	m					n • l	n ñ l					ŋ	•		
Semivowels	w	w	• r* • rr*						r	•			y	y		

Note: E = English; S = Spanish; • = no equivalent in the other language; */r/ and /rr/ in Spanish (trill and flap); (θ) dialectal difference.

Vowels

	Spanish front	central	back			English front	central	back
high	/i/		/u/		high	/i/ /ɪ/		/u/ /ʊ/
mid	/ɛ/		/ɔ/		mid	/e/ /ɛ/	/ə/ /ɚ/	/o/ /ɔ/
low		/a/			low	/æ/		/a/

Another major difference is the use of specific determiners (articles). Spanish has a full set of number and gender forms to show agreement with the following noun. For example, an English speaker may say, "*The* frogs are jumping" or "*The* rabbit is jumping," using the same determiner, whereas the Spanish speaker must differentiate both the gender and number of the determiner. Thus, these sentences are "*Las* ranas están saltando" and "*El* conejo está saltando." A similar pattern occurs with the indefinite articles *a* or *an* in English. Only number is marked for possessives, however. For example, *su carro* means 'his or her car', but *sus carros* may also mean 'their cars'. In this case, the possessive is more marked in English than in Spanish. These contrasts are presented in Table 3-2.

In Spanish, adjectives are placed for the most part after the noun; in English, they are placed before the noun. Adjectives in Spanish also agree in number and gender with the noun that they modify, as for example, la casa *blanca* 'the *white* house' and los gatos *negros* 'the *black* cats'.

English has six basic pronouns (I, you, he, she, we, and they) and makes a gender distinction for the third person singular; Spanish not only has equivalent distinctions, but also marks the plurals. In addition, Spanish differentiates a formal and informal you; *tú* is the familiar form, and *Usted* (abreviated *Ud.*) is the formal form.

Both languages have the same four basic transformations: active, passive, negative, and interrogative. In Spanish, however, the word order differs for the negative and in the passive form, and the past participle agrees with the subject in both gender and number. In English, the order for the negative transformation is

Noun phrase + Auxiliary + Negative + Verb + *ing* + Noun phrase functioning as direct object . . . Prepositional phrase

whereas in Spanish, it is

Noun phrase + Negative + Auxiliary + Verb + *ing* + Noun phrase functioning as direct object . . . Prepositional phrase

---

Table 3-2 Articles and Pronouns in Spanish and English

	Spanish		*English*	
	Singular	*Plural*	*Singular*	*Plural*
Articles				
Definite				
Masculine	el	los	the	the
Feminine	la	las	the	the
Neuter	lo			
Indefinite				
Masculine	un	unos	a/an	some
Feminine	una	unas		any
Pronouns				
Masculine	su	sus	his	their
Feminine	su	sus	her	their
Neuter	su	sus	its	their

For example, *la niña* no está tomando *su leche* is 'the girl *is not drinking* her milk'. In English, the order for a passive transformation is

Auxiliary + Verb + *ed*

whereas in Spanish it is

Auxiliary + Verb [Aux + V + ...] + *ido* (*idos*) or *ida* (*idas*)

depending on whether the participle refers to masculine or feminine, singular or plural. For example, la niña está *empujada* por el niño or los niños están *empujados* por la niña is translated as 'the girl is *pushed* by the boy' or 'the boys are *pushed* by the girl'.

In addition, there are three possible conjugations in Spanish: verbs ending in *ar* such as *caminar* 'to walk', *er* such as *comer* 'to eat', and *ir* such as *discutir* 'to discuss'. The past participle for verbs like "camin*ar*" is "camin*ado*" and for verbs like "discut*ir*" is "discut*ido*" with no change in the vowel marking the infinitive. For verbs like "com*er*" the vowel changes and the participle becomes "com*ido*." Although the passive form is less commonly used in Spanish, it has been included in many research projects to mirror the forms that have been studied in English.

The importance of inflections is further noted in the different verb forms. In Spanish, as many as 47 distinct forms can be differentiated. With Spanish verbs, the speaker makes a distinction for the

1. finity (i.e., all sequences of lexical units can be considered possible, but are not equally probable). For example, the word *arrow* in the sentence *I think I'll* . . . has a close to zero probability contrasted with the sentence *I think I will shoot my bow and* . . . (Stockwell, Bowen, & Martin, 1965, p. 5).

2. tense-aspect (i.e., the speaker distinguishes when an action began and when it ended). For example, in *la niña tomaba leche* 'the girl would drink milk' (imperfect), the action happened several times in the past; in *la niña tomó leche* 'the girl drank milk' (preterite), the action happened only once in the past.

3. mood. Spanish differentiates five moods: the infinitive, indicative, future, subjunctive, and imperative.

4. person.

5. number.

In English, only three of these features are preserved: tense, person, and number (Table 3-3).

Clearly, Spanish makes many more distinctions in inflectional categories than does English. In studying the acquisition of inflectional categories in English and

Table 3-3 Inflectional Categories in Spanish and English

	Spanish		English	
Class	Number of Distinct Forms	Inflectional Categories	Number of Distinct Forms	Inflectional Categories
Number	2	Number	2–4	Number, possession
Adjectives	2–5	Number, gender	1	
Pronouns	5–6	Number, gender, case, status	1–5	Number, case, gender
Verbs	46–47	Finity, tense, mood, person, number	4–5	Tense, limited person, number

Spanish, however, most investigators have concentrated on tense and number. Very few have focused on gender, case (type of pronoun), or status [level of formality such as "tú" vs. "ud."], and still fewer have studied mood. Furthermore, most studies have focused on a few selected uses of a feature. For example, the use of the subjunctive mood in Spanish is very complex. It is frequently optional and serves to express nuances of doubt as perceived by the speaker. Clinicians should be aware that the acquisition of the form does not imply the acquisition of the rules for all of its appropriate uses.

Dialect Variations in the Spanish Language

It is sometimes difficult to define and contrast dialect from language and standard varieties from nonstandard varieties because there may be several definitions for each term (Hidalgo, 1987). It is commonly believed that the prestige of a language is closely linked to the general acceptance of a standard variety. Prestige, in turn, is linked to several key attributes: (1) historical actuality, (2) standardization, (3) variety, and (4) homogenicity (Stewart, 1962). A standard language is the social or regional variety that acquired prestige for political and economic reasons. It is probably the language spoken by a community privileged to have an army and a navy. National ideals and traditions may also play a role in defining a standard variety, however. These factors may affect language groups differentially. In Scandinavia, for example, Norwegian, Swedish, and Danish are considered distinct languages, although they are mutually intelligible. In contrast, Chinese is often described as a compendium of dialects when, in fact, many of these dialects are not mutually intelligible—even though they are linked by the same writing system. Thus, many researchers prefer to consider the standard variety an ideal rather than a fact (Escobar, 1976). Nonetheless, speakers from educated communities continue to make judgments about the acceptability of the speech of others. In turn, linguists can identify those features that speakers from educated communities will not accept.

The Spanish system is complex because of its wide geographic distribution. It is spoken as the majority mother tongue in 20 countries throughout the world and as the principal minority tongue in several other countries, most notably in the United States and Paraguay. (Most Paraguayans speak both Spanish and Guaraní.) This wide geographic distribution has led to substantial phonological and lexical variations.

Phonological Variations

Guitart (1981) defined the "educated" Spanish variety spoken on the American continent as free of both deletion and certain types of "phonetic variability," although some variations may be acceptable. For example, this variety may include the elision of certain consonants: /s/ and its weakening to /h/, as in /gatoh/ for *gatos* 'cats' (frequent in Puerto Rican and Cuban Spanish); /d/ in the final position, as in *verdad* 'truth', or even in the medial position, as in /mercao/ instead of *mercado* 'market' (in rural Panama and Mexico). At times, the /s/ at the end of a word is assimilated onto the next, as in /lop perros/ for *los perros* 'the dogs'.

Another variation involves the /rr/, which becomes either alveolar or velar. For example, Puerto Ricans often pronounce the /rr/ in *perro* 'dog' as in the French production of the /r/ (velar). Also, /l/ may replace /r/ in the medial position, as in /puelta/ for *puerta* 'door' (Navarro, 1974). This variation may also occur in Cuban Spanish. Even within the Caribbean islands, there are many variations in the pronunciation of these consonants.

Variations in the Spanish spoken on the American continent also include the substitution of /ʤ/ for /y/ in Argentina; for example, *pollo* 'chicken' may be pronounced /poʤo/. In northern Mexico, this phoneme is often vocalized. For example, a word such as *mayo* 'May' is pronounced /maio/.

Variations in phonology also occur in the Spanish spoken in the Southwest of the United States (Sánchez, 1972). For example, the /y/ in *botella* 'bottle' is omitted, becoming /botea/, and there are variations in the pronunciation of /r/, /rr/, and /s/ among other phonemes. Variations in the Spanish spoken in the United States may result from contact with English. For example, it is not uncommon to hear words such as *cuchara* 'spoon' pronounced with the /ʃ/ instead of /tʃ/, although the phoneme exists in the language.

Thus, in determining if a student has difficulty with phonology, the clinician should first consider the origin of the student. It is helpful to take a careful history and to converse with the family in order to detect the student's linguistic background. Although dialect variation is most remarkable at the phonological level, it can have an impact on grammar as well. For example, in the Southwest, a form such as *rompido* may commonly be used for *roto* 'broken' (past participle). Examples of phonological, lexical, morphological, and syntactical variations in Puerto Rican Spanish and Spanish from the Southwest of the United States are listed in Exhibits 3-1 and 3-2.

Lexical Variations

In a study of the lexical variations of 47 terms related to the office and other common contexts, Marrone (1974) found that educated informants from major cities in the Spanish-speaking world used 352 different words. For example, the word *ballpoint pen* had 19 distinct variants from *biro* in Argentina to *pluma atómica* in Mexico and *plumilla* in Venezuela.

Exhibit 3-1 Some Features of Puerto Rican Spanish

Phonological Variations
- reduction of /d/ following /l/ or /n/—*grande: grane* 'large'; *caldo: calo* 'broth'; *espalda: espala* 'back'
- weakening of /d/—*chorreado: chorreao* 'spurting'; *picuda: picua* 'beaked'
- aspiration of medial /s/ preceding /p/, /t/, and /k/—*respeto: repeto* 'respect'; *pestaña: petaña* 'eyelash'; *escapa: ecapa* 'runs away'
- phoneme /s/ in medial position pronounced almost as /θ/ like in Andalusia, Spain (in certain regions of the island)—*paso: paθo* 'step'; *rosa: roθa* 'rose'
- phoneme /r/ substituted by /l/—*puerta: puelta* 'door'; *cuerpo: cuelpo* 'body'; *tarde: talde* 'afternoon'
- phoneme /rr/ pronounced like French velar /r/—*perro: pexo* 'dog'; *rosa: xosa* 'rose'
- nasalization of /n/—*carbón: carboh* 'coal'; *joven: joveh* 'young'

Lexical Variations
- *palo:* tree
- *chiringa:* kite
- *nene, nena:* boy, girl
- *pichón:* bird
- *bañera:* bathtub
- *motora:* motorcycle
- *bomba:* balloon
- *chalina:* tie

Grammatical Variations
- use of subjunctive form instead of past tense: *Lo compremos (compramos) hace un año* 'We bought it a year ago'.
- different form for future tense: *Ella salirá (saldrá) mañana* 'She will go out tomorrow'.
- reduction of *es-* in *estoy, estaba, estaremos* (i.e., forms of the verb *to be*). The latter is common in other Spanish-speaking countries.

Source: Examples from *El Español en Puerto Rico* by T. Navarro, 1974, Rio Piedras, Puerto Rico: Editorial Universitaria, Universidad de Puerto Rico.

Exhibit 3-2 Southwest U.S. Spanish Dialect Variations

Phonological Variations
- Loss of initial syllables—*está bien: tá bien* 'he/she is well'; loss of other syllables—*necesita: necita* 'he/she needs'; loss of final syllables—*para: pa'* 'for'; loss of final consonants—*verdad: verda* 'truth'; *sed: se* 'thirst'
- reduction of diphthongs in accented syllables—*treinta y cinco: trenta y cinco* 'thirty-five'; *pues: pos* 'then'
- addition of syllables in word initial position: *gastar: agastar* 'to spend'
- aspiration of /f/—*fuimos: juimos* 'we went'
- changes in stress—*mendigo: méndigo* 'beggar'; *seamos: seámos* 'we are'
- changes in position of a consonant—*pared: pader* 'wall'; *estómago: estóngamo* 'stomach'

Lexical Variations
- loan words from English with Spanish phonology—*mapiador* 'mop'; *chequear* 'to check'
- extension of meaning—*alfombra: carpeta* (from the influence of *carpet*)
- Caló or Pachuco influence—*camisa: lisa* 'shirt'; *policía: chota* 'police'*

Morphological and Syntactical Variations
- regularization of irregular verbs—*roto: rompido* 'broken'; *vuelto: volvido* 'returned'
- overmarking, as in the plural forms of words ending in *a* or *e*—*pies: pieses* 'feet'; *papás: papases* 'fathers'
- use of archaic 16th century forms—*vió: vide* 'saw'; *traje: truje* 'brought'; *mismo: mesmo* 'same'
- use of indicative instead of subjunctive with conditional forms—*Si tuviera $1,000 dólares, iría a México: Si tuviera . . . iba a México* or *Si tenía . . . iba a México* 'If I had $1,000 dollars, I would go to Mexico'
- making all nouns ending with *a* feminine—*el problema: la problema* 'the problem'
- elision of articles before vowels—*el agua: l'agua* 'the water'
- deletion of prepositions—*comencé a trabajar: comencé trabajar* 'started to work'
- methathesis or regularization and deletion—*hablaste: habalste, hablates* 'you spoke'
- change of stress—*pidamos: pídamos* 'we ask'

*Caló is a variation of Spanish spoken in the Southwest. It is predominantly used by young male Chicanos.

Source: Examples from "Nuestra Circumstancia Lingüística" by R. Sánchez, 1982, *El Grito*, 6, pp. 45–74.

Spanish-Speaking Countries. In many countries, indigenous languages are still very widely spoken (Table 3-4). In Bolivia, for example, only 35% of the population speaks Spanish as the mother tongue. A large percentage of the population speaks one or two of the Amerindian languages, Quechua and Aymara. Mexican Spanish is influenced to some degree by Nahuatl, one of the principal indigenous languages spoken in the country (Lope-Blanch, 1977). Words such as *cacahuate* 'peanut', *papalote* 'kite', and *aguacate* 'avocado' come from Nahuatl. Other terms in Mexican Spanish are derived from English because of geographic and political ties. In some cases, the English word is integrated into Spanish as a loan word, such as *lonche* 'lunch' (packed in a bag). Although languages are constantly evolving, the acceptance of a loan word may be slow, especially for lexical items that have an equivalent in the language. Examples abound: *parquear* 'to park' and *retirarse* 'to retire' (in the sense of leaving a job). The influence of other European languages spoken in some of the countries, such as Italian and German in Argentina, is also important.

Regional U.S. Dialects. The Spanish spoken in the U.S. Southwest, particularly in the New Mexico/Colorado area, includes lexical variations that originated from Caló and 16th century variants. Caló, also referred to as Pachuco, is a nonstandard variety most often spoken by adolescent males and the criminal element (Rosensweig, 1973; Trejo, 1968). It originated with the gypsies in Spain (Salillas, 1896), but has now infiltrated the entire Spanish-speaking world. Many Caló terms are widely understood, such as *chavalo* 'youth'. Caló is constantly evolving,

Table 3-4 Distribution of the Spanish Language

Countries	Total Population	No. of Mother Tongue Speakers	Percentage
Argentina	30,100,000	28,800,000	95
Bolivia	6,500,000	2,275,000	35
Chile	11,665,000	10,956,000	94
Colombia	28,700,000	27,740,000	96
Costa Rica	2,693,000	2,666,000	99
Cuba	9,945,000	9,899,000	99
Dominican Republic	6,400,000	6,272,000	98
Ecuador	9,700,000	9,021,000	93
El Salvador	5,500,000	5,335,000	97
Guatemala	7,687,000	4,300,000	56
Honduras	4,480,000	4,345,000	97
Mexico	76,800,000	62,976,000	82
Nicaragua	3,326,000	2,328,000	70
Panama	2,117,000	1,693,000	80
Paraguay	3,458,000	3,389,000	92
Peru	20,000,000	13,600,000	68
Uruguay	3,050,000	2,950,000	96
Venezuela	15,601,000	15,190,000	97
Spain	38,500,000	28,105,000	73

Source: Data from *Statistiques sur la Language Maternelle Majoritaire des Pays et Territoires du Monde* by G.D. McConnell and B. Roberge, 1987, Centre International de Recherches sur le Bilinguisme.

and its main function is secrecy. Forms from the 16th century can be heard, especially in New Mexico: *mismo: mesmo* 'same' and *trajo: trujo* 'brought'.

Other variations in the Spanish spoken in the Southwest occur in the rural Spanish of individuals with limited education. Many Mexicans tend to settle in that area of the United States, and those who do are among the subgroups most likely to have had limited formal education. Such variations may also appear in the language spoken by some immigrants from Puerto Rico and Central America, but the Spanish spoken by those originating from Cuba and South America tends to be among the more standard varieties.

Assessment of Dialect Variations

The implications of standard and nonstandard dialect variations in assessment are clear. Clinicians must establish the dialect variation that may be operating with a particular student through interviews with parents and other members of the community. At the simplest level, country of origin and level of education will roughly establish dialect variation. Parent interviews also provide opportunities to gather actual data on the dialect variants to which children may be exposed, however, as dialect will influence the assessment of syntactic development. This set of data can also be collected when working with an interpreter/translator. In this case, it is very important to consider dialect variations to avoid a misdiagnosis.

PRIMARY RESEARCH ON ACQUISITION OF SPANISH SYNTAX

Because primary research on the acquisition of English is so extensive, clinicians who need to determine whether an English-speaking child has a language disorder have a wide array of resources at their disposal (Bloom & Lahey, 1978; Fey, 1986; Lahey, 1988; Menyuk, 1988). Information is available on the form, content, and use of language. Moreover, the availability of a variety of testing instruments, many with norm-referenced data, enables clinicians to compare the skills of individual children against other children's performance for screening and assessment purposes. Clinicians assessing the language development of a Spanish-speaking child have a much more limited bank of research data in the different dimensions of language, however. Most of the primary research in Spanish has been conducted only in the last two decades.

Design of Research Studies

Studies of language acquisition in Spanish may be characterized as either longitudinal or cross-sectional in design. Longitudinal studies, by definition, involve data collection for a period of at least a few months and may continue for several years (Montes-Giraldo, 1971, 1974). Usually, these are diary studies, which require data collection at regular intervals from a very small group of children (Table 3-5). More common is the cross-sectional design, in which data are collected at one point in time from a larger group of children at several different ages (Table 3-6) (Gili y Gaya, 1972; Merino, 1982). A third type of design, the cross-sequential, integrates the features of both longitudinal and cross-sectional studies by collecting data over several years from groups of children of different ages. This design has not yet been used in studies of Spanish acquisition.

Each design carries with it advantages and disadvantages. The principal advantage of a longitudinal study is that it allows the investigator to outline the sequential stages of development of specific features. For example, Beléndez (1980) focused her study on the verb system and the effect of repetition on its acquisition. She studied four Puerto Rican boys, ranging in age from 17 to 20 months, over a period of 3 to 20 months in a naturalistic environment. When the study ended, their ages ranged from 22 to 37 months. A significant disadvantage of such a study concerns its generalizability and representativeness. Because the sample of subjects is small, it is possible to make only a general assumption about the acquisition pattern of specific grammatical features.

The principal advantage of a cross-sectional study design is sample size. Children are studied at one point in time only, and data are collected from a larger

Table 3-5 Research on Syntactic Development in Spanish Diary Studies

Investigator	Number	Age	Years of Study	Socio-economic Status	Site	Focus
Montes-Giraldo (1971, 1974)	4	0–5:0 years	5	High	Bogotá, Colombia	Syntax
Vivas (1979)	4	2:0–3:6 years	1 month	Middle	Kansas (Latin Americans)	Morphological order
Belendez (1980)	4	2:0–3:0 years	3–20 months	Middle	Puerto Rico	Verbs
Eisenberg (1982)	3	2:0–4:0 years	2 months	Low	Berkeley, CA (Mexicans)	Input
Truex (1982)	6	15–48 months	1 month	Low	Baja, CA (Mexico)	Mother-child interaction
Pardo (1984)	1	28–39 months	1 month	Low	Berkeley, CA (Mexicans)	Reflexives

Table 3-6 Cross-Sectional Studies on the Acquisition of Spanish Syntax

Investigator	Number	Age (Years and Months)	Elicitation Method	Socioeconomic Status	Site
Gili y Gaya (1960, 1972)	50	4:0–7:0	Description of pictures	Low & middle	Puerto Rico
Kernan & Blount (1966)	92	5:0–12:0	Berko nonsense words	Low	Rural Mexico
González (1970, 1975)	27	2:0–6:0	Guided conversation	Low	Texas (Mexicans)
Brisk (1972, 1974)	7	5:0–5:11	Guided conversation	Low	Urban/rural New Mexico
Burt, Dulay, & Hernández-Chávez (1975)	1376	5:0–8:0	Questions/BSM (Bilingual syntax measure (Level I)	Low & middle	U.S. and Coahuila, Mexico
Echeverría (1975)	55	5:0–10:0	Comprehension using toys	Low & middle	Concepción, Chile
Brisk (1976)	21	6:0–7:0	Use of articles	Low	Boston and Córdoba, Argentina
Ferreiro, Ochenin-Girard, Chipman, & Sinclair (1976)	276	4:0–11:0	Comprehension using toys	N/A	Buenos Aires and Córdoba, Argentina
Edelsky & Muina (1977)	80	7:0–10:0	Comprehension using toys	Low & middle	Mexico City
Linares, Orama, & Sanders (1977)	30 normal; 30 language-disordered	3:0–3:11	Structured conversation	N/A	Puerto Rico
Blake (1980)	184 children; 54 adults	4:0–12:0	Guided conversation, written test	Middle	Mexico City
Cohen (1980)	50	3:0–7:0	Guided conversation	Middle	San Francisco
Dale (1980)	122	5:0–8:0	Berko nonsense words	Low	Miami (Cubans)
Galván (1980)	66	5:0–16:0	Guided conversation	Low	Rural Morelos, Mexico

Study	N	Age	Task	SES	Location
Williamson & Rodríguez (1980)	27	6:0–7:0	Structured conversation	Low & middle	Mexico City
Gudeman (1981)	59	4:0–Adult	Imitation, comprehension, production	Low	Rural Panama
Merino (1982)	50	4:0–8:0	Comprehension, production with pictures	Low & middle	Oaxaca, Mexico
Parra (1982)	80	2:0–12:0	Conversation with pictures (structured)	Low & middle	U.S. (Mexicans)
Olarte (1985)	90	2:6–4:6	Cued responses to comprehension and expression	Low, middle, high	Bogotá, Colombia
Romero (1985)	6	3:6–4:7	Story retelling, structured conversation	Middle	Puerto Rico
Kvaal, Shipstead-Cox, Nevitt, Hodson, & Launer (1988)	15	2:0–4:8	Structured conversation	Middle & low	San Diego, CA

group. Thus, universal patterns of development can be more easily identified. The underlying assumption of a cross-sectional study is that the specific language features used by older children indicate the development of language in younger children. Unusually immature or precocious children at any one age in the sample shift the pace at which a particular feature appears to be acquired, however. For example, González (1975), who collected data from 27 children between the ages of 2 and 6, reported that the periphrastic future (i.e., *ir + a* + infinitive) *voy a nadar* 'I am going to swim' was established in the $4^1/_2$-year-olds, but not in the 5- to 6-year-olds. A cross-sequential design would reveal whether the "apparent" regression of the older children (5 to 6 years old) was due to immaturity of the subjects within that age group or simply resulted from the younger children's natural tendency to analyze memorized chunks of data, as is commonly reported in the acquisition of the past morpheme in English.

Comparability is a key issue in the use of primary language acquisition research to establish the timing of acquisition. Not only are studies of language development in Spanish few in number, as mentioned earlier, but also they vary substantially in terms of the setting where data were collected, the features analyzed, the design of the study, and the method of elicitation, as well as the age, class, and language history of the subjects (see Tables 3-5 and 3-6). Each one of these variables may be sufficient to affect expectations for so-called normal language development. For example, a child from a rural background in Mexico who has had very limited formal schooling may use dialect variants that, when compared to data from an urban sample, appear to signal delay.

Table 3-7 lists the ages at which specific grammatical features were produced by the subjects in the different studies. Only those features studied by at least two researchers are included. Research on Spanish speakers in the United States was largely excluded from Table 3-7 because of the effect that English can have on the normal acquisition of Spanish. However, comparisons were made with some studies conducted in the United States, namely, González (1970), Brisk (1972), and Cohen (1980), because the samples included children who were monolingual Spanish-speaking and not yet enrolled in school.

Because of the wide range of techniques and scoring protocols employed in different studies, a feature has been listed in Table 3-7 as acquired only when the researcher has reported that at least 80% of the subjects at any given age have mastered it. Some authors used different criteria for acquisition; González (1970, 1978a, 1978b), for example, did not list a feature if it was not used by all subjects of a certain age. The use of the 80% criterion permitted comparisons of 14 features across two or more studies. Ten features were acquired within one specific year span (i.e., 4:0 to 5:0 or 5:0 to 7:0), indicating a high degree of agreement on the age at which children acquire a particular feature. In some instances, there were larger discrepancies because of the subjects' age range in a particular sample. For ex-

Table 3-7 Age of Acquisition of Selected Grammatical Features (Production)

Feature	Age of Acquisition (Years and Months)	Investigator
Noun Phrase		
Short plural /s/	4:0	Merino (1982)
	5:0	Dale (1980)
	5:0–7:0	Kernan & Blount (1966)
	7:1–9:0	Gudeman (1981)
Long plural /es/	4:0	Merino (1982)
	8:0	Dale (1980)
	11:0–12:0	Kernan & Blount (1966)
Gender (noun adjective)	4:0	Merino (1982)
	6:0	González (1975)
Gender (direct object pronoun)	5:0	Brisk (1972, 1974)
	5:0–7:0	Merino (1982)
Verb Phrase		
Number	4:0–5:0	Merino (1982)
	5:0	Dale (1980)
	5:0–7:0	Kernan & Blount (1966)
	7:1–9:0	Gudeman (1981)
Progressive	2:0–2:6	González (1970, 1972)
	3:0	Cohen (1980)
	4:0	Merino (1982)
Regular preterite	2:0–2:6	González (1970, 1972)
	3:0	Cohen (1980)
	4:0	Merino (1982)
	5:0	Dale (1980)
	7:1–9:0	Gudeman (1981)
	11:0–12:0	Kernan & Blount (1966)
Irregular preterite	4:0–5:0	Merino (1982)
	11:0–12:0	Kernan & Blount (1966)
Present perfect	4:0	Merino (1982)
	6:0	González (1975)
	11:0–12:0	Kernan & Blount (1966)
Present subjunctive	4:0	Blake (1980)
	4:0	González (1975)
	4:0	Cohen (1980)
	4:0	Merino (1982)
Optative	4:0	Merino (1982)
Purposive	5:0–6:0	Merino (1982)
Word Order		
Active	4:0	Merino (1982)
	5:0–6:0	Gudeman (1981)
Passive	5:5–8:3	Echeverría (1975)
	7:0–8:0	Merino (1985)
	12:4; Adults	Gudeman (1981)
Indirect object	7:0–8:0	Merino (1972, 1974)
	9:0–12:4	Gudeman (1982)
Conditional (yes/no)		
	5:0	Brisk (1972, 1974)
	6:0	González (1975)
	6:0	Merino (1982)

ample, the regular preterite (*abrió* 'he/she/it opened') was reportedly established between the age of 2 and 2¹/₂ years (González, 1970). Cohen (1980), whose youngest subjects were 3 years old, reported the use of the preterite in at least 90% of his subjects at 3 years of age. Merino (1982) made similar observations in her youngest subjects, who were 4 years old. This indicates that, like the past tense in English, the preterite is a feature that develops early in Spanish.

The discrepancies in results across studies may be due to several factors, such as elicitation technique, language variation, and effect of bilingualism.

Elicitation Technique

Specific grammatical features have been studied by means of a variety of methods, such as keeping diaries of children's spontaneous speech (Montes-Giraldo, 1974), using the Berko nonsense word cued response technique (Kernan & Blount, 1966), and even administering written tests (Blake, 1980). Not surprisingly, differences in technique can have an effect on the ages at which particular language features appear to be acquired. For example, when Kernan and Blount (1966) tested their subjects with nonsense words, such as *suechó*, they found that the children did not really master the preterite until age 11. As previously noted, however, González (1970) found that the 2¹/₂-year-olds in his study were using the form consistently. Similarly, the 4-year-old group in the Merino study (1982) reached 85% mastery of long plurals, whereas even the oldest subjects in the Dale (1980) and the Kernan and Blount (1966) studies failed to reach the criterion. In the latter two studies, the nonsense word technique was utilized, which taps other skills such as metalinguistic awareness. Metalinguistic awareness is the ability to reflect on language as a code to think about language and comment on it. Therefore, when making inferences about primary research, clinicians should analyze the elicitation technique used and the subjects' experience in responding to the different tasks. Also, they should consider the criterion that the researchers have established to determine that a certain feature has been mastered.

Language Variation

Some of the very earliest studies on language acquisition were conducted in Spanish-speaking countries (Gili y Gaya, 1960; Kernan & Blount, 1966; Montes-Giraldo, 1974), but the largest number, until very recently, were carried out in the United States (Brisk, 1972; González, 1970, 1975, 1978a, 1978b; Martínez-Bernal, 1972; Merino, 1976). Even when the studies are conducted in similar settings, the results may differ in the reported age of acquisition of specific features; such discrepancies may sometimes be attributed to dialect variation. Much remains to be learned about the dialects spoken in many communities, however. In general, dialectology focuses on language varieties of individual communities through studies of the language of a relatively small number of informants. A child's speech may or may not be representative of a given dialect.

The studies listed in Tables 3-5 and 3-6 were conducted in a variety of settings; some were rural, while others were urban. The children in these studies spoke dialect variations from several countries, including Mexico (Merino, 1982), Puerto Rico (Romero, 1985), Colombia (Olarte, 1985), and the United States (Kvaal et al., 1988; Pardo, 1984). Dialect variation may affect the nature and pace of acquisition of certain grammatical features. Often, the rural children in these study samples came from families with few economic and educational resources and from communities in which the local adult variety differs from the standard form of the language. Thus, for example, Gudeman (1981) reported that her un-schooled adult subjects in rural Panama performed significantly more poorly than did the older school children (aged 7, 9, and 12 years) in her sample. These un-schooled subjects may have performed poorly because of a lack of experience with testing situations or a lack of familiarity with structures that seldom occur in casual speech. For instance, Gudeman used features such as passive voice (e.g., *el carro es chocado por el avión* 'the car is run by the plane') and the indicative future tense (e.g., *la niña se bañará* 'the girl will take a bath'). These forms may be very uncommon among uneducated speakers, as these speakers are likely to use simpler or more active forms that convey the same meaning (e.g., *el avión chocó con el carro* and *la niña se va a bañar*) in their everyday speech (Pousada & Poplack, 1982). It is, of course, a truism that even educated speakers violate gen-erally accepted standard Spanish rules occasionally.

The morphological variation of the preterite second person singular in which *hablaste* 'you spoke' becomes *hablastes* or *hablates* is so well-known among standard Spanish speakers that it is seldom misconstrued as an indication of lan-guage delay. Other variants may be less well-known, however. For example, with hypothetical situations, such as *si yo fuera grande, iría solita* 'if I were older, I would go by myself', standard Spanish requires the use of the conditional mood, yet Spanish dialect varieties may use the imperfect past tense of the indicative mood, *si yo era grande, iba solita*, as well as other forms. Other examples of this nature appear in Exhibits 3-1 and 3-2. All these forms have been frequently re-ported in Chicano Spanish studies. They also occur in rural Mexican Spanish (Peñalosa, 1980; Sánchez, 1972). This indicates once again that it is necessary to exercise caution in distinguishing a dialect variation from a language disorder.

Effect of Bilingualism

Differential exposure to the bilingual child's two languages (Merino, 1976), attitude (Elías-Olivares, 1976), and the sociolinguistic characteristics of the com-munity itself are likely to affect both the pace and the nature of language acquisi-tion. Leopold (1949), in what continues to be one of the best documented case studies of early bilingualism, traced the ups and downs of his daughter, Hildegard, in acquiring both English and German while living in the United States and sporadically visiting Germany. A similar switching of dominance over time has been reported for Spanish-English bilingual children who live in bilingual families (Fantini, 1982) or bilingual communities (Padilla & Liebman, 1982). It is generally expected that, as children mature linguistically, they will exhibit greater and more accurate control of the grammar of the language. In cases of normal temporary regression, however, children may test the hypotheses about a particular marker and revert to a seemingly more immature form. A classic English example is the replacement of the irregular *went* by *goed*.

In the majority of instances, older bilingual subjects outperform younger ones. Yet, studies of bilingual subjects in the United States tend to report uneven improvement in Spanish as the children get older. For example, Merino (1976) found that younger children outperformed older ones at significant levels in their use of certain grammatical forms, in spite of the fact that the subjects had been balanced bilinguals at school entry. Similarly, Dale (1980) reported that the ability of bilingual Cuban children to apply morphological rules to real and nonsense words did not improve between the first and second grades. Furthermore, by the third grade, the bilinguals were better able to use morphological rules in English than in Spanish. Martínez-Bernal (1972) reported that bilingual 5- and 6-year-old children in New Mexico could follow morphological rules better than could the 7- and 8-year-olds. It is possible that bilingual children lose their ability to use certain grammatical features in their first language as they acquire a second language. Often, it is due to lack of practice in speaking the language. Thus, the research findings reported in the studies can best be applied with younger children who come from primarily monolingual Spanish-speaking settings or with older children who are recent arrivals from a Spanish-speaking country. With older bilingual children who have also been exposed to English, comparisons should be made with caution. Additional background data such as the type of exposure and use of each language should be gathered.

Specific Outcomes of Research Studies

Comprehension

Studies on the comprehension of grammatical features with Spanish-speaking children are even more rare than are those on the production of grammatical features. A list of those studies appears in Table 3-8.

Echeverría (1975) adopted C. Chomsky's (1968) technique of using dolls and objects to measure Chilean children's understanding of passives. He also tested their comprehension of the Spanish equivalents of *ask*, *tell*, and *promise*. In general, comprehension preceded production. Some features, however, were ex-

Table 3-8 Age of Acquisition of Specific Grammatical Features (Comprehension)

Feature	Age of Acquisition (Years and Months)	Investigator
Short plural	4:0–5:0	Merino (1982)
	5:2–6:2	Gudeman (1981)
Number in verb phrase	5:0–6:0	Merino (1982)
	7:1–9:0	Gudeman (1981)
Regular preterite	6:0–7:0	Merino (1982)
	6:2–7:1	Gudeman (1981)
Word order (active)	4:0	Merino (1982)
	5:2–6:2	Gudeman (1981)
Word order (passive)	7:0–8:0	Merino (1982)
	8:0–9:0	Echeverría (1975)
	9:0–12:4	Gudeman (1981)
	5:0	Keller (1976)

pressed correctly with greater consistency than they were comprehended. Keller (1976) studied the development of the passive in bilingual 3- to 5-year-old Puerto Rican children and found that, after a rise in comprehension to 55% at approximately 3 years and 8 months of age, the children's performance dropped; even the 5-year-olds attained a score of only 42% in the correct use of these features. For the most part, results for comprehension are highly consistent across settings and techniques. As illustrated in Table 3-8, the age discrepancy across studies is only 1 to 2 years at the most, with some exceptions. These exceptions are attributed to method of investigation and, very likely, in the case of passives, to the subjects' infrequent exposure to the grammatical feature in conversation.

Expression

It is difficult to pinpoint the exact ages at which certain grammatical features develop based on the studies that have been reviewed. It is possible to make a determination of those that develop early or late, however. The features that develop early (before age 6 years) are

1. number in the noun phrase, sometimes labeled short plural (*-os/as*), as in *gato: gatos* 'cat: cats' or *rana: ranas* 'frog: frogs'. The short plural is somewhat easier to master than is the long plural, as in *lápiz: lápices* 'pencil: pencils'. Most 4-, 5-, and 6-year-olds have mastered this feature. All the studies reviewed focused on common use of these forms. It may be hypothesized that more complex forms of the plural such as *rubí: rubíes* 'ruby: rubies' may have a later onset.

2. number in the verb phrase, as in *las ranas saltan* 'the frogs jump'. This feature is somewhat more difficult to learn, but also appears to develop early. According to most studies, it is in full control of most 5- to 7-year-olds.

3. gender in a noun adjective or direct object pronoun combination, as in *la camisa blanca* 'the white shirt' and *yo la compré* 'I bought it', making reference to the white shirt.

4. preterite, such as *la rana saltó* 'the frog jumped'. Very young Spanish-speaking children seem to have control of this feature, just as very young English-speaking children do.

5. irregular past tense or preterite, as in *la niña puso eso* 'the girl put that' and *ella lo trajo* 'she brought it'.

6. present progressive, as in *está saltando* 'he/she/it is jumping'.

7. certain forms of the subjunctive, such as the optative, as in *quiere que coma* 'he/she wants him/her to eat', and the purposive, as in *abra la puerta para que entre* 'open the door so that he/she can get in'.

It is more problematic to compare the features that develop later, generally after the age of 6 years, across studies because of the infrequency of their use.

1. the subjunctive. Although the subjunctive is an early feature in its simplest forms (optative and purposive), mastery of all forms and uses of the subjunctive continues through adolescence (Blake, 1980). For example, in certain adjective or adverbial clauses, such as *no hay cosa que sirva* 'there isn't a thing that would be useful' or *esperarán hasta que terminen* 'they will wait until they finish', the subjunctive develops later.

2. certain forms of the conditionals, as in *si el tren no fuera grande, no cabría* 'if the train wasn't big enough, it/he/she would not fit' or *a menos que la niña se agache, el gato la va a arañar* 'unless the girl kneels down, the cat will scratch her'.

3. certain word orders, such as indirect object, as in *el niño le enseña la pelota à la niña* 'the boy shows the girl the ball', and the passive, as in *el oso fué atacado por el águila* 'the bear was attacked by the eagle'.

4. comprehension of certain features, such as relative clauses, as in *el niño que viste es mi primo* 'the boy that you saw is my cousin' (Ferreiro et al., 1976; Merino, 1982). Although children as young as 3 years old have been reported to produce relative clauses, this feature continues to develop through the elementary grades (Gili y Gaya, 1972; Merino, 1982). As Clark (1985) pointed out, relative clauses are particularly difficult. Children very fre-

quently produce them in spontaneous conversation, but it is extremely difficult to elicit these clauses through drawings or even props. Consequently, children are unable to display their full linguistic competence.

NORMATIVE RESEARCH ON THE ACQUISITION OF SPANISH SYNTAX

A battery of tests entitled Sistema de Evaluación sobre la Acquisición de la Lengua Española (SEALE) was developed in a collaboration between the University of California at Davis (Merino & Figueroa, 1984) and the Office of Special Education in Mexico (Merino, Figueroa, Gómez-Palacio, Rangel Hinojosa, & Jackson-Maldonado, 1987). It included tests on several areas of language: (1) syntax (i.e., comprehension and production), (2) articulation, (3) semantics (i.e., naming and definitions), and (4) communicative competence. The battery was developed in three phases. The first phase involved a preliminary study conducted in California to refine the administration procedures and to identify problem items. In the second phase, the pilot study version of the battery was administered to a sample of 240 Mexico City children between the ages of 2 and 11 years, with 20 subjects at each age level. Based on statistical analyses of the data obtained, including reliability and validity studies, the SEALE was refined, shortened, and used in a third study. In this third phase, the norming version of the second phase was administered to a randomly stratified sample of Mexico City public school children. The subjects were drawn from the total population, in which the proportion of children with certain characteristics, such as sex and age, is known. A total of 800 children, ranging in age between 2 and 11 years, and a small sample of adult subjects participated in the final phase of the study.

Content and Statistical Data on Syntax Development

The items included in tests of syntax development were largely drawn from a battery of comprehension and expression subtests previously developed by Merino (1976), the Bilingual Language Acquisition Scales (BLAS). These scales were designed to test subjects' comprehension and expression of specific grammatical features in Spanish. Many of the items from the BLAS had been used in earlier research with bilingual and monolingual normal and language-disordered Spanish-speaking children (Merino, 1976, 1982, 1983b; Merino & Lyons, 1984). The BLAS consists of 56 comprehension items and 56 production items. In the comprehension subtest, the child is asked to point to one of three pictures that corresponds to the target item tested. The production subtest is administered following Lee's (1969) elicitation technique; the child listens to two sentences that are illustrated in two different pictures and then is asked to produce one of them. Essentially, it is a delayed imitation task with considerable visual support.

As part of the normative study carried out in Mexico City, several validity studies were conducted. The degree of correlation between performance on the syntax scales and performance on the WISC-RM (Wechsler Intelligence Scale—Revised) (WISC-R Spanish norms developed in Mexico City) and achievement (Mexican version of the Kaufman battery of tests) was determined. The WISC-RM (Wechsler, 1974) consists of a verbal and a performance section. Each includes several subtests. The child's intelligence scale is derived from the results of each section. The Kaufman Assessment Battery for Children (K-ABC) tests children ages $2\frac{1}{2}$ to $12\frac{1}{2}$ in four areas: sequential processing, simultaneous processing, mental processing composite (sequential plus simultaneous), and achievement. The test includes sociocultural norms which can be applied to interpret scores of minority children (Kaufman & Kaufman, 1982). Also, several reliability studies, including internal consistency, interscorer, test-retest, alternate forms, and interexaminer reliability tests, were conducted.

1. There was no significant correlation between the results obtained with the syntax scales and the results obtained with the WISC-RM.
2. There was a moderately significant relationship between the results obtained with the syntax scales and with the Kaufman; it was stronger for reading than for mathematics.
3. There was a high degree of internal consistency; Chronbach's alpha coefficient was in the 0.90s for the scales as a whole.
4. Test-retest reliability was also high (0.90 in production and high 0.80s for comprehension) when examiners and raters were held constant.
5. Interexaminer effect was not significant.
6. Alternate form reliability studies indicated a high degree of consistency across forms, with correlation coefficients in the 0.80s and 0.90s.

The use of these norms would be tentative only for a U.S. population of bilingual subjects. Their application is most appropriate for children who have recently arrived in the United States from Mexico City. In recent years, the Mexico City population has drawn so heavily from all the provinces of Mexico that the use of these norms with other recent arrivals from Mexico may be defensible. The more a child's background differs from that of the Mexico City normative population, however, the more difficult it becomes to apply the norms in absolute terms. Even so, the norms can be useful in distinguishing grammatical features that are acquired early from those that are acquired late.

Outcomes of the Normative Study

The norming procedures make it possible to trace the mastery of a certain feature by 50% to 80% of the subjects. Consistent with the developmental research that has been discussed, the SEALE showed that the following features are acquired before the age of 6 years:

- number in short plurals, which is well established by age 5 years.
- number in verb phrases, which is established by 4 years of age and used correctly by most 6-year-olds.
- gender in noun adjectives, which is established by age 4 years.
- preterite. At least 50% of the children in the sample had mastered the preterite at age $3^1/2$ or even younger (González, 1970, 1972). Differences may be due to the type of verb. Some may be easier to conjugate than others. For example, -*ar* verbs may be easier to conjugate than are -*er* and -*ir* verbs.
- preterite irregular. Again, children at age $3^1/2$ years were able to use the feature correctly; it was not completely mastered until age 5 years, however.
- present progressive. It is developed as early as age 2 or $2^1/2$ years.
- subjunctive (optative), which is fully developed by age 5 years.

The normative study showed that the following features are also acquired before the age of 6 years:

- periphrastic future, as in *la niña va a bailar* 'the girl is going to dance'. It has been reported to develop as early as age 4 years in 80% of the children.
- past participle regular, as in *la niña está cansada* 'the girl is tired'. The development begins at $3^1/2$ years and is completely mastered by slightly over age 6 years.
- imperative negative, as in *no te canses* 'don't get tired'. This feature is also observed as early as $3^1/2$ years and is well established by age 6 years.
- conditional (yes/no), as in *si el avión no sube, se va a estrellar* 'if the plane does not go up, it will crash'. It is established between ages 5 and 6 years.
- active transformation, as in *la niña ve la muñeca* 'the girl is looking at the doll'. This feature is well established by age 4 years.

In the 6- to 11-year-old age group, the SEALE, like earlier research findings, indicated that the following features are acquired:

- number in long plural, which is not established at the 80% level until 6 years of age.

- subjunctive (purposive). Although research studies by Blake (1980) and Merino (1982, 1983a) found that children sometimes used this form at age 4 years, in this sample it was not well established until age 8 years.
- conditional (*a menos que*), which is not well established until age 9 years.
- indirect object. Approximately 50% of the children did not acquire this feature until age 6 years; it was not completely mastered by at least 80% of the children until age 9 or 10 years.
- relative clauses. Only 50% of children aged 8 years produced the feature correctly; not until age 11 years was there mastery by 80% of the children.

In addition, the SEALE showed that the following features are acquired between the ages of 6 and 11 years:

- prepositions (position). Their distinct use is not well established until age 6 or 7 years, perhaps because of the many words that are prepositions. For example, *in* can be translated as *dentro de* or *adentro de*; *on*, as *encima de*, *arriba de*, or *sobre*.
- relatives (*que* and *quien*), as in *yo quiero el que está adentro* 'I want the one that is inside'. Only 50% of the 5-year-olds use the form correctly, and it is not well produced until age 6 years.
- present perfect, as in *ella ha bailado demasiado* 'she has danced too much'. This feature was established early, but was sometimes not well produced until after age 6 years. It could be due to the lesser frequency of this feature in spoken language.
- past participle irregular, as in *estaba puesto afuera* 'it was placed outside'. At times, this feature is not established until age 7 years.
- passive transformation, as in *la muñeca fué comprada hace mucho tiempo* 'the doll was bought a long time ago'. This feature is not established at the 80% level until age 7 or 8 years.
- comparative sentences with *big* and *little*, *wide* and *narrow*, as in *el niño es más grande que la niña* 'the boy is bigger than the girl'. Sentences with these adjectives in comparative relationships were initially used by 50% of 6-year-olds and were mastered at the 80% level by children aged 9 years or older.

Features that were mastered partially by the older group included the pluperfect preterite (e.g., *ella había amado* 'she had loved') and past purposive (e.g., *el señor sacó un libro para que leyera* 'the man got a book out so that he would read'), as well as the contrafactuals (i.e., conditional forms) that research studies had shown to be acquired later.

The results of the SEALE generally agree with the results of the primary re-search regarding the time that different language features are acquired, except for some forms of the subjunctive (e.g., purposive). The data make it clear that certain features may appear earlier than others, but that their mastery by 80% of children in an age group may take somewhat longer, depending on the feature itself, the elicitation technique, and other variables.

Order of Acquisition

It is important to determine not only at what age children acquire different grammatical features, but also whether there is a natural sequence in the acquisi-tion. Research in English indicates that children and adults acquire grammatical features in a predictable order. Since Brown (1973) reported the "amazingly con-stant" developmental order of the 14 morphemes, others have obtained similar findings in cross-sectional studies among monolingual English speakers (e.g., de Villiers & de Villiers, 1978). Kessler (1975) demonstrated a significant similarity in the natural sequence in which language-disordered subjects acquire the features of English. Menyuk (1975), however, indicated that the differences are qualitative rather than quantitative; that is, some features may develop later than expected, others do not develop at all, while still others develop in different ways. Further-more, studies on the order of acquisition of English as a second language among children (Dulay & Burt, 1974) and adults (Bailey, Madden, & Krashen, 1974) indicate that second-language learners appear to have an "accuracy order" of their own (Larsen-Freeman, 1978). Thus, "order" must be evaluated with caution. For example, language-disordered children use more attributive relations (Bloom, 1980) and use terms that denote existence and action more frequently than other functions (Freedman & Carpenter, 1976; Leonard, Bolders, & Miller, 1976).

Comparisons of data on the Spanish verb system collected by different investi-gators suggest that there is a high degree of consistency in the order in which some verb forms are acquired (Dato, 1975). There has been little research on the acqui-sition order of Spanish grammatical features carried out with different types of subjects and similar elicitation techniques, except for Gudeman (1981) and Merino (1976, 1982). Both investigators collected data on similar features with subjects from Panama and Mexico, respectively. Merino obtained data from nor-mal bilinguals in the United States, monolinguals in Mexico, and both language-disordered and normally developing bilinguals in the United States. The language-disordered group was made up of children who had difficulty acquiring previously identified easy-to-acquire grammatical features in the second language and who had resided at least 2 years in the United States.

Table 3-9 lists the order of acquisition in normally developing monolingual Spanish-speaking children from Mexico and the United States, as well as bilingual

Table 3-9 Rank Order of Acquisition of Different Grammatical Features in Spanish (Monolinguals from Mexico and the United States and Bilinguals in the United States)

Feature	Monolinguals (Mexico and U.S.)	Bilinguals (U.S.)
Active	1	2
Gender: noun adjective	2	8
Short plural	3	4.5*
Long plural	4.5*	4.5*
Regular preterite	4.5*	4.5*
Irregular preterite	6	7
Optative subjunctive	7	10
Purposive subjunctive	8	12
Gender: direct object pronoun	9	4.5*
Number in verb phrase	10	1
Conditional (if)	11	9
Passive	12	11
Indirect object	13	13
Other forms of conditionals	14	14

* Note: These features are all acquired in the same order; r=.74, p<.01.

Source: Data from Merino 1982 and 1983b

subjects in the United States. The easiest feature for the monolingual subjects to acquire was the active form, and for the bilingual subjects it was number in verb phrase form. There were similarities between the two groups in the rank order use of different types of plural, as well as the regular and irregular preterite. Also, features that developed later in monolingual subjects, such as different uses of conditionals, passive, and indirect object, developed later in bilingual subjects as well. Subjects from Mexico and Panama developed the use of different features in slightly different order (Table 3-10) depending on the grammatical feature. Active was always the easiest, and number in verb phrase and indirect object were more difficult for the younger subjects in both countries. There were variations for the other features. Active was also the easiest for the older subjects and passive the most difficult, with variations for the other features.

There are similarities across the monolingual subjects from Mexico, the monolingual subjects from the United States, and the bilingual language-disordered subjects from the United States (Merino, 1982, 1983b) in the use of the irregular preterite, optative subjunctive, and most of the later developing features, such as conditionals, passive, and indirect object (Table 3-11). There are variations in the early developing features, however. For example, the bilingual U.S. sample uses

Table 3-10 Rank Order Correlations in Performance of Monolinguals in Mexico and Panama

Feature	Mexico*	Panama†
	Subjects Aged 4–6 Years	
Active	1	1
Progressive	2	3
Short plural	3	4
Regular preterite	4	2
Number in verb phrase	5	6
Indirect object	6	5
	Subjects Aged 9:1–12:4	
Active	1	1
Progressive	2	3
Preterite	3	2
Number in verb phrase	4	5
Passive	5	6
Indirect object	6	4

*Data from Merino (1982, 1983b)
†Data from Gudeman (1981)
Note: In both cases, r=77, p<0.01.

some features, such as gender in direct object pronoun and number in verb phrase, much earlier than do the other two groups. Thus, it is not possible to make generalizations. Even so, the research findings are helpful in delineating some general patterns of development.

It is also important to determine if the development of specific features is related to the frequency of their use. Brown (1973) found no relationship between the order of acquisition of the grammatical features that he studied and the frequency of their use by the parents of the English-speaking subjects. Larsen-Freeman (1978) found that, for second-language speakers, there was a significant correlation between their order of development and the frequency of use, however. Data on the frequency of grammatical features in spoken Spanish have been compiled in only two studies, one with children and the other with adults. Gili y Gaya (1960) reported that, in their natural speech, first- through fourth-grade children most frequently used the present tense (36% of the verbs), followed by the preterite (20.6%). The passive with the auxiliary *ser* as in *fué herido* 'he was wounded' occurred only once among the fourth-grade subjects. The pluperfect subjunctive, as in *yo hubiera querido ir* 'I would have liked to go' was also rare. When Pousada and Poplack (1982) examined the frequency of verb tenses in adult Puerto Rican

Table 3-11 Rank Order Correlations in Normal Monolingual and Language-Disordered Spanish Speakers in Mexico and Bilingual Subjects in the United States

Feature	Monolingual (Mexico)[1]	Language- Disordered (United States)[2]	Bilingual (United States)[3]
Active	1	1.5	5
Gender: noun adjective	2	8	10.5
Present progressive	3	5	5
Short plural	4.5	1.5	5
Present perfect	4.5	5	8
Long plural	6.5	10	5
Regular preterite	6.5	3	5
Irregular preterite	8	7	9
Optative subjunctive	9	11.5	10.5
Purposive subjunctive	10	13	14
Gender: direct object pronoun	11	9	1.5
Number in verb phrase	12	5	1.5
Conditional (if)	13	11.5	12
Passive	14	15.5	16
Indirect object	15	14	13
Other conditionals	16–18	15–18	15–18

rs=.73, p<0.01 Monolingual (Mexico) and bilingual (United States).
rs= .83, p<0.01 Monolingual (Mexico) and language-disordered (United States).
r = rank order correlations
Source: Data from (1) Merino 1982; (2) and (3) Merino 1983b.

Spanish speakers in New York, they found that, in this sample also, the present was by far the most frequently used tense (49.5%), followed by the preterite (13.9%), the imperfect (8.3%), and the present subjunctive (3.9%). Merino (1982), in her study with children from Oaxaca, had similar results. Some of the differences noted between the studies done with monolingual English speakers and those done with Spanish speakers could be the particular features analyzed and the setting in which data were collected.

In summary, research and normative data on the development of specific grammatical features in Spanish indicate that, indeed, certain forms are mastered earlier than others. This information is very helpful in determining if a language disorder may exist. It must be used carefully, however; the clinician must consider other aspects as well, such as the background of the student, the use and exposure to language, the perceptions of parents and teachers, and observations of the student's interaction in different settings.

PRIMARY RESEARCH IN THE ACQUISITION OF SPANISH PHONOLOGY

Like studies on the syntactical development of Spanish-speaking children, studies on the phonological development of these children have been done both longitudinally and cross-sectionally.

Longitudinal Studies

Only two longitudinal studies have been conducted thus far. Montes-Giraldo (1971) followed the development of his four children over a 5-year period, while Mackey and Barton (1980) studied three children aged 19 months for only a 7-month period. Each study focused on slightly different phonological features. Montes-Giraldo documented the types of substitutions that his children produced for vowels and consonants. Mackey and Barton focused on the acquisition of voicing contrasts in initial stops. Although these studies are valuable because they report specific phonological processes, their applicability to larger groups of children remains limited.

Cross-Sectional Studies

Of the six major cross-sectional studies that have been reported thus far, four were conducted with monolingual Spanish-speaking children in Spanish-speaking countries (De la Fuente, 1985; Linares, 1981; Melgar, 1976; Merino, 1983a). Two others, while focusing on monolingual children, were conducted in the United States so that the children may have been exposed to English, even though they were considered Spanish dominant (Jiménez, 1987; Mason, Smith, & Hinshaw, 1976). Linares (1981) also compared the phonological development of children who were considered bilingual in Spanish and English with monolingual Spanish-speaking children from Mexico (Chihuahua).

Mason and associates (1976) used an articulation test that they had devised (Medida Española de Articulación [MEDA]) with a total of 199 boys and 225 girls aged 4 to 9 years in a school district in San Diego County located near the Mexican border. The children were asked to respond by completing a sentence such as *El perro está . . .* 'the dog is . . .' or answer a question *¿Qué es esto?* 'What is this?' Phonemes were considered acquired at a certain age if 90% of children in that age group pronounced the targeted sound correctly. Consonants, blends, and diphthongs were tested.

Using an instrument similar to the MEDA, but with different words and drawings, Melgar (1976) studied the articulation skills in 200 monolingual Mexican children ranging from 3 to $6^{1}/_{2}$ years of age. The subjects were 109 boys and 91 girls who were randomly selected from five day care centers in Mexico City. In this study also, a 90% criterion was used to determine whether a phoneme had been acquired by each age group.

Linares (1981) tested the control of consonants in 97 children between the ages of 3 and 6 years in Chihuahua, Mexico, and in 148 monolingual and bilingual Spanish-speaking children between the ages of 5 and 8 years in New Mexico. The Spanish Articulation Test, an experimental test that consists of 40 black and white drawings, was used for elicitation. Again, results were reported on the basis of 90% production at specified age levels.

Merino (1983a) used the MEDA to study the articulation skills of 58 children between the ages of 4 and $8^1/2$ years in Oaxaca, Mexico. All the children were enrolled in a private Catholic school. The 90% criterion was also used in this study to determine whether a phoneme had been acquired by the children in each age group.

De la Fuente (1985) tested the acquisition of Spanish consonants in 55 monolingual Spanish-speaking Dominican children between the ages of 2 and $6^1/2$ years. The children were asked to provide the label for pictures that illustrated a common term in which the target phoneme occurred. If a child failed to respond, the examiner asked questions such as "What is this?", asked either/or questions, or finally asked for a repetition of the word wanted. The children were producing all the consonants by the age of 3 to $3^1/2$ years and reached 90% mastery at approximately the age of 6 to $6^1/2$ years.

In a study conducted in Northern California, Jiménez (1987) investigated the acquisition of Spanish consonants in 120 Spanish-speaking children of Mexican descent, ranging in age from 3 years to 5 years and 7 months. All the children came from Spanish-speaking homes, and Spanish was their primary language. She reported that, even by the age of 5 years, two consonant phonemes (i.e., /s/ and /rr/) had not been mastered at the 90% level.

Major Findings on Phonological Development

Although the studies differ in the setting where the data were collected, in the number and origin of children in each group, and in the elicitation techniques used, they lead to two general conclusions. First, because of their exposure to English, Spanish speakers in the United States may reach the 90% criterion a bit later than do their counterparts. For example, Mason and associates (1976) reported that their subjects did not master the /rr/ (e.g., in *perro* 'dog' and *ropa* 'rope') until age 7 years, while Merino (1983a) and Melgar (1976) reported its acquisition by age 6 years. Also, the children did not pronounce the /d/ in final position as in *verdad* 'truth' until age 9 years, although this error may be due to the fact that this phoneme is produced only in careful speech by adults (Harris, 1969).

The children in the Jiménez (1987) study produced several phonemes later than did the children in the Merino or Melgar studies.

Second, although there is some variation, there is general agreement across studies about the age at which specific phonemes develop. Most studies have focused on the age of mastery for particular phonemes, with 90% as the criterion. As has been noted in studies on the phonological development of English speakers, however, establishing valid guidelines that can be used as cut-off points with which to diagnose problems is not an easy task. It is much more practical to evaluate the production of a sound as it is correctly articulated by 50% of the subjects and trace it until it is developed in 90% of the group (Sander, 1972).

The development of the different consonants that can be compared across the Melgar (1976), Merino (1983a), and Jiménez (1987) studies is represented in Figure 3-1. The bar begins at the point where more than 50% of the children could produce a phoneme and ends at the point where 90% of the subjects in an age group could produce the target sound. Where the studies disagreed, the later age for mastery appears in the bar graph. The majority of consonant phonemes are well established by age 5 years, with the exception of /s/ and /rr/. Those studies that focused on consonant blends (Mason et al., 1976; Melgar, 1976; Merino, 1983a) indicate that, although some clusters are mastered by age 4 years, others may not develop until age 6 or 7 years. This mirrors findings obtained with English-speaking children.

Discrepancies between studies can be attributed in part to the position of the consonant in the word or the type of word. For example, the late acquisition of /x/ (notation for English equivalent of /h/), as in *reloj* 'watch', may be due to its position in the word. Jiménez (1987) did not include this position of the phoneme in her target words and found that the /x/ was developed by age 5 years. Similarly, /l/ may appear to develop later because it was tested in a word such as *árbol* 'tree' as opposed to *sol* 'sun', which is an easier word to pronounce (Mason et al., 1976; Merino, 1983a). Another source of difference may be dialect variation. For example, the MEDA tests the /gl/ sound in *globo* 'balloon'. In Mexico and much of Central America, however, the word *vejiga* is a possible variant. Several of the children in Merino's sample from Oaxaca used the word *vejiga* first and had to imitate the less familiar word *globo*. The use of multisyllabic words can also cause problems for children who are trying to pronounce sounds that, if contained in shorter units, would present no difficulty. In the Oaxaca study, several children stumbled over *mariposa* 'butterfly'. Jiménez used the simpler word *pera* 'pear' to test the /r/.

Trends in Phonological Assessments

The research findings reported to date are most useful with children who are recent arrivals from a Spanish-speaking country or with very young children

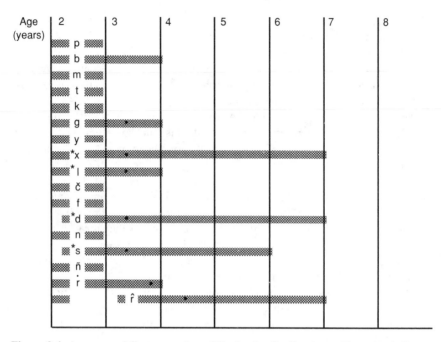

Figure 3-1 Average and Customary Age of Production for Consonant Phonemes in Spanish. Data from Melgar (1976) and Merino (1983a). *Age discrepancies between the two studies. •Age discrepancies in Melgar and Merino, as compared to Jiménez (1987). According to the latter study, these sounds develop later.

whose exposure to English may still be minimal. Clinicians must always take into account variables such as language loss, dialect, or influence from English in determining whether a particular child has a language problem.

In their future efforts, researchers should continue to collect information from children who are from other Spanish-speaking countries and from those who are less than 3 years old. Multiple items for each individual sound in different word positions should be included. Items selected for elicitation should be of high frequency, should evoke no dialect variants, and should involve concepts that are easy to interpret. The collection of a language sample should be an integral part of investigations in order to identify errors that occur in connected speech. In addition, efforts should continue in documenting the different processes that occur in the course of phonological development. For example, Hodson, Becker, Diamond, and Meza (1989) found that unintelligible Spanish-speaking 4-year-olds made the very same types of errors in Spanish that unintelligible English-speaking children commonly make:

- reduction of consonant sequences, such as /epexo/ for *espejo* 'mirror' (equivalent of /poon/ for *spoon*)
- liquid deviation /ádbol/ for *árbol* (equivalent of /wug/ for *rug*)
- stridency deletion as /lápi/ for *lápiz* (equivalent of /oap/ for *soap*)

Although the control group made similar errors, the percentage of errors that the identified unintelligible subjects made was much more significant. The research in this area has just begun in Spanish and quite likely will continue in the future.

PRAGMATICS AND COMMUNICATIVE COMPETENCE

Recently, there has been an increased interest in the possibility of diagnosing language disorders in bilingual children by assessing their pragmatic skills according to specific criteria (Damico, Oller, & Storey, 1983) or in conjunction with traditional language proficiency measures (Hamayan, 1984). One difficulty with this type of assessment is the wide divergence in the definition of the term *pragmatics* and the allied term *communicative competence*. Bates (1976) held to a broad definition of pragmatics as encompassing the "rules of use." Communicative competence entails the ability to use the linguistic and social convention of a particular language and culture in which the communication occurs (Cheng, 1987).

Most of the research on linguistic communicative competence in Spanish has been done in reference to adult language learners in the acquisition of forms of address as reviewed by Ordas (1984). Some studies have been conducted on bilingual children to determine whether there is a significant relationship between their general communicative competence and their performance on standardized achievement tests. For example, Politzer, Shohamy, and McGroarty (1981) found that some measures of communicative competence, such as inviting a friend to a party, giving directions, or using a map, correlated more significantly with achievement than did a regular language syntax measure. Merino and Lyons (1984) found that this same measure of communicative competence did not differentiate between low and high achieving limited-English–proficient students, however, except in their ability to read English. To differentiate, it may be necessary to administer a greater variety of tasks, such as solving problems, narrating a story, or defending one's point of view about an issue. Clearly, conclusions based on discrete-point tests alone are not always accurate.

Primary research on the development of pragmatics among monolingual Spanish-speaking children is largely limited to a few areas that are not always relevant to clinical conditions. For example, there are more than 20 studies on the use of forms of address in Spanish-speaking subjects (Ordas, 1984). Some research has been undertaken on the classroom discourse and specific language interaction needs of Spanish-speaking children who attend U.S. schools (Day, 1981; Hamayan, 1984; Iglesias, 1984, 1985; Wilkinson, Milosky, & Genishi, 1986). For example, in their study, Wilkinson and associates noted that Hispanic students addressed requests to the entire group rather than a particular person. Most of the time, both bilingual and monolingual children made requests that were direct, on task, and sincere.

As part of the normative study conducted in Mexico, Merino and Bye (1983) developed a test of communicative competence in Spanish based on the earlier work of Bye (1976). This test measured two discourse functions: giving directions and narrating a series of events. The principal visual stimulus used to elicit data was a miniature three-dimensional village with various buildings and houses distributed throughout the town. In the direction-giving task, for example, children aged 4 to 11 years were asked to role-play by calling emergency service personnel to come to their assistance and giving directions to their house. Scoring was qualitative and focused on continuity, the ability to organize the discourse and establish a relationship between the point of origin and the destination; specificity, the amount of detail supplied as directions are given and the implicitness or explicitness of this detail; and functionality, the degree to which the directions provide sufficient information for the listener to arrive at the designated destination. Most children were not able to provide directions until the age of 4 or 5 years; at these ages, the children gave directions that were incomplete, lacked explicit detail, and had a limited continuity in organizational structure. Even at the age of 6 and 7 years, the children gave directions that were more explicit, but continued to lack cohesion and functionality. Only between 8 and 11 years of age did the children begin to give functional directions, although many children continued to exhibit problems (Merino, Figueroa, Bye, Rangel Hinojosa, Romero Contreras, & Gómez-Palacio, 1988).

Thus, communicative competence encompasses the notion of language in use in specific contexts. The child's unique language and social experiences affect the measurement of this competence. There is a great need for more information on how better to match the communication demands of a school setting with the language skills that the child brings to school.

REFERENCES

Anderson, R., & Smith, B. (1986). Phonological development of 2-year-old monolingual Puerto Rican Spanish-speaking children. *Journal of Child Language, 14,* 57–78.
Bailey, N., Madden, C., & Krashen, S. (1974). Is there a natural sequence in adult second language learning? *Language Learning, 24,* 235–244.

Bates, E. (1976). *Language and context: The acquisition of pragmatics*. New York: Academic Press.

Beléndez, P. (1980). *Repetitions and the acquisition of the Spanish verb system*. Unpublished doctoral dissertation, Harvard University, Cambridge, MA.

Blake, R.J. (1980). *The acquisition of mood selection among Spanish-speaking children: Ages 4–12*. Unpublished doctoral dissertation, University of Texas, Austin.

Bloom, L. (1980). Language development, language disorders and learning disabilities: LD3. *Bulletin of the Orton Society, 30*, 115–133.

Bloom, L., & Lahey, M. (1978). *Language development and language disorders*. New York: John Wiley.

Brinton, B., & Fujiki, M. (1989). *Conversational management with language-impaired children: Pragmatic assessment and intervention*. Gaithersburg, MD: Aspen Publishers.

Brisk, M.E. (1972). *The Spanish syntax of the preschool Spanish-American: The case of New Mexican five-year-old children*. Unpublished doctoral dissertation, University of New Mexico,

Brisk, M.E. (1974). A preliminary study of the syntax of five-year-old Spanish speakers in New Mexico. *International Journal of the Sociology of Language, 2*, 69–78.

Brisk, M.E. (1976). The acquisition of Spanish gender by first-grade Spanish-speaking children. In G.D. Keller, R.V. Teshner, & S. Viera (Eds.), *Bilingualism in the bicentennial and beyond* (pp. 143–160). Jamaica, NY: Bilingual Review Press.

Brown, R. (1973). *A first language*. Cambridge, MA: Harvard University Press.

Burt, M., Dulay, H., & Hernández-Chávez, E. (1975). *The bilingual syntax measure*. San Francisco: Harcourt Brace Jovanovich.

Bye, T. (1976). *Aspects of the acquisition of communicative competence: The role of listener-oriented presuppositions in producing directives*. Unpublished doctoral dissertation, University of California, Los Angeles.

Cheng, L.L. (1987). English communicative competence of language minority children: Assessment and treatment of language "impaired" preschoolers. In H.T. Trueba (Ed.), *Success or failure?: Learning and the language minority student* (pp. 49–68). Cambridge, MA: Newbury House.

Chomsky, C. (1968). *The acquisition of syntax in children from 5 to 10*. Cambridge, MA: MIT Press.

Chomsky, N. (1968). *Language and mind*. New York: Harcourt Brace Jovanovich.

Clark, E.V. (1985). The acquisition of romance with special reference to French. In D. Slobin (Ed.), *The cross-linguistic study of language acquisition, Vol 1: The data*. Hillsdale, NJ: Lawrence Erlbaum Associates.

Cohen, A.D. (1975). Assessing language maintenance in Spanish-speaking. In E. Hernández-Chávez, A. Cohen, and A. Beltramo (Eds.), *El lenguaje de los Chicanos* (pp. 202–219). Washington, DC: Center for Applied Linguistics.

Cohen, S.W. (1980). *The sequential order of acquisition of Spanish verb tenses among Spanish-speaking children of age 3–7*. Unpublished doctoral dissertation, University of San Francisco.

Dale, P. (1980). *Acquisition of English and Spanish morphological rules by bilinguals*. Unpublished doctoral dissertation, University of Florida, Gainesville.

Damico, J., & Oller, J.W. (1980). Pragmatic versus morphological/syntactical criteria for language referrals. *Language, Speech, Hearing Services in Schools, 9*, 74–84.

Damico, J., Oller, J., & Storey, M.E. (1983). The diagnosis of language disorders in bilingual children: Surface-oriented and pragmatic criteria. *Journal of Speech and Hearing Disorders, 48*, 385–394.

Dato, D.P. (1975). On psycholinguistic universals in children's learning of Spanish. In D. Dato (Ed.), *Developmental psycholinguistics: Theory and applications* (pp. 235–254). Washington, DC: Georgetown University Press.

Day, C. (1981). Assessing communicative competence. In J.G. Erickson & D.R. Omark (Eds.), *Communication assessment of the bilingual bicultural child* (pp. 179–197). Baltimore: University Park Press.

De la Fuente, M. (1985). *The order of acquisition of Spanish consonant phonemes by monolingual Spanish-speaking children between the ages of 2.0 and 6.5.* Unpublished doctoral dissertation, Georgetown University, Washington, DC.

de Villiers, J.G., & de Villiers, P.A. (1978). *Language acquisition.* Cambridge, MA: Harvard University Press.

Dulay, H., & Burt, M.K. (1974). Natural sequences in child second language acquisition. *Language Learning, 24,* 37–53.

Dulay, H., Burt, M., & Krashen, S. (1982). *The second language.* New York: Oxford University Press.

Dulay, H., Hernández-Chávez, E., & Burt, B. (1978). The process of becoming bilingual. In S. Singh & J. Lynch (Eds.), *Diagnostic procedures in hearing, speech, and language* (pp. 251–303). Baltimore: University Park Press.

Echeverría, M. (1975). *Late stages in the acquisition of Spanish syntax.* Unpublished doctoral dissertation, University of Washington, Seattle.

Edelsky, C., & Muina, V. (1977). Native Spanish language acquisition: The effect of age, schooling, and context on responses to "díle" and "pregúntale." *Journal of Child Language, 4,* 453–475.

Eisenberg, A.R. (1982). *Language acquisition in cultural perspective: Talk in three Mexican homes.* Unpublished doctoral dissertation, University of California, Berkeley.

Elías-Olivares, L. (1976). *Ways of speaking in a Chicago community: A sociolinguistic approach.* Unpublished doctoral dissertation, University of Texas, Houston.

Escobar, A. (1976). *Language.* Lima, Peru: Instituto de Investigaciones.

Fantini, A. (1982). *Language acquisition of the bilingual child: A sociolinguistic perspective.* Brattleboro, VT: The Experiment Press.

Ferreiro, W., Ochenin-Girard, C., Chipman, H., & Sinclair, H. (1976). How do children handle relative clauses? *Archives Psychologiques, 44,* 229–265.

Fey, M. (1986). *Language intervention with young children.* Austin, TX: PRO-ED.

Freedman, P.P., & Carpenter, R.L. (1976). Semantic relations used by normal and language impaired children at stage I. *Journal of Speech and Hearing Research, 19,* 784–795.

Galván, J.L. (1980). *The development of aspectual relationship in Spanish-speaking children.* Unpublished doctoral dissertation, University of Texas, Austin.

Gili y Gaya, S. (1960). *Funciones gramaticales en el habla infantil.* Publicaciones pedagógicas, Serie II, No. 24. Rio Piedras: Universidad de Puerto Rico.

Gili y Gaya, S. (1972). *Estudios de lenguaje infantil.* Barcelona: Bibliograf.

González, G. (1970). *The acquisition of Spanish grammar by native Spanish speakers.* Unpublished doctoral dissertation, University of Texas, Austin.

González, G. (1972). Analysis of Chicano Spanish and the problem of usage. *Aztlán, 3,* 223–231.

González, G. (1975). The acquisition of grammatical structures by Mexican-American children. In E. Hernández-Chávez, A.D. Cohen, & A.F. Beltramo (Eds.), *El languaje de los Chicanos* (pp. 220–237). Washington, DC: Center for Applied Linguistics.

González, G. (1978a). *The acquisition of Spanish grammar by native Spanish-speaking children.* Rosslyn, VA: National Clearinghouse for Bilingual Education.

González, G. (1978b). The speech of a Chicano child: Spanish grammatical transformation at age 2–6. In A.G. Lozano (Ed.), *Bilingual and biliterate perspectives.* Boulder, CO: University of Colorado.

González, G. (1980). *The acquisition of verb tenses and temporal expression in Spanish age 2–4:6.* Bilingual Education Paper Series. Los Angeles: National Dissemination and Assessment Center, California State University.

Gudeman, R.H. (1981). *Learning Spanish: A cross-sectional study of the imitation, comprehension and production of Spanish grammatical forms by rural Panamanians.* Unpublished doctoral dissertation, University of Minnesota, Minneapolis.

Guitart, J. (1981). The pronunciation of Puerto Rican Spanish in the mainland: Theoretical and pedagogical considerations. In G. Valdés, A. Lozano, & R. García-Moya (Eds.), *Teaching Spanish to the Hispanic bilingual* (pp. 46–58). New York: Teachers College Press, Columbia University.

Hamayan, E. (1984). Assessment of language proficiency of exceptional bilingual students: An integrative approach. *Workshop on Communicative Disorders and Language Proficiency: Assessment, Intervention and Curriculum Implementation.* Los Alamitos, CA: National Center for Bilingual Research.

Harris, J.W. (1969). *Spanish phonology.* Cambridge, MA: MIT Press.

Hidalgo, M. (1987). On the question of "standard" vs. "dialect": Implications for teaching Hispanic college students. *Hispanic Journal of Behavioral Sciences, 9,* 375–395.

Hodson, B., Becker, M., Diamond, F., & Meza, P. (1989). Phonological analysis of unintelligible children's utterances: English and Spanish. In *Occasional papers on linguistics: The uses of phonology.* Carbondale: Southern Illinois University Press.

Iglesias, A. (1984). Assessing communicative performance of LEP children in the classroom. *Workshop on Communication Disorders and Language Proficiency: Assessment, Intervention, and Curriculum Implementation.* Los Alamitos, CA: National Center for Bilingual Research.

Iglesias, A. (1985). Cultural conflict in the classroom: The communicatively different child. In D.N. Ripich & F.M. Spinelli (Eds.), *School discourse problems* (pp. 79–96). Austin, TX: PRO-ED.

Jiménez, B. (1987). Acquisition of Spanish consonants in children aged 3–5 years, 7 months. *Language, Speech, and Hearing Services in Schools, 18,* 357–363.

Kaufman, A.S., & Kaufman, N.L. (1982). *Kaufman assessment battery for children: Interpretive manual.* Circle Pines, MN: American Guidance Service.

Keller, G. (1976). Acquisition of the English and Spanish passive voices among bilingual children. In G.D. Keller, R.V. Teschner, & S. Viera (Eds.), *Bilingualism in the bicentennial and beyond* (pp. 161–168). New York: Bilingual Press.

Kernan, K., & Blount, B.G. (1966). The acquisition of Spanish grammar by Mexican children. *Anthropological Linguistics, 8,* 1–14.

Kessler, C. (1975). Postsemantic processes in delayed child language related to first and second language learning. In D.P. Dato (Ed.), *Developmental psycholinguistics: Theory and applications* (pp. 159–192). Washington, DC: Georgetown University Press.

Kvaal, J., Shipstead-Cox, N., Nevitt, S., Hodson, B., & Launer, P. (1988). The acquisition of 10 Spanish morphemes by Spanish-speaking children. *Language, Speech, and Hearing Services in Schools, 19,* 384–394.

Lahey, M. (1988). *Language disorders and language development.* New York: Macmillan.

Larsen-Freeman, D.E. (1978). An explanation for the morpheme accuracy order of learners of English as a second language. In E.M. Hatch (Ed.), *Second language acquisition: A book of readings* (pp. 371–379). Rowley, MA: Newbury House Publishers.

Lee, L. (1969). *Northwestern Syntax Screening Test (NSST).* Evanston, IL: Northwestern University Press.

Leonard, I., Bolders, J., & Miller, J.A. (1976). An examination of the semantic relations reflected in the usage of normal and language-disordered children. *Journal of Speech and Hearing Research, 19,* 371–392.

Leopold, W. (1949). *Speech development of a bilingual child: A linguist's record. Vol. 3. Grammar and general problems.* Evanston, IL: Northwestern University Press.

Linares, T. (1981). Articulation skills in Spanish-speaking children. In R.V. Padilla (Ed.), *Ethnoperspectives in bilingual education research III.* Ypsilanti, MI: Eastern Michigan University.

Linares, T., Orama, N., & Sanders, L.J. (1977). Evaluation of syntax of three-year-old Spanish-speaking Puerto Rican children. *Journal of Speech and Hearing Research, 20,* 350–357.

Lockwood, W.B. (1972). *A panorama of Indo-European languages.* London: Hutchinson and Company.

Lope-Blanch, J.M. (Ed.). (1977). *Estudios sobre el español hablado en las principales ciudades de América.* Mexico, D.F.: Universidad Autónoma de México.

McConnell, G.D., & Roberge, B. (1987). Statistiques sur la langue maternelle majoritaire des pays et territoises du monde. Quebec, Canada: Centre International de Recherches sur le Bilinguisme.

Mackey, M., & Barton, D. (1980). The acquisition of the voicing contrast in Spanish: A phonetic and phonological study of word-initial stop consonants. *Journal of Child Language, 7,* 433–458.

Marrone, N. (1974). Investigación sobre variaciones léxicas en el mundo hispano. *The Bilingual Review, 1,* 152–173.

Martínez-Bernal, J.A. (1972). *Children's acquisition of Spanish and English morphological systems and noun phrases.* Unpublished doctoral dissertation, Georgetown University, Washington, DC.

Mason, M., Smith, B., & Hinshaw, M. (1976). *Medida española de articulación (MEDA).* San Ysidro, CA: San Ysidro School District.

Melgar de González, M. (1976). *Cómo detectar al niño con problemas del habla.* Mexico, D.F.: Editorial Trillas.

Menéndez Pidál, R. (1926). *Orígenes del español.* Madrid: Hermando.

Menyuk, P. (1975). Children with language problems. What's the problem? In D. Dato (Ed.), *Developmental psycholinguistics: Theory and applications* (pp. 129–144). Washington, DC: Georgetown University Press.

Menyuk, P. (1988). *Language development.* Glenview, IL: Scott, Foresman & Co.

Merino, B.J. (1976). *Language acquisition in bilingual children: Aspects of syntactic development in English and Spanish by Chicano children in grades K–4.* Unpublished doctoral dissertation, Stanford University.

Merino, B.J. (1982, October–November). *Language development in Spanish as a first language: Implications for assessment.* Paper presented at the National Conference on the Exceptional Bilingual Child, Phoenix, AZ.

Merino, B.J. (1983a). *Developmental milestones for children learning the Spanish sound system.* Unpublished manuscript. Davis, CA: University of California.

Merino, B.J. (1983b). Language development in normal and language handicapped Spanish-speaking children. *Hispanic Journal of the Behavioral Sciences, 5,* 379–400.

Merino, B.J., & Bye, T. (1983). *Escala de competencia comunicative/Scale of catibve competence.* Davis, CA: University of California.

Merino, B.J., & Figueroa, R.A. (1984). *Report on the development of a transnational language assessment system for Spanish-speaking children.* Unpublished report to U.S. MEXUS. Davis, CA: Department of Education, University of California.

Merino, B.J., Figueroa, R.A., Bye, T., Rangel Hinojosa, E., Romero Contreras, S., & Gómez-Palacio, M. (1988). *Batería de evaluación de la lengua española para niños mexicanos de 3 a 11 años.* Mexico, D.F.: Dirección General de Educación Especial.

Merino, B.J., Figueroa, R.A., Gómez-Palacio, M., Rangel Hinojosa, E., & Jackson-Maldonado, D. (1987). *Sistema de evaluación sobre la adquisición de la lengua española (SEALE).* Mexico, D.F.: Oficina de Educación Especial, Secretaría de Educación Pública.

Merino, B.J., & Lyons, J. (1984). *Components of language proficiency and their relation to academic achievement.* Final Report to the Kellogg Foundation and the Public Service Research and Dissemination Program.

Montes-Giraldo, J.J. (1971). Acerca de la apropriación por el niño del sistema Fonológico español. *Boletín del Instituto Caro y Cuervo, 31,* 14–40.

Montes-Giraldo, J.J. (1974). Esquema ontogénico del desarrollo del lenguaje y otras cuestiones del habla infantil. *Boletín del Instituto Caro y Cuervo, 29,* 254–270.

Navarro Espinosa, A., & Rodríguez Castellano, L. (1933). La frontera del andaluz. *Revista de Filología Española, 20,* 225–277.

Navarro, T. (1974). *El español en Puerto Rico.* Rio Piedras: Editorial Universitaria, Universidad de Puerto Rico.

Olarte, G. (1985). *Acquisition of Spanish morphemes by monolingual, monocultural Spanish-speaking children.* Unpublished doctoral dissertation, University of Florida, Gainesville.

Ordas, R. (1984). *Variables in use of pronouns of address in Spanish.* Unpublished manuscript. Davis, CA: University of California.

Ortíz, M. (1980). The acquisition of Spanish as a native language. In H. Dulay, M. Burt, & D. McKeon (Eds.), *Testing and teaching communicatively handicapped Hispanic children: The state of the art in 1980.* Sacramento, CA: Department of Education, Office of Special Education.

Padilla, A., & Liebman, E. (1982). Language acquisition in the bilingual child. In J. Fishman & G. Keller (Eds.), *Bilingual education for Hispanic students in the United States.* New York: Teachers College Press, Columbia University.

Pardo, E. (1984). *Acquisition of the Spanish reflexive: A study of a child's overextended forms.* Unpublished doctoral dissertation, Stanford University.

Parra, R. (1982). *The sequential order of acquisition of categories of Spanish adjectives by Spanish-speaking children of age 2 to 12 years.* Unpublished doctoral dissertation, University of San Francisco.

Peñalosa, F. (1980). *Chicano sociolinguistics.* Rowley, MA: Newbury House.

Politzer, R.L., Shohamy, E., & McGroarty, M. (April 1981). *Validation of linguistic and communicative oral language tests for Spanish-English bilingual programs.* Paper presented at the Colloquium on Validation of Oral Proficiency Tests, Ann Arbor, MI.

Pousada, A., & Poplack, S. (1982). No case for convergence: The Puerto Rican Spanish verb system in a language contact situation. In J.A. Fishman & G.D. Keller (Eds.), *Bilingual education for Hispanic students in the United States* (pp. 207–237). New York: Teachers College Press, Columbia University.

Ripich, D.N., & Spinelli, F.M. (1985). *School discourse problems.* San Diego: College Hill Press.

Romero, M. (1985). *Verb acquisition in Spanish as a native language in Puerto Rico.* Unpublished doctoral dissertation. New York: New York University.

Rosensweig, J.B. (1973). *Calo: Gutter Spanish.* New York: E.P. Dutton.

Salillas, R. (1896). *El delincuente español: El lenguaje.* Madrid: V. Suárez.

Sánchez, R. (1972). Nuestra circumstancia lingüística. *El Grito, 6,* 45–74.

Sander, E.K. (1972). When are speech sounds learned? *Journal of Speech and Hearing Disorders, 37,* 55–63.

Spaulding, R. (1975). *How Spanish grew.* Berkeley, CA: University of California Press.

Stewart, W. (1962). An outline of linguistic typology for describing multilingualism. In F. Rice (Ed.), *Study of the role of second languages in Asia, Africa and Latin America* (pp. 14–25). Washington, DC: Center for Applied Linguistics.

Stockwell, R.P., Bowen, J.D., & Martin, J.W. (1965). *The grammatical structures of English and Spanish.* Chicago: University of Chicago Press.

Trejo, A.D. (1968). *Diccionario etimológico latinoamericano del léxico de la delincuencia.* Mexico, D.F.: Editorial Hispano Americana.

Truex, N.W. (1982). *An interactive concept of language development with reference to Spanish.* Unpublished doctoral dissertation. University of California, Los Angeles.

Van Naerssen, M. (1980). How similar are Spanish as a first language and Spanish as a foreign language? In R. Scarcella & S.D. Krashen (Eds.), *Research in second language acquisition.* Rowley, MA: Newbury House.

Vivas, D. (1979). Order of acquisition of Spanish grammatical morphemes: Comparison to some cross-linguistic methodological problems. *Kansas Working Papers in Linguistics, 4,* 77–105.

Wechsler, D. (1974). *Manual for the Wechsler Intelligence Scale—Revised.* New York: Psychological Corporation.

Wilkinson, L.C., Milosky, L.M., & Genishi, C. (1986). Second language learners' use of requests and responses in elementary classrooms. *Topics in Language Disorders, 6*(2), 57–70.

Williamson, R., & Rodríguez, O. (1980). Asking and telling, a problem of language acquisition: Some data from Mexican children. *Rassegna Italiana di Linguistica Applicata, 12,* 73–90.

Chapter 4

Language Communication and Sociocultural Patterns in Hispanic Families

Henriette W. Langdon

As they grow up, children are influenced first by their families and the community, later by the schools that they attend. Although children spend only a portion of their day in school, this institution plays an important part in their lives. It is the place where they acquire new knowledge and where, in order to be successful, they must follow particular discourse rules that are specific to that setting.

The importance of communication rules within any given setting was not recognized until the mid-1970s (Bates, 1976). Subsequently, the focus of research began to shift from language form to language use. As a result, greater emphasis has been given to the identification of specific discourse rules in specific settings, and the language used to communicate at home has often been found to vary significantly from the language used to communicate at school. Mainstream children are at an advantage over their minority peers. Their parents are more familiar with school expectations, and they have greater access to different institutions and networks that can facilitate the educational process. In sum, they and their families are more familiar with the discourse rules of the school system than are language minority children and their families.

Many Hispanic children must cross the language barrier as they adapt to a totally new set of communication rules upon entering school for the first time or even after having attended school in their own home country. For example, they may understand that it is appropriate to exchange information with other students while completing a project, but not realize that such an exchange is inappropriate during an examination. Also, expectations about what children need to say and when they need to say it vary from teacher to teacher and from setting to setting. This has been observed in different classrooms and therapy rooms with English-speaking children (Spinelli & Ripich, 1985) as well as across different types of bilingual classrooms where mixed groups of limited-English–proficient (LEP) and Anglo children are placed (Iglesias, 1985a, 1985b). Specifically, teachers may allow students to initiate conversation only in certain contexts, but not others, and often encourage short rather than elaborate answers. Thus, there is a need for greater understanding among teachers and other school staff members of their own expectations and of children's communication needs, particularly for those children who come from a family with different communication styles and experiences, and for those who may also have language or learning difficulties. The function of the school should be "not only to teach English to those students but also to provide them with opportunities for learning a greater range of oral and written language uses" (Heath, 1986, p. 144).

The mismatch between what children have experienced at home and what is expected of them at school, coupled with a language barrier, is the cause of academic failure for many of those in minority groups. There is no simple explanation, however, for the fact that only 50% to 55% of Mexicans and 60% of Central and South Americans in the United States complete high school by the age of 34 years (Current Population Reports, 1990). As Walker (1987) noted, "Experiences of the Hispanic student at school would be impossible to compile—indeed, (and fortunately) its variety and complexity render such a task overwhelming" (p. 15).

In the past, lack of learning was blamed on the child or the school. Now, the belief is that it is necessary to consider the interaction of culture, language, and cognition within the child's learning environment (Trueba, 1988, 1989). According to the "zone of proximal development" defined by Vygotsky (1962), children learn skills by interacting with a more competent and experienced member of their culture. At first, the child receives support from an adult or more competent child in accomplishing a task. Later, the child is slowly left to accomplish the task independently with less control from the adult. Not all experiences are gained in this fashion, however. Children also learn by simply observing or modeling. They are influenced by their parents' attitudes toward formal schooling and education.

DEFINING ETHNOGRAPHY

Spindler and Spindler (1987) defined an ethnographic study as the study of "how natives behave and how they explain their behaviors. An ethnography, strictly speaking, is an orderly report of this recording. Natives are people in situations anywhere—including children and youth in schools—not just people who live in remote jungles or cozy pleasant villages" (p. 17). An ethnographic study can be carried out through participant observations, interviews, videotaping and audiotaping, journal writing, and many other techniques (Trueba, 1989, p. 176). There are established criteria for such a study, however (Spindler & Spindler, 1987, pp. 18–21; Trueba, 1989, pp. 176–177).

1. The observations must be systematic and contextualized, as well as carried out in a natural environment.

2. The observer must refrain from any hypothesis about what is observed until the study is completed.
3. The focus must be on communicative interactions.
4. The researcher must be knowledgeable of the sociocultural context in which the interaction is taking place.
5. The researcher should remain objective about what is observed and should not impose a personal perspective.

There are only a limited number of ethnographic studies available on Hispanics living in the United States. Most of the research dates from the last decade and has been carried out on recent immigrants, principally those from Mexico. Furthermore, the majority of these studies focused on families of low-to-middle or low socioeconomic status, so generalizations cannot be made for Hispanics as a group or even for one specific subgroup, such as Mexicans or Cubans. Nevertheless, the ethnographic information provided by such studies is helpful in the educational assessment of Hispanic children and adults.

LANGUAGE COMMUNICATION PATTERNS IN SELECTED HISPANIC HOMES

Understanding the nature of communication between Hispanic adults and children helps clinicians and educators determine whether any differences in their language patterns reflect a possible disorder, a different set of experiences, or simply a lack of exposure to specific situations. It also helps clinicians suggest to the family the best ways to help a child who may have language and learning difficulties.

Parent-Child Interactions

Hispanics do not always translate actions into words. Parents may not comment or verbalize about ongoing events. For example, while engaged in a daily activity such as cooking, shopping, or completing household chores, the parent does not necessarily pair the actions with words and offer step-by-step directions (e.g., "First we are going to cut the tomatoes, potatoes, and celery into little pieces; then we are going to boil some water and add the vegetables with a little salt and pepper"). Parents and older siblings tell the children what to do. In turn, children's responses are rewarded with comments such as "good," "fine," "wrong," or "bad." Parents do not understand the value of playing and consider it a pastime that distracts the children from completing their household chores; consequently, they seldom participate in their children's play (Delgado-Gaitán & Trueba, 1991). Moreover, children are asked not to interrupt while adults are talking. In many families, children interact verbally more often with peers or siblings than with their parents or other adults. The lack of parent-child interaction may be attributed in part to the increasing pressure on both parents to work outside the home.

The amount of time that parents spend reading to their children is proportional to the amount of their own formal education. Laosa (1982) found a positive correlation between a mother's number of years of schooling and her children's level of preliterate skills. Also, the higher the educational level of the mother, the more opportunities that a child has to respond to questions and comments. Although the families that Heath (1986) observed did not read books to the children, they often told the children stories and adventures about their own lives. Many of these stories included details about real events and about historical figures. This practice is also common among American Indians (Rietz, 1986). Delgado-Gaitán and Trueba (1991) observed that adults in Hispanic families read school bulletins. Few adults read as a leisure activity or read storybooks to their children, but several children were observed to read to one another. Furthermore, those children who seemed more advanced in reading helped those who were having difficulties.

Adult-Child Interactions

Hispanic adults interact primarily with other adults at social gatherings. During certain pastimes that they may share with children, such as TV viewing, adults do not comment on what is occurring. Once again, they do not translate actions into words. With today's life pressures, however, many parents and adults from many language and social backgrounds allow children to watch TV alone while they themselves are engaged in different activities.

Adults do not ask children for their interpretation of events or emotional evaluations. For example, when there is a choice of actions, adults do not ask children to voice their preferences (Heath, 1986). Even so, when children are assigned certain tasks, they may be able to negotiate how and when the tasks are to be completed (Delgado-Gaitán, 1987a; Delgado-Gaitán & Trueba, 1991). Children generally have responsibilities at home, such as caring for younger siblings while the parent is occupied with another task or is absent, and it may be that a child's ability to negotiate and voice preferences varies from situation to situation.

Children are exposed to a great deal of vocabulary, especially that related to names of different relatives and their relationship to one another. The emphasis on family word names reflects the importance given to the family as a unit. In fact, many Hispanic children are raised to give a higher priority to cooperation with family members than to individual achievement. In cases of distress, the family remains cohesive. Naturally, the degree of family cooperation varies from situation to situation, but it appears stronger among Hispanic families than it is among many Anglo groups (Guendelman, 1983).

Hispanic children are not asked to repeat facts or to foretell what they will do. Thus, it may be uncommon for any adult to ask a child to retell what happened on any occasion during which both of them were present. It would be considered more natural if the child was recounting the event to someone else who was not present. This particular information is important because mainstream teachers frequently ask children to verbalize that which was previously shared by teacher and children. This technique permits the teacher to check the child's comprehension and assimilation of the material presented in the classroom. This form of questioning is also common in language proficiency testing. For example, on the Language Assessment Scales (De Avila & Duncan, 1983) and the Idea Language Proficiency Test (Ballard & Tighe, 1982), the examiner asks the child to retell a story that is known to both of them in order to verify comprehension and analyze expressive skills. The Hispanic child may not perform well on a task of this nature because of a lack of experience in displaying shared knowledge. Therefore, examiners should verify the range of past experiences of a child being tested, as the test may require a language use that the child must learn in order to succeed on the test. If a child does not readily answer questions about a shared event or does not initiate a conversation, the examiner cannot assume that the child has a language problem.

Nonverbal Communication Patterns

Systematic research in the area of nonverbal communication among Hispanics is scarce. Yet, gestures, facial expressions, pauses, intonation patterns, vocal patterns, and spatial arrangements convey meaning and intent. Leubitz (1973) identified four functions of nonverbal communication: to relay a message and to augment, contradict, or replace verbal communication.

Although there are always individual differences, the nonverbal features of communication patterns among Hispanics generally fall into two main categories: (1) those relating to the person's identity and relationship to others and (2) those relating to the meaning of what is being said. Among those features in the first group are

- an appreciation of the uniqueness of an individual, which is valued among Hispanics. An individual's inner qualities are referred to as the person's *alma* 'soul' or *espíritu* 'spirit'. An Anglo may feel that this characterization of a person is almost too sentimental.
- respect for individuals because of their advanced age and experience. For example, a mechanic with a great deal of experience may be called *maestro* 'teacher, master' (Condon, 1986). Thus, it is advisable for clinicians to address a parent, adult, or older patient with *Ud.* (formal *you*) in a professional-

client relationship—never with the form *tú* (familiar or informal *you*). The clinician may address a young child or adolescent with "tú," however.

- handshaking, which is routinely done upon greeting someone, both among men and women. Occasional hugging and kissing is appropriate when the persons know each other.

- initiation of conversation with personal questions rather than business talk. Hispanics may interpret opening a conversation without a personal note as rude.

- awareness of many lasting and close relationships. Among Hispanics, family takes precedence over everything else, even a job, school, or friendships. In the Anglo world, the emphasis is often on remaining loyal to a job, even if it is stressful to the family.

- children's use of gestures as they speak, which may be much greater than the use of gestures among other non-Hispanic children. This use of gestures should not be interpreted as a communication disability (Kayser, 1990).

Those nonverbal features relating to the meaning of what is being said include

- the use of *mañana* 'tomorrow'. The word *mañana* does not necessarily mean the next day; rather it may mean in the future. Anglos are much more time-bound, driven by schedules and deadlines than are Hispanics (Condon, 1986). Hispanics often comment that it is difficult for them to adjust to the tightness of schedules in the Anglo world. For many Hispanics, people and their needs take precedence over precise schedules or appointments (Penfield, 1989).

- the use of politeness forms. Hospitality is wholehearted. Terms denoting politeness may be somewhat exaggerated, however, such as *Está Ud. en su casa* 'You are in your own home'. The meaning conveyed is really, "Please feel as if this is your own home." When scolded, children are forbidden to look at adults; also, when talking with adults, they may look away to show their respect. Out of politeness, a patient may not openly disagree with the professional, but may only pretend to follow the prescribed recommendations—even when there is no language barrier.

- the use of *sí, como no* 'yes, indeed'. Such a comment does not mean that the person agrees with what is said, but rather is an acknowledgment that the person is attentive and listening.

The nonverbal characteristics of communication described have been observed not only in Hispanics, but also to some extent in other cultural groups, such as Asians (Cheng, 1987). Although this information provides clinicians with an increased awareness of some nonverbal features that may occur in their communications with Hispanic persons, they must remain aware of differences due to the subgroup or individual characteristics.

SCHOOLING IN HISPANIC COUNTRIES

Recent immigrant children and adolescents who are attending schools throughout the United States may come from a variety of Spanish-speaking countries. The clinician or teacher who works with these students should have an overview of the operation of schools in those countries in order to understand the general expectations and instructional strategies used there.

As can be noted from Table 4-1, Hispanic countries vary widely in the literacy rates of their populations (Dostert, 1989; Skabelund & Sims, 1990). Furthermore, each country defines the term *literacy* differently. In some, being literate means being able to fill out a basic form; in others, it means reading and writing at a level that allows individuals to answer questions on their country's culture and history (personal communication, National Office on Literacy, 1990). Therefore, the numbers can be only estimates. Literacy rates are low (65% or below) in Bolivia, El Salvador, Guatemala, Honduras, and Peru. Argentina, Chile, Costa Rica, Cuba, Spain, and Uruguay have the highest rates of literacy (93% and above). Despite the high prevalence of illiteracy, education is compulsory for children from ages 6 or 7 years to ages 12 or 14 years in most countries.

Access to Schooling

Variations can be predicted in the literacy skills of immigrants, migrants, and refugees, depending on their access to formal schooling. Some children did not attend school regularly in their home country because they had to work to supplement the family's income or because they lived in remote, rural areas and had to travel several hours to school. For these very same reasons, many of the adults did not have an opportunity to complete their formal education. This situation is particularly common in Mexico, Bolivia, and Guatemala, but it may occur in other countries as well.

Often, the Native Indians who live in the remote areas do not speak Spanish, which constitutes an additional barrier for them as they seek access to education. The proportion of Indians is significant for Bolivia (70%), Peru (45%), Guatemala (41%), Ecuador (40%), and Mexico (30%). Educating these persons poses immense challenges to these governments. Mexico, for example, has already implemented bilingual programs to meet the needs of more than 3 million indigenous persons, and some sources report that Mexico may have as many as 8 million. A special project has been undertaken to write bilingual textbooks in as many lan-

Table 4-1 Ethnic Composition, Educational Standards, and Literacy Rates in Hispanic
Countries

Country	Ethnic Composition	Educational Standards	Literacy Rate (%)
Argentina (35 million)	98% Whites 2% Mestizo	Compulsory, age 6–14 years; free secondary and higher education	94
Bolivia (7.3 million)	70% Indian 20% Mestizo 10% Caucasian	Limited access to education	63
Chile (13.6 million)	95% European 5% Mestizo	Compulsory, age 5–18 years; free throughout	94
Colombia (27 million)	58% Mestizo 20% European 14% Mulatto 4% Black 4% Negro-American/Indian	Compulsory, age 6–12 years, but not free; number of rural schools increasing	80
Costa Rica (2.9 million)	96% Caucasian 4% Mestizo or Black	Compulsory education in primary grades; secondary free	93
Cuba (11.3 million)	51% Mulatto 37% Caucasian 11% Black	Compulsory education in primary grades	93
Dominican Republic (7.2 million)	73% Mestizo 16% Caucasian 11% Black	Compulsory education in primary grades	74
Ecuador (10 million)	40% Mestizo 40% Indian 10% Black 10% Caucasian and Oriental	National government in control of schools	85
El Salvador (6.3 million)	92% Mestizo 4% Indian 4% Caucasian	Free education; many private schools; in rural areas, literacy rate of 30%	65
Guatemala (9 million)	59% Ladinos* 41% Indian	Half of eligible primary age children not in school, despite availability of programs	50

Country	Ethnic Composition	Educational Standards	Literacy Rate (%)
Honduras (4.9 million)	90% Mestizo 5% Black 5% Indian	Compulsory, age 7–14 years, but many not in school	56
Mexico (89 million)	60% Mestizo 30% Indian 10% Caucasian	Compulsory, age 7–15 years; increase of 14% in literacy rate last 5 years	88
Nicaragua (3.4 million)	69% Mestizo 17% Caucasian 9% Black 5% Indian	Compulsory, age 7–14 years; shortage of teachers, Cuban teachers recruited	88
Panama (2.4 million)	70% Mestizo 14% Black 9% Caucasian 7% Indian	Compulsory, age 7–15 years	85
Paraguay (3.8 million)	95% Mestizo 5% Caucasian	Education compulsory and free, but many private schools	81
Peru (22 million)	45% Indian 37% Mestizo 15% Caucasian 3% Black and Oriental	Compulsory and free, age 6–17 years	54
Puerto Rico (3.5 million)	98% Mestizos 2% Caucasian	Compulsory and free, age 8–18 years	89
Spain (40 million)	Mediterranean and Nordic descent	Compulsory, age 6–14 years; free, but most operated by religious and private organizations	97
Uruguay (4 million)	90% Caucasian 5% Mestizo 5% Black	Compulsory, age 6–12 years; free, necessary to pass special examination for secondary	94
Venezuela (19 million)	83% Mestizo 10% Caucasian 5% African 2% Indian	Compulsory, age 7–14 years; free	90

* *Ladino*, Mestizo and westernized Indians.

Sources: Data from *Culturgram for the '90s* by G.P. Skabelund and S.M. Sims, 1990. Provo, UT: Brigham Young University, and *Latin America 1989* by P.E. Dostert, 1989, Washington, D.C.: Stryker-Post Publications.

guages as possible in Mexico. As of 1984, some textbooks had been adapted in 12 Indian languages and 26 dialects from the total of 125 to 150 languages and dialects spoken by approximately 56 Indian groups (Miller, 1984). In contrast, most of the Argentinean population resides within a metropolitan area, speaks Spanish, and, thus, has easier access to schooling.

Priorities and policies set by the local governments also affect access to schooling and, thus, literacy rates. For example, the Cuban Revolution of 1959 increased educational opportunities for most of its population so that, after 30 years, the literacy rate is quite high. In 1956, only 50.4% of the children aged 6 to 12 years had been enrolled in school; in 1971 to 1972, the percentage had risen to 96.4% (Richmond, 1985). The Cuban government expected that, by 1990, most citizens will attain a ninth-grade education. In contrast, a young child immigrating from Puerto Rico, which is influenced by the U.S. educational system, may have had only limited schooling due to access to educational institutions. This occurs when the family has resided in a rural area of the island. Frequent moves from the island to the mainland may disrupt a child's education. This may also be the case with immigrants from other countries of the world.

School Systems in Hispanic Countries

The basic school systems in many of the Spanish-speaking countries of Latin America have many characteristics in common (Brock, 1985). Some characteristics pertain to the accessibility to education; others, to the relationship between the public and the private sectors; still others, to the quality of education. As mentioned earlier, children in rural areas frequently receive intermittent schooling because of the long distances that they must travel between their homes and the school site. In addition, teachers in those areas may not attend the schools on a consistent schedule. Secondary schools are often completely inaccessible to those children. Additionally, public schools must compete with the private sector that offers schooling to the middle and upper classes. The quality of education is often dependent on the social class and ethnic background of the students. Parents who have the financial means may opt to send their children to private school. Education is often of better quality and children may receive religious education sought by their parents. Many minorities, such as Indians and Blacks, do not receive appropriate education. Standards for teachers may be low, especially in rural areas; students are often forced to repeat grades because of ineffective teaching strategies. Furthermore, special education is almost nonexistent.

Many Hispanic adults have had very limited opportunities to pursue an education. The "literacy" of many consists only of the ability to sign their names. Therefore, local governments should assist in providing schooling for these persons. Those who reside in rural areas and who do not speak Spanish have even more limited access to resources. Local governments report that they are attempting to address these issues by campaigning for *alfabetización* 'literacy' (Miller, 1984). When those programs are indeed available, they must focus on the needs of the students.

Schooling in Mexico

Public schools in Mexico, which charge no tuition, are usually attended by the low-to-middle socioeconomic groups. Middle- and upper-class Mexicans and many of the Europeans residing in the country send their children to parochial schools or to bilingual French, German, or American private schools. The curriculum is the same for all public schools in Mexico, but is different for each of the parochial and bilingual schools.

Although the number of preschool programs is increasing, they are mostly private; only a few are supported by the government. Primary school includes six grades, while secondary school includes three grades. A college preparatory education requires 3 more years of high school. Each bilingual private school, which has the same grade structure, offers a curriculum conducted in varying proportions of the primary and secondary languages. After completing high school, the student is ready to enter the university. A rigorous entrance examination is required, however; only one of every three examinees passes the test. A graduate from a parochial or bilingual school must take the university entrance examination as well. Vocationally trained students may attend special technical schools.

Teachers are trained in normal schools (i.e., teachers' colleges), which are different from universities. Until approximately 10 years ago, a prospective teacher could begin the normal school without completing a college preparatory education. Today, however, the prospective teacher must complete the entire course of education.

Because of Mexico's proximity to the United States, both public and private schools emphasize instruction in English as a second language. Some schools offer English as part of their curriculum in the elementary grades; others initiate instruction in English at the junior high school level. Any student entering the university must possess at least a minimal ability to read material in English. Technical books in Spanish are scarce or outdated. University lectures are supplemented by English texts. Prospective employers often give preference to those applicants who are bilingual in English.

Classroom Size and Management. Classrooms may have as many as 58 students, who are not grouped by ability. The teacher has no assistant. Discipline and authority are stressed. When adults enter the classroom, the children greet them by standing.

Teaching Methodology. The curriculum is subject-based. Each grade studies a different topic and follows an integrated curriculum. For example, family is the theme in first grade. Concepts introduced in reading are reviewed in social studies and applied in math and science. Teachers write the work on the blackboard. Then one or two students go to the blackboard to do the activity, and the other students in the classroom write the lesson in their notebooks. Teachers seldom promote children's literature, and students do not usually take books home from a school library. Generally, the children read in chorus rather than on an individual basis.

Penmanship is emphasized from the very beginning of school. Memorization is stressed. Students are generally asked to retell the information that the teacher provided rather than to synthesize the material that was covered in a lesson. Examinations consist for the most part of fill-in-the-blank and essay questions, only infrequently including multiple choice questions.

Teaching Alternatives. Very limited teaching alternatives are available. Repeating a grade is often used as the remedy for a child's academic problems, particularly in the rural areas. In fact, it is not uncommon for a student to have repeated a grade two or more times. Only recently has there been a systematic way to refer children to special education. For example, Mexico City has nine centers to which students can be referred for assessment, but testing is a value judgment based on Spanish adaptations of U.S. tests. About 85 schools have special programs, not nearly enough for a total school population of approximately 8 million.

Parents are not generally asked to participate in school matters to the same degree as in the United States. Teachers are considered the experts, and their skills are seldom questioned. Some students have been denied access to school because of a lack of space. The 1985 earthquake in Mexico City damaged many school buildings, and some undamaged schools operated on two or three sessions. The government is now attempting to offer an education to all children, however.

Schooling in Puerto Rico

The educational system in Puerto Rico is somewhat influenced by the U.S. system. Elementary school includes kindergarten through the 6th grade; junior high school, the 7th through the 9th grade; and high school, the 10th through the 12th grade. As in Mexico, most preschools are privately run. The quality of public education is variable. It is better in larger districts because of the greater availability of funds. Many middle- and upper-class children attend private schools. To enter a university, the prospective student must take a test similar to the Scholastic Achievement Test (SAT). Some state universities are considered better than private ones.

All schools, whether public or private, strive to be bilingual. English is taught for 1 hour a day, beginning in first grade, although students do not usually become fluent until high school. In college, professors lecture in both Spanish and English. As mentioned earlier, many technical textbooks at that level are available in English only. Sports do not play as important a role in the school curriculum as they do in the United States. Computers are not widely utilized in the schools.

Most classes have approximately 25 students in each. Teachers and professors are never questioned. They are considered experts, and students are expected to show them respect. A few special programs for children with learning disabilities or low intellectual functioning are available, but only in the major cities of the island. In small towns, children with a variety of learning problems are placed in the regular program.

There are significant differences between the Puerto Ricans who live on the island and those who emigrate or travel back and forth from the mainland. For example, those who settle in large cities on the mainland, such as New York, frequently have limited resources. They live in low-rent apartments called *caserías*. It is estimated that, of all the Hispanic subgroups, Puerto Ricans have the greatest proportion of families living below the poverty level (33% in contrast to 26% for the total Hispanic group). Also, among those families, there is the greatest proportion of female-headed households (65%, as opposed to 52% for the total Hispanic group). Many of the moves back and forth to the island are motivated by economic conditions (Valdivieso & Davis, 1988). Despite their problems, Puerto Ricans have always had strong ties with their families. These ties appear to be deteriorating, however, especially on the mainland. Economic pressure and the high rate of divorce are contributing factors.

Guatemala's Rural Education: A Case Study

In addition to their responsibility toward the mainstream population, schools in the Spanish-speaking world have an obligation to educate those children whose primary language is not Spanish. In Guatemala, some 20 Mayan languages with approximately 70 additional dialects are spoken (Kaufman, 1976). Although the case study of Indian children's schooling occurred in Guatemala, similar events take place in Mexico and other Spanish-speaking countries in which a large population of Indians reside.

In her description of the schooling of Indian children in Guatemala, Richards (1987) stated that Spanish is the language of power and that the ability to speak Spanish gives the person the necessary status and prestige to succeed in the mainstream society. However, as Richards noted, "Because [Indian] children are exposed to few appropriate Spanish-language contexts outside the confines of the school, their opportunity to develop the skills they may have learned in school is severely limited" (p. 118). Many children become discouraged and leave school early. Much of the teaching methodology lacks a contextual base. For example, instruction in Spanish as a second language consists of choral recitation and drill.

By the time the students are sorted through the sieves of "Castellaniza-ción" (learning Spanish) and first grade, they have learned to copy well and have mastered the classroom behavior rules. But although they may have gained control of the sound system in Spanish, the students remain every bit as reluctant to utter Spanish in any form other than choral word-for-word repetition (and the enthusiasm for this activity has significantly waned). When students are put on the spot and are asked to respond individually to a question posed by the teacher, they either freeze, then lower their eyes, and, by their avoidance, express total ignorance of the answer, or they answer the question (which usually has been simplified to elicit a one-word response) in a meek, muffled, reluctant and embarrassed way. (Richards, 1987, p. 126)

As Richards indicated, it is difficult to speculate on the students' eventual proficiency in Spanish. It depends largely on the opportunities that they will have to interact with Spanish-speaking persons. The particular community described by Richards has a handful of elementary school graduates. No one has acquired a secondary education yet. Furthermore, the people do not have the resources to send their children away for further education.

HISPANICS' ATTITUDES TOWARD EDUCATION

Members of the Hispanic culture have varying attitudes toward education and schooling. Often, their attitudes are bound to social class. Middle-class immigrants appear to adapt more easily to new institutions and to the operation of schools. As Trueba (1989) commented, however, the constant flow of immigration may obscure the true extent to which Hispanic parents accept and support their children's bilingual education. Some families are eager to learn English and maintain Spanish. Others continue to speak Spanish but are not sure of the value of learning English. Still others may be opposed to enrolling their children in a bilingual program because they feel their children should learn only English at school.

Hispanic parents encourage their children to learn, but they do not always know which competencies to emphasize. Parents who themselves failed in school may promote more values of family tradition and culture. Maestas and Erickson (1989) found that parents would help their children with schoolwork if they were given specific instructions to follow, however. In most cases, parents make their children feel responsible for their own learning and encourage them to listen to and respect the teacher.

Although Mexicans born in Mexico have fewer years of schooling than do those born in the United States, second-generation Mexicans may have a negative view of school. Few remember successful public school experiences. Despite this fact, they desire a good education, even a college education, for their children

(Romo, 1984). Mothers who are more educated have particularly high aspirations for their children. Recent immigrants believe that schooling will provide better opportunities for the next generation, and they encourage their children to learn English so that they will feel better settled in the new country (Romo, 1984; Suárez-Orozco, 1987).

None of the studies mentioned specifically addresses gender differences in aspiring to complete a formal education. Until perhaps 20 years ago, there was minimal encouragement for women in Hispanic countries to seek a career. At the present time, however, it appears that more Hispanic women are pursuing an education. Their participation in the work force is also greater today, as it is in the United States. Nevertheless, in some families, women are still assigned traditional roles.

> A second-grade Hispanic girl, the oldest of four children (the rest were all boys), was not achieving in school. Extensive testing indicated that she had no learning problems. When she applied herself, she was able to perform quite well. At home, this girl was a great helper, and her mother trusted her with many household responsibilities. The girl's parents encouraged her to do well in school, as they themselves did not have very much schooling. The child appeared to have strongly identified with her mother, however, and had no motivation to apply herself. In this case, it was suggested that the girl work closely with a Spanish-speaking aide whom she liked; this adult served as a model for her by also working in cooperation with her family.

In some families, girls are not permitted to play outside because they are girls and need to be protected. Sometimes, only boys participate in specific outings with their father.

Although Puerto Ricans are U.S. citizens and, therefore, can travel freely from the island to the mainland, they have difficulty adjusting to the U.S. school system. Figler (1979) found that it was necessary to contact Puerto Rican parents personally to encourage their involvement in school issues. Many times, these parents were not aware of what their children were doing in school or what programs were available; as a result, many parents had misconceptions about bilingual education. Their lack of involvement and information about their child's schooling has been attributed to

1. the language barrier. Notes and notices may be written in Spanish, but the language used is often too official.
2. insufficient confidence in interacting with school personnel, even if the staff members speak Spanish, because of the parents' own limited schooling.

3. fear that being called to school means the child has some problems.

Although no specific ethnographic studies have been carried out with Cubans, it is important not to generalize. Many of the first Cuban immigrants to the United States were primarily from the middle and upper classes, and they had a high regard for education. Successive migrations brought in persons from lower socio-economic groups who may have attitudes more similar to those of the other Hispanic subgroups that have been discussed, however (Queralt, 1984).

HISPANICS' ATTITUDES ABOUT HANDICAPPING CONDITIONS

A family's reaction to a handicapping condition that afflicts a child is a personal matter. Some families find it easier to understand that a child is "handicapped" when the handicap is a visible physiological one, such as a cleft palate, blindness, or deafness, rather than a learning or language disability in which the manifestations are not as apparent. In either case, a handicap constitutes a hardship for any family.

"Visible" Handicaps

Among many Hispanic and other minority groups, there is a tendency to attribute a child's "visible" handicap to an external, nonmedical reason (Cheng, 1990; Meyerson, 1983, 1990; Weddington, 1990). Meyerson (1983, 1990) reported that several Chicano mothers attributed their children's cleft palate to an eclipse during pregnancy. Some mothers may attribute the problem to a *susto* 'a frightful situation' during pregnancy, to *mal puesto* 'witchcraft', or *mal ojo* 'evil eye'. Still other mothers reported that their child's affliction was a direct punishment for some wrongdoing in the course of their own childhood. Among Cubans, a child's physical or mental problem is often attributed to *empacho* 'indigestion', *desmayo* or *desvanecimiento* 'fainting spell', *decaimiento* 'lack of energy', or even *barrenillo* 'obsessive thinking' during pregnancy (Queralt, 1984). Mothers have often been known to ask if one or another event during pregnancy could have caused their child's speech or language problem, especially when there is a physical manifestation (e.g., cleft palate or cerebral palsy).

A belief in folk medicine as part of a medical treatment process is common among some less acculturated Hispanics. The healing process is described as *curanderismo* and is practiced by *curanderos* 'healers' (Mexico) and *espiritistas* 'spiritualists' (Puerto Ricans). As Meyerson (1990) reported, these *curanderos* use a combination of intense concern, rituals, herbs and herbal teas, oil massage, amulets, and prayers. Thus, some groups seek medical care from physicians for physical problems, but seek psychological support from a *curandero*. Again, generalizations about a group or certain types of persons may create a bias, but the clinician working with Hispanic families should be aware that these families may adhere to such beliefs.

Some research is available on the attitudes of Hispanics toward institutionalization and their acceptance of their child's hearing impairment. Meyerson (1983) and Figler (1979) reported that some Hispanic families strongly resist the institutionalization of severely handicapped children. Often, these children are referred to as *enfermitos* 'little sick ones'. Because of the acceptance of their fate and their large family network, Hispanic families care for these children at home more often than do others. In comparing Puerto Rican families residing on the mainland with handicapped children and families with normally developing children, however, Figler (1979) found that the first group experienced more stress. Having a handicapped child enhanced the families' ties to the mainland with its access to various educational and medical establishments. Foremost, this attitude eliminated their initial intent of staying only temporarily on the mainland. Families with handicapped children relied more on community level support; they were more involved with welfare agencies and had more contacts with the school, but had less contact with relatives in Puerto Rico and had no plans to return to the island.

Fishgrund, Cohen, and Clarkson (1987) reported that Hispanics have more difficulty than do other minority groups in accepting their child's handicap, such as a hearing loss. Contrary to the conclusions reached by Figler (1979), these researchers found that Hispanics do "shop" around for help more than do other groups. They more often seek religious-based avenues in their efforts to remedy the problem. Many return to their homeland temporarily. These authors also noted that Hispanics have more difficulty keeping appointments and understanding the roles of the different agencies that they must consult. For example, they find small, local *clínicas* 'clinics' less threatening than are services offered within a large medical center or hospital.

In some Hispanic families, strict adherence to schedules takes second place to socialization with friends and relatives, even when the schedules involve medical treatment (Meyerson, 1990). A missed appointment may be due to a lack of transportation or possible economic repercussions, however. For example, a day or a few hours away from work for a medical or clinical appointment may mean lost wages (Rodríguez, 1983). Also, an appointment may be missed because of a failure to understand the urgency of the problem or the need for repeated visits (e.g., for a speech-language or hearing evaluation). Visiting a clinician for therapy that requires regular appointments may be particularly difficult for some parents to understand, because progress is often slow and may not be immediately apparent. It is important for the clinician to explain the intervention clearly and delineate some expectations.

"Invisible" Handicaps

There are very few data on Hispanic parents' views of "invisible" handicaps. Anecdotal evidence suggests that less visible problems, such as speech, language, or language-learning disabilities (i.e., educational problems) are sometimes more difficult for Hispanic parents to accept, however. Matsuda (1989) reached a similar conclusion in a study of Asian parents. This attitude may vary according to the age of the child and the severity of the problem. Because the child may be able to perform as expected at home most of the time, the parent may not always view the language or educational handicap as significant.

In one of the few studies conducted with Hispanic families who had children in resource or pull-out programs, Gallegos and Gallegos (1988) found that Hispanic parents of children with learning problems did not feel that their children were "handicapped." Like their Anglo counterparts in the study, these parents believed that their children would outgrow the problem and would be able to do whatever they desired as adults. Parents who have had limited schooling themselves may not believe that, indeed, a language-learning difficulty is a true problem, especially when the child with the "problem" is able to read and write in Spanish and/ or English better than the parents can. In many instances, however, these same parents consent to placing their child in a special program, trusting the good intentions of school personnel, but not fully understanding the situation.

Hispanic parents respect teachers highly. Often, they feel that "teachers know best and educational decisions are the school's job" (Gallegos & Gallegos, 1988; Stein, 1983). Many Hispanic parents' preoccupations at meetings are more on the behavior than on the performance of their children, at least initially. As a result, Hispanic parents' involvement in the development of an individual education program for their child is generally less than that of Anglo groups (Gallegos & Gallegos, 1988; Lynch & Stein, 1987; Maestas & Erickson, 1989; Stein, 1983). Hispanic parents tend to leave these decisions to school personnel. They do not understand the process of identification well and feel incapable of supporting their child's program at home unless they are given specific directions. Parents from other minority or even mainstreamed groups may share these feelings, however.

HISPANICS' ATTITUDES TOWARD BILINGUALISM

An important variable in evaluating and planning programs for LEP or bilingual children is their family's attitude toward the use of each language. Thus, some children may appear less proficient in Spanish because of a lack of practice or language loss rather than a language disability. Still others may not be learning English as fast as they might because their families are ambivalent about accepting the new language and culture. Therefore, it is very important to collect information on motivation and attitudes toward maintenance of the first language and learning patterns in the second.

Loss of the primary language generally occurs within two or, at the most, three generations of immigration (Veltman, 1988). Some subgroups may use the primary language longer than do others, however, depending on their feeling about the migration experience. Laosa (1982) and Walker (1987) indicated that Spanish, for example, is maintained more frequently when the reason for migration is political rather than economic, which would explain the greater prevalence in the use of Spanish by first-generation Cuban and Central American immigrants. Occupation may also affect language maintenance; some immigrants must struggle to keep a job, so they may not have the energy to learn a new language. In other situations, parents may continue speaking the primary language, but the children may lose it as they learn English. Society at large or other factors cause children to devalue their primary language and put pressure on them to acquire the new language.

As previously mentioned, immigrant parents encourage their children to learn English because they view the process of the new language acquisition as a way to better their lives (Delgado-Gaitán, 1987a, 1987b; Delgado-Gaitán & Trueba, 1991; Romo, 1984; Suárez-Orozco, 1987). Even when families use Spanish at home, however, it is lost eventually. Several studies have shown that the use of Spanish decreases as the use of English increases (Peñalosa, 1980). In addition, many communities or families may switch back and forth from one language to the other within the same conversation. Code-switching has often been erroneously taken for language confusion. Thus, there is great variation in the degree of bilingualism.

If Both Parents Are Bilingual

The degree of the parents' bilingualism may substantially affect the child's language use. Parents should be encouraged to express themselves on various topics in the language of their choice. For example, some bilingual parents may feel more at ease explaining events, scolding, or comforting in one language than in the other. A communication breakdown may occur if parents feel pressed to change their language use so that it conforms with the mainstream culture. As a result, children lose their native language, but the parents do not necessarily acquire the competence to express themselves fully in the second language. To maximize the use of each language, it may be beneficial to communicate in one or the other language when addressing specific topics. For example, English may be used to discuss school and job matters, whereas Spanish may be used to express personal feelings. The family must make the ultimate choice on the use of each language.

If Only One Parent Speaks English

The type of use of each language may affect family dynamics, especially if the children attend schools where the majority of students are English-speaking. Eventually, as they spend more time in school or with English-speaking peers, the children may speak English more fluently than Spanish. If only one parent speaks English, the children may turn to that parent when they have a problem or need to discuss an issue. The parent who is not fluent in English may begin to lose the ability to communicate with the family. It is important that the bilingual parent maintain a balance by encouraging the children to speak Spanish at home as much as possible to allow the participation of the monolingual parent. At the same time, the parent who does not speak English should be encouraged to learn more English to increase his or her receptive skills. In this manner, the children maintain their Spanish, and the entire family can understand the parent who is not fluent in English.

If Neither Parent Speaks English

It is not advisable for a family to learn to communicate in English at the expense of their Spanish. Switching to a language in which the family's skills are weaker may cause a loss of communication between parents and children. Rodríguez (1982) noted that his parents' compliance with a suggestion to switch to English to facilitate his adjustment to school resulted in such a loss of communication. The parents' English was never proficient enough to enable them to express more complex ideas. Rodríguez's Spanish could never develop because of a lack of practice in using the language. Cummins (1981) indicated that, when they use their native language naturally, parents increase their children's pride in their own culture and language. This is particularly important when a child has a language disorder in Spanish. More exposure to English does not necessarily resolve the problem. Rather, reinforcement of concepts in the native language appears to facilitate the acquisition of language in general.

Cummins (1981) cited cases in which parents had switched to the majority language to help their children with language and learning problems. Those children whose parents maintained their native language eventually performed better than did those whose parents tried to use the second language (Bhatnager, 1980; Chesarek, 1981). The parents who used the second language were not able to express more complex ideas and were not good language models for their children. This finding corroborates the theory of "common underlying proficiency" (Cummins, 1981). Two languages have common underlying characteristics, such as expressing similar concepts and functions, even though the surface structures (words and word order) are different. In other words, skills are transferable across languages.

If Parents Have Only a Receptive Knowledge of English

If the children speak English and the parents answer in Spanish, reinforcing in Spanish what the children have said will enable them to preserve and expand their understanding of Spanish. When they have more natural opportunities to use Spanish, their expressive abilities will develop faster and more completely. For example, one child who had been exposed to French since birth could understand the language, but would answer only in English. After attending a 3-hour immersion program in French for 3 weeks at age 6, she began using complete and long sentences in the French language. Thus, when given the time, opportunity, and motivation, children who have a good understanding of a language may develop expressive skills very quickly.

Cummins (1984) gave the following advice to educators: (1) "Never advise minority parents to switch to English at home. This may lower the quality of interaction between parents and children." (2) "Communicate to minority children that bilingualism is a special achievement to be valued and developed" (p. 267). It may be difficult for educators to follow these suggestions, but doing so not only will help preserve the identity of the persons and their communication with their families, but also will emphasize the value of bilingualism.

HISPANICS' ATTITUDES TOWARD OTHER HISPANIC SUBGROUPS

It is erroneous to assume that members of a minority group will always have a positive attitude toward other members of the group. For example, Delgado-Gaitán (1987a) reported that the parents whom she interviewed wanted their children to do well in school to prevent them from becoming *cholos* (i.e., youths of Hispanic origin who are school truants and dropouts). These youths cause great shame to other members of the Hispanic community by stigmatizing the entire group. Also, Romo (1984) noted that there is some antagonism between the more assimilated Mexican-Americans who speak English and recent Mexican immigrants. The more assimilated group resents the immigrants because they take jobs away from them, and contact between these two groups is often minimal. More assimilated and more proficient English-speaking Hispanics have less and less contact with their own language minority group. There is even antagonism between different groups of black Hispanics.

It is difficult to predict the attitude of one subgroup toward another based on their common linguistic background. Variables such as length of residence and reason for migration to the United States do not determine the attitude of one group toward another. Attitudes may stem from the failure of society at large to accept persons who are different and who are not proficient in English. Perhaps, if there were more acceptance and tolerance for language and cultural diversity (as there may be in certain areas), there would be less antagonism among members of minority groups. Unfortunately, in their efforts to conform to their peers, children begin to forget their first language and culture before they acquire the second language (Trueba, 1989). As a result, these children often have limited proficiency in either language. Ethnographic studies with a Spanish-speaking community in the Colorado area clearly show that a decrease in contact with peers of the same linguistic group and a lack of reinforcement in primary language use at home contribute to a loss of fluency in the native language and a loss of respect for the primary culture (Commins, 1989; Commins & Miramontes, 1989).

CASE STUDIES

Manuel

An 11-year-old dominant Spanish speaker, Manuel is a fifth grader in northern California. His school does not have a bilingual program, and his class is conducted exclusively in English. Language minority students are instructed in English as a second language (ESL) for 30 minutes each day. Those students who need additional assistance receive small group instruction from the bilingual aide. All individualized help is offered in English, although the classroom aide uses some Spanish to clarify concepts. Manuel has been in the fifth grade for 9 months, which is the length of his residence in the United States, and both his teacher and the aide are concerned about his progress. Despite individual attention and instruction, Manuel has gained very few skills in English. His teacher reports that he is inattentive at times and does not follow group instructions well. On some occasions, he tends to rebel; at other times, however, he is helpful and friendly. He can understand some basic directions when they are contextualized, as in "bring the yellow book that is on top of the shelf." He does not know the alphabet and is able to recognize in English only the words *stop, school, restroom,* and *grade.* A screening done in Spanish by the aide indicated that he does not know the alphabet in Spanish either; furthermore, he can recognize only a few Spanish words. His mathematical skills are depressed, but he can solve addition and subtraction problems up to 10. He can recognize numbers to 100 and can write them when they are named in Spanish. He can also manipulate numbers up to 50 when they are named in English. Although Manuel cannot read, he has very good handwriting and can copy words as well as sentences very neatly onto paper.

Manuel had attended the same school 3 years earlier. At that time, his first school experience in the United States, he remained in the second grade for only 1 month. Prior to this placement, he had attended school sporadically in Mexico when he did not have to help his parents with fieldwork. He came from an impoverished rural town, and the school was a two-room building with approximately 60 children, ranging in age from 7 to 14 years. Manuel had to walk for almost an hour to get to the school. During the rainy season, the school was inaccessible because of large puddles of water. The teacher would not come to school in those instances. Thus, the students lost many school attendance days.

Home Visit and Parent Interview

A clinician made a home visit to gather information on language input, to determine the parents' expectations for Manuel, and to gain greater understanding of his background and health history. The interview questions selected were not used in any rigid manner. When the parent volunteered personal information, the clinician took the opportunity to ask further questions for clarification. In order to keep the interview within a certain time frame, however, an effort was made to stay on task. This process can also be followed with the assistance of an interpreter.

Manuel's parents, Mr. and Mrs. B., are migrant workers. They were interviewed in their home, a barrack in the middle of fields where numerous crops are grown. Manuel lives with his parents and a 3-year-old sister. He has two other sisters, aged 7 and 9 years, but they were left behind in Mexico in the care of their maternal grandparents. Mr. and Mrs. B. reported that they had been in and out of the United States the past several years because of job opportunities. Their schooling had been interrupted for economic reasons; they had to help their own parents with fieldwork. Mrs. B. had completed only first grade, while Mr. B. had been able to complete four grades. Neither of them seemed to have had learning problems, but they are not proficient in English.

Reading material is minimal in Manuel's home. There are a few magazines in Spanish, but no newspapers or books. The family owns a TV set. They reported watching the Spanish channel exclusively, although Manuel and his sister enjoy "Sesame Street." The house consists of only one room, and its furnishings are very humble. Manuel sleeps on the floor next to his sister on an old mattress. His parents sleep on a couch in the same room. Adjacent to the main room is a nook for a small kitchen, which is furnished with a stove, table and chairs, and a tiny refrigerator. Bathroom facilities are in an outhouse. The home is clean and tidy, and the clinician was offered coffee before the interview.

Manuel had been born at home with the assistance of a midwife. There were no complications at birth, and developmental milestones occurred within normal time limits. Mr. and Mrs. B. did not feel that Manuel had a language problem. Recent screenings at Manuel's school had indicated normal hearing and vision acuity. Mrs. B. remarked that Manuel had nice printing skills, but she knew that he could not read many words in Spanish. Although she had not been able to have conferences with the teacher in Mexico, she realized that Manuel could not read as well as his own sisters. She did not feel Manuel had a problem with memory. She indicated that, if Mr. B. showed him some words, Manuel was able to retain them.

Although Mr. B. never read to Manuel or his sisters, he told them stories about his own childhood while they were engaged in home activities. He said that he liked to tell stories "from his head" and that the children enjoyed listening.

Mr. and Mrs. B. were hoping to stay permanently in the United States. They were in the process of completing their immigration papers. They realized the value of schooling and wanted Manuel to succeed in school. Often, they made comments such as *Queremos que aprenda pa' que agarre mejor trabajo que nosotros* 'We want him to learn so he can get a better job than we can'. They were grateful for the visit and expressed regret that they were unable to visit the school. The notes that they received from the school were in English. Manuel was not able to translate them because he himself did not know what they said. The principal did not speak Spanish, but the secretary was bilingual and had talked with the family a few times. Mr. and Mrs. B. felt embarrassed about calling her, however; they were afraid to disturb her.

Testing Procedure and Observations

The school appraisal team decided to request a Spanish language assessment to rule out a language-based problem. The district hired a bilingual Spanish-speaking speech and language consultant. In conjunction with the assessment, this clinician interviewed the parents at their home, observed Manuel in the classroom and on the playground, and worked with him on an individual basis. During the one-to-one interaction, Manuel was given two language proficiency tests: the Bilingual Syntax Measures (Level II) (BSM; Burt, Dulay, & Hernández-Chávez, 1980), and the Idea Language Proficiency Test (Level I) (IPT; Ballard & Tighe, 1982). Some other discrete-point tests were also administered, and a language sample was recorded through an informal conversation in which they discussed different topics. On a one-to-one basis, Manuel was very cooperative with the clinician. He enjoyed the individual attention and, when asked specifically, stated that he liked speaking in Spanish. Manuel reported that he had no other peers he could play with after school. His afternoons were spent completing homework and helping the family with chores and work in the fields.

Manuel seemed unhappy working with the aide on some of the assigned vocabulary words. The activity required him to name pictures. No other child participated with him. He had difficulty repeating and remembering the words in English. The aide did not use manipulatives (objects) or other materials (made out of paper or felt) to illustrate the words, but used only the pictures and followed the very rigid instructions suggested by the manual that came with the kit. The aide reported that other students who had come from similar linguistic and sociocultural backgrounds had learned the vocabulary faster than Manuel was learning it. Manuel cooperated reluctantly. This was evident by his seating posture; he was half lying on the table. He was happier when he was asked to copy words and short sentences into his notebook. He also enjoyed solving mathematical problems, an activity in which he could be successful.

On a whole class art activity, Manuel excelled. The students were asked to make a drawing of their choice with watercolors. Manuel's final product was one of the best in the class. His attention to detail and choice of colors were outstanding. Manuel had drawn some children playing soccer, one of his favorite sports. During this activity, Manuel had minimal interaction with the other children in the classroom. He was heard making occasional short requests in English, such as "I need water," and "give me the yellow color."

Results of testing, observations, and analysis of the language sample indicated that Manuel could follow directions well. He could sustain a conversation by responding appropriately to comments and questions. When he was read brief stories, he could answer different questions about what he had heard. He had more difficulty when asked to give a title to the story or to define words. His vocabulary knowledge was approximately that of a second grader. For example, he could recognize the picture representing words such as *human* and *artist*, but he had difficulty with the words *discussion*, *island*, and *nutritious*. He could define words such as *temple* and *invisible*, however. Manuel expressed himself with correct grammar and syntax. On the BSM, he scored as fully proficient in Spanish. He did not perform as well on the other proficiency test, the IPT, because of unfamiliarity with some vocabulary words. Also, he did better retelling a story that he had heard from the clinician than recounting the plot of a TV show, for example; more details and better sequencing skills were evident. The clinician had preformulated the story structure, which aided its recall. Overall, Manuel was able to use language to convey basic ideas, interpret meaning, and hypothesize. On the other hand, he had gaps in vocabulary and concepts, and he was unable to verbalize extensively in recounting narrative details. It appeared, however, that lack of exposure and lack of experience were interfering with his performance.

Manuel's word recognition repertoire was very limited. At the beginning of the session, the clinician asked him to list the words he wished to learn to read in Spanish. The words he selected were *pelota* 'ball', *jugar* 'to play', *colorear* 'to color', *cuentas* 'mathematical problems', and *casa* 'house'. The clinician rehearsed these words several times with him. After a few minutes, Manuel could read all of them. He was asked to make up sentences using the words, and these were written on the board. His reading retention was good. At the end of the testing session, Manuel was able to read all the words; he even volunteered to copy the sentences into his notebook. He did this activity quickly, neatly, and accurately. He asked the clinician if she would work with him the following day and showed disappointment when she said that she could not.

Interpretation of Findings

When reviewing a case such as Manuel's, it is not easy to determine whether the reason for his lack of progress is a learning difficulty. It is necessary to consider his past and present experiences at home, in his country of origin, and in the United States. His performance in one environment is not a sufficient basis for any assumptions.

Past School Experience. Manuel's schooling in Mexico was sporadic and was initiated in the United States with a new language. Subsequently, schooling continued in his native country in his primary language, but was inconsistent because of his own and the teacher's irregular attendance. Manuel can copy well, but reading is difficult for him. His exposure to literacy is minimal; it is also possible that the teaching methodology has not been adequate. Essentially, Manual has been taught to reproduce what others tell him.

Present School Experience. Manuel has gained some skills in solving computation-type mathematical problems. Very likely, this type of task is more meaningful to him. He has not learned very much English during the one-to-one instruction or in school. The lessons have followed a very rigid format, and the content has been far from his interests and needs. Furthermore, he has been singled out every day to receive individual instruction. His verbal interactions with peers in the classroom and outside school grounds are limited. Until he gains some oral skills in English, reading in English will be very difficult and meaningless. Because his experiences at home and in the community have been restricted, his range of language use is somewhat limited.

The brief diagnostic teaching lesson showed that Manuel learns better when the vocabulary at hand is within his frame of interest. It may be too early to decide that this particular approach to reading is the best teaching technique for him. It should be tried for some time, however. Unfortunately, educators may become impatient with one methodology when the students do not learn immediately. Trueba (1989) noted that teaching does not always produce instant results.

Manuel Himself. Manuel learns better in cooperative activities and excels in art. He can communicate adequately and express a number of language functions in Spanish. He does not understand certain concepts, however, and he lacks the vocabulary and language-based skills necessary to provide a cohesive and extensive story. He has not had opportunities to practice this type of "meta" language use at home or school. Manuel is receiving academic teaching in English where his proficiency is very weak. His frustration is noted by his distractibility and occasional lack of discipline. His willingness to learn is apparent in his request that the clinician return the next day and his disappointment when she cannot.

Parents. Manuel's parents have not been able to help him with school-related tasks. Most of the information that they have received from the school was written in a language that they do not know. Feeling inadequate and poorly schooled themselves, they are reluctant to contact the school—even the Spanish-speaking personnel. Nevertheless, they demonstrated their interest by granting an interview to the Spanish-speaking clinician. They expressed their wish for their son to have a better education so that he can have more opportunities in life. Although she has had limited schooling herself, Mrs. B. described her concern to the clinician quite accurately. She does not question the teaching, nor is she concerned that something may be "wrong" with her son. She is hopeful that the school will be instrumental in helping him.

Strategies: Program Modifications

Although it is not yet possible to conclude that Manuel has a learning disability, gathering the sociocultural data and observing Manuel in his school setting help the clinician to design a more appropriate program for him. Some suggestions are to

- offer literacy skills development in Spanish in a small group of students. If there are no other students in the class who could benefit from the program, place Manuel in a group with students from other grades.
- involve Manuel in cooperative learning activities in his class, not only for art, but also for mathematics and science. Create situations in which there is a greater need for verbal exchanges between him and his group, such as making it necessary for the children to ask questions of one another in order to solve a problem. These activities will help Manuel develop comprehension and expression skills in English. Once he has acquired sufficient oral language skills, it will be easier for him to learn academically related material in English.
- encourage Manuel to share what he learns with his parents by communicating through a dialogue journal (Westby & Costlow, 1991). Manuel can recount what he has learned. His parents can write a note back or send a message with him. The Spanish-speaking aide can be very instrumental in this process.
- invite Manuel's parents to participate in special activities and parent night events. Ask if one of them can help in the classroom. Ascertain if there is an interpreter or a bilingual person who can facilitate communication in the school.
- encourage Manuel to invite a friend from school who has some skills in Spanish to his home to promote exchanges between peers.

Unless these areas are addressed, it is impossible to be certain that Manuel has a language-learning disability. Progress must be carefully monitored.

Lupe

The second of five children who range in age from 7 years to 3 months, Lupe is 5 years old. Her parents are from El Salvador and have been in the United States for 10 years. They returned to their homeland only once, when Lupe was 4 years old. The visit lasted 8 months. Mr. G., Lupe's father, works in construction; in El Salvador, he had the equivalent of a junior college certificate in accounting. Mrs. G., a homemaker, completed eighth grade. Both Mr. and Mrs. G. speak English well, although Mrs. G. prefers reading in Spanish. The language used at home is Spanish. In fact, Mr. and Mrs. G. never speak English to their children, except when there are persons present who do not speak Spanish. Although Mr. G. has a fairly good salary, the family qualifies under Medicaid for glasses or hearing aids at no cost.

Lupe was a premature baby. She was born in New Mexico in a hospital at 6 months of gestation. She had to have heart and lung surgery, and she remained in an incubator in intensive care for 3 months. Upon her release from the hospital, she had gained weight and was doing well. During her first year of life, a visiting nurse monitored her development. Mrs. G. reported that Lupe did progress fairly well during that time, but seemed behind in gross motor development. She had difficulty rolling and sitting, even with support. She began physical therapy at 8 months of age. Intervention was successful and, although she did not walk until she was 2 years old, her progress was steady. She was subsequently dismissed from the program, and no follow-up was suggested.

Identification of Further Problems and Evaluation Process

At age 3 years, Lupe was using only a few words and communicated primarily with gestures. Because of her mother's concern, Lupe underwent an audiological workup for the first time. A moderately severe sensorineural loss was identified, with a 65-dB loss in the speech range in the left ear and a 55-dB loss in the right ear. Hearing aids were fitted, but a follow-up visit revealed that Lupe was not using them consistently. Mrs. G. claimed that hearing aids "were not doing any good." Apparently, Lupe could hear and respond to her mother equally well with and without the aids. The clinician stressed the importance of wearing the aids to Mrs. G. Although a formal speech and language evaluation was not conducted at that time, Mrs. G. brought Lupe back to the clinic for four sessions. She was offered counseling to discuss her feelings about the use of the aids and was also given ideas on ways to help Lupe develop language skills. These sessions were conducted in English by a monolingual clinician, as Mrs. G.'s skills in English were judged sufficient to follow up on the recommendations.

In addition to a speech and language delay, Lupe also had difficulties with fine and gross motor skills. She was enrolled in a special preschool program for multiply handicapped children, but a formal language assessment was not conducted. Her attendance in the program was soon interrupted by her family's visit to El Salvador, however. Upon her return to the United States, she was almost 5 years old. Mrs. G. brought her back to the audiologist and reported once again that the aids did not seem to make a difference in Lupe's ability to hear. Yet, Lupe's speech had improved, despite the inconsistent use of the aids. Lupe was using two-word combinations and sometimes expressed herself with longer sentences, although it was difficult to understand her because of her numerous sound substitutions and omissions. She had also acquired some isolated English words and phrases such as *hi*, *bye-bye*, *fine*, and *thank you*. Her younger siblings had surpassed her in language skills, however. Mrs. G. indicated that she had not been pleased with the previous school placement. She said that the children had seemed "sick," and she believed that her daughter had more skills than the rest of the class. Lupe played well with her siblings, but she interacted with no other children.

The hearing assessment and aid evaluation indicated that Lupe's aids had been fitted correctly. A Spanish speech and language assessment was recommended. It was conducted on a diagnostic basis throughout eight sessions and informally as Lupe was unable to respond to the available normed tests in Spanish. The eight sessions were conducted in Spanish during 3 consecutive months. The sessions were also intended to offer Mrs. G. support and counseling to accept Lupe's hearing loss, as well as ideas to reinforce Lupe's language skills. In addition, the clinician assisted Mrs. G. in seeking a school placement for Lupe.

Mrs. G. was not always able to bring Lupe to the sessions as scheduled. Appointments were canceled because of Mrs. G.'s numerous responsibilities at home. She had no child care support when one of her children was too sick to be brought to the sessions. When she missed a session, she would call a few days later and apologize to the receptionist. If the Spanish-speaking clinician called her on the day that she had missed the session, her telephone was unanswered. Mrs. G. always apologized to the clinician at the next session. At the fourth session, Mrs. G. reported that she had misplaced Lupe's hearing aids. The clinician advised her to look for them before trying to order new ones. Mrs. G. still had not found them by the following session. She insisted that the aids were not making any difference, although she claimed that she tried to make Lupe wear them for at least a few hours every day. At last, Mrs. G. found the aids the following week.

By the sixth session, Lupe had been placed in a special day class for the hearing-impaired. She was receiving speech and language therapy in Spanish, as well as assistance with fine motor and gross motor areas in English to increase her listening skills in that language. Mrs. G. seemed pleased with the program. The clinician and the classroom teacher consulted frequently to ensure that Lupe was receiving the assistance that she needed.

The classroom teacher reported that she also had to remind Mrs. G. to fit Lupe with the hearing aids. To offer Mrs. G. further support, the clinician asked if she would talk to another Hispanic mother who had found it difficult at first to accept her child's hearing loss. Although Mrs. G. agreed, she demonstrated her discomfort the following session. She interpreted it as an accusation of negligence. Some time was spent explaining the purpose of that parent contact. Also, efforts were made to demonstrate to Mrs. G. that Lupe was indeed making progress. At last, Mrs. G. began noting differences at home and seemed pleased with Lupe's progress. Mr. G. had never participated in the sessions, although the clinician encouraged his attendance. Mr. G. occasionally drove Lupe and her family to the clinic, but always remained in the car. Mrs. G. had several excuses for not inviting him.

Interpretation of the Case and Follow-up

During all sessions, the clinician put forth a great deal of effort to help Mrs. G. note Lupe's strengths. Mrs. G. had very few expectations of her daughter and often made negative comments. Yet, she did not feel that Lupe was as severely handicapped as some of the children who were enrolled in the first class. Slowly, Mrs. G. began reporting that Lupe was wearing the aids more consistently and that she was noticing improvement. At the end of the last session, Lupe's speech was much clearer than it had been 3 months before. Mrs. G. herself admitted being able to understand her better and, for the first time, she began making positive comments about her daughter. She also indicated that she was pleased with the school program. Although Lupe was 6 years old at the time, her language skills were more like those of a 4-year-old. She was improving steadily, however. Monthly sessions with the clinician were scheduled to monitor Lupe's progress.

In this case, it was possible to witness a positive outcome to the initial problem. It was necessary, however, for the clinician to take different steps and give more personal time and patience in helping this family.

- Mrs. G. had difficulty accepting Lupe's need to use the hearing aids to make progress in language development. The clinician gave her more time and repeated explanations on the importance of the aids. Another parent's assistance was necessary to stress this point.
- The clinician had to be more accepting of Mrs. G.'s missed appointments and understand that they were not attributable to a lack of cooperation. Rather, some family obligations and, perhaps, a misunderstanding of Lupe's problem were the main causes.
- The clinician had to take more initiative in leading Mrs. G. through the steps of finding an adequate school program for Lupe. Mrs. G. was not knowl-

edgeable of the system nor did she have the resources to search for a more appropriate school program.

Clinicians and staff working with Hispanic students must understand their cultural values and concerns in coming into contact with a different language, another country, and new institutions (e.g., school, clinic, or hospital). This, in turn, will help clients benefit from the services offered by speech-language clinicians, as well as by audiologists and other health care providers.

REFERENCES

Ballard, B., & Tighe, P. (Eds.). (1982). *Idea language proficiency test (IPT Level I)*. Brea, CA: Ballard Tighe.

Bates, E. (1976). *Language in context*. New York: Academic Press.

Bhatnager, J. (1980). Linguistic behavior and adjustment of immigrant children in French and English schools in Montreal. *International Journal of Applied Psychology, 29*, 141–158.

Brock, C. (1985). Latin America: An educational profile. In C. Brock & H. Lawlor (Eds.), *Education in Latin America*. London: Croom Helm.

Burt, M., Dulay, H., & Hernández-Chávez, E. (1980). *The bilingual syntax measure (Level II)*. San Francisco: Harcourt Brace Jovanovich.

Cheng, L.L. (1987). English communicative competence of language minority children: Assessment and treatment of language "impaired" preschoolers. In H.T. Trueba (Ed.), *Success or failure? Learning and the language minority student* (pp. 49–68). Cambridge, MA: Newbury House.

Cheng, L.L. (1990). Asian American cultural perspectives on birth defects: Focus on cleft palate. *The Cleft Palate Journal, 27*, 294–299.

Chesarek, S. (March, 1981). *Cognitive consequences of home or school education in a limited second language: A case study in the Crow Indian bilingual community*. Paper presented at the Language Proficiency Assessment Symposium. Virginia: Airlie House.

Commins, N.L. (1989). Language and affect: Bilingual students at home and at school. *Language Arts, 66*, 29–43.

Commins, N.L., & Miramontes, O.B. (1989). Perceived and actual linguistic competence: A descriptive study of four low-achieving Hispanic bilingual students. *American Educational Research Journal, 26*, 443–472.

Condon, J.C. (1986). ". . . So near the United States." In J.M. Valdés (Ed.), *Culture bound* (pp. 85–93). New York: Cambridge University Press.

Cummins, J. (1981). The role of primary language development in promoting educational success for language minority students. In California State Department of Education (Ed.), *Schooling and language minority students: A theoretical framework* (pp. 3–49). Los Angeles: Dissemination and Assessment Center, California State University at Los Angeles.

Cummins, J. (1984). *Bilingualism and special education: Issues in assessment and pedagogy*. Clevedon, England: Bilingual Matters.

Current Population Reports. (1990). *The Hispanic population in the United States: March 1990*. Washington, DC: U.S. Bureau of Census.

De Avila, E., & Duncan, S.E. (1983). *Language assessment scales.* Monterey, CA: McGraw-Hill.

Delgado-Gaitán, C. (1987a). Parent perceptions of school: Supportive environment for children. In H. Trueba (Ed.), *Success or failure? Learning and the language minority student* (pp. 131–155). Cambridge, MA: Newbury House.

Delgado-Gaitán, C. (1987b). Traditions and transitions in the learning process of Mexican children: An ethnographic view. In G. Spindler & L. Spindler (Eds.), *Interpretive ethnography of education: At home and abroad* (pp. 333–359). Hillsdale, NJ: Lawrence Erlbaum Associates.

Delgado-Gaitán, C., & Trueba, T. (1991). *Crossing cultural borders.* New York: Falmer Press.

Dostert, P.E. (1989). *Latin America 1989.* Washington, DC: Stryker-Post Publications.

Figler, C. (1979). *A comparative study of Puerto Rican families with and without handicapped children.* Unpublished doctoral dissertation, University of Massachusetts, Amherst.

Fishgrund, J.E., Cohen, O.P., & Clarkson, R.L. (1987). Hearing impaired children in Black and Hispanic families. *Volta Review, 89,* 59–67.

Gallegos, A., & Gallegos, R. (1988). The interaction between families of culturally diverse handicapped children and the school. In S. García & R.C. Chávez (Eds.), *Ethnolinguistic issues in education* (pp. 125–132). Lubbock, TX: College of Education, Texas Tech University.

Guendelman, S. (1983). Developing responsiveness to the health needs of Hispanic children and families. *Social Work in Health Care, 8,* 1–15.

Heath, S.B. (1986). Sociocultural contexts of language development. In California State Department of Education (Ed.), *Beyond language: Social and cultural factors in schooling language minority students* (pp. 143–186). Los Angeles: Evaluation, Dissemination and Assessment Center, California State University.

Iglesias, A. (1985a). Communication in the home and classroom: Match or mismatch? *Topics in Language Disorders, 5*(4), 29–41.

Iglesias, A. (1985b). Cultural conflict in the classroom. In D.N. Ripich & F.M. Spinelli (Eds.), *School discourse problems* (pp. 79–96). San Diego, CA: College Hill Press.

Kaufman, T. (1976). *Proyectos de alfabetos.* Guatemala: Editorial Pineda Ibarra.

Kayser, H. (1990). Social communicative behaviors of language-disordered Mexican-American students. *Child Language Teaching and Therapy, 6,* 255–269.

Laosa, L.M. (1982). School, occupation, culture and family: The impact of parental schooling on the parent-child relationship. *Journal of Educational Psychology, 74,* 791–827.

Leubitz, L. (1973). *Nonverbal communication: A guide for teachers.* Skokie, IL: National Textbook.

Lynch, E.W., & Stein, R.C. (1987). Parent participation by ethnicity: A comparison of Hispanic, Black, and Anglo families. *Exceptional Children, 54,* 105–111.

Maestas, A.G., & Erickson, J.E. (November 1989). *Mexican immigrant parents and the education of their handicapped children: Factors that influence parent involvement.* Paper presented at the American Speech-Language-Hearing Association Annual Convention, St. Louis.

Matsuda, M. (1989). Working with Asian parents: Some communication strategies. *Topics in Language Disorders, 9*(3), 45–53.

Meyerson, M.D. (1983). Genetic counseling for families of Chicano children with birth defects. In D.R. Omark & J.G. Erickson (Eds.), *The bilingual exceptional child* (pp. 285–298). San Diego, CA: College Hill Press.

Meyerson, M.D. (1990). Cultural considerations in the treatment of Latinos with craniofacial malformations. *The Cleft Palate Journal, 27,* 279–288.

Miller, R. (1984). *The primary schools of Mexico.* Los Gatos, CA: Paradox Press.

Peñalosa, F. (1980). *Chicano sociolinguistics: A brief introduction.* Cambridge, MA: Newbury House.

Penfield, J. (1989). *The Hispanic student: Questions and answers.* Highland Park, NJ: Penfield Associates.

Queralt, M. (1984). Understanding Cuban immigrants: A cultural perspective. *Social Work, 29,* 115–121.

Richards, J.B. (1987). Learning Spanish and classroom dynamics: School failure in a Guatemala Maya community. In H.T. Trueba (Ed.), *Success or failure? Learning and the language minority student* (pp. 109–130). Cambridge, MA: Newbury House.

Richmond, M. (1985). Education and revolution in socialist Cuba: The promise of democratization. In C. Brock & H. Lawlor (Eds.), *Education in Latin America.* London: Croom Helm.

Rietz, S.A. (1986). Preserving Indian culture through oral literature. In J. Reyhner (Ed.), *Teaching the Indian child: A bilingual/multicultural approach* (pp. 255–280). Billings, MT: Eastern Montana College.

Rodríguez, J. (1983). Mexican Americans: Factors influencing health practices. *The Journal of School Health* (special issue): 136–139.

Rodríguez, R. (1982). *Hunger of memory: The education of Richard Rodríguez.* Boston: David R. Godine.

Romo, H. (1984). The Mexican origin population's differing perceptions of their children's schooling. *Social Science Quarterly, 65,* 635–649.

Skabelund, G.P., & Sims, S.M. (Eds.). (1990). *Culturgram for the '90s.* Provo, UT: Brigham Young University

Spindler, G., & Spindler, L. (Eds.) (1987). *Interpretive ethnography of education: At home and abroad* (pp. 17–33). Hillsdale, NJ: Lawrence Erlbaum Associates.

Spinelli, F.M., & Ripich, D.N. (1985). Discourse and education. In Ripich, D.N. & Spinelli, F.M. (Eds.), *School Discourse Problems* (pp. 3–10). San Diego, CA: College Hill Press.

Stein, R.C. (1983). Hispanic parents' perspective and participation in their children's special education programs: Comparisons by program and race. *Learning Disability Quarterly, 6,* 432–438.

Suárez-Orozco, M. (1987). Towards a psychosocial understanding of Hispanic adaptation to American schooling. In H.T. Trueba (Ed.), *Success or failure? Learning and the language minority student* (pp. 156–168). Cambridge, MA: Newbury House.

Trueba, H.T. (1988). English literacy acquisition: From cultural trauma to learning disabilities in minority students. *Linguistics and Education, 1,* 125–152.

Trueba, H.T. (1989). *Raising silent voices: Educating the linguistic minorities for the 21st century.* Cambridge, MA: Newbury House.

Valdivieso, R., & Davis, C. (1988). *U.S. Hispanics: Challenging issues for the 1990's.* Washington, DC: Population Reference Bureau, Inc.

Veltman, C.J. (1988). *The future of the Spanish language in the United States.* Washington, DC: Hispanic Policy Development Project.

Vygotsky, L.S. (1962). *Thought and language.* Cambridge, MA: MIT Press.

Walker, C. (1987). Hispanic achievement: Old views and new perspectives. In H.T. Trueba (Ed.), *Success or failure? Learning and the language minority student* (pp. 15–32). Cambridge, MA: Newbury House.

Weddington, G.T. (1990). Cultural considerations in the treatment of craniofacial malformations in African Americans. *The Cleft Palate Journal, 27,* 289–293.

Westby, C.E., & Costlow, L. (1991). Implementing a whole language program in a special education class. *Topics in Language Disorders, 11*(3), 69–84.

Chapter 5

Acquisition and Development of a Second Language in the Spanish Speaker

Henriette W. Langdon and Barbara J. Merino

The acquisition of two languages, or bilingualism, can occur sequentially or simultaneously. Sequential or consecutive bilingualism occurs when a child "acquires a second language (L_2) early in childhood but after the basic linguistic acquisition of the mother tongue (L_1) has been achieved" (Hammers & Blanc, 1989, p. 10). Simultaneous bilingualism takes place "when a child develops two mother tongues from the onset of language which we call language A (LA) and language B (LB) as, for example, the child of a mixed-language family" (Hammers & Blanc, 1989, p. 10). Some researchers have stipulated a specific age, the age of 3 years, as the demarcation for sequential as opposed to simultaneous bilingualism (Vihman & McLaughlin, 1982). (Bilingualism is referred to as being simultaneous when the child has acquired the two languages before the age of 3 years.)

It is difficult to estimate the percentage of the approximately 23 million Hispanics presently in the United States who still speak Spanish at home. Based on a study conducted in the mid-1970s, López (1982) reported that approximately 70% to 75% of Hispanics continue using Spanish. In view of the fact that 50% of the increase in the number of Hispanics in the United States between 1970 and 1990 was due to immigration, it is reasonable to assume that Hispanics in the United States are at different stages of learning English. Also, a great proportion may remain essentially monolingual in Spanish for a number of reasons, such as lack of access to educational institutions, lack of confidence in their ability to learn another language, or, simply, occupations and living arrangements that do not require the use of English.

Many definitions of the term *bilingual* have been proposed. One of the most global is that "bilingualism is the mastery of two or more languages. It is a relative term since individuals vary greatly in types and degrees of language proficiency" (*Encyclopedia Britannica*, cited in Harding & Riley, 1986, p. 22). The lack of agreement among researchers, linguists, and teachers on the definition has led to conflicting data from studies on this population.

The construct of language proficiency has spurred as much discussion as the construct of intelligence. For some, language proficiency involves a single unitary factor that includes a variety of language abilities displayed by fully competent speakers (Oller, 1978, 1979). Others define it according to terminology borrowed from linguistics, claiming that language proficiency includes two aspects (i.e., receptive and expressive skills) and four processes (i.e., speaking, listening, reading, and writing). Each skill and process is connected to three basic language areas: (1) syntax, including morphology; (2) semantics and phonology; and (3) pragmatics. Hernández-Chávez, Burt, and Dulay (1978) also incorporated into their model sociolinguistic performance—the ability of the speaker, as an individual and a member of a speech community, to communicate in social situations.

Cummins (1981b, 1984) proposed a framework of communicative proficiency that incorporates a developmental perspective, takes into account differences between the language demands of the classroom and those of nonacademic settings, and captures the relationship between proficiency in the first language and proficiency in the second language. Accordingly, he proposed a model in which two continua intersect. One continuum represents the degree of cognitive demand involved in the communication task, and the other represents the extent to which context contributes to expressing and receiving meaning. Thus, all communication tasks can be placed in one of four quadrants (Figure 5-1). Quadrant A tasks are the least cognitively demanding; those in Quadrant D are the most demanding. In addition, two types of language proficiency are differentiated: (1) the language proficiency noted in a context-embedded face-to-face situation, which is referred to as basic interpersonal communicative skills (BICS), and (2) the language proficiency acquired in a context-reduced (academic) situation, which is referred to as cognitive academic language proficiency (CALP). Second-language learners usually acquire the first type of language proficiency (BICS) within 2 years of contact with the second language, whereas they may require 5 to 7 years of exposure before the second type of language proficiency (CALP) is comparable to that of a native speaker.

As mastery is developed, the degree of difficulty that an individual can manage moves from bottom to top along the vertical continuum. For example, producing sounds in certain words may be difficult for a 3-year-old at first; therefore, the task would be placed along Quadrant B. As the child becomes more proficient in the language, the task would be placed along Quadrant A. Similarly, the task of mastering basic sentence structures may begin along Quadrant B for second-language learners, but move to Quadrant A as these learners progress in acquiring the language (Cummins, 1981b). As another example, school-based tasks that are

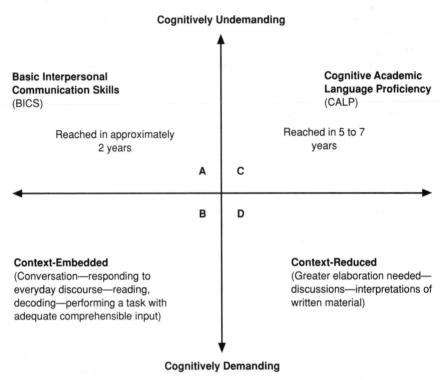

Figure 5-1 Defining Second-Language Proficiency. *Source:* From *Schooling and Language Minority Students: A Theoretical Framework* (p. 12) by California State Department of Education, Office of Bilingual Cultural Education, 1981, Los Angeles: Evaluation, Dissemination and Assessment Center, California State University. Copyright 1981 by California State University. Adapted by permission.

context-reduced are often "cognitively demanding" to the student. With the use of appropriate instructional strategies, the material should eventually become "cognitively undemanding," and its difficulty would move from Quadrant D to Quadrant C.

It is rare to find individuals who have completely mastered all components of two languages with the same degree of skill. Generally, bilinguals are more dominant in one language for specific components. For example, although bilingual persons may be able to carry on a conversation on many topics with the same degree of ease in two languages, they may prefer writing on certain topics in one of the two languages. Each bilingual individual is a unique case, and the variations add to the complexity of assessing the language proficiencies of bilinguals who may have a language disorder.

SEQUENTIAL BILINGUALISM

Most normally developing children acquire their first language with no difficulty, provided that they have opportunities to listen and interact in that language. Although there are differences in the pace of acquisition, most children go through similar stages. Second-language development parallels monolingual development if the two languages are developing simultaneously (Harding & Riley, 1986; Saunders, 1982). On the other hand, the development of sequential bilingualism may follow a greater diversity of stages and rates, depending on both learner characteristics and the environment in which the second language is acquired.

A Theoretical Framework for Second-Language Acquisition

Schumann (1978) has proposed that any theory of second-language acquisition must answer three basic questions: (1) how second-language acquisition occurs, (2) what is acquired, and (3) why second-language acquisition succeeds or fails. Krashen (1981, 1982) proposed five hypotheses to explain this process: (1) the acquisition-learning distinction hypothesis, (2) the monitor hypothesis, (3) the input hypothesis, (4) the natural order hypothesis, and (5) the affective filter hypothesis.

How Second-Language Acquisition Occurs

Krashen (1981, 1982) proposed three hypotheses that address the way in which learners acquire a second language. First, Krashen made a distinction between acquisition and learning. Acquisition is unconscious, both in the process and the product. Children, for example, are not aware that they are acquiring a first language, nor can they describe the rules of the language that they have acquired. Learning, on the other hand, pertains to conscious knowledge about language, its rules, and ways to talk about these rules (metalinguistic awareness). Learners use metalinguistic awareness skills to a greater or lesser degree in the course of learning a second language, depending on their exposure to formal language instruction. The conscious knowledge of being exposed to and using two languages has been described in most of the literature on early bilingualism, however; children are aware of which language is being spoken from a very early age.

Acquisition is responsible for fluency in the language. In contrast, the role of learning is to monitor or edit communications before speaking or writing, as in self-correction (Krashen, 1981, p. 58). Monitoring is not an effective approach to second-language acquisition for three reasons. First, there is no time in conversation to use grammatical rules consciously. Yet, it is not uncommon for second-language learners to stop and correct their utterances. Second, only rarely do language users focus on the grammatical rules, except in writing. Even in writing, the primary goal is self-expression rather than form, unless precision is essential to convey information on a particular topic to a particular audience. Third, monitoring requires a complete knowledge of grammatical rules. Such a thorough knowledge is practically impossible to develop, as only partial rules have been written on only a few of the world's languages.

In the input hypothesis, Krashen suggested that learners progress to the next stage of language comprehension (i) by understanding a bit beyond their current comprehension level ($i + 1$). In addition, "learners acquire structures by understanding messages and not by focusing on the form of the input and analyzing it" (Krashen, 1981, p. 58). Context and extralinguistic information ensure comprehension. A variable time during which the learner does not express very much is referred to as the silent period.

One of the major criticisms of Krashen's three hypotheses is that they appear to be more readily applicable to the natural process of acquiring a second language rather than to learning a second language in the classroom setting (Hammerly, 1985). In reality, explanations of grammar rules may be important in certain contexts, but not so important in others. For example, study of the conscious use of grammatical rules in teaching a second language to adults has yielded mixed results. According to Salica (1981) and Wren (1982), teachers' highlighting errors through questioning increased the rate of self-correction among older students. In a study conducted in Canada, however, Spada (1987) found that knowing formal rules had no effect on adult learners of English as a second language. McDonald, Stone, and Yates (1977) reached the opposite conclusion; they found that explaining grammar rules had a positive effect on second-language acquisition in several adult ESL classes in the United States. The variation in results may be due to the different learning styles of the students. Some may want to learn how certain grammatical rules operate, while others may not. It is important, therefore, that teachers understand the needs of their students.

The concept of comprehensible input in learning a second language has also been criticized because defining that role may be difficult at particular stages of language development. Krashen based his hypothesis on four phenomena: (1) "motherese" (language used by parents to ease interaction with their children); (2) "foreigner talk" (adaptation of two persons' communication who have uneven language proficiency within one given language); (3) the silent period that those who are acquiring a second language go through in natural informal settings; and (4) applied studies of second-language acquisition in the classroom (Krashen, 1981). In the latter, comprehensible input is emphasized in the form of visuals, gestures, and manipulatives, and language production is consciously delayed (Asher, 1979; Winitz & Reeds, 1973).

As attractive as the Krashen theory sounds and as useful as it may be for teachers in understanding second-language acquisition in a holistic sense, its testability remains in doubt (Politzer, 1989). Furthermore, as comprehensible input is difficult to define, it is equally difficult to apply in teaching a second language. Setting standards for a methodology based on this hypothesis may present problems because of the variety of ways in which students react to materials or context designed to render the input more comprehensible. To understand the nature of comprehensible input, teachers could be encouraged to experiment with visuals and manipulatives when presenting new vocabulary. The fact is that, without comprehensible input, language learners will not rapidly gain skills in a second language. The lack of comprehensible input is an important factor in many students' inability to learn a second language, even at the elementary level. Teachers who note that their students are not advancing as fast as expected should make certain that they are providing sufficient comprehensible input.

The use of sheltered English, a newer method of teaching English to students with limited English proficiency, incorporates subject matter to match the students' linguistic skills. The language used in the classroom is tailored to the students' proficiency. Further language skills are developed through instruction of content areas. Thus, the comprehensible input is derived not only from the language used, but also from subjects that are familiar to the students in their primary language. When it is necessary to explain grammatical rules, the teacher should make every attempt to involve the student in the process actively by asking for a response in which the student is to perform an action or to use the grammatical form that is being reinforced. In the total physical response approach (Asher, 1979), language is developed through physical (motor) responses from the students. As the students listen to language, they initially respond by moving their body or by performing different physical tasks. Eventually, they are able to use those commands or questions to ask others to perform the same tasks. This approach has been found to be most effective in the initial stages of second-language learning. In the natural approach (Krashen & Terrell, 1983), language input rather than practice is emphasized. Written materials, props, and manipulatives serve as sources of comprehensible input. In the later stages, the lessons are structured to allow the students to respond with increasingly more complex answers.

According to Swain (1985), the catalyst for second-language acquisition is comprehensible *output* or the opportunities that learners have to generate both verbal and nonverbal output. Second language learners are engaged in situations where their responses are verbalized as often as possible. They also interact with persons who are either more proficient or are native speakers of that language. She described the various roles that comprehensible output has in facilitating acquisition. First, because it is an indicator of the amount of input being understood, it generates greater amounts of comprehensible input. Second, it provides opportunities to test hypotheses about language (Schachter, 1983). Third, it provides opportunities for the meaningful use of language. Swain based her claim on the fact that immersion students in the French-English programs in Canada had some degree of success in acquiring nativelike proficiency in spoken French. Apparently, these students had limited access to peers whose primary language was French so that they could practice the language. Because output is greater when there is a need to sustain a conversation, the context in which exchanges take place must be challenging and interesting. Ramírez and Merino (1990) found that referential questions (i.e., those requiring genuine communication) yielded greater output than did display questions (i.e., questions designed to produce known information). Thus, there should be functional opportunities to enhance language output to facilitate higher levels of second-language proficiency.

Finally, Long (1981), as well as Long and Porter (1985), contended that comprehensible input is not sufficient to explain higher levels of second-language proficiency. There must be opportunities for the learners to negotiate in the language. Thus, learners should practice the new language in small groups as much as possible. The level of accuracy maintained in unsupervised groups is similar to that maintained in the presence of the teacher. Furthermore, levels of fluency are higher in heterogeneous groups (Ellis, 1984; Pica, Doughty, & Young, 1986). Further research is needed to determine the optimum size, composition, and internal organization of the groups, however.

What Is Acquired

Krashen (1981, 1982) addressed the specific content of what is acquired in the second-language acquisition process in his fourth hypothesis, the natural order hypothesis, which pertains to the acquisition of grammatical forms in a predictable manner. Not every learner will acquire the forms in the very same order, however. Some forms tend to develop earlier than do others. The most widely studied grammatical forms in English are the 14 morphemes described by Brown (1973). Individuals who are acquiring English as a second language also seem to follow a natural order in acquiring those very same grammatical morphemes (Krashen & Terrell, 1983, pp. 28–29). Dulay and Burt (1974) found that children whose primary language was Chinese or Spanish acquired the very same grammatical morphemes in English following a similar order, despite the differences in their first languages. Morpheme studies on other language groups have generally shown similar results (e.g., Kessler & Idar, 1977 [Vietnamese]; Mace-Matluck, 1978 [Spanish, Illokano, and Tagalog]; Makino, 1980 [Japanese]), although there are exceptions (Hakuta, 1976 [Japanese]). The order in which adults who speak a variety of first and second languages tend to acquire those morphemes is similar to the order in which children acquire them (Bailey, Madden, & Krashen, 1974). The order is not exactly the same as for English as a first language, however (Table 5-1). As Krashen and Terrell (1983, p. 29) indicated, the natural order may not sur-

Table 5-1 Comparison of Average Order of Acquisition of Grammatical Morphemes between English As a Second Language (Children and Adults) and English As a First Language

English As a Second Language	English As a First Language
-*ing* (progressive)	-*ing* (progressive)
Plural*	Plural*
Copula (to be)	Irregular past*
Auxiliary (progressive)	Article*
Article (*a, the*)	Regular past*
Irregular past*	Singular (-*s*) (third person)*
Regular past*	Possessive*
Singular (-*s*) (third person)*	Copula
Possessive (-*s*)*	Auxiliary

Note: Variations are possible.

This order is derived from an analysis of empirical studies of second-language acquisition in a 1981 study by Krashen. Most studies show significant correlations with the average order.

Copula and auxiliary are acquired relatively later in first-language acquisition than in second-language acquisition. For other morphemes (*), the order is similar between first- and second-language acquisition.

Source: From *The Natural Approach: Language Acquisition in the Classroom* (p. 29) by S.D. Krashen and T.D. Terrell, 1983, Englewood Cliffs, NJ: Prentice Hall. Copyright 1983 by Prentice Hall. Reprinted by permission; data for English as a first language from *A First Language: The First Stages*, by R. Brown, 1973, Cambridge, MA: Harvard University Press.

face during the administration of grammatical tests; it is more likely to appear in conversation.

In addition to morphology, syntactical forms, such as the negative, have been studied extensively. In acquiring the negative, both children and adults seem to go through similar stages in which they use intermediate forms that resemble those found in the different stages in English monolingual language development, such as "I no want envelope" for "I don't want the envelope." Cancino, Rosansky, and Schumann (1978) studied the development of the negative in a sample of six subjects (two adults, two adolescents, and two children) who all were native speakers of Spanish learning English. Although the subjects acquired the structures in a similar order, there were differences attributed to the age of the acquirer and the pace (rate) of acquisition. Thus, the order of acquisition of specific forms is partially known, but information on the process of their acquisition is still insufficient.

Although there is a certain order to the acquisition of structures in English as a second language, it is not practical to build a second-language curriculum on the forms as they seem to appear. As Krashen (1981) stated, "The existence of the natural order does not imply that we should teach second language along this order, focusing on earlier acquired items first and later acquired items later. Indeed there is a good evidence that language teaching aimed at acquisition should not employ a grammatical syllabus" (p. 57). The knowledge available on the order of acquisition can orient clinicians on what grammatical forms are most likely to develop earlier than others, but it is necessary to interpret the information carefully by taking into account each individual's unique characteristics and exposure to the second language.

Why Second-Language Acquisition Succeeds or Fails

The fifth hypothesis developed by Krashen (1981, 1982), the affective filter hypothesis, pertains to the subconscious attitude of the learner toward the acquisition of the second language. It includes three components: motivation, self-confidence, and anxiety. Krashen and Terrell (1983, p. 38) indicated that people who have a positive self-image and motivation seek more input and acquire more than do others exposed to the same input. Thus, to ensure maximal learning, students need to receive adequate comprehensible input in an environment that fosters self-confidence and reduces feelings of anxiety.

Critical Period in Second-Language Acquisition

The study of a critical period in second-language acquisition is important for both theoretical and practical reasons. Theoretically, the notion of a critical period is at the heart of understanding second-language acquisition and is one of the principal factors that distinguishes it from first-language acquisition. Practically, it figures prominently in clinicians' decisions about the nature and choice of a language for intervention purposes.

Research on adult-child differences in second-language acquisition has produced a consensus on three points (Krashen, Long, & Scarcella, 1979). First, adults proceed more quickly through the very early stages of phonological, syntactical, and morphological development. Second, when time and exposure are controlled, older children move through the stages of syntactical and morphological development at a faster pace than do younger children. Third, those who begin to acquire a second language as young children usually achieve higher levels of oral proficiency in accent and syntax (in the long run) than do those who begin as adults.

Acquisition of Phonology

Most long-term studies in which the success of second-language speakers who began their acquisition as children has been compared with that of second-language speakers who began as adults show an advantage for children. For example, Asher and García (1969) asked junior high school students to judge native Spanish speakers in three different age groups (1 to 6 years, 7 to 12 years, and 13 to 19 years) in their accents in English. They were most likely to consider as native speakers of English those who began their exposure during the earliest ages and the least likely to consider as native speakers those who began in the oldest group. Other studies with different language groups (e.g., Seliger, Krashen, & Ladefoged, 1975) produced similar results. The same pattern has been noted in individuals' ability to discriminate sounds in the presence of white noise (Oyama, 1978), although length of exposure to the language was not a factor in the latter study. Yet, different results have been found with short-term studies (e.g., Asher & Price, 1967; Snow & Hoefnagel-Höhle, 1977, 1978). Even though the older learner may have an initial advantage in the acquisition of grammatical forms and vocabulary, the younger acquirer ultimately mastered pronunciation better. Thus, it is realistic to expect that older learners, with some exceptions, may have a less nativelike pronunciation in the second language.

Non-native speakers frequently may make a false or negative impression because of their "foreign accent" (Biederman, 1989). Perceptions vary from language to language, however. For example, a French accent may be considered "charming," whereas a Spanish accent may be considered "thick" (Cheng, 1990b, p. 2). Older learners may wish to reduce the degree of their "foreign accent" through one of several programs, such as those developed by Compton and Hutton (1978) or Sikorski (1987). Motivations for reducing an accent range from a desire to sound like a native of the country, to a need to be more intelligible on the telephone (where no contextual or other nonverbal clues are available), to a simple hope to increase the chances for a better career.

The practice of accent reduction is becoming more popular in the field of speech-language pathology. Intervention may be recommended if the impact of the native language reduces the individual's intelligibility. If a child or adult is intelligible to most people, however, intervention may not be warranted unless desired by the individual. With the ever increasing diversity of the population in the United States, native speakers of English and other languages should learn to understand accents in English beyond those identified as U.S. regional accents.

Acquisition of Morphology and Syntax

Most studies that correlate the age of immigrants when they arrive in a host country with their attainment of morphology and syntax indicate that the younger groups have an advantage over adults (Patkowski, 1980; Snow & Hoefnagel-Höhle, 1978). Older students have an advantage over young ones in the initial stages of second-language acquisition, however. Snow and Hoefnagel-Höhle (1978), for example, found that the 11- to 15-year-olds acquired skills in morphology and syntax faster than did the 6- to 10-year-olds. Ervin-Tripp (1974) found that the 7- to 9-year-olds outperformed the 4- to 6-year-olds. Thus, expectations about normal progress in second-language acquisition should be defined in reference to age and the language dimension considered. Younger children may progress faster in their acquisition of pronunciation, whereas older children seem to have an advantage in acquiring the morphology and syntax of the language. Attitude toward the new language may also be an important factor.

Development of Pragmatics and Semantics

Language involves considerably more than the transmission of language forms. The term *pragmatics* refers to the ways in which these forms are used to express particular meanings and to perform the particular functions of language in its social contexts. A culture-bound communication style may affect social, academic, and professional success. For example, there is increasing evidence that, for the most part, Hispanics learn best in a "cooperative" environment (De Avila, Cohen, & Intili, 1981), whereas Asian children may prefer to receive their information directly from the teacher (Cheng, 1987).

The distinction between a literal and a nonliteral context is not always obvious, particularly in a cross-cultural setting where the participants must share both knowledge of the form and understanding of the situation for the communication to be completed successfully. As Cheng (1990a) indicated, "The failure to distinguish between literal and non-literal intention is particularly subject to misinterpretation and intolerance across cultural groups" (p. 268). Examples such as "it's in the bag" (what bag?) or "she drives me up the wall" (how can you drive up a wall?) demonstrate the basis of this problem.

One of the essential functions of language is in establishing and maintaining social interaction. Conversation consists of several different parts, including the selection of a topic of conversation, initiating the conversation, taking turns in speaking, maintaining the topic, and closing the conversation (Wolfram, in press). Although few clinicians can define "effective" communication from the American perspective, they must understand that American values and beliefs may significantly affect communication behaviors. For example, the American aspiration to be a "classless" society often leads to a more informal communication style that is atypical in other cultures. Also, because Americans are highly time- and results-oriented, they expect quick responses. The American belief in rugged individualism and competition corresponds to a direct and assertive communication style; to Americans, other styles may suggest evasiveness or incompetence. Hispanics may define effective communication very differently, however.

Not many researchers have examined the process of acquiring specific pragmatic skills, such as fluency or topic maintenance, in a second language. In one of the few studies that have been done, Damico, Oller, and Storey (1983) tried to determine the types of errors that best identified children with possible language disorders by comparing the performance of 10 bilingual (Spanish-English) $6^1/_2$- to $8^1/_2$-year-olds on their pragmatic skills and surface language errors (articulation and syntax). The children's language samples were analyzed according to seven types of pragmatic errors: (1) linguistic nonfluencies, defined as "speaker's production disrupted by repetitions, unusual pauses, and other hesitations" (Damico et al., 1983, p. 388); (2) revisions; (3) delays before responding; (4) nonspecific vocabulary; (5) inappropriate responses; (6) poor topic maintenance; and (7) need for repetition. The children were studied over a 7-month period. Those who had made a greater percentage of errors overall in both languages made less progress in academic and language areas in English than did those who made fewer errors. Furthermore, pragmatic errors were better predictors of the students' academic and language performance over time than were language surface errors (articulation and syntax).

Replication of this study with other children has yielded inconclusive results. Ortíz and Polyzoi (1988) gave the same tasks used in the study conducted by Damico and associates (1983) to a sample of 120 kindergarten-aged children that included four groups: language-handicapped children, learning-disabled children, nonhandicapped achievers, and nonhandicapped underachievers. Many linguistic nonfluencies were noted in all groups in English (more than in Spanish), but no differences could be identified in the other parameters. The researchers postulated that the failure to identify differences could be due to the procedure used to count and weigh the errors.

A study by Saenz, Iglesias, and Alemán (1989) with 18 college-educated Hispanic students indicated that hesitations were present in great proportions of their speech in English—54%, compared to 30% in the study of Damico and associates (1983). Thus, this type of error could not have differentiated individuals with language problems from those without language problems at this age level (college). Some caution in interpretation is warranted, however. For one reason, the elicitation techniques were different in the two studies. For another, the types of errors in the study by Damico and associates were more varied. Nevertheless, more information is needed to define the range of fluency-type errors that can be expected of second-language learners. In addition, it would be helpful to determine (1) what range of nonfluent speech can be expected in a second-language learner as a function of the type and exposure to a second language and (2) whether a certain proportion of nonfluent speech is symptomatic of a language disorder.

Meara (1980) noted that there has not been any systematic research on semantics. Most of the work on vocabulary acquisition has concentrated on vocabulary instruction rather than on vocabulary acquisition, although a few studies have attempted to differentiate the type of vocabulary words acquired. Studies tend to concentrate on word association ability in second-language learners with "no particular coherent or coordinated research strategy" (Meara, 1980, p. 120). Many questions remain unanswered: Are some words more readily acquired than are others in a second language? Can any stages of development be identified? Are there any phonetic or morphological restrictions in acquiring specific words?

Pace of Acquisition

Some researchers have taken the position that it is impossible to establish norms for second-language acquisition because there are too many variables to account for and control (Dulay, Hernández-Chávez, & Burt, 1978). Such variables include age, differences in input (Beebe, 1985), motivation (Gardner & Lambert, 1972), personality (Strong, 1983; Wong Fillmore, 1976), level of first-language development (Cummins, 1981b), and sociocultural distance and social status (Ogbu & Matute-Bianchi, 1986; Schumann, 1978). Most of the studies on the pace of second-language acquisition have focused on these variables in isolation.

While recognizing these difficulties, other researchers have attempted to compare the performance of second-language learners with that of native speakers, taking into account the type and time of exposure to the language. In the French immersion program in Canada, for example, English-speaking Canadians receive instruction in French from the time they enter school until they complete high school. After approximately 3 years, half of the instruction is provided in English, and half is provided in French. Teachers are native French speakers who also know English. These English-speaking students are isolated from their French-speaking peers in the classroom, however, and instruction is tailored to a second-language context. These programs have been carefully monitored, and the students' progress has been compared to that of students who attend monolingual English programs in Canada and French programs in France. In a review of research spanning more than 20 years, Swain (1985) concluded that immersion students perform as well as native French speakers in reading and mathematics after 5 to 6 years, but their skills in speaking and writing are not nativelike, even after the completion of high school.

Cummins (1981a) reached somewhat different conclusions after studying more than 1,200 Canadian students with limited English proficiency in kindergarten through ninth grade. Cummins (1981b) found that they could master the basic interpersonal communication skills (BICS) in approximately 2 years. Yet, it took them 5 to 7 years to reach the level of native speakers in gaining meaning for less contextualized sources, such as reading, referred to by Cummins as cognitive academic language performance (CALP). Very likely, these students' contact with native speakers of English enhanced their ability to interact verbally.

This type of research is less documented with language minority children who are acquiring English in the United States. Most of the data available are based on cross-sectional samples rather than longitudinal studies (Krashen & Biber, 1988). In most cases, researchers found that it took students from 3 to 6 years to perform at the 50th percentile in English in academic areas. This finding is consistent with those of an earlier longitudinal study conducted by Merino and Lyons (1987). These researchers found that only half of their sample (13 of 26) were performing at the 50th percentile in reading after 3 to 5 years of formal exposure to English, whereas a slightly greater number (19 of 26) were performing at that level in mathematics. In all of these programs, students received instruction in both languages in equal proportions.

Collier (1987) found somewhat similar results in a cross-sectional study of 1,548 limited-English–proficient (LEP) students from middle-class backgrounds who were performing at grade level in their native language upon their entry into the U.S. schools. The students came from a variety of language backgrounds, principally Spanish, Korean, and Vietnamese. The school offered instruction in English as a second language on a pull-out basis only. Holding the length of residence constant, Collier found that 8- to 11-year-olds were the fastest achievers; they required 2 to 5 years to reach 50% in national norms in all academic areas. Those in the 5- to 7-year-old age group were 1 to 3 years behind the 8- to 11-year-olds. Adolescents who were 12 to 15 years old experienced the most difficulty, requiring as much as 6 to 8 years to attain grade level norms.

The length of time necessary for children, adolescents, and adults to acquire a second language depends on the area considered. For example, as mentioned earlier, adolescents and adults may initially acquire morphological and syntactical skills in the second language more rapidly, but those who begin learning a second language at a younger age will attain higher levels of performance in the second language. The level of achievement depends on many factors. For example, Krashen (1982) noted the major changes associated with cognitive and affective development occur as a child progresses through puberty. Combined with differences in exposure to a second language, these changes exert a great influence on the rate and degree of attainment in the second language. More research is needed to determine the factors that accelerate or interfere with the process of acquisition of specific language dimensions and processes.

SIMULTANEOUS BILINGUALISM

The development of two languages from infancy, or simultaneous bilingualism, has been of interest to researchers since the early 1900s. Most studies of this phenomenon have been conducted by parent researchers, typically linguists, who study their children in additive bilingual contexts (Leopold, 1970; Ronjat, 1913). In additive bilingualism, both languages are prestigious in the community, and the children are likely to reap the maximum cognitive and social benefits of their bilingualism (Lambert, 1975). There are very few studies of simultaneous bilingualism in subtractive situations, where one language, typically the home language, is not held in high esteem by the broader community (Merino, 1983b; Padilla & Liebman, 1975).

The literature on simultaneous bilingualism is not very extensive, but it covers a wide variety of research topics (Grosjean, 1982; Hammers & Blanc, 1989; Redlinger, 1979; Vihman & McLaughlin, 1982). Moreover, there are variations in the languages studied, the environment in which they are acquired, the length of

Table 5-2 Studies on Simultaneous Bilingualism

Investigator	Language	Age of the Child (Years and Months)
Each parent speaks one language to the child.		
Ronjat (1913)	German (M) French (F)	Birth to 4:10
Leopold (1970)*	English (M) German (F)	2:0 to 15 years
von Raffler-Engel (1965)	Italian (M) English (F)	Birth to 5:0 years
Saunders (1982)	English (M) German (F)	Birth to 7–8 years
Parents use a common language different from that of the community.		
Pavlovitch (1920)	Serbian in France	Birth to 2:0 years
Burling (1973)**	English in India	1:4 to 3:4
Oksaar (1971)	Estonian in Sweden	Birth to 4 years
Fantini (1978)	Spanish in the U.S.	Birth to 5 years
Vihman (1981)	Estonian in the U.S.	About 1 to 5 years
Parents use a second language that they do not know well at specific times of the day.		
Past (1976)	Spanish in the U.S.	Birth to 2nd grade
Dimitrijević (1965)	English in Yugoslavia	Birth to teen age
Parents speak two languages without making a dichotomy.		
Bergman (1976)	English and Spanish	One to 2 years
Padilla & Liebman (1975)	English and Spanish	Three children (1:5 to 2:2)
Lindholm & Padilla (1978)	English and Spanish	19 children 2:0 to 6:0
Huerta (1977)	English and Spanish	2:1 to 2:10

M = mother; F = father

*Research compiled from 1939 to 1949 (1970 reference contains all 4 volumes originally published separately by Northwestern University Press).

**Burling's work was originally published in *Word, 15,* 45–68 (1959).

the studies, and the language areas investigated (Table 5-2). Studies are limited in both quantity and replication for any given language. Studies with Spanish-English bilingual children have been conducted by Bergman (1976), Fantini (1978), Huerta (1977), Lindholm and Padilla (1978), Padilla and Liebman (1975), and Past (1976).

Family Organization of Bilingual Input to the Children

Bilingual families vary a great deal in the way they use their languages in the home (Arnberg, 1984; Grosjean, 1982; Harding & Riley, 1986; Schmidt-Mackey, 1977; Vihman & McLaughlin, 1982). There are four possible strategies: (1) separation by person (i.e., each parent speaks a different language to the child); (2) separation by place (i.e., the parents speak one language, the community the other); (3) separation by time (i.e., the family uses each language during a predetermined segment of the day); and (4) parental use of the two languages without differentiation as to person, place, or time.

Separation by Person

The earliest account of the strategies that a bilingual family followed in promoting the two languages dates from the early 1900s. Grammont, a French psychologist, counseled his friend Ronjat, a linguist married to a German, to separate the two languages by person: *"une personne, une langue."* Louis, their child, communicated in French with his father and in German with his mother (Ronjat, 1913). Families that consciously engineer bilingualism frequently use this strategy. One of the best documented records of a bilingual child is a longitudinal study conducted by Leopold (1970) of his daughter Hildegard, who grew up principally in the United States. The father spoke German; the mother, English. Hildegard thought it so natural that she was surprised to realize that not everyone's father spoke German. Relatively few studies of this nature have been undertaken to date.

Separation by Place

It is common for immigrant families to use one language in the home and the other in the community. As older siblings begin to use the language of the community in the home, younger siblings acquire it from them. Fantini (1978) described in detail how his two children, Carla and Mario, who were bilingual in Spanish and English, consciously selected one language over the other, depending on the particular circumstances. At times, however, when they felt close to a person, they would use Spanish words even though the majority language in that particular environment was English.

Separation by Time

Some bilingual families speak one of the two languages at a designated time, such as after lunch or during dinner. In the case of Past (1976), neither he nor his wife spoke Spanish well, but they both interacted in the language with their daughter Mariana during certain segments of the day. To further expose her to the language, she was encouraged to watch TV in Spanish. Her parents also taught her to read in Spanish at a very young age. When she entered kindergarten, she was enrolled in a bilingual program. By second grade, she could apparently read well in the two languages and express herself fairly fluently in Spanish.

No Differentiation for Person, Place, or Time

In some families, the two languages are spoken whenever the speakers see fit, letting the topic, setting, or persons determine the language used. This strategy seems to be common in families that have not made a conscious effort to nurture bilingualism. At times, this situation arises simply because the parents cannot adhere to a more rigorous strategy. Bergman (1976), Lindholm and Padilla (1978) , and Huerta (1977) reported that switching back and forth from one language to the other did not affect the rate of acquisition or quality of either of the languages, perhaps because of the community's support of bilingualism in these cases. The observations may have been different under other conditions.

The best strategy may well be the one that seems most natural to the family (Grosjean, 1982). Typically, the two languages develop in a parallel fashion under favorable circumstances (i.e., adequate input and support by the family and community). Certain linguistic features, such as grammar, vocabulary, or verbal fluency, may be better developed in one or the other language at any given stage, however, depending on exposure and practice of that particular language.

Child's Awareness of Two Languages

Bilingual children may become aware of using two languages as early as 15 months of age (Bergman, 1976) and as late as $3^{1}/_{2}$ years of age (von Raffler-Engel, 1965). The ability to differentiate two languages depends on the children's metalinguistic awareness, that is, whether the child is able to attend to the language in which something is said rather than to what is said (van Kleeck, 1984). The ability of children to become aware of two languages has been documented in languages as diverse as Afrikaans and English (Ianco-Worral, 1972). However, children in the Ianco-Worral study were older, 4 to 9 years of age.

Different researchers have described awareness of speaking two languages in a variety of ways (Table 5-3). For example, there is some base awareness on a child's ability to respond in the language in which the child is addressed or to initiate a conversation in the language of the speaker with whom the child is interacting. Thus, one 2-year-old girl, in discussing an upcoming family party, told her

Table 5-3 Bilingual Children's Awareness of Two Language Systems

Investigator	Languages	Manifestation	Age (Years and Months)
Bergman (1976)	Spanish/English	Child responds in language addressed.	1:3
Ronjat (1913)	French/German	Child says *"comme papa"* and *"comme maman"* when asked which language is spoken.	1:9
Pavlovitch (1920)	French/Serbian	Child speaks in the appropriate language with any speaker of a language.	2:0
Leopold (1970)	English/German	Same as above	2:0
Burling (1973)	English/Garo	Same as above	2:3
Fantini (1978)	English/Spanish	Same as above	2:5
von Raffler-Engel (1965)	English/Italian	Child translates.	3:6
Vihman (1981), Vihman & McLaughlin (1982)	English/Estonian	Two levels of awareness	2:0 and 4:0

mother, *"Va a venir mucha gente"* and then turned to her monolingual father and said, "Many people are coming today." Von Raffler-Engel (1965) reported the oldest age of awareness, but it was based on the child's ability to translate from one language to the other consistently. Vihman and McLaughlin (1982) summarized this point by stating, "Although differentiation may be said to have begun at about age 2, awareness of the fact that words could be labeled by language and translated appeared to come slightly later, while consciousness of the bilingual situation as a whole seemed to dawn only at the end of the fourth year, with explicit awareness of his own bilingual capacities acknowledged a few months later" (p. 46). Thus, very young children are able to switch from one language to the other, but they are not aware of doing this until approximately age four years. The child's level of awareness of two codes is dependent on many factors, including the proficiency of the parents and caregivers, and the language use patterns of the community.

Process of Simultaneous Language Acquisition

Saunders (1982) described the process of simultaneous language acquisition by suggesting that there are three main stages. Stage 1 occurs at the age of 1 to 2 years. Initially, the children use one word at a time. Very often, they use a word from one language, but not the other language to designate an object or concept. The frequency of occurrence of the word while interacting in a particular language, the phonological composition of the word, or both may determine which word is selected. For example, one child who was being raised bilingually in French used *pain* instead of *bread* and *ananas* instead of *pineapple* when she began saying single words. These words not only were more frequently used in French in her environment, but also were simpler to produce. Vihman and McLaughlin (1982) gave similar examples from the diaries of parents using different combinations of languages. For example, Vihman noted that one of her children, raised in an Estonian-English environment, used the word *puzzle* instead of *noistatus*. In all situations, however, the children were able to understand the words in both languages.

In Stage 2, which occurs at the age of 2 to 3 years, the two languages continue to develop; however, the syntactical system may remain undifferentiated for a while. For example, one young girl who had been raised bilingually in Polish and Spanish heard her brother say, *"Queta, jéchame más"* 'Queta, do drive me some more' to which she responded, *"Ya te jeché bastante"* 'I have driven you enough'. The root originates from the morphological ending (*jechać:* to drive [Polish], *me:* to me [Spanish]). The root is *jechać* with the "é", which denotes past tense in Spanish. Both sentences had the appropriate structure, but the children were using the root of the verb from one language (i.e., Polish) and a morphological ending from the other language (i.e., Spanish). Although this does not occur with every utterance, such combinations are not unusual at this stage.

After approximately age 3 years, the child enters Stage 3. As their vocabulary increases, children typically use the appropriate syntax and grammar to express themselves in each language. Yet, it is not uncommon for them to use words from one language within sentences from the other. This is also common in adults who speak two languages. It does not mean that the individuals have a problem, but only that the topic or situation was conducive to using a term in another language.

Language Acquisition and Delay among Bilingual Children

Perhaps the most frequent concern of parents is the effect of bilingualism on language acquisition and delay. Both Ronjat (1913) and Leopold (1970) discussed this issue and concluded in their studies of their respective children that there was no difference in the pace of language acquisition between their children and monolingual children. Neither one of them conducted a systematic comparison with monolingual children, however.

Swain (1972), studying French-English bilingual children in Canada, found that they acquired the use of the interrogative *est-ce que* form later than did monolingual French-speaking children (Grégoire, 1947) and English-speaking children (Klima & Bellugi, 1973). In French, there was a gap of 8 months (age 3:2 compared to 2:6). In English the gap was 6 months (age 3:8 compared to 3:2). Yet, Padilla and Lindholm (1976), in their study of Spanish-English bilingual children, found no differences between their sample and monolingual children in the use of negative and interrogative forms, nor in the mean length of utterance.

The variation in results may be due to individual differences. It may also be that linguistic development is parallel in any given two languages for certain structures, but not for others. There is scant systematic research in which the language development of bilingual children is compared to that of monolingual children. In a study conducted in Montreal with 35 bilingual children matched with a control group of monolingual children, Doyle, Champagne, and Segalowitz (1978) found that the groups progressed at a different pace; bilinguals had a less extensive vocabulary, but they outperformed the monolingual group in verbal fluency in English.

Language loss, which is common even among young bilinguals, may also influence linguistic development. Leopold (1970) reported that there were periods in which his daughter seemed dominant in English or German; they coincided with the family's visits to Germany. Burling (1973) reported on the loss of Garo (spoken in the Garo Hills in India) in his son Stephen, who learned the language while the family resided in India. Stephen was almost 3 years old when he left India. At that time, he was a fairly well balanced bilingual. Once the family returned to the United States, he lost the language; even comprehension became problematic because of lack of exposure and opportunities to practice the Garo language.

LANGUAGE INTERDEPENDENCE BETWEEN SPANISH AND ENGLISH

As previously discussed, many grammatical features develop similarly in second-language learners of English, irrespective of the nature of their first language (Bailey, Madden, & Krashen, 1974; Cancino, Rosansky, & Schumann, 1978; Dulay & Burt, 1974). Yet, Fathman (1975), Hakuta (1976), and Zehler (1982) found that certain structures may not develop as readily in English because they do not exist or are marked/expressed differently in the first language. For example, Uguisu, Hakuta's subject, did not acquire articles and plurals until late because they are not marked in Japanese.

In the 1950s and 1960s, contrastive analysis (pointing out phonological and grammatical differences between the first and second languages) prevailed in second-language curricula because it was believed to increase proficiency in the second language. It soon fell into disfavor, however, when second-language acquisition studies seemed to indicate that there were common strategies for second-language acquisition, independent of the native language. In fact, Dulay and Burt (1972, 1973) concluded that most errors of second-language learners resemble those of first-language learners in acquiring English. They indicated that only 5% of errors were due to native language interference. Thus, the type of error may not be as important as the quantity of those errors. As Langdon (1977, 1983) found, students who had been identified as language-disordered made very much the same types of errors as did the normally developing students, but there were indeed significant differences between the normal and language-disordered groups in the quantity of errors that they made.

In general, it is easier to identify phonetic than grammatical interference. Several linguistic forms that language-disordered children may use structurally resemble those that children learning English as their first language use. Clinicians working with Spanish-speaking children should have an inventory of possible phonological and grammatical forms that are transfers from Spanish to English.

Consonants

As can be noted on Table 5-4, 17 of the 24 English consonants in addition to the three /s/ clusters do not exist in Spanish in the final position of words. Furthermore, 8 of those consonants do not exist in any position in Spanish words, although some Spanish phonemic variations have allophones for /dʒ/ (Argentina) and /θ/ (Castile). In addition, some of the phonemes have different variants. For example, the Spanish /d/ in certain configurations resembles the pronunciation of the English /ð/ in the middle position of words such as *lado* 'side' and *pardo* 'brown'. Other sounds are pronounced differently in the two languages. For example, /t/ and /d/ in Spanish are dental, whereas they are alveolar in English. Also, often some of the plosives in the initial position such as /p/, /t/, and /k/ are pronounced without aspiration in Spanish, resulting in substitutions such as /bin/ for /pin/. Consonant clusters that begin with /s/ exist in the middle position only in Spanish. Other less frequent English clusters that occur in the final position do not exist in Spanish either; for example, Spanish has no /rd/ or /rm/ as in /lard/ and /harm/. Although /r/ exists in both languages, it is formed differently. In English, it is a palatal glide, whereas in Spanish it is dental with two possibilities: /r/ as in *pera* 'pear' or trilled /rr/ as in *ropa* 'clothing'.

Vowels

There are 12 different vowels in English, but only 5 equivalent vowels in Spanish (Table 5-5). In addition, there are differences in stress and intonation that affect the pronunciation of vowels.

In English, there are accented and unaccented syllables, whereas in Spanish and other Romance languages all syllables receive equal time and full vowel pronunciation; Spanish does not have the phonological characteristic known as vowel

Table 5-4 English Consonants and Cluster Sounds That Do Not Exist in Spanish

Initial	Medial	Final	Examples
z	z	z	zebra, scissors, houses
v	v	v	vest, harvest, have
ð	ð	ð	them, bathing, bathe
dʒ	dʒ	dʒ	joke, judging, cage
ʃ	ʃ	ʃ	ship, pushing, cash
–	ŋ	ŋ	fingers, ring
θ	θ	θ	think, toothbrush, path
–	ʒ	ʒ	vision, garage
		b	cab
		p	hip
		g	bug
		m	came
		t	cat
		k	coke
		t	catch
		f	safe
		tʃ	catch
st, sp, sk		st, sp, sk	store, spin, skate; cast, wasp, desk
sl, sw, sn			slave, swim, snail

Table 5-5 English Vowels That Do Not Exist in Spanish

English	Spanish				English	Spanish
be	p*i*so	*i		u*	cool	puso
s*i*t		I		U	foot	
name		e		o	go	
bet	p*e*so	* ɛ	ɚ murde*r*	ɔ*	law	*o*so
hat		æ	ə ab*o*ve	*a**	father	p*a*so

*Equivalents exist in Spanish

reduction. Stress patterns are also different in the two languages. English has four stress patterns (i.e., primary, secondary, tertiary, and weak), whereas Spanish has essentially two stress patterns (strong and weak). In addition, there are differences in intonation patterns; English generally has a mid-high-low pattern, whereas Spanish has a low-mid-low pattern. As a result of all these factors, English and Spanish have different rhythms.

Common Phonetic and Grammatical Errors

It is common for a Spanish-speaking person to make such phonological errors as

/s/ for /z/	sebra for zebra
/ʃ/ for /tʃ/	shair for chair
/tʃ/ for /ʃ/	chip for ship
/d/ for /ð/	den for then
/t/ for /θ/	tief for thief, bat for bath
/f/ for /v/	fan for van
/b/ for /v/	berry for very, cabe for cave
/ʊ/ for /u/	pull for pool
/i/ for /ɪ/	cheap for chip
/ə/ for /ou/	call for coal
/esp/ for /sp/	Espanish for Spanish

Grammatical errors that Spanish speakers may make in English include

- omission of the auxiliary "is", as in "he going" vs. "he's going" (This error is common in the process of acquiring English as a first language.)
- transference of the possessive form, as in "the coat of the boy" vs. "the boy's coat" (*el abrigo del niño*)
- incorrect negative form (transference from Spanish), as in "he not play anymore" vs. "he doesn't play anymore" (*ya no juega*)
- incorrect interrogative form "how the story helps?" vs. "how does the story help?" (*¿Cómo ayuda la historia?*)
- incorrect use of pronouns as in "she is putting a towel on his head" vs. ". . . on her head" (In Spanish, the same pronoun is used for masculine and feminine.)
- substitutions of some prepositions, as in "on" for "in" (*en*) and confusion between "of" and "from" (*de*)
- word order difficulty with adjectives, as in "the house red" vs. "the red house" (*la casa roja*)

- lack of agreement of subject and verb, as in "the girl are playing" vs. "the girls are playing"
- omission of "to" in the second verb, as in "I go play" vs. "I go to play"
- omission of article, as in "the ant came back to grass" vs. "the ant came back to the grass"
- omission of pronoun, as in "then flew back" vs. "then he flew back" (in Spanish, pronouns are omitted unless particular reference is made)
- addition of pronouns, as in "the bird he came, too" vs. "the bird came, too"
- incorrect use of negative, as in "No help him" vs. "Don't help him"

The clinician must carefully note these phonological and grammatical/syntactical errors that can be attributed to the influence of Spanish.

CODE-SWITCHING AND ITS ROLE IN LANGUAGE ASSESSMENT

The alternation of two languages in conversation among bilinguals is a natural phenomenon prevalent in many communities, not only in the United States, but also throughout the world. It has been investigated most widely among bilinguals who speak English and one of the European or African languages, such as English and German (Clyne, 1967), English and Italian (Di Pietro, 1977), English and Norwegian (Haugen, 1969), English and Swedish (Hasselmo, 1970), English and Kikuyu (Scotton, 1979), and English and Swahili (Mkilifi, 1978).

Code-switching is usually defined as the alternation or switching of two different languages at the word, phrase, clause, or sentence level (Valdés-Fallis, 1981, p. 95). Timm (1975, 1989) distinguished code-switching from interferences by indicating that in code-switching entire linguistic units from one language are attached onto units of another language. This type of switch is illustrated in the sentence *"Pero verdad que* it was worth it" (But the truth is that it was worth it; Valdés-Fallis, 1981, p. 95); the English phrase *it was worth it* is pronounced according to English phonological rules, and the Spanish portion follows Spanish phonological rules. Code-mixing is a category of code-switching. It consists of short insertions from one language into an utterance in the other language. Most often these are labels, action words, or words that describe an attribute (Cheng & Butler, 1989).

Gumperz and Hernández-Chávez (1970), Lance (1979), Mahecha (1990), and Valdés-Fallís (1976, 1981, 1982), among others, have studied code-switching between Spanish and English. The Spanish-English code-switching that is frequently heard in the Southwest is referred to as "Tex-Mex" in the English-speaking community and *"hablar apochado"* in the Spanish-speaking community. There is a continuum in the use of code-switching, ranging from standard Spanish to standard English (Elías-Olivares, 1976). In between are Popular Spanish,

Español Mixtureado, Caló (Pachuco), and Chicano English. Español Mixtureado (also called Pocho or Tex-Mex) uses a Spanish base with many English borrowings and code-switches (Grosjean, 1982, p. 331). Very often, however, code-switching may have pejorative connotations.

Timm (1989) outlined several characteristics of speech communities in which code-switching is likely to occur: (1) the two languages have been in contact for several generations; (2) a majority of the speakers in the speech community are bilingual; and (3) the language use patterns of the community are not rigid or compartmentalized. As Timm (1989) indicated, however, it is important to distinguish learner's code-switching from competent code-switching. (See also Mahecha [1990].) Learners frequently alternate languages at the word or phrase level, particularly in the beginning stages of second-language acquisition when they are pushed to communicate in their weaker language. For example, a learner may say, "*Yo quiero* get out" (I want to get out). This process is different from proficient code-switching, in which the speakers are highly skilled in both languages and alternate languages for reasons other than a lack of a specific word.

Timm (1975) indicated that both linguistic and nonlinguistic constraints operate in code-switching. There are two main linguistic constraints. First, there is a free morpheme constraint; a switch cannot take place between the stem of a word and its affix. For example, the word *jeché* mentioned earlier is not an example of code-switching, but perhaps of borrowing. In this case, the word was composed of the stem of one language (Polish) and the ending of the other (Spanish). There are also constraints for idiomatic expressions, set phrases, and discourse elements that function as affixes (Grosjean, 1982, p. 325). Second, the word order immediately before and after a switch point must be possible in both languages. Examples given by Poplack (1979) that Grosjean (1982, p. 326) cited are

English: I /told him/ /that/ /so that/ /he/ /would bring it/ /fast/
Spanish: *(Yo)* /le dije/ /eso/ /pa' que/ /él/ /la trajera/ /ligero/
Switch: I told him that *pa' que la trajera ligero*

Switches can take place at the slashes. In her sample, Poplack found only 1% of code-switches violated these two linguistic constraints. Some exceptions may apply, however, depending on factors such as the length of the phrase and the semantic or pragmatic unit of the segments.

According to Grosjean (1982), there are several nonlinguistic constraints that explain the reason for code-switching: (1) filling a linguistic need for a lexical item, phrase, or stretch of discourse; (2) quoting someone; (3) marketing and emphasizing the group identity; (4) conveying confidentiality; (5) excluding someone from conversation; (6) changing the role of the speaker (i.e., raising the speaker's status); (7) adding authority; (8) showing expertise; and (9) using a word or phrase that may not have an equivalent in the other language.

Very few studies have been conducted on the development of code-switching in children. Those that have been done have shown a great deal of variation. Some researchers have reported a very limited incidence of code-switching; for example, Swain (1974) found a 4% incidence in a study of French-English bilingual children, while Lindholm and Padilla (1976) found a 2% incidence in bilingual Spanish-English children. On the other hand, Vihman (1981) reported that her 20-month-old son switched codes in 34% of instances. Several factors may explain such variations: (1) differential exposure to the two languages, (2) the definition of mixing or code-switching selected by the researcher, and (3) the amount of code-switching used by the adults around the child. Children may switch languages not only for the same reasons that adults do, but also because of a perception that an adult lacks proficiency in the language (McClure, 1981). As normal as code-switching is among bilinguals, however, its overabundance may signal dominance of one language over another or a possible lack of competence in either language (Cheng & Butler, 1989).

LANGUAGE LOSS

Children and Adolescents

It is common for second-language learners to lose their first language if its use is discontinued. Language loss has been described as a common phenomenon in an additive environment (Leopold, 1970); however, it is often thought of as resulting in "semi-lingualism" in a subtractive context. For the most part, middle-class parents who note the shift in proficiency in their bilingual children have tended to view it as a natural consequence of the type of input that the child receives as the environment changes (McLaughlin, 1987). Language loss in the subtractive environment may be erroneously considered symptomatic of a language disability. Often, in both additive and subtractive situations, the child may be proficient in social situations in the first language, but have more difficulty in performing on decontextualized tasks, such as comprehending written text. This phenomenon is even more pronounced if the child had not been exposed to the more academically oriented tasks in the primary language. It may also occur with adults who have rare opportunities to interact in the language.

When evaluating the primary language of a child, clinicians should always consider language loss. Finding out the extent to which each language is used and the environment in which it is used is very important. For example, Merino (1983b) found that loss of the primary language may be due to school and/or peer group pressure. In many cases, the family must "salvage" the primary language at home in order to maintain and nurture the communication between family members, especially between parents and children. Wong Fillmore (1991) described cases of language loss in preschool children who spoke a variety of first languages. These children often acquired English at the expense of their primary language. In some cases, their speaking English did not affect communication with their parents, but in others, there was a significant breakdown in verbal interaction. Some children who returned to their home country needed several years to regain their native proficiency. Thus, societal pressures have reinforced the learning of the second language at the expense of the first language.

Adults

Aging may have an impact on the language skills of a bilingual individual. Research on the effects of aging has increased in the last decade or so, although it has focused primarily on the monolingual population. One reason that research on this topic has been limited is that changes are much slower in late puberty and during adulthood. Research on bilingual individuals usually follows research on monolingual individuals. Therefore, research on bilinguals has been equally scarce for the adolescent and adult groups. One of the practical outcomes of such research is that it is helpful in assessment and intervention for neurologically based language problems following a stroke, trauma, or progressive disease (e.g., Alzheimer's or any dementia). With the bilingual population, the research is complicated by all the variables that relate to the acquisition and use of two or more languages (Hyltenstam & Obler, 1989). Accurate information on a patient's pretraumatic language skills is necessary, however, in order to select the more efficient intervention techniques (Holland, 1983).

Obler, Albert, and Lozowick (1986) noted that only three studies of aging in intact or aphasic bilingual adults have been conducted thus far. The first study, conducted by Clyne (1977), is a case report on an older German-English bilingual woman, whose proficiency in English had declined in association with increased traces of her German accent and words. The research provided no information on her health status, however. The second study consisted of a review of 107 cases of bilingual aphasics selected from the literature (Albert & Obler, 1978). One of the important findings of the review was that, in individuals who had acquired aphasia prior to age 65 years, the language that they used at the time of the injury recovered first, regardless of their principal language. In patients older than 65 years, there was no clear parameter of recovery. The third study, conducted by Bergman (1980), indicated that elderly bilinguals had more difficulty with comprehension tasks involving temporally distorted stimuli than did monolinguals.

Since that time, Obler and associates (1986) have compared the performance of 11 Yiddish-English bilinguals with that of 32 monolinguals of similar age (mean age for both groups, 73 years), health, and education. The subjects were given a number of language tasks, such as naming and providing antonyms; some more figurative tasks, such as idiom and proverb interpretations; and two visual memory tasks. No significant group differences were found for most tasks. The bilingual group did better on word fluency and one of the visual tasks. The monolingual group was better at reciting the alphabet, counting, and interpreting proverbs. It is possible that differences would have been more significant if the subjects had been younger.

Obler and associates (1986) raised some important questions regarding the language performance of older bilingual persons. For example, what attributes of the language history of the individuals (e.g., their age, manner of second-language acquisition) interact with the rate or pattern or language attrition? Is there a critical period during which, if a second language has been acquired, there is less chance of loss? These and other questions remain unanswered, but must be taken into account in evaluating the language performance of bilinguals, especially after trauma or any progressive disease that may affect communication in adults. Also, more information is needed on the sociolinguistic issues of aging in a pluralistic society (Holland, 1983).

DEFINING A LANGUAGE DISORDER IN BILINGUAL CHILDREN

A language disorder may manifest itself at different ages and stages in the course of children's development. For example, an infant may have difficulty in acquiring an oral system of communication, while an elementary school–aged child may be able to express basic needs, but still have problems in narrating a story with a logical sequence. Typically, this child may also have reading and writing problems. An older student may have learned basic reading skills, but have difficulty with more complex material. This student may have difficulty in integrating the information to make generalizations and set hypotheses. Also, there may be weaknesses in comprehending more figurative language, such as metaphors, idioms, and humor.

In some cases, the language disorder is a manifestation of a traceable condition, such as a hearing or vision impairment. It could have a neurological base, as in cerebral palsy, or it could be the result of autism or mental retardation. In most cases, however, the source of the problem cannot be easily detected, and this lack of a clearly identifiable cause makes it even more difficult for parents to accept that their child has a problem. The parents of many bilingual Hispanic students, for example, often attribute their child's problem to the process of second-language acquisition. In addition, if the student decodes words (often without really understanding the text), parents with limited literacy skills themselves find it difficult to understand the reason for the student's lack of success in school. It is particularly delicate when problems are not identified until the student is in the upper grades.

Although there is a vast literature on the nature and identification of language disorders in English-speaking monolingual children (e.g., Carrow-Woolfolk & Lynch, 1982; Fey, 1986; Lahey, 1988; Simon, 1985; Wallach & Butler, 1984), a very limited number of studies have been conducted to define the nature of a language disorder in Spanish-English bilingual children. A total of six studies have specifically addressed this issue. Two of them focused on the subjects' performance in Spanish only (i.e., Ambert, 1986; Linares-Orama, 1977), whereas the other four focused on the children's language performance in both languages (i.e., Damico, Oller, & Storey, 1983; Kayser, 1990; Langdon, 1977, 1983; Merino, 1983a). These studies differ not only in their focus and the areas investigated, but also in the ages and Hispanic origin of the subjects. For example, Linares-Orama (1977) and Ambert (1986) used their subjects' elicited language samples, but they analyzed their data differently. Linares-Orama, who worked with Puerto Rican preschool children, used the developmental sentence scoring procedure created by Lee (1974) and adapted for Spanish by Toronto (1972, 1976). Ambert also worked with Puerto Rican children (although her subjects were 5 to 12 years of age) and analyzed the children's phonology, syntax, and semantics. The ages and methodologies used in the Langdon (1977, 1983) studies and Merino (1983a) study were also different. Kayser (1990) described specific observations of her three Mexican-American subjects in different contexts. Despite these differences among studies, they provide important information.

A language disorder in a Spanish-speaking child may manifest itself in areas similar to those in which a language disorder manifests itself in an English-speaking child. The children's linguistic skills deviate from the norm when their performance is compared with results of studies done with Spanish-speaking monolingual children. Ambert found that several students identified as language-disordered made articulation errors; others made grammatical and syntactical errors, such as omitting articles and pronouns that should have been mastered by children of their chronological age. Also, the order of words in the sentences was not always correct, nor did the verb always agree with the subject, as in *el sapo no pueden hablar* 'the toad are not able to speak' for *el sapo no puede hablar* 'the toad is not able to speak'. The subjects also made semantic errors; they did not use the correct label for many common words (*radio* 'radio' for *teléfono* 'telephone'), denoting word finding difficulties. In addition, the children had difficulty retelling stories, narrating personal experiences, following directions, discriminating sound differences, and recalling auditory information. Linares-Orama (1977) found that preschoolers' mean length of utterance was shorter for those children who had an identified language disorder than for normally developing children.

A language disorder may be more evident in the dominant language, but is present in the other language as well. There may be significant differences across normally developing and language-disordered children in the number of errors that they make on different types of language tasks. For example, Langdon (1977,

1983) found that the children with a language disorder made more errors in all areas tested (i.e., articulation, auditory discrimination, comprehension, and expression) than did their normally developing counterparts—in both Spanish and English.

It is important to conduct a thorough assessment in different areas of language. Merino (1983a) found that her sample did not differ from the normally developing group in comprehension, but there were differences in the expressive areas. Damico and associates (1983) found that assessment of form was not sufficient in detecting language problems; pragmatic criteria were needed for an accurate diagnosis. Kayser (1990) found that basing conclusions on the results of discrete-type testing incorrectly identified as language-disordered students who simply may have been having more difficulty learning a second language.

Results of the studies mentioned above indicate that a language disorder in a primary or dominant language manifests itself in similar areas as compared to a second language. The language disorder may be more or less evident depending on the individual's length and type of exposure to the second language. Thus, it is important to evaluate the individual in all linguistic areas (form, content, and use) in *both* languages to gain a truer picture of this individual's linguistic competence.

REFERENCES

Albert, M., & Obler, L. (1978). *The bilingual brain: Neuropsychological and neurolinguistic aspects of bilingualism.* New York: Academic Press.

Ambert, A. (1986). Identifying language disorders in Spanish speakers. In A.C. Willig & H.F. Greenberg (Eds.), *Bilingualism and learning disabilities* (pp. 15–33). New York: American Library Publishing.

Arnberg, L. (1984). Mother tongue playgrounds for preschool bilingual children. *Journal of Multilingual and Multicultural Education, 5,* 65–84.

Asher, J. (1979). *Learning another language through actions: The complete teachers' guidebook.* Los Gatos, CA: Skyoak Productions.

Asher, J., & García, R. (1969). The optimal age to learn a foreign language. *Modern Language Journal, 8,* 334–341.

Asher, J., & Price, B. (1967). The learning strategy of Total Physical Response: Some age differences. *Child Development, 38,* 1219–1227.

Bailey, N., Madden, C., & Krashen, S. (1974). Is there a "natural sequence" in adult second language learning? *Language Learning, 21,* 235–243.

Beebe, L.M. (1985). Choosing the right stuff. In S.M. Gass & C.G. Madden (Eds.), *Input in second language acquisition* (pp. 104–114). Rowley, MA: Newbury House.

Bergman, C. (1976). Interference vs. independent development in infant bilingualism. In G. Keller, R. Teschner, & S. Viera (Eds.), *Bilingualism in the bicentennial and beyond* (pp. 86–96). New York: Bilingual Press/Editorial Bilingüe.

Bergman, M. (1980). *Aging and the perception of speech.* Baltimore: University Park Press.

Biederman, P.W. (1989, November 23). Dialectician puts accent on the stars. *Los Angeles Times.*

Brown, R. (1973). *A first language: The early stages.* Cambridge, MA: Harvard University Press.

Burling, R. (1973). Language development of a Garo and English-speaking child. In C.A. Ferguson & D.A. Slobin (Eds.), *Studies of child language development* (pp. 69–90). New York: Holt, Rinehart & Winston.

Cancino, H., Rosansky, E., & Schumann, J. (1978). The acquisition of the English auxiliary by native Spanish speakers. *TESOL Quarterly, 15,* 421–430.

Carrow-Woolfolk, E., & Lynch, J.I. (1982). *An integrative approach to language disorders in children.* New York: Grune & Stratton.

Cheng, L.L. (1987). *Assessing Asian language performance.* Gaithersburg, MD: Aspen Publishers.

Cheng, L.L. (1990a). Recognizing diversity. *American Behavioral Scientist, 34*(2), 263–278.

Cheng, L.L. (1990b). *Multicultural and multiethnic diversity and higher education.* Unpublished manuscript, San Diego State University, San Diego.

Cheng, L.L., & Butler, K. (1989). Code-switching: A natural phenomenon vs. language deficiency. *World English, 8,* 293–309.

Clyne, M. (1967). *Transference and triggering.* The Hague, Netherlands: Marinus Nijhoff.

Clyne, M. (1977). Bilingualism of the elderly. *Talanya, 4,* 45–56.

Collier, V. (1987). Age and rate of acquisition of second language for academic purposes. *TESOL Quarterly, 21,* 739–764.

Compton, A., & Hutton, J. (1978). *The Compton-Hutton phonological assessment.* San Francisco: Carousel House.

Cummins, J. (1981a). Age on arrival and immigrant second language learning in Canada: A reassessment. *Applied Linguistics, 2,* 132–149.

Cummins, J. (1981b). The role of primary language development in promoting educational success for language minority students. In Office of Bilingual Bicultural Education, California State Department of Education (Ed.), *Schooling and language minority students: A theoretical framework* (pp. 3–49). Los Angeles: Evaluation, Dissemination and Assessment Center, California State University.

Cummins, J. (1984). *Bilingualism and special education.* Clevedon, England: Multilingual Matters.

Damico, J.S., Oller, J.W., & Storey, M.E. (1983). The diagnosis of language disorders in bilingual children: Surface-oriented and pragmatic criteria. *Journal of Speech and Hearing Disorders, 46,* 385–394.

De Avila, E., Cohen, E., & Intili, S.K. (1981). Interdependence and management in bilingual classrooms. Palo Alto, CA: Center for Educational Research.

Dimitrijević, N. (1965). A bilingual child. *English Language Teaching, 20,* 23–28.

Di Pietro, R. (1977). Code-switching as a verbal strategy among bilinguals. In F. Eckman (Ed.), *Current themes in linguistics: Bilingualism, experimental linguistics and language typologies.* Washington, DC: Hemisphere Publishing.

Doyle, A., Champagne, M., & Segalowitz, N. (1978). Some issues in the assessment of linguistic consequences of early bilingualism. In M. Paradis (Ed.), *Aspects of bilingualism.* Columbia, SC: Hornbeam Press.

Dulay, H., & Burt, M.K. (1972). Goofing: An indicator of children's second language strategies. *Language Learning, 22,* 235–252.

Dulay, H., & Burt, M.K. (1973). Should we teach children syntax? *Language Learning, 23,* 245–258.

Dulay, H., & Burt, M.K. (1974). Natural sequences in child second language acquisition. *Language Learning, 24,* 37–53.

Dulay, H., Hernández-Chávez, E., & Burt, M.K. (1978). The process of becoming bilingual. In S. Singh & J. Lynch (Eds.), *Diagnostic procedures in hearing, language and speech* (pp. 305–326). Baltimore: University Park Press.

Elías-Olivares, L. (1976). *Ways of speaking in a Chicano community: A sociolinguistic approach.* Unpublished doctoral dissertation, University of Texas, Austin.

Ellis, R. (1984). Can syntax be taught? A study of the effects of formal instruction on the acquisition of WH questions by children. *Applied Linguistics, 5,* 138–155.

Ervin-Tripp, S. (1974). Is second language learning like the first? *TESOL Quarterly, 8,* 111–127.

Fantini, A. (1978). Bilingual behavior and social cues: Case studies of two bilingual children. In M. Paradis (Ed.), *Aspects of bilingualism.* Columbia, SC: Hornbeam Press.

Fathman, A. (1975). *Language background, age, and the order of English structures.* Paper presented at the TESOL Convention, Los Angeles.

Fey, M.E. (1986). *Language intervention with young children.* Boston: College Hill Press.

Gardner, R.C., & Lambert, W.E. (1972). *Attitudes and motivation in second language learning.* Rowley, MA: Newbury House.

Grégoire, A. (1947). *L'apprentissage du langage.* Gembloux: Duclot.

Grosjean, F. (1982). *Life with two languages: An introduction to bilingualism.* Cambridge, MA: Harvard University Press.

Gumperz, J., & Hernández-Chávez, E. (1970). Cognitive aspects in bilingual education. In W. Whitely (Ed.), *Language use and social change.* London: Oxford University Press.

Hakuta, K. (1976). A case of a Japanese child learning English. *Language Learning, 26:* 321–351.

Hammerly, H. (1985). *An integrated theory of language teaching and its practical consequences.* Burnaby, British Columbia, Canada: Second Language Publications.

Hammers, J., & Blanc, M. (1989). *Bilinguality and bilingualism.* New York: Cambridge University Press.

Harding, E., & Riley, P. (1986). *The bilingual family: A handbook for parents.* New York: Cambridge University Press.

Hasselmo, H. (1970). Code-switching and modes of speaking. In G. Gilbert (Ed.), *Texas studies in bilingualism.* Berlin: Walter de Gruyter.

Haugen, E. (1969). *The Norwegian language in America: A study in bilingual behavior.* Bloomington: Indiana University Press.

Hernández-Chávez, E., Burt, M.K., & Dulay, H. (1978). Language dominance and proficiency testing: Some general considerations. *NABE Journal, 3,* 41–54.

Holland, A. (1983). Nonbiased assessment and treatment of adults who have neurologic speech and language problems. *Topics in Language Disorders, 3*(3), 67–75.

Huerta, A. (1977). The acquisition of bilingualism: A code-switching approach. *Sociolinguistic Working Paper, 39,* 1–33.

Hyltenstam, K., & Obler, L.K. (1989). *Bilingualism across the lifespan.* New York: Cambridge University Press.

Ianco-Worrall, A. (1972). Bilingualism and cognitive development. *Child Development, 43,* 1390–1400.

Kayser, H. (1990). Social communicative behaviors of language-disordered Mexican-American students. *Child Language Teaching and Therapy, 6,* 255–269.

Kessler, C., & Idar, I. (March 1977). *The acquisition of English syntactic structures by a Vietnamese child.* Paper presented at the Los Angeles Second Language Acquisition Forum, Los Angeles.

Klima, E., & Bellugi, U. (1973). Syntactic regularities in the speech of children. In D.I. Siobin (Ed.), *Studies of child language development* (pp. 333–354). New York: Holt, Rinehart & Winston.

Krashen, S.D. (1981). Bilingual education and second language acquisition theory. In Office of Bilingual Bicultural Education, California State Department of Education (Ed.), *Schooling and language minority students: A theoretical framework* (pp. 51–79). Los Angeles: Evaluation, Dissemination and Assessment Center, California State University.

Krashen, S.D. (1982). *Principles and practice in second language acquisition.* Elmsford, NY: Pergamon Press.

Krashen, S.D., & Biber, D. (1988). *On course: Bilingual education's success in California.* Sacramento: California Association for Bilingual Education.

Krashen, S.D., Long, M., & Scarcella, R. (1979). Age, rate and eventual attainment in second language acquisition. *TESOL Quarterly, 13,* 573–582.

Krashen, S.D., & Terrell, T. (1983). *The natural approach: Language acquisition in the classroom.* Elmsford, NY: Pergamon Press.

Lahey, M. (1988). *Language disorders and language development.* New York: Macmillan.

Lambert, W. (1975). Culture and language as factors in learning and education. In A. Wolfgang (Ed.), *Education of immigrant students.* Toronto: The Ontario Institute for Studies in Education.

Lance, D. (1979). Spanish-English bilingualism in the American Southwest. In W. Mackey & J. Ornstein (Eds.), *Sociolinguistic studies in language contact.* The Hague, Netherlands: Mouton.

Langdon, H.W. (1977). *Determining a language disorder in a bilingual Spanish-English population.* Unpublished doctoral dissertation, Boston University.

Langdon, H.W. (1983). Assessment and intervention strategies for the bilingual language disordered student. *Exceptional Children, 50,* 37–56.

Lee, L. (1974). *Developmental sentence analysis.* Evanston, IL: Northwestern University Press.

Leopold, W. (1970). *Speech development of a bilingual child,* vols 1–4. New York: AMS Press.

Linares-Orama, N. (1977). Evaluation of syntax in three year old Spanish-speaking Puerto Rican children. *Journal of Speech and Hearing Research, 20,* 350–357.

Lindholm, K.J., & Padilla, A.M. (1978). Language mixing in bilingual children. *Journal of Child Language, 8,* 327–335.

Long, M. (1981). Input, interaction and second language acquisition. In H. Winitz (Ed.), *Native language and foreign language acquisition* (pp. 259–278). New York: New York Academy of Sciences.

Long, M., & Porter, P.A. (1985). Group work, interlanguage talk, and second language acquisition. *Language Learning, 19,* 207–228.

López, D. (1982). *The maintenance of Spanish over three generations in the U.S.* Los Alamitos, CA: National Center for Bilingual Research.

Mace-Matluck, B. (May 1978). *Order of acquisition: Same or different in first and second language learning.* Paper presented at the Annual Meeting of the International Reading Association, Houston, TX:ERIC DOC: 159–633.

Mahecha, N. (1990). *Perception of pre-switch cues by Spanish-English bilinguals.* Unpublished doctoral dissertation, City University of New York, New York.

Makino, T. (1980). *Acquisition order of English morphemes by Japanese adolescents.* Tokyo: Shinozaki Press.

McClure, E. (1981). Formal and functional aspects of the code-switched discourse of bilingual children. In R.P. Durán (Ed.), *Latino language and communication behavior.* Norwood, NJ: Ablex Publishers.

McDonald, F., Stone, M., & Yates, A. (1977). *The effects of classroom interaction and student characteristics on the acquisition of proficiency in English as a second language.* Princeton, NJ: Educational Testing Service.

McLaughlin, B. (1987). *Theories of second language learning*. London: Edward Arnold.

Meara, P. (1980). Vocabulary acquisition: A neglected aspect of language learning. In V. Kinsella (Ed.), *Surveys 1* (pp. 120–126). New York: Cambridge University Press.

Merino, B.J. (1983a). Language development in normal and language handicapped Spanish-speaking children. *Hispanic Journal of Behavioral Sciences, 5,* 379–400.

Merino, B.J. (1983b). Language loss in bilingual Chicano children. *Journal of Applied Developmental Psychology, 10,* 477–494.

Merino, B.J., & Lyons, J. (1987). The problem of exit criteria in second language learners: California as a case study. *Association of Mexican American Educators Journal, 8,* 5–25.

Mkilifi, M. (1978). Triglossia and Swahili-English bilingualism in Tanzania. In J. Fishman (Ed.), *Advances in the study of societal multilingualism*. The Hague, Netherlands: Mouton.

Obler, L., Albert, M., & Lozowick, S. (1986). The aging bilingual. In J. Vaid (Ed.), *Language processing in bilinguals: Psycholinguistic and neuropsychological perspectives* (pp. 221–231). Hillsdale, NJ: Lawrence Erlbaum Associates.

Ogbu, J.U., & Matute-Bianchi, M.E. (1986). Understanding sociocultural factors: Knowledge, identity and school adjustment. In Bilingual Education Office, California State Department of Education (Ed.), *Beyond language: Social and cultural factors in schooling language minority students* (pp. 73–142). Los Angeles: Evaluation, Dissemination and Assessment Center, California State University.

Oksaar, E. (1971). Zum Spracherwerb des Kindes in zweisprachiger Umgebung. *Folia Linguistica, 4,* 330–358.

Oller, J.W., Jr. (1978). The language factor in the evaluation of bilingual education. In J.E. Alatis (Ed.), *Georgetown University round table on language and linguistics* (pp. 410–422). Washington, DC: Georgetown University Press.

Oller, J.W., Jr. (1979). *Language tests at school: A pragmatic approach*. New York: Longman.

Ortíz, A., & Polyzoi, E. (1988). Language assessment of Hispanic learning disabled and speech and language handicapped students: Research in progress. In A.A. Ortíz & B.A. Ramírez (Eds.), *Schools and the culturally diverse exceptional student: Promising practices and future directions* (pp. 32–44). Reston, VA: Council for Exceptional Children.

Oyama, S. (1978). The sensitive period and comprehension of speech. *Working Papers in Bilingualism, 16,* 1–17.

Padilla, A.M., & Liebman, E. (1975). Language acquisition in the bilingual child. *The Bilingual Review/La Revista Bilingüe, 3,* 122–152.

Padilla, A.M., & Lindholm, K.J. (1976). Development of interrogative, negative and possessive forms in the speech of young Spanish-English bilinguals. *The Bilingual Review/La Revista Bilingüe, 3,* 122–152.

Past, A. (1976). *Preschool reading in two languages as a factor in bilingualism*. Unpublished dissertation, University of Texas, Austin.

Patkowski, M. (1980). The sensitive period for the acquisition of syntax in a second language. *Language Learning, 30,* 449–472.

Pavlovitch, M. (1920). *Le langage enfantin: Acquisition du serbe et du français par un enfant serbe*. Paris: Champion.

Pica,T., Doughty, C., & Young, R. (1986). The linguistic and conversational performance of experienced and inexperienced teachers. In R.R. Day (Ed.), *Talking to learn: Conversation in second language acquisition* (pp. 85–98). Rowley, MA: Newbury House.

Politzer, R. (Summer 1989). *A researcher's reflections on bridging dialect and second language learning: Discussion of problems and solutions*. Paper presented at Spanish for Success, a summer institute for secondary school teachers of Spanish who teach native Spanish-speaking students, University of California, Davis.

Poplack, S. (1979). Sometimes I'll start a sentence in Spanish Y TERMINO EN ESPAÑOL: Towards a typology of code-switching. Centro de Estudios Puertorriqueños. *Working Papers, 4,* 1–79.

Ramírez, D., & Merino, B.J. (1990). Classroom talk in English immersion early-exit and late-exit transitional bilingual education programs. In R. Jacobson & C. Faltis (Eds.), *Language distribution issues in bilingual schooling.* Clevedon, England: Multilingual Matters.

Redlinger, W.E. (1979). Early developmental bilingualism: A review of the literature. *The Bilingual Review/La Revista Bilingüe, 6,* 11–30.

Ronjat, J. (1913). *Le développement du langage observé chez un enfant bilingue.* Paris: Champion.

Saenz, T.I., Iglesias, A., & Alemán, G. (November 1989). *Fluency in Spanish college-educated Hispanics.* Paper presented at the American Speech-Language-Hearing Association Convention, St. Louis.

Salica, C. (1981). *Testing a model of corrective discourse.* Unpublished master's thesis, University of California, Los Angeles.

Saunders, G. (1982). *Bilingual children: Guidance for the family.* Clevedon, England: Multilingual Matters.

Schachter, J. (1983). A new account of language transfer. In S. Gass & L. Selinker (Eds.), *Language transfer in language learning* (pp. 98–111). Rowley, MA: Newbury House.

Schmidt-Mackey, I. (1977). Language strategies of the bilingual family. In W. Mackey & T. Andersson. *Bilingualism in early childhood.* Rowley, MA: Newbury House.

Schumann, J. (1978). The acculturation model for second language acquisition. In R. Gringras (Ed.), *Second language acquisition and foreign language teaching* (pp. 27–50). Arlington, VA: Center for Applied Linguistics.

Scotton, C. (1979). Codeswitching as a "safe choice" in choosing a lingua franca. In W. McCormack and S. Wurm (Eds.), *Language and society.* The Hague, Netherlands: Mouton.

Seliger, H., Krashen, S.D., & Ladefoged, P. (1975). Maturational constraints in the acquisition of second languages. *Language Sciences, 38,* 20–22.

Sikorski, L. (1987). *Proficiency in oral English communication (assessment battery).* Santa Ana, CA: Lorna D. Sikorski & Associates.

Simon, C. (Ed.). (1985). *Communication skills and classroom success: Assessment of language learning disordered students.* San Diego, CA: College Hill Press

Snow, C., & Hoefnagel-Höhle, M. (1977). Age differences in pronunciation of foreign sounds. *Language and Speech, 20,* 357–365.

Snow, C., & Hoefnagel-Höhle, M. (1978). Age differences in second language acquisition. In E. Hatch (Ed.), *Second language acquisition* (pp. 333–381). Rowley, MA: Newbury House.

Spada, N. (1987). Relationships between instructional differences and learning outcomes: A process-product study of communicative language teaching. *Applied Linguistics, 8,* 137–161.

Strong, M. (1983). Social styles and the second language acquisition of Spanish-speaking kindergartners. *TESOL Quarterly, 17,* 241–258.

Swain, M. (1972). *Bilingualism as first language.* Unpublished doctoral dissertation, University of California, Irvine.

Swain, M. (1974). Child language learning and linguistic interdependence. In S. Carey (Ed.), *Bilingualism biculturalism and education.* Edmonton: University of Alberta Printing Department.

Swain, M. (1985). Communicative competence: Some roles of comprehensible input and comprehensible output in its development. In S.M. Gass & C.C. Madden (Eds.), *Input in second language acquisition.* Rowley, MA: Newbury House.

Timm, N. (1975). Spanish-English code-switching. El porqué y how-not-to. *Romance Philosophy, xxviii*(4), 473–482.

Timm, N. (Summer 1989). *Bilingual code-switching: An overview of research.* Paper presented at Spanish for Success, a summer institute for secondary school teachers of Spanish who teach native Spanish-speaking students, University of California, Davis.

Toronto, A. (1972). *A developmental Spanish analysis procedure for Spanish-speaking children.* Unpublished doctoral dissertation, Northwestern University, Evanston, IL.

Toronto, A. (1976). Developmental assessment of Spanish grammar. *Journal of Speech and Hearing Disorders, 41,* 150–171.

Valdés-Fallis, G. (1976). Social interaction and code-switching patterns: A case study of Spanish/English alternation. In G. Keller, R. Teschner, & S. Viera (Eds.), *Bilingualism in the bicentennial and beyond* (pp. 53–85). New York: Bilingual Press/Editorial Bilingüe.

Valdés-Fallis, G. (1981). Code switching as deliberate verbal strategy: A microanalysis of direct and indirect requests among bilingual Chicano speakers. In R. Durán (Ed.), *Latino language and communicative behavior.* Norwood, NJ: Ablex Publishing Corporation.

Valdés-Fallis, G. (1982). Social alternation and code-switching patterns: A case study of Spanish-English alternation. In J. Amastae & L. Elías-Olivares (Eds.), *Spanish in the United States: Sociolinguistic aspects* (pp. 209–229). New York: Cambridge University Press.

van Kleeck, A. (1984). Metalinguistic skills: Cutting across spoken and written language and problem-solving abilities. In G.P. Wallach & K.G. Butler (Eds.), *Language learning disabilities in school-age children* (pp. 128–153). Baltimore: Williams & Wilkins.

Vihman, M.M. (1981). Phonology and the development of the lexicon: Evidence from children's errors. *Journal of Child Language, 8,* 239–264.

Vihman, M.M., & McLaughlin, B. (1982). Bilingualism and second language acquisition in preschool children. In C.J. Brainerd & M. Pressley (Eds.), *Verbal processes in children: Progress in cognitive development research* (pp. 35–57). New York: Springer Verlag.

von Raffler-Engel, W. (1965). Del bilinguismo infantile. *Archivio Glottologica Italiano, 50,* 175–180.

Wallach, G., & Butler, K. (Eds.). (1984). *Language learning disabilities in school-age children.* Baltimore: Williams & Wilkins.

Winitz, H., & Reeds, J. (1973). Rapid acquisition of a foreign language by the avoidance of speaking. *International Review of Applied Linguistics, 11,* 295–317.

Wolfram, W. (in press). Grammatical, phonological and language use differences across cultures. In L. Code & V. Deal (Eds.), *Communicative disorders in multicultural populations.* Rockville, MD: American Speech-Language-Hearing Association.

Wong Fillmore, L. (1976). *The second time around: Cognitive and social strategies in language acquisition.* Unpublished doctoral dissertation, Stanford University, Stanford, CA.

Wong Fillmore, L. (1991). Language and cultural issues in early education. In S.L. Kagan (Ed.), *The care and education of America's young children: Obstacles and opportunities* (pp. 30–49). The 90th Yearbook of the National Society for the Study of Education. Chicago: Chicago University Press.

Wren, D. (1982). A case study of the treatment of oral errors. *Selected Papers in TESOL, 1,* 90–103. Monterey, CA: Monterey Institute of International Studies.

Zehler, A.M. (1982). *The reflections of first-language–derived processes in second language acquisition.* Unpublished doctoral dissertation, University of Illinois at Urbana-Champaign, Urbana.

Chapter 6

Defining Bilingual Education in the United States

Henriette W. Langdon and Li-Rong Lilly Cheng

As stated earlier, the number of language minority students in the United States has increased significantly in the last two decades. In 1970, 20% of U.S. public school students belonged to a minority group; by 1986, the percentage had increased to almost 30%. In California alone, the number of limited-English–proficient (LEP) students in the public schools increased from one-quarter million in 1979 to three-quarter million in 1989, representing a growth of 300% in 10 years. In sum, of the nation's student population, ethnic minority students constitute approximately 50% in California and 33% nationwide (Cheng, 1990).

The educational attainment of minorities in the United States is not keeping pace with their growth in numbers. If left uncorrected, this situation will create serious problems for society as a whole (Grant, 1989). Schools and institutions of higher education must examine instructional techniques, identify areas of concern, and design programs to enhance learning. This must be done so that all students will achieve in terms of equity and excellence (Allen, 1987). As Collison (1988) indicated, the United States must renew its commitment to the advancement of minority groups; otherwise, the future prosperity of the nation may be jeopardized.

One effort to meet the needs of this linguistically different nation was marked by the passage of the Bilingual Education Act, or Title VII of the Elementary and Secondary Education Act, which was signed by President Lyndon Johnson in 1968. The Act had two main objectives: (1) to develop programs that utilized two languages as an instructional medium and (2) to maintain the foreign language resources of the United States. Bilingualism and bilingual education are not new concepts in the educational history of the United States, however. Whereas second-language acquisition research has been conducted with a variety of language combinations (e.g., English-French, English-Spanish, English-German), bilingual education in the United States has been mostly implemented and researched with Spanish, as Hispanics have been the largest language minority group in the United States.

Language minority students are often referred for assessment because of language difficulties that do not necessarily stem from a basic language disorder, but may be caused by inappropriate program implementation. According to Cummins (1984), these problems are often "pedagogically induced" (p. 223). Understanding the roots of bilingualism and bilingual instruction is important in assessing the educational history and needs of non-native individuals. Therefore, speech-language clinicians must be knowledgeable of the different bilingual program options. In addition, they must understand the basis of the current debate over these programs and its effect on the education of all students.

With such a linguistically and culturally diverse population represented in the school system today, speech-language clinicians must be aware of the various attitudes represented in these groups. The different cultural backgrounds, the varying attitudes toward school and educators, the lack of exposure to educational systems, and the lack of knowledge about community resources are some of the reasons that it is imperative to counsel ethnic parents. It is critical that college and university training programs for speech-language clinicians address the realities of serving people who are diverse in terms of cultural orientation, economic standing, and academic background.

HISTORICAL PERSPECTIVE AND LEGISLATION

Tolerance and support for other languages and multiculturalism in the United States have fluctuated from the times of the Continental Congress in 1774 to the present. The period from 1774 to World War I was a time when there was significant support for bilingual education. Following World War I, however, this support declined because of feelings of nationalism (Ambert & Meléndez, 1985). "It was expected that immigrants would learn English, forget their native language and integrate into the 'American ways' of life" (p. 5). Attitudes changed again after political events of the late 1950s at home and abroad, such as the launching of the Sputnik satellite by the Soviet Union, previously considered a technologically less advanced nation; Fidel Castro's assumption of power in Cuba, which resulted in a flood of middle- and upper-class Cuban immigrants to the United States; and the Civil Rights Movement of the 1960s (Ambert & Meléndez, 1985). The feeling that the United States needed to increase its contact with other nations by encouraging instruction in other languages and by providing non–English-speaking students with the right to receive an appropriate education led to the passage of the Bilingual Education Act of 1968 (U.S. Code Title 20, 1968) .

Implementation of Bilingual Education Act at the Federal Level

As of 1968, the federal government had an official document supporting the implementation of bilingual programs for all students. Shortly before the passage of the Act, however, some bilingual schools had been established, principally in Florida, which was heavily populated by the recent Cuban immigrants. There was no research base to support these programs, and teachers who were also immigrants relied on their previous experience in their home country with a curriculum developed by Robinett and Rojas, two English as a second language (ESL) instructors from Puerto Rico (Hakuta, 1986). The program involved instruction in Spanish and English on an equal basis, and the languages themselves were taught during two different segments of the day. The students' high reading scores in both languages and strong parental support proved that the program was successful. This model was a prototype of a maintenance program; both languages were used as a medium of instruction throughout at least elementary school.

Maintenance programs are almost nonexistent today. They have been replaced by transitional programs, in which the native language is used as a vehicle to learn academic subjects and the second language (English) is emphasized to enable the student to follow an English-only curriculum as soon as possible. Such programs are viewed as compensatory rather than complementary. Results of research studies such as those of the American Institutes of Research (AIR) conducted by Danoff, Coles, McLaughlin, and Reynolds (1977, 1978) and later on by the studies of Baker and de Kanter (1983), as well as political pressure, were largely responsible for the shift from maintenance to transitional programs.

In transitional programs, the students are instructed through the native language for 3 years, generally kindergarten through second grade. English is introduced gradually, and support from the first language is subsequently dropped. For many students, however, 3 years of exposure to English is not sufficient to acquire the skills necessary to learn academic subjects exclusively in English. The students may acquire the basic interpersonal communication skills (BICS) of the language, but not the cognitive/academic language proficiency (CALP) to succeed in an English-only curriculum. As previously discussed, students vary a great deal. It may take as much as 2 or 3 years for someone to acquire the basic communication skills of a language and 5 to 7 years to acquire the necessary language skills to succeed academically in the second language (Cummins, 1981, 1984).

Implementation of Bilingual Education Act at the State Level

The Bilingual Education Act contained no clear guidelines on ways to implement bilingual programs, which resulted in great confusion. The Act did provide monies for experimentation with bilingual programs, although the school systems were under no obligation to use them (Hakuta, 1986). As Senator Carl Yarborough noted, "It is not the purpose of the bill to create pockets of different languages throughout the country . . . not to stamp out the dominant language, but just to try to make those children fully literate in English" (Crawford, 1989, p. 32). From the very beginning, however, the ultimate goal for bilingual programs established under the Act appeared to help the students gain skills in English, with no regard for the maintenance of their primary language.

As a result of class action lawsuits filed by several language minority groups, including Mexican-American, Puerto Rican, Khmer, and Chinese parents who felt that their children were not receiving adequate education, several states (beginning with Massachusetts in 1971) have enacted laws to promote bilingual education (Table 6-1). *Lau v. Nichols* (1974) had one of the greatest impacts on state laws to protect the rights of language minority students. It was initiated in San Francisco by Cantonese-speaking parents whose children were not succeeding in school because of the language barrier. The case was debated in both the lower federal courts and the U.S. Supreme Court. Although the Justices did not mandate a specific teaching methodology, they required the district to rectify the situation. As Crawford (1989) reported, Justice William O. Douglas said, "No specific remedy is urged upon us. Teaching English to the students of Chinese ancestry who do not speak the language is one choice. Giving instructions to this group in Chinese is another. There may be others. Petitioners ask only that the Board of Education be directed to apply its expertise to the problem and rectify the situation" (p. 36). Subsequently, the San Francisco Board of Education signed a decree to provide bilingual education to the city's Chinese, Filipino, and Hispanic children.

The U.S. Office of Civil Rights soon complied with this U.S. Supreme Court ruling by requiring bilingual education for those students who were not able to progress because of their unfamiliarity with the English language. In 1975, Terrell Bell, then U.S. Commissioner of Education, announced the *Lau* Remedies, which were guidelines drafted to identify and evaluate LEP students, to suggest instructional interventions, and to delineate teachers' standards that must be met according to specific timetables. The Remedies were very specific; ESL instruction was not considered sufficient to meet the students' linguistic needs. Although the *Lau* Remedies did not at first have the legal status of federal regulations, they had government support and eventually became the *Lau* Regulations in 1980. Numerous class action lawsuits were necessary before appropriate programs for LEP students were fully implemented in different states or localities: *Diana v. California State Board of Education* (1970), *Serna v. Portales Municipal Schools* (1972) in New Mexico, *Rio v. Read* (1977) in Long Island, New York, and *United States v. State of Texas* (1981). Several districts adopted bilingual education for fear of a loss of federal funding.

Table 6-1 Bilingual Education Legislation

State	Permits	Prohibits*	No Statute
Alabama		+	
Alaska	+		
Arizona	+		
Arkansas		+	
California	+		
Colorado	+		
Connecticut	+		
Delaware		+	
D.C.			+
Florida			+
Georgia			+
Hawaii			+
Idaho			+
Illinois	+		
Indiana	+		
Iowa	+		
Kansas	+		
Kentucky			+
Louisiana	+		
Maine	+		
Maryland			+
Massachusetts	+		
Michigan	+		
Minnesota	+		
Mississippi			+
Missouri			+
Montana			+
Nebraska		+	
Nevada			+
New Hampshire			+
New Jersey	+		
New Mexico	+		
New York	+		
North Carolina		+	
North Dakota			+
Ohio			+
Oklahoma		+	
Oregon	+		
Pennsylvania			+
Rhode Island	+		
South Carolina			+
South Dakota	+		
Tennessee			+
Texas	+		
Utah	+		

State	Permits	Prohibits*	No Statute
Vermont			+
Virginia			+
Washington	+		
West Virginia		+	
Wisconsin	+		
Wyoming			+

*Bans are no longer enforced.

Source: Data from *Bilingual Education: History, Politics, Theory, and Practice* by J. Crawford, 1989, Trenton, NJ: Crane Publishing Company, Inc., and from *Bilingual Education and Bilingual Special Education* by S. Fradd & W. Tikunoff, 1987, Boston, MA: College Hill Press.

Course of the Bilingual Education Act

Six years after its initial implementation, in 1974, the Bilingual Education Act was reauthorized with full support from the federal government. The law was amended to require schools receiving grants to include instruction in the children's native language and culture to "the extent necessary to allow a child to progress effectively through the education system" (Crawford, 1989, p. 37). Support for a maintenance program was short-lived, however, for the results of the AIR studies (Danoff et al., 1977, 1978) had demonstrated that the programs were not promoting the acquisition of English and that the maintenance approach contributed to isolation and segregation of students. Congress amended the Bilingual Education Act in 1978 to support the transitional method only. In 1978, the target population to receive support from bilingual education included those students who would be considered of limited proficiency in English in any combination of the four processes (i.e., understanding, speaking, reading, and writing). To avoid segregation, the law required a classroom composition of a 60:40 ratio of monolingual English-speaking students to second-language learners.

In 1981, Bell, who had issued the Remedies only 6 years earlier, stated, "Instruction is state and local responsibility . . . we will protect the rights of children who do not speak English well, but will do so by permitting school districts to use any way that has been successful" (Crawford, 1989, p. 42). The repeated lack of enforcement of specific bilingual programs and an increasingly diverse linguistic and cultural population in the schools seemed to have ignited, once again, a greater sense of nationalism. Currently, bilingual education is viewed only as an alternative teaching approach for LEP students. It no longer serves to promote and enhance literacy in two languages.

Senator Sam Hayakawa presented a legislative initiative in 1981, declaring English the official language of the United States. The bill died in the 98th Congress, but new versions have appeared at each subsequent Congress. The English Language Amendment (ELA) to the Constitution would declare English the official language in any given state and, ultimately, in the nation, if two-thirds of the states passed such legislation. The ELA bills presently pending in Congress designate English as the official language of the United States, but implementation is left to Congress. Thus far, 17 states have designated English as their official language (Table 6-2). Other states have bills pending.

The impact of the state laws has been primarily symbolic, as federal mandates related to issues such as civil rights, equal opportunity, affirmative action, and bilingual education supersede state laws. Further details on the pros and cons of the ELA, as well as the implications for the speech-language clinician, are presented in Appendix 6-A.

Table 6-2 Official Language States: 1990

State	Year	Legislation
Alabama	1990	Constitutional Amendment
Arkansas	1987	Statute
California	1986	Constitutional Amendment
Colorado	1988	Constitutional Amendment
Florida	1988	Constitutional Amendment
Georgia	1986	Resolution
Hawaii*	1978	Constitutional Amendment
Illinois	1969	Statute
Indiana	1984	Statute
Kentucky	1984	Statute
Mississippi	1987	Statute
Nebraska	1923	Constitutional Amendment
North Carolina	1987	Statute
North Dakota	1987	Statute
South Carolina	1987	Statute
Tennessee	1984	Statute
Virginia	1981	Statute

*Officially bilingual—Native Hawaiian and English as coequal languages.

Source: From *English Only Legislation in Multicultural America: A State and Federal Update* by the Mexican American Legal Defense and Educational Fund and the Joint National Committee for Languages, 1990, Washington, D.C.: Joint National Committee for Languages.

OUTCOMES OF BILINGUAL EDUCATION

The Debate: Programs That Do and Do Not Work

Contrary to common belief, bilingual education was not instituted to promote bilingualism. As Hakuta (1986) stated, "It gives some measure of official public status to the political struggle of language minorities, primarily Hispanics" (p. 191). The phrase *bilingual education* implies that students will receive their education in two languages. Of 1.7 million LEP students aged 5 to 14, however, O'Malley (1982) found that only 23% were in bilingual programs. The others were in English-only classrooms with ESL instruction (11%) or remedial English instruction (66%). The National Clearinghouse for Bilingual Education (1985) indicated that a very negligible proportion of schools offer continued instruction in the native language of bilingual students. In many ways, instead of promoting bilingualism and biculturalism, greater emphasis has been placed on mainstreaming. With Hispanics, for example, the children's language proficiency is switched from monolingual Spanish to monolingual English as rapidly as possible. Thus, becoming bilingual is essentially bypassed (see Figure 2-2).

The issue of bilingual education continues to be a source of controversy, despite evidence that it may be effective when implemented appropriately. The controversy was initiated following the release of the AIR studies (Danoff et al., 1977, 1978) and the reports of Baker and de Kanter (1983), indicating that bilingual education had a negative impact on the academic achievement of Hispanic LEP students. A careful analysis of the reports reveals that their conclusions were based on a heterogeneous group of programs, however. For example, the AIR studies involved 38 programs and more than 7,000 students in 150 schools. The reading and mathematics scores of elementary school-aged children enrolled in bilingual programs were compared with the scores of others who were not attending a bilingual program. Baker and de Kanter reviewed 300 studies, half of which were primary evaluations of actual programs. The programs varied in many aspects, from their philosophy toward bilingual education to actual instructional methodology. One principal conclusion of these studies and reports was that there is insufficient evidence to recommend a maintenance approach and, because students were isolated from the mainstream in that approach, a transitional method was preferable. Also, the researchers advocated more local control by the school districts. These suggestions matched the political trends of the late 1970s and early 1980s, which emphasized more local government control.

On the basis of a meta-analysis, Willig (1985) challenged the conclusions of the reports. This statistical analysis accounted for 183 variables that the previous studies had not considered, such as student and teacher characteristics, methods of instruction, and language of the achievement test. Willig found small to moderate differences among the students' achievements that favored bilingual instruction. Furthermore, she found that, in the AIR studies, as many as two-thirds of the students who were in the monolingual classrooms (comparison groups) had previously been in bilingual programs. Thus, in fact, the students in monolingual classrooms had received instruction in Spanish and were outperforming their counterparts whose exposure to English was still minimal. Subsequently, the statistical methodology of Willig's study was criticized. For example, Willig had used averaging techniques by which mean effect sizes, or differences between programs that were too small to be statistically significant, were combined. In fact, the results of the AIR studies (Danoff et al., 1977, 1978) and the reports of Baker and De Kanter (1983) based themselves more on the design of the studies reviewed than they did reflect the true characteristics of the programs analyzed (Crawford, 1989, p. 94). As Hakuta (1986) said, "The outcome of a study depends on how bilingualism is defined and what methodology is used" (p. 41).

This research debate highlights the importance of defining terms correctly and choosing appropriate designs to confirm or reject any given hypotheses. Nevertheless, there is evidence that bilingual programs can enhance students' language and academic performance in English, if adequately implemented. One of the positive outcomes of studies such as the AIR studies and Baker and de Kanter reports is that they stressed the lack of consistency in the definition and implementation of bilingual education programs.

Case Studies Project

The California State Department of Education undertook a project to improve school practices rather than to demonstrate the effectiveness of bilingual education. Thus, for example, there were no comparison groups. The instructional model was based on information on second-language acquisition research (Office of Bilingual Bicultural Education, California State Department of Education, 1981). The researchers had devised five important principles:

1. The development of both the native language and English should have a positive impact on academic achievement.
2. Language proficiency needs should be reflected in both BICS and CALP.
3. Improvement of the native language should have positive effects on the acquisition of oral and written skills in the second language (i.e., teachers should avoid mixing English and the native language during instruction).
4. Sufficient comprehensible input should be offered in English.
5. Attention should be given to the status of the students and their interaction with teachers and other students.

Of 134 schools initially identified as candidates for the project, 5 were selected. The project was implemented following a specific schedule (Table 6-3).

Certain subjects were taught in Spanish; others, in sheltered English (i.e., language tailored to the students' proficiency) or mainstream English. Further language teaching was done through content areas. The students were gradually integrated with mainstream English-speaking students after their skills were evaluated with a variety of instruments, including the California Test of Basic Skills (CTBS), to assess academic skills and a test of conversational English, the Student Oral Language Observation Matrix (SOLOM). In most cases, bilingual teacher shortages were accommodated by language grouping. Although budgetary prob-

Table 6-3 The Case-Studies Curriculum Model

Phase	Spanish	Sheltered English	Mainstream English
I. Non-English–Proficient (K–grade 1)* (SOLOM 5–11)	Language Arts Mathematics Science/Health Social Studies	ESL	Art Music Physical Education
II. Limited-English–Proficient (grades 2–3)* (SOLOM 12–18)	Language Arts Social Studies	ESL Mathematics Science/Health	Art Music Physical Education
III. Limited-English–Proficient (grades 3–4)* (SOLOM 19–25)	Language Arts	Transitional Language Arts Social Studies	Art Music Physical Education Mathematics Science/Health
IV. Fully-English–Proficient (grades 4–6)* (SOLOM 25+)	Language Arts (extended Spanish activities)		Art Music Physical Education Mathematics Science/Health Social Studies Language Arts

*Typical grade level for each phase.

Source: From *Bilingual Education: History, Politics, Theory, and Practice* (p. 133) by J. Crawford, 1989, Trenton, NJ: Crane Publishing Company. Copyright 1989 by Crane Publishing Company. Reprinted by permission of James Crawford.

lems made it necessary to discontinue program funding after 3 years, the researchers in charge of the program design were able to provide strong evidence of significant positive correlations between initial Spanish reading proficiency and English reading proficiency 2 years into the program (Tempes, 1986). Thus, those
students who had a good foundation in Spanish could successfully perform English literacy-based activities.

Successful Bilingual Programs

Krashen and Biber (1988) analyzed the effectiveness of seven bilingual programs in California selected on the basis of three criteria: (1) translation was not
used when the curriculum was taught in the first language; (2) the development of
literacy in the first language was enhanced; and (3) there was ample opportunity
for comprehensible input in English. Although the results must be evaluated with
care because the study was not longitudinal, the researchers demonstrated that the
LEP students in these programs ultimately outperformed other LEP students. On
the average, it took at least 3 years for students to attain reading skills in English at
the 50th percentile of the English-speaking monolingual group. It was concluded
that "children who participate in properly designed bilingual programs acquire
English rapidly. They typically achieve at grade level norms for English and math
after three to five years. Furthermore, bilingual education in fact may be the best
English program we have" (Krashen & Biber, 1988, p. 63).

Table 6-4 summarizes aspects of the Canadian immersion programs, transitional programs, and the more recent types of programs implemented in the United
States, such as the case studies and the two-way bilingual programs. The latter
programs are versions of transitional programs, but have six additional features.

1. The length of the program should be 4 to 6 years.
2. Instruction is adjusted to the students' level.
3. Oral language development is done in conjunction with academic subjects.
4. Languages are separated during instruction.
5. Students have opportunities to interact with native speakers.
6. There should be home-school collaboration to reinforce the native language and enhance the need for success in academic subjects. (Crawford,
   1989, p. 167)

Such programs are in operation in California, New York, and Massachusetts. One
fundamental factor differentiating these programs from the immersion programs
in Canada is that the latter have the advantage of greater community support for
bilingualism.

It is evident that the debate over bilingual education as an effective method to

Table 6-4 Description of Bilingual Programs

Program	Government Policy	Parents' Status and Views	Teachers	Curriculum
Immersion in Canada	Enhancement of bilingualism and multiculturalism Promotion of international economic advantage	Additive—Middle class— Parents initiate and support the program. Students' skills in both languages are valued.	All teachers are bilingual. Have the support from the community and administrators. Are offered a uniform preparation.	Students are expected to use both languages. All students begin at the same level of L2. Literacy in both languages is emphasized. Both languages have the same value. No real transition in programs.
Transitional programs	No clear policy Bilingualism is not viewed as an advantage	Programs are viewed as remedial in nature. Generally, bilingualism may be considered as an advantage but is difficult to maintain.	Only some teachers are bilingual. May have community and administrators' support. Training institutions offer great variation in preparation. Requires large numbers of bilingual teachers. Many rely on teacher aides.	Use of L1 until L2 is mastered. Students need to catch up to function in an all-English curriculum. Transition to English is often made when surface language skills (BICS) are judged adequate. Some other programs may transition students when sufficient (CALP) skills are acquired.
Other models in the U.S.	Flexibility at the local level Bilingualism is viewed as an advantage	Socioeconomic status is generally low. Parents' participation is generally promoted but in actuality parents have little to say. *There may be exceptions, however.*	Only some teachers are bilingual. May have community and administrators' support. Training institutions offer great variation in preparation. Requires fewer bilingual teachers. Use of language grouping. More emphasis on teacher cooperation.	Use of L1 and L2 is acquired. L1 is valued. Provision is made for uniformity in language instruction. Transition to English is done only when student has higher language skills in L1 (CALP).

Note: L1, first language; L2, second language.

Source: From *Bilingual Education and Bilingual Special Education: A Guide for Administrators* (p. 36) by S.H. Fradd and W.J. Tikunoff, 1987, Austin, TX: PRO-ED. Copyright 1987 by PRO-ED. Adapted by permission.

instruct language minority students has yet to be settled. This is a problem evident not only in the United States, but also in other countries throughout the world where the number of language minority students is steadily increasing. The differences noted in outcomes from program to program are subject to many methodological variables, as well as to individual instructional and learner differences.

Instructional Variables

The heterogeneous outcomes of the different research studies stem in part from the diverse teaching methodologies used within districts, schools, and even classrooms in bilingual instruction. Even though a program may be referred to as bilingual, the way and the extent to which the two languages are used vary considerably. In the alternate day or altering times model, students are introduced to the same material once in English and again in Spanish on different days; a modification of this approach is the use of each language during separate blocks of time within the same day. In the preview-review model, a lesson is introduced in the first language, then explained in the second language, and subsequently summarized in the first language. In both these models, reading is taught in the stronger language first. The concurrent translation model involves presenting the information in one language and then translating it into the other. Students may have limited incentive to learn the second language, however, because translation is offered in their dominant language. As a result, concurrent translation is in great disfavor.

Each type of program may be supplemented with ESL instruction, which can vary in method from an emphasis on the conscious understanding of the formal rules of grammar to a more conversational approach (Krashen, 1981). Often, programs that are essentially conducted in English, commonly referred to as sink-or-swim programs, are inappropriately called bilingual simply because they are supplemented with ESL instruction. The currently favored transitional programs may also include additional ESL instruction. At first glance, it may appear that teaching more English will be beneficial to the students. Some well designed studies in which researchers have compared different teaching models, such as the Santa Fe Bilingual Program (Leyba, 1978) and the Direct ESL-Bilingual Comparison Study (Legarreta, 1979), suggest that separating times for instruction in each language and eventually giving equal time to each language may be the best bilingual teaching method.

In the immersion programs as they exist in Canada, students learn the second language (French) from the start. Beginning with second grade, the first language (English) is introduced for increasingly longer periods. The particular reasons for the lack of success of these programs in the United States are difficult to identify, although the emphasis on linguistic and cultural assimilation in the U.S. versions of the program may be a factor (Crawford, 1989, p. 70; Fradd & Tikunoff, 1987, p. 119). The U.S. Department of Education commissioned a study on the effectiveness of immersion programs in the mid-1980s. A total of nine districts from states with large Hispanic populations (i.e., California, Texas, Florida, New York, and New Jersey) participated in the longitudinal project, which lasted 8 years, from 1983 to 1991. Its purpose was to compare the effectiveness of Spanish-English transitional bilingual education programs (both early and late exit) with immersion programs from kindergarten through sixth grade. The performance of 2,000 Spanish-English bilingual students in academics and language in English was compared with that of their English-speaking monolingual peers. Other variables, such as teaching methodology and teacher characteristics, were also analyzed. In the immersion program, all instruction was in English, and language development was taught through the various subjects. In the early exit transitional programs, students received instruction in their native language for 30 to 60 minutes a day; the teachers phased out this instruction by second grade. In the late exit transitional programs, students received 40% of their instruction in Spanish through the sixth grade.

In all three programs (i.e., early and late exit transitional programs and the immersion program), LEP students advanced in their language and academic skills in English as fast or faster than did students in the mainstream. A great majority of LEP students were not ready for total mainstreaming until fourth grade or later, although providing instruction in the students' primary language (Spanish) did not slow down their progress in gaining language or academic skills in English (Ramírez, 1991). The outcomes of studies such as this one indicate that the best program options seem to be "well founded" bilingual programs.

Individual Learner Differences

Several individual factors, such as personal learning strategies, social skills, and attitude toward the first and second languages, may affect the learning of a second language in a classroom setting. Because of the overlap between variables that play a role in the acquisition of the second language, all variables should be taken into account when evaluating the success or failure of a bilingual program.

Limited English Proficiency vs. Fluency

It is difficult to define the terms *limited English proficiency* and *fluency* because of varying interpretations of the terms. Most often, districts base their definitions on the results of language proficiency tests (available only in Enlish and Spanish), such as the Bilingual Syntax Measure (BSM, Level I and II; Burt, Dulay, & Hernández-Chávez, 1975, 1980), Idea Language Proficiency Test (IPT, Levels I and II; Ballard & Tighe, 1980, 1982, 1983, 1987), the Language Assessment

Scales (LAS, Levels I and II; De Avila & Duncan, 1977, 1979, 1983), or the Language Assessment Battery (LAB; Board of Education of the City of New York, 1976). All these instruments assess the students' BICS; some, their CALP. The LAB assesses reading and writing skills as well. In practice, the tests are often administered in English only, thus sometimes identifying a student as limited in English proficiency without due information of the student's performance in Spanish.

These same tests are used to determine when students from bilingual programs should enter English-only programs. Frequently, students are enrolled in English-only programs without sufficient documentation that they will be able to learn academic subjects through English only. Furthermore, LEP students may have varying degrees of proficiency in their native language, but this information is not readily available. A knowledge of the level of a student's skills in the native language would be valuable in predicting the likelihood of that student's successful acquisition of the second language, however (Krashen & Biber, 1988; Legarreta, 1979; Leyba, 1978; Tempes, 1986).

Learning Strategies

In 1987, the New York State Board of Regents recommended that teachers become more aware of the effects of different cultural backgrounds on communication and learning. A *Harvard Education Letter* contained the comment that "most educators agree that students approach learning in many different ways and that teachers need to take these differences into account in developing their instructional strategies" (cited in Green, 1989, p. 141). For example, experience plays an important role in recall, as demonstrated by Steffensen, Joag-Dev, and Anderson (1979), who asked university students to read descriptions of weddings in the United States and India. Students from each country could recall more details if the weddings had taken place in their native country. In addition to background information, knowing the rules of a learning situation enhances performance. Durán (1989) indicated that Hispanic students and other minority students' learning ability depends on "knowing certain rules such as when and how to respond to teachers' questions, how to ask for clarifications of information and all in all, how to use language in the activities of a classroom" (p. 155).

The strategies that have been identified in the second-language acquisition and learning process can be divided into two main categories: (1) cognitive strategies that allow the learner to form relationships between linguistic forms and their meaning and (2) metacognitive strategies that allow the learner to monitor and evaluate this process (O'Malley, 1985; Wong Fillmore & Valadez, 1986). There are many individual differences in the use of these two strategies, however. Individual aptitude skills (e.g., verbal memory, auditory perception, pattern recognition), as well as various socially based variables (e.g., personality type, social style, motivation), play a role in influencing these strategies. Often, because of these different personal learning strategies, there is variability in learning a second language among students who have been exposed to the same, very effective teaching strategies. Thus, linguistic, cognitive, and social processes are intimately linked (Wong Fillmore, 1991).

Role of Social Skills

All language learners need social skills that will enable them to initiate and sustain conversations. As Wong Fillmore and Valadez (1986) indicated, language acquisition depends on many socially related factors, such as early experiences, differences in personality, and degree of talkativeness among learners. Some of these factors (e.g., talkativeness) have been found to be of secondary importance for successful language learning, however (Saville-Troike, 1983; Strong, 1982). The proportion of native speakers of the target language in the classroom affects the learning process. In classrooms where there are more learners than natives, peer contact may not be as beneficial; the students are likely to practice their first language rather than the second language. Other characteristics, such as the ability to determine the patterns of language and the willingness to practice, are also important. Some students are reluctant to practice for fear of being wrong; consequently, they practice the language less. These observations are applicable to students of all ages.

Attitude toward the Languages

The attitudes of the learner and the community toward the first and second languages are crucial. In Canada, the attitude toward bilingualism is generally additive; learning another language is viewed for the most part as positive. In the United States, however, bilingualism is not always regarded as an asset; most of the bilingual programs are essentially compensatory in nature. A few programs offer native language instruction for only a few years and then require students to switch to English instruction exclusively. This phenomenon often causes language loss and may diminish communication between parents and children. Unfortunately, too many people in this society regard those who maintain a language other than English as "outsiders." "Bilingualism is not valued here" (Wong Fillmore & Valadez, 1986, p. 678). Yet, many businesses and corporations spend time and money teaching some of their employees a second language to facilitate transactions with officials from other countries. It can almost be said that there is tolerance, but not direct support, for the use of other languages.

Other Factors

One last factor to be taken into account in language acquisition and learning is length of stay in the host country. There appears to be no correlation between the length of residence and language proficiency. Some people who have resided in the United States for several years are still not proficient in English. Others may be new immigrants who are ready to be mainstreamed in 2 years or less. The amount and type of exposure to the second language, as well as the opportunities to interact with native speakers of English or more fluent speakers of the second language, play a significant role in developing language proficiency.

IMPLICATIONS OF BILINGUAL EDUCATION

Effect on Cognitive Development

The relationship between cognitive development and bilingualism has been measured by means of a diversity of procedures. Some researchers have analyzed the subjects' performance on traditional intelligence tests of linguistic and general intellectual skills, while others have focused on tests of divergent thinking, academic performance, and metalinguistic awareness (Swain & Cummins, 1982). Thus, the outcome of two similar studies may vary as a result of the nature of the tasks considered.

Negative Outcomes

In early studies carried out in the 1920s and 1930s with a variety of language combinations (Saer, 1924; Smith, 1923; Smith, 1931, 1939; Yoshioka, 1929), it was concluded that bilingualism had a negative impact on intellectual ability. For example, Goodenough (1926) concluded that the more a foreign language was spoken in the home, the less intelligent the child. As a corollary, she concluded that the child's maintenance of the primary language reflected lower intellectual ability altogether. Such studies were based on inappropriate methodology, however, perhaps partly because testing intellectual skills was a relatively new construct in the 1920s and 1930s. In addition, control of some variables was inappropriate. Subjects were tested in their second language, which was their weaker language, and their length of residence in the United States was not taken into account. Also, the researchers did not consider attitudes, experience with testing, and other cultural variables.

Early studies were not designed carefully enough to determine the impact of bilingualism on different measures of cognitive ability. The main focus of the research centered on whether the differences among individuals and groups reflected heredity or experience, not whether the measures were adequate and equivalent for all individuals tested (Hakuta, 1986). Even today, as Figueroa (1989) pointed out, psychologists are still debating how best to interpret results of intelligence tests on bilingual students—even when results of performance in both languages are available. As he noted, "Tests for non-English speakers in the process of acquiring English are yet to appear" (p. 148). To demonstrate that bilingualism does indeed have a positive impact on intellectual ability, the subject must have reached a certain *threshold* of performance in both languages "in order to avoid cognitive deficits and allow the potentially beneficial aspects of becoming bilingual to influence cognitive growth" (Cummins, 1984, p. 107). Recently, this theory has been somewhat revised to indicate that a certain level of dual language proficiency is necessary before bilingualism can be shown to have a positive effect on the performance of a specific cognitive-type task (Díaz & Klingler, 1991). Therefore, in research to correlate bilingualism and cognitive performance, it is important to control variables such as comparability across groups for IQ, socioeconomic status, and the level of proficiency in both languages.

Positive Outcomes

The Canadian studies reported by Peal and Lambert (1962) were the first to show that bilingualism has a positive outcome on different measures of cognitive development. Even when studies indicate that bilingualism has a positive impact on cognitive and intellectual functioning, however, the subjects' proficiency in two languages is not necessarily the only reason. Other factors, such as attitude, motivation to learn the language, and the community's attitude toward bilingualism, are also important.

Díaz (1983), as well as Swain and Cummins (1982), noted that several researchers have reported correlations between bilingualism and different measures of cognitive/intellectual and linguistic ability. Such measures involved (1) use of more complex sentence structures (Barik & Swain, 1978; Ekstrand, 1978); (2) metalinguistic awareness, including the ability to detect ambiguity in sentences or different meanings of words (Ben-Zeev, 1977; Galambos & Hakuta, 1988); or (3) metacommunicative abilities, such as efficiently explaining rules to listeners, some of whom were blindfolded (Genesee, Tucker, & Lambert, 1976), or identifying facial expressions with greater accuracy (Bain & Yu, 1978). Although most of the studies that have reflected favorably on bilingualism were conducted under conditions in which bilingualism was considered an asset, more recent studies have yielded positive results even in situations that could be considered subtractive. Specifically, Hakuta and Díaz (1985), and Galambos and Hakuta (1988), found in longitudinal studies that bilingualism was positively correlated with the performance of Puerto Rican students on the Raven (1938, 1947) test, a nonverbal test. The students' performance on metalinguistic tasks that required detecting ambiguities in words indicated that students were best able to perform the task when they had reached a certain level of equal proficiency in the two languages. The threshold previously mentioned was valid only for one certain level of bilingual ability. Beyond a certain proficiency level in the two languages, the effect was not as significant.

Language Transfer and Learning

Transfers from one language to another are so obvious that "almost no empirical studies have been conducted to understand the characteristics or even to demonstrate the existence of the transfer of skills" (Hakuta, 1986, p. 218). Studies that validate this assumption include those conducted by Genesee, Hamers, Lambert, Mononen, Seitz, and Starck (1978); Lambert and Tucker (1972); and Swain (1978).

The concept of transfer is related to the hypothesis developed by Cummins (1981, 1984) that there is a common underlying proficiency between two languages. For example, while learning to read in Spanish, the student not only develops skills in Spanish, but also acquires a deeper conceptual and linguistic proficiency that influences the development of English literacy and general academic skills. The metaphor of the "dual iceberg" illustrates this concept (Figure 6-1; Cummins, 1984, p. 143). The two languages both express certain functions, such as sharing information, requesting, denying, predicting, or hypothesizing, for example. Both languages may also include certain concepts, such as liberty, honesty, freedom, sadness, and happiness. These similarities can be described as a common underlying proficiency. The two languages may differ in the sound system and word order, or their surface features, however.

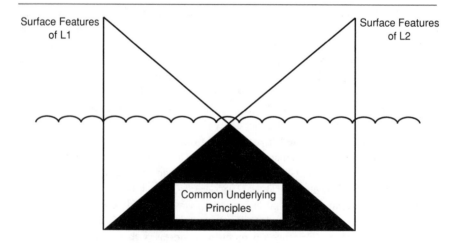

Figure 6-1 Linguistic Interdependence Model. L1, first language; L2, second language. *Source:* From *Empowering Minority Students* (p. 45) by J. Cummins, 1989, Sacramento, CA: California Association for Bilingual Education. Copyright 1989 by the California Association for Bilingual Education. Reprinted by permission.

Although there are data to support the concept of transfer, information is still insufficient to determine the specific school-related skills that transfer most easily and their relationship to language competence (Hakuta, 1986). Students are known to transfer to reading in English much more rapidly if they have practiced reading in their native language so that they better understand the vocabulary included in the text, however. Table 6-5 lists reading skills that are readily transferred from one language to the other. The majority of skills are related to thinking skills, such as getting the main idea, inferencing, or understanding cause and effect (Thonis, 1981, pp. 152–153).

Some academic skills may transfer across languages faster than do others, but no specific sequence has yet been determined. In general, research indicates that high performance in one language readily transfers to the other. This has been documented in both oral and written language (Cummins, 1991). Transfer studies with elementary school-aged Hispanic children have been done on the subjects of academic proficiency (González, 1986; Hakuta & Díaz, 1985; Mace-Matluck & Hoover, 1986; Ramírez, 1985), written skills (Carlisle, 1986), and narrative retelling skills (Goldman, 1985). Salgado (1988) and Guerra (1984) have conducted similar studies with adults.

The concept of transfer is especially important in planning interventions for bilingual students with language or learning disabilities. Very few studies document these students' progress in two languages. The studies that Bruck (1978, 1982) carried out in Canada with immersion students indicated that even language-disordered students could progress in two languages (French and English). Although their progress in each language was slower than that of other students enrolled in immersion programs, they performed as well in English as did language-disordered students who were transferred to monolingual schools. Thus, it appears that, when programs are adequately planned, students with language or learning problems can benefit from learning in two languages. No comparable research has been carried out in the United States, however. Much remains to be done to identify appropriate teaching and learning strategies, as well as conditions that facilitate the transfer of skills across languages—both for normally developing bilingual children and for those who have language and learning problems.

In most cases, bilingual students receive native language support for approximately 3 years before they are transferred to an English monolingual program. This length of time may not be sufficient, however (Cummins, 1984; Krashen & Biber, 1988; Ramírez, 1991). As previously mentioned, LEP students may take 5 to 7 years to attain CALP skills comparable to those of their English-speaking monolingual peers. Even so, many bilingual students are judged ready to learn reading in English when they still have limited BICS in English and limited CALP skills in their own language.

Table 6-5 Cross-Linguistic Transfer of Reading Skills (Thonis, 1981)

	Language—Specific Skill Transfer	Language—General Skill Transfer
Sensory-Motor Transfer		
Visual Skills:		
Figure-ground		X
Attention to detail		X
Perception	X	X
Discrimination	X	X
Memory	X	
Sequencing		X
Eye-hand coordination		X
Fine muscle control		X
Auditory Skills:		
Figure-ground		X
Perception	X	X
Discrimination	X	X
Memory	X	X
Sequencing		X
Spatial Skills:		
Left-to-right orientation	X	X
Top-to-bottom organization	X	X
Spatial integration		X
Writing System Transfer		
Alphabet	X	
Sound-symbol connections	X	
Capitalization	X	X
Punctuation	X	X
Spatial conventions	X	X
Principle and Generalization Transfer		
Understanding that print represents speech		X
Concepts of words, phrases, sentences, paragraphs		X
Comprehension as thinking		
main idea		X
sequence of ideas		X
supportive details		X
inferencing		X
predicting outcomes		X
drawing conclusions		X
seeing cause and effect		X
distinguishing fact from fantasy		X

Source: From *Schooling and Language Minority Students: A Theoretical Framework* (pp. 153–154) by the California State Department of Education, Office of Bilingual Bicultural Education, 1981, Los Angeles: Evaluation, Dissemination and Assessment Center, California State University. Copyright 1981 by California State University. Reprinted by permission.

Exit Bilingual Education Programs

Criteria for exit from bilingual programs vary from district to district, but the student should have at least sufficient oral language communication skills in English, as measured by the language proficiency tests mentioned earlier (BSM, IPT, LAS, LAB) and indicated by teachers' observations, to respond to questions based on lessons presented orally and to ask clarification questions. The student should also be able to read at grade level in Spanish and be able to comprehend text by (1) obtaining the main idea, (2) sequencing ideas, (3) answering inferencing and predicting questions, (4) drawing conclusions, (5) recognizing moods and emotions, (6) understanding cause and effect, and (7) distinguishing fact from fiction (Cummins, 1989; Thonis, 1981).

One of the unfortunate outcomes of learning to read in English without maintaining Spanish is that students may not be exposed to Spanish texts until junior or senior high school, at which time they may have lost experience and opportunities in using and reading their primary language. Some of these students may even have to "relearn" the language. A maintenance program would offer opportunities to nurture the first language while strengthening the second language.

BILINGUAL SPECIAL EDUCATION

Bilingual education has existed in the United States since the founding of the nation, whereas bilingual special education dates only from the early 1970s. Baca and Amato (1989) divided this new field of education into three periods: (1) from 1970 to 1975, an awareness period; (2) from 1975 to 1985, a program development phase; and (3) from 1985 to the present, program refinement and implementation stage. During the first period, a great deal of attention was given to serving second-language learners of English who had learning problems. During the second period, the emphasis was on biased testing and program development, resulting in the application of more appropriate measures when assessing the skills of LEP students. During the third period, there has been a greater focus on the implementation of appropriate programs for students who need both bilingual and special education services.

P.L. 94-142, Education for All Handicapped Children Act (1975), requires that students be tested for learning problems in their primary language, yet there are no specifications on the particular process to follow (Figueroa, Fradd, & Correa, 1989). The phrase *primary language* is often interpreted to mean the language that the students use in school. The simultaneous exposure of bilingual students to Spanish or primary language at school and/or at home is often ignored in the assessment process. This results in an incomplete profile of their linguistic and communicative competence. To date, two institutions, the University of California at Davis and the University of Texas at Austin, have received grants to investigate assessment and intervention issues regarding Spanish-English bilingual students with learning problems. Although located in two different states, both programs have reported similar findings regarding the assessment process.

1. Students are most frequently tested in English only. Scores on language proficiency tests in Spanish are not taken into account, and many of the students' English patterns are erroneously interpreted as the result of a language disorder rather than the process of second-language acquisition.
2. Because students are now classified as learning-disabled or communicatively handicapped, they are no longer placed in classes for the mentally retarded.
3. The background of the students is not considered in the assessment data, and home data are not collected.
4. The tests used to assess the students' abilities are uniform; that is, the same instruments are always used, regardless of the problem.
5. The likelihood of eligibility for special education increases when parents are born outside the United States.
6. More special education is suggested upon reevaluations.

Their findings regarding instructional issues were also similar.

1. Very few bilingual students who are referred for special education have received sufficient native language instruction. Even fewer receive primary language support when enrolled in special education programs.
2. Most referrals take place in the second and third grades. Often, students are referred on the basis of their inability to communicate effectively in English. As they do with mainstreamed students, teachers frequently focus on the students' use of language form (e.g., grammar, pronunciation) rather than on the students' ability to express thoughts and effectively convey information.
3. Programs are rarely modified to offer educational support in the primary language prior to referral for special education.
4. The Individualized Education Programs (IEPs) reflect a very limited attempt to serve the LEP students specifically.
5. In regard to bilingual special education classes, "the most effective ones resemble more the regular bilingual classroom (use of whole language, comprehensible input, cooperative learning and student empowerment) rather than the traditional behaviorist, task-analysis work sheet oriented special education classes" (Figueroa et al., 1989, p. 176).

Systematic documentation on which bilingual special education programs may work best is not yet available. Ruíz (1988) is currently investigating promising teaching strategies for bilingual learning-disabled students in a program that takes into account the students' sociocultural background and its effects on academics and second-language learning. The program includes a curriculum in a meaning-ful context in which the communicative purpose is clear, authentic, and related to the students' personal experiences (Ruíz, 1988). Other programs that have docu-mented successful teaching strategies with language learning-disabled Hispanic students are based on some of the same principles, but the programs have been used only with a relatively small population of students (Westby & Rouse, 1985; Willig & Swedo, 1986).

Recently, the Office of Educational Research and Improvement of the U.S. Department of Education has funded 18 different projects with various universi-ties and agencies throughout the country. The topics range widely, but include assessment and instructional issues for bilingual students. The results very likely will have an impact on determining best practices to work with bilingual students with language and learning disabilities. The projects are coordinated through the University of California at Santa Cruz ("Research Center," 1991).

LOOKING TOWARD THE FUTURE

There is no question that the public school system will continue to face chal-lenges as the U.S. population becomes more and more linguistically and culturally diverse. Bilingual education in this country may not be as successful as it could have been, however, because of the negative attitude toward bilingualism and its implications for the unity of the nation (Hakuta, 1986; Hakuta & García, 1989). Furthermore, economic and political realities play an important role in determin-ing the future of bilingual programs. Even though bilingual education legislation in California has been withheld, numerous bilingual model programs remain in the state (Olsen, 1989). Other successful programs are operating in other parts of the United States, such as Washington, DC, and Arlington, Virginia. The latest linguistic phenomenon, however, is that first languages are quickly replaced by the majority language in the United States (Hakuta, 1986; Veltman, 1988).

Because bilingualism encompasses so many issues—linguistic, cognitive, edu-cational, anthropological, political, and social—it is important that experts in these different fields work collaboratively in their research efforts (Hakuta & García, 1989). It is also crucial that communication between researchers and prac-titioners increase. It can be hoped that the project funded through the University of Santa Cruz in California will achieve this end.

Lack of language skills on the part of U.S. citizens has occasionally hurt their business and even political image. It is time to view bilingualism as an additive rather than subtractive phenomenon. As Crawford (1989) said, "Perhaps some-day, to become Americanized will no longer mean to be monolingual English" (p. 173).

RECOMMENDATIONS FOR SPEECH-LANGUAGE CLINICIANS

Given the ethnic, cultural, and linguistic diversity of the United States, it is difficult for clinicians to develop an in-depth knowledge of each student's language, cultural history, and social background. It is possible to develop cross-cultural communicative competence to promote a warm and supporting environment for all students, however. Excellence in the delivery of speech, language, and hearing services requires a culturally heterogeneous cadre of professionals who are knowledgeable and understanding of related social, linguistic, cultural, educational, and economic factors. As clinicians work with members of specific groups, their understanding and knowledge of those individuals will increase. Clinicians should be challenged with the following questions (Banks, 1990; Banks, Cortés, Gay, García, & Ochoa, 1976).

- Am I prepared to assess and work with the multicultural clients who have various language learning disabilities?
- Have I updated my knowledge and skills with regard to issues of diversity?
- How do I encourage positive interaction between myself and students?
- How do my therapy strategies reflect and accommodate the learning styles of the diverse students?

Although many college and university programs claim that they are addressing cultural training issues, many remain ethnocentric in nature. The importance of considering the affective domain of language minority students and their need to maintain their own cultural identity may not be sufficiently stressed. In order to shift to an attitude that views multiculturalism in a positive light, professionals must enhance and embrace diversity, as well as endorse a shifting of paradigms (Cheng, 1990). Accepting the paradigm shift really means that clinicians must learn about, understand, and respect their culturally diverse students. They must talk with them about their experiences and present a curriculum that is relevant, valid, and realistic (Hilliard, 1990). Instead of looking at the diverse patterns of writing and speaking as deficiencies, clinicians can be enriched by different modes of communicating and different ways with words in sociocultural diversity (Heath, 1983). Thus, rather than focusing on deficiencies, it is necessary to identify strengths and to work based on those strengths. Giving all students the same assessment and therapy is equality; however, they may not all learn well. Equity means giving students what they need in order to achieve equally well.

As we approach an increasingly multiracial and multiethnic twenty-first century, higher education must play an important role in educating and training this and future generations of American students—white and black, yellow and brown, immigrant and nonimmigrant—if we are to continue to meet the human capital needs that our technologically advanced society demands (Oliver & Johnson, 1988).

So, perhaps we can say, "Hablamos los dos" rather than "I speak English, y Ud. habla español."

REFERENCES

Allen, W.R. (1987, May/June). Black colleges vs. white colleges: The fork in the road for Black students. *Change,* pp. 25–34.

Ambert, A.N., & Meléndez, S.E. (1985). *Bilingual education: A sourcebook.* New York: Garland Publishing.

Baca, L., & Amato, C. (1989). Bilingual special education: Training issues. *Exceptional Children, 56,* 168–173.

Bain, B.C., & Yu, A. (1978). Toward an integration of Piaget and Vygosky: A cross-cultural replication (France, Germany, Canada) concerning cognitive consequences of bilinguality. In M. Paradis (Ed.), *Aspects of bilingualism.* Columbia, SC: Hornbeam Press.

Baker, K.A., & de Kanter, A.A. (Eds.). (1983). *Bilingual education: A reappraisal of federal policy.* Lexington, MA: Lexington Books.

*Ballard, W., & Tighe, P. (Eds.). (1980, 1982, 1983, 1987). *Idea oral language proficiency test.* Brea, CA: Ballard and Tighe.

Banks, J.A. (1990). *Transforming the curriculum.* Conference on Diversity. Oakland, CA: California Teacher Credentialing Commission.

Banks, J.A., Cortés, C.E., Gay, G., García, R., & Ochoa, A.S. (1976). *Curriculum guidelines for multiethnic education.* Washington, DC: National Council for the Social Studies.

Barik, H.C., & Swain, M. (1978). Evaluation of a French immersion program: The Ottawa study through grade five. *Canadian Journal of Behavioural Science, 10,* 192–201.

Ben-Zeev, S. (1977). The influence of bilingualism on cognitive development and cognitive strategy. *Child Development, 48,* 1009–1018.

Board of Education of the City of New York. (1976). *Language assessment battery.* Brooklyn, NY: OREA Scan Center.

Bruck, M. (1978). The suitability of early French immersion programs for the language disabled child. *Canadian Journal of Education, 3,* 51–72.

Bruck, M. (1982). Language impaired children's performance in an additive bilingual education program. *Applied Psycholinguistics, 3,* 45–60.

*Burt, M.K., Dulay, H., & Hernández-Chávez, E. (1975, 1980). *Bilingual syntax measure: Level I and level II.* San Francisco: The Psychological Corporation.

*Multiple dates indicate publication of English and Spanish versions of different levels of the test.

California test of basic skills (CTBS). Monterey, CA: CTB/McGraw Hill.

Carlisle, R.S. (1986). The writing of Anglo and Hispanic fourth and sixth graders in regular, submersion, and bilingual programs. (Doctoral dissertation, University of Illinois at Urbana-Champaign). *Dissertation Abstracts International, 47,* 1987.

Cheng, L.L. (1990). Recognizing diversity. *American Behavioral Scientist, 34*(2), 263–278.

Collison, M.N. (1988). Neglect of minorities seen jeopardizing future prosperity. *Chronicle of Higher Education, 34,* A1.

Crawford, J. (1989). *Bilingual education: History, politics, theory and practice.* Trenton, NJ: Crane Publishing.

Cummins, J. (1981). The role of primary language development in promoting educational success for language minority students. In Office of Bilingual Bicultural Education, California State Department of Education (Ed.), *Schooling and language minority students: A theoretical framework* (pp. 3–49). Los Angeles: Evaluation, Dissemination and Assessment Center, California State University.

Cummins, J. (1984). *Bilingualism and special education: Issues in assessment and pedagogy.* Clevedon, England: Multilingual Matters.

Cummins, J. (1989). *Empowering minority students.* Sacramento: California Association for Bilingual Education.

Cummins, J. (1991). Interdependence of first- and second-language proficiency. In E. Bialystok (Ed.), *Language processing in bilingual children* (pp. 70–89). New York: Cambridge University Press

Danoff, M.N., Coles, G.J., McLaughlin, D.H., & Reynolds, D.J. (1977, 1978). *Evaluation of the impact of ESEA Title VII Spanish/English bilingual education program* (Vols 1–3). Palo Alto: American Institutes of Research.

*De Avila, E., & Duncan, S. (1977, 1979, 1983). *Language assessment scales.* Monterey, CA: McGraw-Hill.

Diana v. California State Board of Education. (1970). No. C-70-37, U.S. District Court of Northern California.

Díaz, R. (1983). Thought and two languages: The impact of bilingualism on cognitive development. *Review of Research in Education, 10,* 23.

Díaz, R., & Klingler, C. (1991). Towards an explanatory model of the interaction between bilingualism and cognitive development. In E. Bialystok (Ed.), *Language processing in bilingual children* (pp. 167–192). New York: Cambridge University Press.

Durán, R. (1989). Assessment and instruction of at-risk Hispanic students. *Exceptional Children, 56,* 154–159.

Ekstrand, L.H. (1978). *Bilingual and bicultural adaptation.* Unpublished doctoral dissertation, University of Stockholm.

Figueroa, R.A. (1989). Psychological testing on linguistic-minority students: Knowledge, gaps and regulations. *Exceptional Children, 56,* 145–152.

Figueroa, R.A., Fradd, S.H., & Correa, V.I. (1989). Bilingual special education and this special issue. *Exceptional Children, 56,* 174–178.

Fradd, S.H., & Tikunoff, W.J. (1987). *Bilingual education and bilingual special education: A guide for administrators.* Boston: College Hill Press.

Galambos, S.J., & Hakuta, K. (1988). Subject-specific and task-specific characteristics of metalinguistic awareness in bilingual children. *Applied Psycholinguistics, 9,* 141–162.

Genesee, F., Hamers, J., Lambert, E., Mononen, L., Seitz, M., & Starck, R. (1978). Language processing in bilinguals. *Brain and Language, 5,* 1–12.

Genesee, F., Tucker, G.R., & Lambert, W.E. (1976). Communication skills of bilingual children. *Child
Development, 46,* 1010–1014.

Goldman, S.R. (1985). *Utilization of knowledge acquired through the first language in comprehending
a second language: Narrative composition by Spanish-English speakers.* Washington, DC: U.S.
Department of Education and Minority Language Affairs.

Goodenough, F. (1926). Racial differences in the intelligence of school children. *Journal of Experimental Psychology, 9,* 388–397.

González, L.A. (1986). *The effects of first language education on the second language and academic
achievement of Mexican immigrant elementary school children in the United States.* Unpublished
doctoral dissertation, University of Illinois at Urbana-Champaign.

Grant, B. (1989). *Making an educated decision.* Phoenix: Arizona State University Business School
Magazine.

Green, M.F. (Ed.). (1989). *Minorities on campus: A handbook for enhancing diversity.* Washington,
DC: American Council on Education.

Guerra, V. (1984). *Predictors of second language learners' error judgments in written English.* Unpublished doctoral dissertation, Corpus Christi State University, Corpus Christi, Texas.

Hakuta, K. (1986). *Mirror of language: The debate on bilingualism.* New York: Basic Books.

Hakuta, K., & Díaz, R. (1985). The relationship between degree of bilingualism and cognitive ability:
A critical discussion and some new longitudinal data. In K. Nelson (Ed.), *Children's language.
Vol. 5.* Hillsdale, NJ: Lawrence Erlbaum Associates.

Hakuta, K., & García, E.E. (1989). Bilingualism and education. *American Psychologist, 44,* 374–379.

Heath, S.B. (1983). *Ways with words: Language, life and work in communities and classrooms.* New
York: Cambridge University Press.

Hilliard, A. (1990, February 21). *Validity and equity in the curriculum.* Presentation at San Diego State
University, San Diego, CA.

Krashen, S.D. (1981). Bilingual education and second language acquisition theory. In Office of Bilingual Bicultural Education, California State Department of Education (Ed.), *Schooling and language minority students: A theoretical framework* (pp. 51–79). Los Angeles: Evaluation, Dissemination and Assessment Center, California State University.

Krashen, S.D., & Biber, D. (1988). *On course: Bilingual education's success in California.* Sacramento: California Association for Bilingual Education.

Lambert, W.E., & Tucker, G.R. (1972). *Bilingual education of children: The St. Lambert experiment.*
Rowley, MA: Newbury House.

Lau v. Nichols. 414 U.S. Reports, 563-572 (October Term, 1974).

Legarreta, D. (1979). The effects of program models on language acquisition by Spanish speaking
children. *TESOL Quarterly, 13,* 521–534.

Leyba, C. (1978). *Longitudinal study, Title VII bilingual program, Santa Fe public schools, Santa Fe,
New Mexico.* Los Angeles: Evaluation, Dissemination and Assessment Center, California State
University.

Mace-Matluck, B.J., & Hoover, W.A. (1986). Language, literacy and instruction in bilingual settings:
Issues and implications of findings from a recent longitudinal study. In A. Willig & H.F.
Greenberg (Eds.), *Bilingualism and learning disabilities: Policy for teachers and administrators*
(pp. 169–187). New York: American Library.

National Clearinghouse for Bilingual Education. (1985). Descriptive phase of national longitudinal study completed. *Forum, 7*(3), 1–7.

Office of Bilingual Bicultural Education, California State Department of Education. (1981). *Schooling and language minority students: A theoretical framework*. Los Angeles: Evaluation, Dissemination and Assessment Center, California State University.

Oliver, M.L., & Johnson, J.H., Jr. (1988). The challenge of diversity in higher education. *The Urban Review, 20*, 139–145.

Olsen, L. (Ed.). (1989). *Bridges: Promising programs for the education of immigrant children*. San Francisco: California Tomorrow Publications.

O'Malley, J.M. (1982). *Children's English and services study: Language minority children with English limited proficiency in the United States*. Rosslyn, VA: Inter America Research Associates.

O'Malley, J.M. (1985). Learning strategy applications to content instruction in second language development. In National Clearinghouse for Bilingual Education and the Georgetown University Bilingual Education Service Center (Ed.), *Issues in English language development*. Rosslyn, VA: National Clearinghouse for Bilingual Education.

Peal, E., & Lambert, W.E. (1962). The relation of bilingualism to intelligence. *Psychological Monographs, 76*, (27, Whole No. 546).

Public Law 94-142. Education for All Handicapped Children Act of 1975. 20 USC 1401. *Federal Register, 42*(86), May 4, 1977.

Ramírez, C.M. (1985). *Bilingual education and language interdependence: Cummins and beyond*. Unpublished doctoral dissertation, Yeshiva University, New York.

Ramírez, D. (1991). Longitudinal study of structured English immersion strategy: Early-exit and late-exit transitional bilingual programs for language minority students. *National Association for Bilingual Education (NABE) News, 15*(5), 1.

*Raven, J.C. (1938, 1947). *Coloured progressive matrices*. London: Lewis.

Research center identifies 18 projects. (1991). *National Association for Bilingual Education (NABE) News, 14*(5), 9.

Rio v. Read. 73 *Federal Rule Decisions, 589–603*, 1977.

Ruíz, N. (1988). *The optimal learning environment (OLE) curriculum guide: A resource for teachers of Spanish-speaking children in learning handicapped programs*. Unpublished manuscript, University of California at Davis, Division of Education.

Ruíz, N. (1989). An optimal learning environment for Rosemary. *Exceptional Children, 26*, 130–144.

Saer, D.J. (1924). The effect of bilingualism on intelligence. *British Journal of Psychology, 14*, 25–38.

Salgado, L.J. (1988). *Language proficiency and retention among Hispanic students in community colleges*. Unpublished doctoral dissertation, Seton Hall University, Greensburg, PA.

Saville-Troike, M. (August 1983). *What really matters in second language learning for academic achievement*. Paper presented at the TESOL Summer Institute, Toronto.

Serna v. Portales Municipal Schools. 499 *Federal Reporter*, 2d, 1147–1154 (10th Cir., 1974).

Smith, F. (1923). Bilingualism and mental development. *British Journal of Psychology, 13*, 271–282.

Smith, M. (1931). A study of five bilingual children from the same family. *Child Development, 2*, 184–187.

Smith, M. (1939). Some light on the problem of bilingualism as found from a study of the progress in mastery of English among preschool children of non-American ancestry in Hawaii. *Genetic Psychology Monographs, 21*, 119–284.

Steffensen, M.S., Joag-Dev, C., & Anderson, R.C. (1979). A cross cultural perspective on reading comprehension. *Reading Research Quarterly, 15,* 10–29.

Strong, M. (1982). *Social styles and second language acquisition among kindergartners.* Unpublished doctoral dissertation, University of California, Berkeley.

Student oral language observation matrix. (SOLOM). (1981). *Individual learning plan.* Sacramento, CA: California State Department of Education.

Swain, M. (1978). Home-school language switching. In J.C. Richards (Ed.), *Understanding second and foreign language learning: Issues and approaches.* Rowley, MA: Newbury House.

Swain, M., & Cummins, J. (1982). Bilingualism, cognitive functioning and education. In V. Kinsella (Ed.), *Surveys 1.* Melbourne, Australia: Press Syndicate of the University of Cambridge.

Tempes, F. (1986). *Case studies in bilingual education: Second year report* (1984–1985). U.S. Office of Bilingual Education and Minority Languages Affairs (Federal Grant #GOO8303723).

Thonis, E.W. (1981). Reading instruction for language minority students. In Office of Bilingual Bicultural Education, California State Department of Education (Ed.), *Schooling and language minority students: A theoretical framework* (pp. 147–181). Los Angeles: Evaluation, Dissemination and Assessment Center, California State University.

U.S. Code Title 20, 880b, 460. (text of the Bilingual Education Act, 1968).

United States v. State of Texas, 506 F. Supp. 405 E.D. Tex (1981).

Veltman, C. (1988). *The future of the Spanish language in the United States.* Washington, DC: Hispanic Policy Development Project.

Westby, C., & Rouse, G. (1985). Culture in education and the instruction of language learning disabled students. *Topics in Language Disorders, 5*(4), 15–28.

Willig, A.C. (1985). A meta-analysis of selected studies on the effectiveness of bilingual education. *Review of Educational Research, 55,* 269–317.

Willig, A.C., & Swedo, J.J. (1986, April). *Improving teaching strategies for exceptional Hispanic limited English proficient students: An exploratory study of task engagement and teaching strategies.* Paper presented at the annual meeting of the American Educational Research Association, Washington, D.C.

Wong Fillmore, L. (1991). Second language learning in children: A model of language learning in social context. In E. Bialystok (Ed.), *Language processing in bilingual children* (pp. 49–69). Cambridge: Cambridge University Press.

Wong Fillmore, L., & Valadez, C. (1986). Teaching bilingual learners. In Witroch, M.C. (Ed.), *Handbook of research in teaching* (3rd ed.) (pp. 648–683). New York: Macmillan.

Yoshioka, J.G. (1929). A study of bilingualism. *Journal of Genetic Psychology, 36,* 473–479.

Appendix 6-A

Further Comments on the English Language Amendment (ELA)

In delineating the pros and cons of the English Language Amendment (ELA), members of the Committee on Cultural-Linguistic Differences and Disorders of Communication of the American Speech-Language-Hearing Association (ASHA; 1988, 1989) listed the following points:

Pros

1. A single national language is a unifying economic, political and social force.
2. A common language facilitates economic and social development because skills and expertise are more easily shared and applied.
3. English is already recognized nationally and internationally as the language of the United States.
4. The ELA may encourage the review and improvement of current practices in bilingual and ESL programs.

Cons

1. The ELA may nullify the necessity and rationale for bilingual education.
2. The ELA may undermine the civil liberties of LEP and non-LEP citizens in the United States.
3. The ELA may discourage the often mandated and costly translation of government documents, such as voting ballots.
4. The ELA may restrict access of non-English speakers to necessary services, such as health and fire/police protection.
5. The ELA may negate the historical importance and value of contributions from other languages and cultures to American life.

6. The ELA may discourage acceptance of social dialects and regional pronunciation differences.

IMPLICATIONS FOR SPEECH-LANGUAGE CLINICIANS

The negative implications of ELA passage for the practicing clinician would be multiple. For example, decreased numbers of academic programs to prepare clinicians to provide services for bilingual clients may increase the misidentification of language differences as language disorders. Violations of P.L. 94-142, which requires assessment in the primary language of the client, may increase. Incentives for trained bilingual individuals in the field of speech and language pathology and audiology may decrease (due to lack of funding). Dissemination of consumer informational pamphlets, materials, and resources written in other languages may be prohibited.

In addition, the implementation of the ELA would undermine ASHA's concerted effort to meet the growing challenges of working with a multilingual and multicultural population. The following programs and resources were created by ASHA specifically for this end:

1. Available materials, including a multicultural resource library and a directory of bilingual speech and language pathologists and audiologists (1990–1991) to facilitate the identification of local service providers.
2. Further certification requirements. Beginning in 1993, the standards for the Certificate of Clinical Competence (CCC) for speech-language pathologists and audiologists call for coursework that addresses "issues pertaining to normal and abnormal human development and behavior across the life span and to the culturally diverse populations" (American Speech-Language-Hearing Association, 1990, p. 33). To address this need, ASHA has been conducting different workshops for practicing clinicians and university faculty.
3. Incentives to learn a foreign language. As of 1991, ASHA members may enroll in self-study programs to acquire basic skills in any of three languages (ie.g., Spanish, Japanese, or Mandarin Chinese). This program was developed by the ASHA's Committee on Cultural-Linguistic Differences and Disorders of Communication to enhance clinicians' ability to relate to some of their clients with greater cultural and linguistic understanding.

Proponents of the ELA recognize the importance of other languages, but their main concern is for all U.S. citizens to master the English language. Failing to give an equal status to other languages tends to devalue the linguistic and cultural heritage of others, however. As Crawford (1989) and Cummins (1989) advocated, a more humane and effective educational approach is to build on the skills and knowledge that children already have in another language.

REFERENCES

American Speech-Language-Hearing Association. (1990–1991). *Directory of bilingual speech-language pathologists and audiologists.* Rockville, MD: American Speech-Language-Hearing Association.

American Speech-Language-Hearing Association *(ASHA) Journal.* (1990). November, p. 9.

Committee on Cultural-Linguistic Differences and Disorders of Communication. (1988). Pros and cons of the ELA. *American Speech-Language-Hearing Association, 30,* 56.

Committee on Cultural-Linguistic Differences and Disorders of Communication. (1989). The English language amendment. *American Speech-Language-Hearing Association, 31,* 80–81.

Crawford, J. (1989). *Bilingual education: History, politics, theory and practice.* Trenton, NJ: Crane Publishing.

Cummins, J. (1989). *Empowering minority students.* Sacramento: California Association for Bilingual Education.

Chapter 7

Speech and Language Assessment of LEP/Bilingual Hispanic Students

Henriette W. Langdon

The speech-language clinician who is assessing the language proficiency of a mainstreamed English-speaking student first determines whether a speech-language problem exists by gathering information from various sources (e.g., parents, teachers, or other professionals who know the student) and supplementing this information by means of direct interaction with the student or observation of the student in one or more settings. If the student has a speech-language problem, the clinician assesses its nature and severity by using any number of standardized tests, often including specific measures of language form, content, and use. The assessment may also include the elicitation of a language sample and its analysis. If the student is eligible for speech-language services, the clinician uses the assessment data to write specific speech-language goals and objectives to meet the student's communication needs.

The steps that a speech-language clinician follows in assessing the language proficiency of a Spanish-speaking Hispanic student are similar, but three main factors can complicate the process. First, the clinician may not be proficient in Spanish. Second, standardized tests for Spanish-speaking students are limited in number and scope; furthermore, their validity and reliability are limited. Third, although various authors (Damico, 1991; Erickson & Iglesias, 1986; Kayser, 1989b; Langdon, 1989b; Mattes & Omark, 1984) have suggested procedures for conducting assessments with cultural and linguistic minority students, these procedures have not been validated. Yet, all these authors advocate observations of the student in several contexts, using various interactants, supplemented by reports and information from parents and teachers or other professionals who know the student in order to determine if the student has a speech-language problem.

In a study comparing the content of speech-language reports done with English-speaking monolingual and limited-English–proficient (LEP) students, Langdon (1989b) found no significant difference in the assessment procedures used. For the most part, the clinicians used the results of standardized tests to determine eligibility for speech-language services for students from both groups. Very few clinicians analyzed the impact of the cultural, linguistic, or experiential backgrounds of the students. Furthermore, only a limited number of clinicians considered their observations of the students in various settings or the input provided by the students' parents as part of the assessment process.

USE OF INTERPRETERS/TRANSLATORS

The practice of using an interpreter/translator for speech-language assessment and testing in the clinical or school setting has been neglected by the literature. At the present time, there is no research-based information on the best ways to work with an interpreter, who conveys information from one language to the other in the oral modality, or a translator, who conveys information in the written modality. Some of the "best practices" reported in the field of international conference, legal, and medical interpretation, as well as interpretation for the deaf, may be useful in speech-language assessment, however (Cheng, Langdon, & Davies, 1991; Langdon, 1989a).

Specific Procedures

Working with an interpreter/translator requires additional preparation time and training, on the part of both the clinician and the interpreter/translator. Therefore, it is essential to ask a bilingual individual to serve as an interpreter/translator well in advance. The clinician should meet with the interpreter/translator prior to a parent conference or testing/assessment of the student to plan the content and format of the interaction.

The clinician should be present during the testing (administration of standardized or adapted test items, including the elicitation of a language sample) to observe the behavior of the student and the reactions of the interpreter/translator. Also, some points may need further clarification, even after a briefing has taken place. If possible, it is wise to have a separate session before the testing date so that the student can become accustomed to having both the clinician and the interpreter/translator in the same room. Such a session is particularly helpful if the student is shy, but it may be impractical because of time constraints.

After the testing/assessment or conference session, the clinician and the interpreter/translator should discuss what occurred.

An interpreted or translated test should not be scored unless it has been normed on the given population and the manual indicates that it can be administered by a trained assessor. Rather, the clinician should make notations on how and when the student was able to provide accurate responses and when the student had difficulties. Thus far, limited studies have been conducted to determine the effects of another professional's presence when a test is administered in Spanish or in any other language by an interpreter/translator. Swanson and DeBlassie (1979) compared the performance of Spanish-dominant bilingual students on the Wechsler Intelligence Scale for Children—Revised (WISC-R, 1974) in English under different conditions, one of which involved the use of an interpreter. They could not draw firm conclusions because there were no data available on the subjects' initial language proficiency, but it appeared that the presence of the interpreter may have created a "halo" effect; the scores obtained when the tests were administered through an interpreter were higher than those obtained when the tests were administered in Spanish only.

Role of the Interpreter/Translator

It is important that the person who is to serve as interpreter/translator in a speech-language assessment has both oral and written ability in the two languages. Oral proficiency alone is not sufficient. The interpreter/translator should also be familiar with technical vocabulary used in the field of speech-language pathology, testing procedures, and the purpose of any given test. Weddington and Meyerson (1983) recommended that interpreters/translators receive very specific training. In no instance should a person with no previous exposure to testing be asked to serve as an interpreter/translator. Often, it is erroneously assumed that the need for bilingualism supersedes the need for an understanding of the complexity of testing, particularly in another language. It is preferable to select a person who has training in a field related to speech, language, and hearing (e.g., a teacher, educator, or health professional). The least desirable person is a family member or another student fluent in both languages.

The interpreting/translating must be as accurate as possible. The interpreter/translator must remain neutral and cannot become emotionally involved with the case.

Interpreting and translating are not easy tasks. Specialized training is necessary to become an international conference interpreter for the United Nations, an interpreter for the deaf, or, in some states, a court interpreter. These careers have been officially recognized as professions. The interpreting/translating process in the educational and clinical fields, such as speech-language pathology or audiology, has not yet received the recognition that it deserves, however, and is not yet considered a "professional" occupation. With the ever increasing multicultural and multilingual U.S. population, more trained interpreters/translators will be needed in these fields. Both the clinician and interpreter/translator should have an ongoing dialogue on how best to facilitate the contact with students whose language proficiency is to be assessed and how best to communicate with the students' families.

LANGUAGE PROFICIENCY

Oral Language Proficiency Tests

Speech-language clinicians typically do not administer oral language proficiency tests, such as the Bilingual Syntax Measure (BSM; Burt, Dulay, & Hernández-Chávez, 1975, 1980), the Idea Oral Language Proficiency Test (IPT; Ballard & Tighe, 1980, 1982, 1983, 1987), or the Language Assessment Scales (LAS; De Avila & Duncan, 1977, 1979, 1983). These tests are generally administered by bilingual school personnel. Clinicians must understand the information that can be obtained from these tests and the limitations of the data provided by them, however, as the results of oral language proficiency tests are often the only language-based data that are collected to determine a student's overall communicative competence in any given language. The results of oral proficiency tests are used to make decisions about the student's eligibility for bilingual education or readiness for mainstreaming into an English-only instruction classroom.

The administration of a language proficiency test is essential if the parent or legal guardian indicates on the home language survey that a language other than English is used in the home (Exhibit 7-1). In California, school districts use any of the three tests that have been mentioned to rate the language proficiency of students on a scale from 1 to 5, with a range of 1 to 3 considered limited English proficiency and 4 to 5 considered near fluency or fluency. Some states, such as New York, use the Language Assessment Battery (LAB; Board of Education of the City of New York, 1976), which also contains reading and writing portions. The student who is not proficient in English should also be tested in Spanish, but Spanish tests are not always administered because of the lack of available bilingual Spanish or, for that matter, designated personnel to obtain this important information. The results of Spanish testing would be very helpful in determining and comparing the student's proficiency across languages, however.

The results of oral language proficiency tests must be interpreted with care for various reasons. First, the level of difficulty of each language version of the tests is not equivalent (Merino & Spencer, 1983). Second, the results of these tests have a very low predictive correlation with academic achievement (Ulibarri, Spencer, & Rivas, 1981). Finally, there is no significant correlation across the three proficiency tests mentioned, because each one includes a variety of language tasks that make it possible to assess different aspects of language form and content but offer very limited opportunities to assess language use. The BSM, for example, focuses on the students' ability to use correct grammatical forms. In contrast, the IPT in-

Exhibit 7-1 Home Language Survey

(To be completed by the parent or guardian)

ENGLISH VERSION

1. Which language did your son or daughter learn when he or she first began to talk?
2. What language does your son or daughter most frequently use at home?
3. What language do you use most frequently to speak to your son or daughter?
4. Name the languages in the order most often spoken by the adults at home.

SPANISH VERSION

1. ¿Cuál idioma aprendió primero cuando su hijo/a empezó a hablar?
2. ¿Cuál idioma usa principalmente su hijo/a cuando conversa en la casa?
3. ¿Cuál idioma usa Ud. con más frecuencia cuando habla con su hijo/a?
4. ¿Cuál idioma hablan los adultos con más frecuencia en la casa? (Indique el orden de frecuencia.)

---

volves labeling skills, understanding of specific concepts, comprehension of short paragraphs, and sentence repetition tasks. The LAS proficiency tests consist of tasks designed to determine the students' ability to discriminate small differences in sounds between pairs of words, to repeat words and short phrases, to label pictures, to retell a story, and to understand specific sentences. A few of these tests also provide information about the students' metalinguistic abilities. For example, on both the LAS and IPT, the students are asked to determine if two words sound the same or different. On the IPT, they must repeat the grammatically correct sentence from a choice of two sentences (one is grammatically incorrect). Thus, the term *oral language proficiency* is defined differently in each one of the oral proficiency tests.

Many of the skills necessary to respond successfully to the test items require specific learning and experience. If students fail to answer some of these items, the examiner must determine whether lack of exposure or practice may be the principal reason. Regrettably, many school districts continue to devise programs based solely on the outcome of tests, with minimal consideration of input from staff and parents and without any collection of oral and written samples from the students, where appropriate. The test results are also used to determine the student's language dominance. Thus, if an LEP bilingual student is referred to special education assessment, it is often recommended that the more in-depth testing be conducted only in the language that is considered dominant. Assessing a bilingual student's proficiency in only one language provides an incomplete profile of the student's communicative competence.

In an effort to supplement the information obtained through oral language proficiency tests, the speech-language clinician should explore the experiences of the student in general and should devise language-related tasks for LEP/bilingual students that will have greater academic predictive value. To obtain more information on the students' experiences, it is helpful to interview parents and to observe the students in order to document their opportunities to communicate and interact outside their immediate family and to evaluate their exposure to print. Heath (1986) found that those language minority students who had more opportunities for extended experiences used more specific, precise, topic-centered language. One effective technique to learn about the student's experiences is to ask the parent to describe the student's typical weekend day. The experience that the student has had with print is also very important. Curtis (1986) and Lomax and McGee (1987) indicated that knowledge about print may be an important precursor to word identification (see Exhibit 7-2 later in this chapter).

Research efforts to identify other language-related tasks that will yield a better predictive measure of the LEP/bilingual student's academic performance are continuing. The first relates to using a Cloze procedure, the second bases itself on the students' sense of story. A Cloze procedure is one in which the student is requested to fill in words from a passage where every fifth to seventh word has been omitted. Laesch and van Kleeck (1987) devised a Cloze procedure that was found to correlate much more significantly with students' scores on the California Test of Basic Skills(CTBS) than did their scores on the LAS, which had also been used. In their 1987 study, the Cloze procedure involved completing sentences about subject matter familiar to the students. Thirty third-grade bilingual Mexican-American students from Texas participated in the study.

Fitzgerald and Spiegel (1986) investigated the relationship between sense of story and academic achievement, specifically reading comprehension, and found a strong positive correlation between these two variables. To assess the sense of story in LEP/bilingual students, Jax (1988a, 1988b) developed a method to score their narrative skills by using a wordless book. Jax considered seven areas of story grammar, including items described by Peterson and McCabe (1983). It was predicted that those students who obtained high story construction scores would also achieve at higher levels of reading comprehension. Although the hypothesis was confirmed with a small sample of students from Southern California (56 fourth-grade students), it needs further validation with a larger number of subjects. Both studies indicated, however, that scores on oral language proficiency tests, such as the LAS, are insufficient to predict students' academic achievement.

To determine the student's oral language proficiency in English or, for that matter, Spanish, the clinician may want to use a checkoff list, such as that presented in Table 7-1. It includes four different language development stages, their definitions, and the use of language associated with that particular stage of language proficiency. In addition, samples of the student's classroom work in English should be examined and compared to the classroom work of others who are

Table 7-1 Different Stages in English Language Development

Stage	Title	Definition	Activity	Vocabulary
1	Preproduction: silent period (6–10 months exposure to the language)	Minimal comprehension, no verbal production	Listen, point, move, choose, match, mime, act out, draw	500 receptive words
2	Early production (3¹/₂ months exposure to 1 year)	Limited comprehension; one- or two-word response; some phrases, short sentences	Name, list, categorize, label, respond with one or two words	1,000 receptive words (10% expressive words)
3	Speech emergence, tele-graphic speech (1–3 years exposure to the language)	Good comprehension; errors in pronunciation and grammar; simple sentences, but limited vocabulary	Describe, define, explain, recall, retell, summarize, role-play, compare, contrast	7,000 receptive words
4	Intermediate fluency (3–4 years exposure to the language)	Excellent comprehension, few grammar errors	Give opinions, defend, debate, justify, examine, analyze, create, evaluate, read, write	12,000 receptive words

succeeding in a monolingual English classroom to determine if the student is ready to follow an English-only curriculum.

Speech and Language Tests Available in Spanish

The speech-language clinician typically assesses the communicative competence of students by analyzing the three language dimensions: form, content, and use. Traditional speech and language tests in English focus on language form (e.g., phonology, morphology, or syntax) or on language content (e.g., vocabulary and concepts). Numerous tests that focus on only very specific areas (discrete point) are available. The areas of language comprehension and expression are also covered in most tests and reports.

In recent years, recognition of the relationship between oral and written language has made it necessary for the clinician to examine the significance of language in communication and in learning academic subjects. New awareness of the importance of language use, termed *pragmatics*, has led to the design of a variety of testing materials, such as Evaluating Communicative Competence: A Functional Pragmatic Procedure Test (Simon, 1987), the Test of Language Competence (Wiig & Secord, 1985), and the Test of Problem Solving (TOPS; Zachman, Jorgensen, Huisingh, & Barrett, 1984). A great number of these tests explore the student's metalinguistic ability as well. No one test can tap the vast array of language competencies, however.

Test development in Spanish has not kept pace with that in English. Most tests focus on assessment of form and content and were developed only in the last 15 years. None focuses on the development of language use. Table 7-2 lists the different tests, both the Spanish and the English versions, according to the major area tested. The publication of some of the tests, such as the Del Rio Language Screening Test (Toronto, Leverman, Hanna, Rosenzweig, & Maldonado, 1975) and the Toronto Test of Receptive Vocabulary (Toronto, 1977), has been discontinued, and the pace at which new test materials are being designed in Spanish has slowed in the last 3 to 5 years. The greater emphasis in developing English language proficiency skills in LEP students may be responsible for this lack of interest in developing other Spanish test materials.

Characteristics of Speech and Language Tests in Spanish

The number of speech and language tests that measure any given skill in Spanish, such as knowledge of concepts or use of specific grammatical forms, is limited. Moreover, the sampling and norming of the tests that do exist were carried out primarily on early elementary school–aged children; only a very few tests are available for the preschool and older-than-10 age groups.

Table 7-2 Spanish Speech and Language Test Instruments

Area	Spanish	English Equivalent
General proficiency	Bilingual Syntax Measure (BSM) Idea Language Proficiency Test (IPT) Language Assessment Scales (LAS)	Bilingual Syntax Measure (BSM) Idea Language Proficiency Test (IPT) Language Assessment Scales (LAS)
Articulation	Medida Española de Articulación (MEDA) Austin Spanish Articulation Test Melgar Test Assessment of Phonological Processes (Spanish) Spanish Articulation Measures	Goldman-Fristoe Articulation Test Assessment of Phonological Processes (English) ALPHA Articulation Test (Lowe 1986)
Receptive vocabulary	Test de Vocabulario en Imágenes Peabody (TVIP) Del Rio (Subtest) Toronto Receptive Vocabulary Ber-Sil Receptive Vocabulary (Beringer 1977)	Peabody Picture Vocabulary Test (PPVT) (Dunn & Dunn 1981) Del Rio (Subtest) Toronto Receptive Vocabulary Peabody Picture Vocabulary Test (PPVT)
Expressive vocabulary	Woodcock-Johnson (Subtest) Expressive One-Word Picture Vocabulary Test (EOWPVT) Dos Amigos	Woodcock-Johnson (Subtest) Expressive One-Word Picture Vocabulary Test (EOWPVT) Dos Amigos (Critchlow 1974)
Concepts	Preschool Language Scale (PLS) Test of Auditory Comprehension of Language (TACL) Illinois Test of Psycholinguistic Abilities (Spanish version) (ITPA) (Subtest) (Kirk et al 1980) Pruebas de Expresión Oral y Percepción de la Lengua Española (PEOPLE)	Preschool Language Scale (PLS) Test of Auditory Comprehension of Language (TACL) (Carrow 1974) Illinois Test of Psycholinguistic Abilities (ITPA) (Subtest) (Kirk et al 1968)
Sentence comprehension	Screening Test of Spanish Grammar (STSG)	Northwestern Syntax Screening Test (NSST) (Lee 1971)
Oral directions	Del Rio (Subtest) Brigance (Subtest)	Del Rio (Subtest) Brigance (Subtest)
Sentence repetition	Del Rio (Subtest) Brigance (Subtest) Pruebas de Expresión Oral y Percepción de la Lengua Española (PEOPLE)	Del Rio (Subtest) Brigance (Subtest) Woodcock-Johnson (Subtest)
Sentence expression	Structured Photographic Expressive Language Test (SPELT)	Structured Photographic Expressive Language Test (SPELT) (Werner & Kresheck 1989)

Note: References to authors and dates of publication may be found at the end of the chapter. Acronyms have been added for tests that are commonly referred to by their acronym.

The norming of most tests was conducted with specific bilingual populations who had particular exposure to Spanish and English (e.g., the Pruebas de Expresión Oral y Percepción de la Lengua Española (PEOPLE) [Mares, 1980]) or with Spanish-speaking monolingual students outside the United States (e.g., the Test de Vocabulario en Imágenes Peabody (TVIP) [Dunn, Padilla, Lugo, & Dunn, 1986] and the Woodcock Language Proficiency Battery [Woodcock, 1981]). Even though some of the tests, such as the Woodcock test, have "adjusted U.S. norms," they must be interpreted with care. In many cases, measures of validity and reliability are insufficient. According to Toronto and Merrill (1983), who discussed some of the procedures necessary to norm a test for any given population, a test is valid only when it has been standardized on a population with characteristics similar to those of the individual tested. In addition, the construct validity and reliability of the test must be documented. Construct validity (e.g., the extent to which a test is said to measure a theoretical concept) includes criterion validity (i.e., the degree to which scores on the test agree with or predict a given criterion measure) and content validity (i.e., confirmation that the content of the test adequately represents that which was to be measured). Reliability studies provide information on internal reliability (i.e., consistency of the items of a test with the entire test), interscorer reliability (i.e., stability of scores when the same test is administered by different clinicians), alternate form reliability (i.e., comparability and equivalency of all forms), and test-retest reliability (i.e., same scores obtained when the test is administered a second time after a short interval). Appendix 7-A lists the most commonly used speech and language tests in Spanish. Clearly, very few tests comply with all the statistical measures that have been described.

Several of the Spanish tests are adaptations or translations of the English versions, and Spanish norms are unavailable. On the Spanish version of the Structured Photographic Expressive Language Test (SPELT; Werner and Kresheck, 1989), for example, most tested grammatical forms are direct translations of the English version. The authors provided suggestions on ways to develop norms for the test. Although there is value in developing local norms, this is a time-consuming process that requires additional commitment from staff and extra funding. Also, no matter how cautiously local norms are developed, such a test must always be interpreted carefully. In the case of the SPELT, grammatical forms that are developmentally more appropriate in Spanish should have been selected.

Tests of Written Language and Metalinguistic Abilities

The number of formal tests designed to assess reading and writing in Spanish is still limited. Some of the most commonly used materials are listed in Appendix 7-B. As can be noted, there are many variations in the areas tested and the scoring procedures. In addition, many of the tests lack data on validity and reliability. Results from these tests may be difficult to interpret and of limited value for intervention—except to determine the severity of a student's problem and the student's eligibility for certain programs. A more practical approach is to test curriculum-based reading and writing skills using the students' basal readers (Table 7-3). Furthermore, because formal reading and writing tests tend to give grade level scores without allowing for a more in-depth analysis of what the student can or cannot do with the process of reading or writing, some informal inventories are helpful (Exhibits 7-2 and 7-3).

Table 7-3 Selected Basal Spanish Readers

Reader	Levels	Comment
Economy Spanish Reading Series Amato, Basque, Allen, & Kiraithe, 1987 Economy Company Oklahoma City, OK	Preprimers– 5th grade	Pre-reading activities, including songs, poems, science projects; evaluation of content at the end of each unit; some supportive materials included. Placement tests; criterion-referenced tests at the end of each unit that focus on different areas, such as word analysis, comprehension.
Hagamos Caminos Ada & Olave, 1986 Adison Wesley Publishing Co. Menlo Park, CA	Levels 1–6	Development of oral language skills; syllabic emphasis on reading skills; acquisition of language promoted through integration of songs, rhymes, literature, and poetry.
Lectura en Dos Idiomas Ramos, 1985 Santillana Publishing Co. Northvale, NJ	Readiness–5th grade	Phonetic approach; criterion-referenced tests at the end of each unit. Auditory-visual approach to learning. Every lesson emphasizes hearing, saying and writing.
Mil Maravillas Guzmán, Long, Marías, Santiago, Somoza, & Tinajero, 1986 Macmillan Publishing Company New York, NY	Preprimer–5th grade	Syllabic approach to teaching reading; many supportive materials for oral language teaching and group activities; frequent testing with different suggested strategies for administration.
Programa de Lectura en Español Barrera & Crawford, 1987 Houghton Mifflin Boston, MA	Kindergarten– 6th grade	Literature-based reader; integration of reading, language, and writing.

Exhibit 7-2 Informal Assessment of Reading Skills

Area	Beginning	Secure	Date SP	EN

Book Awareness
Listens to stories
Looks at books as a self-initiated activity
Holds the book right side-up
Turns pages in sequence
Recognizes where print begins on page
Recognizes where print ends on page
Moves eyes and finger across the print while
    attempting to read

Print and Word Awareness
Points to letters in words
Tracks to find a word
Points to a word according to length (more
    syllables, then longer word)
Recognizes common words in stories
Talks about own reading ("that's dog, and it
    starts like my name David")
Uses phonetic cueing with familiar words
Transfers reading behavior from known
    words to unknown ones
Attempts to read the selection
Knows which words are in Spanish and
    which ones are in English

Reading Patterns
Reads familiar predictable texts
Reads unfamiliar pattern texts
Reads familiar unpatterned texts
Reads a variety of texts
Reads for enjoyment

Literary Genres Preferred by the Student
Legends
Fantasy, fairy tales
Fiction
Biographies
Classic books
Poems
Plays

Area	Beginning	Secure	Date SP EN
Reading Strategies			
Self-corrects (report in percentages)			_____
Types of errors: semantic			_____
syntactic			_____
Reading Comprehension			
Recalls main idea			_____
Recalls details			_____
Can list events in the story			_____
Understands cause and effect			_____
Can relate ideas to own experiences			_____
Can discuss how idea relates to other persons' experiences			_____

SP, Spanish; EN, English. Circle what student can do and date; use a different color pen for each language.

Source: From "Predictable Literature Selections and Activities for Language Arts Instruction" by G. Heald-Taylor, 1987, *The Reading Teacher, 17,* pp. 7–12. Copyright 1987 by the International Reading Association. Adapted by permission.

In assessing academic areas, it is also important to include information on the students' metalinguistic abilities. As Wallach and Miller (1988) indicated, school activities require a great deal of metalinguistic awareness. Although children are able to demonstrate some such awareness at a very early age, metalinguistic skills do not fully emerge until they have had some formal schooling. From the very early grades, students "are asked to compare sentences, to count the number of words in a sentence, to listen to the first sound in a word, to identify a rhyming word, and to decide which sentence is the 'proper' way to say something" (Wallach & Miller, 1988, p. 9).

Miller (1986) devised a list of tasks to assess the students' metalinguistic abilities based on the different Piagetian stages of cognitive development. The clinician can use the following series of informal tasks to assess the metalinguistic awareness of Spanish-speaking 3- to 5-year-olds and to determine whether training can improve their performance; the tasks suggested are somewhat similar to those tested in Miller (1986, p. 33).

1. *Rhyming words.* Request that the child provide rhymes for the following Spanish sounds:

        —ana: rana, sana, cana, lana
        —ata: mata, rata, lata, bata
        —ala: ala, bala, mala, pala, sala, jala

Exhibit 7-3 Informal Assessment of Writing Skills

Area	Beginning	Secure	Date SP	EN
Content Organization Form	Single events. Simple ideas that are not always related. Irrelevant details. No generalizations. Overuse of "and" and "then." Omitted punctuation.	Sense of story noted. Relevant details provided. Purpose of writing clearly stated. Variety in sentence length and structure. Correct punctuation.		
Vocabulary	Use of general nouns (e.g., man, thing) and verbs (e.g., want, have).	Precise vocabulary. Concise expression of ideas with no excess of words.		
Spelling	Omission, addition of letters.	Correct spelling.		
Handwriting	Poor letter formation. Erasures. Illegible writing. Slow and laborious.	Readable text. Neat, carefully done. Spacing in letters and paragraphs adequate.		

SP, Spanish; EN, English. Circle what student can do and date; use a different color pen for each language.

Source: Information from *Evaluating and Improving Written Expression* (pp. 12–13), by J. Hall, 1981, Boston: Allyn and Bacon.

Ask for definitions or explanations of a couple of words that have a meaning; determine if the child can detect that some words, such as *tana* or *vana*, have no meaning. Repeat the same task with the —*ash*, —*et*, and —*ot* sounds in English.

2. *Playing with words.* Pick a word and request that the child substitute the first sound by letters in alphabetical order.

Spanish: bola, cola, dola, fola, gola, hola, jola, lola, mola, . . .
                barro, carro, darro, farro, garro, jarro, larro, marro, . . .
                bima, cima, dima, fima, gima, lima, mima, nima, . . .
English: bam, cam, dam, fam, gam, ham, jam, lam, . . .
                bit, cit, dit, fit, . . .
                bop, cop, cop, dop, . . .

3. *Breaking words into syllables and constructing words from syllables.* Give the child the words one at a time, and ask that the words be broken down into syllables. Begin the task by providing an example.

Spanish: *banana* ba - na - na
                guitarra, estrella, cobija 'guitar, star, blanket'
English: television te - le - vi - sion
                chocolate, animals, elephant

Give the student syllables that form a true word. Ask that the word be "re-constructed."

Spanish: te - lé - fo - no *teléfono* 'telephone'
          cum - ple - años *cumpleaños* 'birthday'
          co - ra - zón *corazón* 'heart'
          mu - cha - cho *muchacho* 'young man'
English: cro - co - di - le — crocodile
          te - le - phone — telephone
          po - lice - man — policeman

Older children, aged 6 to 10 years, can be given the same tasks, plus the following:

1. *Recognizing words with more than one meaning.* Name words that have two meanings. (There are fewer such words in Spanish than in English.) If the student cannot think of the two meanings, provide some sentences to clarify the meanings.

   Spanish: *café* 'coffee' and 'coffee shop'.
            Ayer mi mamá tomó un café en la mañana 'My mother had a
                 cup of coffee yesterday morning'.
            Después de la escuela, vamos al café 'After school, we'll go to the coffee
                 shop'.
            banco 'bank' and 'bench'
            En el parque nos sentamos en el banco 'We sit on the bench in the park'.
            Puse mi dinero en el banco 'I put my money in the bank'.
            nada 'nothing' and 'swim'
            Ella nunca sabe nada 'She never knows anything'.
            Hace mucho calor, entonces nada 'It's warm, so do swim'.

   In English, words such as *glasses*, *sink*, and *light* can be used.

2. *Solving riddles.* Give the following riddles (Simon, 1987, p. 97) and ask the student to provide an answer.

   Spanish: *Soy bueno para tomar, soy blanco, y mi nombre suena como eche. ¿Qué soy?*
                 (leche) 'I am good to drink, I am white, and my name rhymes with
                 eche. What am I? (milk)'
            Tengo dos manos y números del 1 al 12. Mido el tiempo. ¿Qué soy? (reloj) 'I
                 have two hands and numbers from 1 to 12. I measure time. What
                 am I? (clock, watch)'
            Estoy hecho de vidrio, uso electricidad, y ayudo a encender la luz. ¿Qué soy?
                 (foco) 'I am made out of glass, I use electricity, and I help light a
                 room. What am I? (bulb)'
   English: I am worn on the face, I have a frame, and I help people see. What am I?
            I am soft and white, I am square, and I come in a box. You use me for your
                 nose. What am I?
            I am a container, and I am used to hold hot liquids. People drink from me.
                 What am I?

3. *Translating.* Ask the student to translate words and sentences from Spanish to English and from English to Spanish.

Spanish: *casa* 'house', *hermano* 'brother', *mesa* 'table'
           Mi maestra está tomando un vaso de leche 'My teacher is drinking a glass of milk'.
           Ayer pintamos unas flores rojas y blancas 'Yesterday we drew some red and white flowers'.
           No hice mi tarea porque no tuve tiempo 'I didn't do my homework because I didn't have time'.

English: chair *silla*, teacher *maestro*, food *comida*
           I go to my house after school. *Voy a mi casa después de la escuela.*
           My mother went to the big store. *Mi mamá fue a la tienda grande.*
           I didn't come to school because I was ill yesterday. *No vine a la escuela porque estaba enfermo(a) ayer.*

These tasks allow the clinician to determine whether the student is aware of the two languages, can tell which language is which, and can take the point of view of the listener.

OBTAINING A LANGUAGE SAMPLE IN SPANISH

A language sample is an effective tool in assessing a student's language use (Lahey, 1988; Prutting, 1983). It may be a time-consuming process, however, because the sample must be representative of the student's communication skills and the scoring may be laborious. Yet, "the language sample is the only procedure which provides an opportunity to assess communication in real live contexts with real live communicative partners who need to communicate. The language sample remains a most valued clinical tool" (Prutting, 1983, p. 90). The interaction between the clinician and the subject must be structured to some extent in order to obtain the desired information. For example, it is unreasonable to say that the student cannot use a particular verb form if the context was not conducive for the elicitation of that form. Likewise, it should not be concluded that a student cannot narrate if there was no opportunity to do so.

The number of utterances necessary to obtain a representative sample of the individual's language skills remains a source of debate among researchers. Lee (1974), Prutting (1983), and Tyack and Gottsleben (1974) recommended obtaining 100 utterances, whereas Muma (1978) and Wren (1985) recommended as many as 200 or 300. Given the fact that the numerous responsibilities of a clinician leave limited time, the number of utterances may not be as important as the variety of topics. In the case of a bilingual student, more time will be required because a sample in each language is necessary in most cases.

The topics of conversation or activities (tasks) that are used to elicit the sample must be controlled to allow comparisons of data across individuals with similar experiential and linguistic backgrounds. To address the issue of what topics and tasks are most likely to elicit a typical language sample, Wren (1985) presented several tasks to three groups of English-speaking children aged 6 to 7 years. Two groups had language difficulties; the third did not. Wren was interested in determining whether one or a combination of tasks would yield the most typical language from the children. Wren elicited the samples by means of free play with puppets, storytelling from pictures, explanation of a game (Candyland), the use of a viewmaster (e.g., asking the student to explain which picture was being referred to), preparation for a birthday party (e.g., using props), and a sentence-building activity to elicit sentences with specific words. The birthday party activity elicited the most utterances from all three groups, because the clinician asked the largest number of structured questions during this task to elicit specific syntactical structures. More complex language was obtained from the explanation of the game; during this task, the control group used the largest number of embedded sentences (sentences that include a dependent clause). The birthday party, stories from pictures, and the viewmaster activity were the most helpful in differentiating the language skills between the different groups. The findings of the study indicated that a variety of activities should be devised in order to obtain a truly representative sample, however.

In following these recommendations to elicit the most representative sample possible from preschool and elementary school students, the clinician may

- use puppets and toys, guiding the conversation to create certain situations.
  1. Use a toy car, and speculate where it might go. Then it has a flat; what would happen?
  2. Create a scene with a birthday party.
  3. Use a doll house, and comment about what is happening.
  4. Use broken toys to enhance a dialogue.
- ask the child what he or she did that same day or the day before; inquire about the child's family, favorite pastimes, or toys.
- ask the child if he or she knows a story or wants to retell something seen on TV. If the child cannot, read a story aloud and ask him or her to retell it to another child or a puppet. With upper elementary school children, use wordless books.
- request that the child explain the rules of his or her favorite game (board or sport). If the child cannot, explain one and have the child explain it to another child.
- play barrier games to determine how the child follows and gives directions.
- ask the child to explain how he or she performs different actions.
  1. preparing a sandwich
  2. wrapping a present

3. sending a letter
4. using a telephone

Older students participate in similar activities but are also requested to provide definitions of words, to solve riddles, and to explain absurdities. In addition, the clinician creates situations in which the student must use particular language functions, such as negotiation. Thus, the clinician who needs a language sample from an older student may

- ask the student to explain the rules of his or her favorite sport.
- request comments about a TV show or film.
- ask for definitions of words such as *temperature, peace, invisible, promise,* or *inform.*
- assess the student's ability to explain absurdities.
  1. *A medianoche el sol estaba brillando fuerte* 'At midnight the sun was shining very brightly'.
  2. *El hombre ciego estaba mirando a los pájaros* 'The blind man was looking at the birds'.
  3. *La esposa del soltero es muy guapa* 'The bachelor's wife is very pretty'.
- ask what the student would do if he or she were invisible, had won the lottery, or had all the power in the world.
- determine how the student would persuade his or her parents to let him or her take the family car to a party or persuade friends to order one particular brand of pizza.
- inquire about the student's plans upon graduation from high school; ask what he or she needs to know to be successful in a particular career.
- analyze the way in which the student retells the content of a story read aloud.
- request that the student make up a story using a wordless book.

With these techniques, which include a variety of situations and allow the clinician to expand certain topics based on the student's interests and comments, the clinician can obtain a representative sample in 30 minutes of interaction with the subject. For the bilingual student, the language samples must be obtained one language at a time.

The atmosphere in which a language sample is obtained must be as natural and comfortable for the student as possible. It is important to let the student lead some of the conversation. The type of interaction between the clinician and the student should be documented (e.g., who participated and was the interaction successful). For example, a more representative sample may be obtained in the presence of a known adult, particularly with preschool children or students who are very shy, or in the presence of a peer. Collecting the sample in the student's home may result in a more valid measure of verbal skills.

The person who interacts with the student should be fluent in Spanish and experienced in conversing with children; some children may be reluctant to use Spanish because they realize that the examiner is not fluent in the language. It is sometimes helpful to encourage the student to imagine that the interaction is occurring in a place where Spanish is customarily spoken. On some occasions, it is helpful to give the family an audio cassette to record the home interaction. This practice may lead to some constraints at first, because the family is conscious of being recorded; however, they soon forget the recording and begin to interact naturally. Another technique is to ask the family to videotape one characteristic set of interactions. These processes help the family to understand the nature of the problem and also to become more involved in the assessment. It also helps the clinician to become familiar with the family's interaction patterns and topics of conversation (Langdon, 1988).

Frequently, code-switching has erroneously been interpreted as a sign of language mixing or even a language disorder. Code-switching may reflect the typical language patterns spoken in the home, however. If code-switching is accompanied by periods in which the individual is searching for words, there are many pauses and hesitations, and this interferes with successful communication, a problem may be present.

DECISION-MAKING PROCESS

Should the Student's Language Competence Be Assessed?

In a school setting, it is often the speech-language clinician who is consulted to determine whether a student should be assessed. Langdon (1989b) found that the reasons for the referrals of Hispanic students were generally a concern about a language delay in English, Spanish, or both languages, often accompanied by slow academic progress. Before undertaking a full-scale assessment, the clinician should investigate certain areas, such as length of residence (Langdon, 1989b; Ortíz & García, 1988). If the student has resided in the United States for less than a year, he or she may simply need some additional time to acquire English. The student's attendance should also be verified. Frequent absences not only disrupt the educational process, but also decrease the opportunities of many LEP students for exposure to English. If a student who has been in the United States for less than a year is having problems in Spanish, however, a referral may be warranted.

Documentation of the types of programs that a student has attended is important to determine if the student has received optimal second-language learning opportunities. For example, has sufficient comprehensible input been offered? Has the student had enough interactions with native speakers of the second language? Also, have different teaching methods been tried to improve the student's learning? As Cummins (1984) noted, it takes an average of 2 years for a second-language learner to reach basic interpersonal communication skills (BICS). Up to 7 years may be necessary for that student's cognitive academic language proficiency (CALP) to equal that of monolingual peers. Ultimately, the clinician may want to verify that the student has been making steady progress in language acquisition and in academic areas over time.

In exploring the need for a complete speech-language assessment, the clinician should ascertain whether the student has had previous experience with certain school-related activities. For example, the clinician should determine whether a young student has seen family members read and write, has been read to, and has answered questions about the content; whether the older elementary or secondary student has had opportunities to do independent research, knows how to use the library to look for specific information, and has taken examinations. Comparisons with siblings and peers are very helpful.

A health and developmental history helps determine if the student has a health-related problem, such as a hearing loss, that may interfere with academic progress. The care of such a health problem should precede any form of testing.

All this information can be gathered by reviewing the student's cumulative record and by consulting his or her teachers and family. Various types of questionnaires may be useful in obtaining input from teachers and parents. A modified version of the teacher questionnaire designed by Erickson and Omark (1981) has proved very helpful (Exhibit 7-4). To record data about the student's use of the two languages, the questions can be divided into two columns, one for observations when the interaction is in Spanish and the other for observations when the interaction is in English.

A parent questionnaire can be completed at the time of the clinician's initial contact with the family (Exhibit 7-5). Completing a questionnaire during a telephone or face-to-face interview allows the clinician or interpreter to ask for clarification or additional information about the child's background and the parents' perception of the child's performance at home. Depending on the answers provided, the assessment team may decide that further assessment is not indicated at that time. For example, if the child has attended school for only a short time, a full-scale assessment may be postponed—provided that the child's performance at home is comparable to that of siblings or other children the same age.

Some questions require particular tact. Obtaining information on the student's length of stay in the United States is important, for example, but the clinician must realize that some parents may come to the United States to establish themselves and leave the children behind in the care of grandparents or other relatives. The child emigrates later and may experience some difficulty in adjusting to the new

Exhibit 7-4 Teacher Questionnaire

Please check all the areas that apply to the student whom you are referring. Indicate the language(s) where you note a difficulty. Thank you.

(Spanish) (English)

1. Frequently chooses to play alone
2. Is usually quiet
3. Chooses to sit in areas outside the mainstream of activity (i.e., in the back of the room)
4. Frequently fails to follow directions, needs repetition
5. Listens, but does not seem to comprehend
6. Appears to hear some things, but not others
7. Has trouble retaining information
8. Frequently misunderstands words
9. Gets nervous when asked to respond orally
10. Avoids speaking during "sharing" time
11. Rarely volunteers to answer questions in class
12. Prefers to speak to friends in _____
13. Rarely asks for clarifications
14. Frequently speaks in words or short phrases
15. Speaks in incomplete sentences
16. Gives inappropriate responses
17. Uses inappropriate vocabulary to express ideas
18. Has difficulty recalling words (hesitates, pauses)
19. Is unable to tell a story in sequence
20. Draws attention to self by speech
21. Speaks in a way that is unclear and difficult to understand
22. Omits or substitutes sounds in words
23. Speaks in extremely loud or soft voice
24. Stutters or stammers frequently
25. Has a "raspy" or "hoarse" voice

Source: From *Communication Assessment of the Bilingual-Bicultural Child* (p. 269) by J.G. Erickson and D.R. Omark, 1981, Baltimore, MD: University Park Press. Copyright 1981 by J.G. Erickson and D.R. Omark. Adapted by permission.

---

family life. If a parent hesitates to give an answer concerning the family's length of stay in the United States, the clinician can reformulate the question as "Have you been in this country for more than 2 years, and has your child lived with you all this time?" *¿Ha vivido en este país más de dos años, y su hijo/a ha vivido con Ud. todo el tiempo?* Similarly, to avoid embarrassing the parent, who may have had very limited formal education, the interviewer may ask about the parent's education by saying, "How many years of schooling did you have an opportunity to complete in your country?" *¿Cuántos años tuvo Ud. oportunidad de asistir a la escuela?*

Exhibit 7-5 Parent Interview Questionnaire

Name of student: _____

Birthdate: _____ Age: _____ Place of birth:_____

Grade: _____ School:_____ Teacher: _____

Name of interpreter: _____ Language: _____

Date: _____

A. SOCIAL AND FAMILY HISTORY:

A.1. How long in the U.S. mainland   Father: _____ Mother: _____ Student: _____

A.2. How many persons living in the household: _____

Name   Age   Relationship

_____

_____

_____

_____

_____

_____

                                              1   2

A.3. Language(s) spoken to student by (1)   Father: _____

      Language(s) spoken by student to (2)   Mother: _____

                                    Siblings: _____

                            Other relatives: _____

A.4. Father's occupation: _____ Education: _____

      Mother's occupation: _____ Education: _____

Parents' proficiency in English: Mother: _____   Father: _____

A.5. Has any family member had any language and/or learning difficulty: Y   N

Please explain: _____

A.6. Trips to country of origin (indicate length of stay, where applicable):

_____

B. PARENT/FAMILY OBSERVATIONS ABOUT THE STUDENT:

B.1.   Does you child have problems following directions?   Y   N
B.2.   Does your child have problems understanding what you say?   Y   N
B.3.   Do you have problems understanding your child?   Y   N
B.4.   Does your child relate ideas in sequence?   Y   N
B.5.   Does your child express events that will be happening?   Y   N
B.6.   Does your child express events that might happen (predict)?   Y   N
B.7.   Is your child told stories?   Y   N
B.8.   Do you comment about what you read or tell your child?   Y   N
B.9.   Do you and your family read: Please specify what: _____   Y   N
B.10. Please specify your child's interests: _____
B.11. Does you child have behavior problems?   Y   N
B.12. Does your child have difficulties in making friends?   Y   N
B.13. Does your child have difficulty in learning new concepts?   Y   N

C. SCHOOL HISTORY:

C.1. Was your child in school in your home country?   Y   N
Please explain: _____
C.2. Any problems observed?   Y   N
Please explain: _____
C.3. Grade attained: _____
C.4. Has your child attended preschool in the U.S. or your home country?   Y   N
Please explain: _____
C.5. Have there been any school attendance problems?   Y   N
C.6. Have you had to move frequently?   Y   N
Please explain: _____

D. HEALTH AND DEVELOPMENTAL INFORMATION:

D.1. Problems with vision?   Y   N
D.2. Problems with hearing?   Y   N
D.3. Problems with allergies?   Y   N
D.4. Any significant illnesses?   Y   N
D.5. Any hospitalizations?   Y   N
D.6. Medications in the past or present?   Y   N
D.7. Any difficulties in learning to walk?   Y   N
D.8. Any problems in learning to talk?   Y   N
D.9. Any problems while mother was pregnant or at time of delivery?   Y   N
D.10. Indicate location of delivery: home, hospital, clinic. (Circle one.) Birth weight: _____
Please explain if answer is *yes* for any of the above questions: _____
_____
_____

Please describe one of your child's typical days (e.g., what does he or she do, what does he or she play with).
_____
_____
_____
_____
_____

ADDITIONAL COMMENTS: _____
_____
_____
_____

If the student's residence in the United States has been stable and the educational program has been modified to accommodate the student's linguistic and academic needs, but with limited success, it may be appropriate to refer the student for a speech and language assessment. Even when the parents report that the student has no problems, but the teachers suspect a difficulty, the clinician may wish to observe the student in the school setting and, if necessary, at home. The observations allow the clinician to compare specific behaviors of the child with the behaviors of other children of the same age, as well as to verify reports from parents, teachers, or other professionals who know the child (Lahey, 1988). It is also helpful to observe the student's interactions with other adults and peers in different situations and settings (e.g., classroom, playground, lunch room) and to document differences over time (e.g., a month). If progress is limited, further assessments are warranted. In this case, the clinician must identify the severity of the problem, the most affected language dimensions (i.e., form, content, or use), and the relationships between the communication problem and other areas (e.g., reading and writing).

Should the Student's Proficiency Be Assessed in One or Both Languages?

To determine if a Hispanic student should be tested in two languages, the clinician first takes the student's language classification on proficiency tests as a general guideline. In addition, the clinician may use the following criteria:

1. The student responds in Spanish when spoken to by family or caregivers.
2. Informal communication with adults and peers indicates that the student can understand Spanish, but responds appropriately in either Spanish or English. Even under these circumstances, assessment should be conducted to determine the level and type of comprehension skills in Spanish.
3. The student is enrolled in a bilingual program.

Testing communicative competence in both languages permits the clinician to determine whether the student's skills in one or the other language are superior for certain language uses. Neglecting one language, even the one in which the student has weaker skills, would give an inaccurate appraisal of the student's general language competence. Testing the student in either language when it appears to be frustrating should be avoided. Any testing attempts should be properly documented, however.

Alternating from one language to the other may be appropriate when the student's language skills in both languages are very weak (Chamberlain & Medeiros-Landurand, 1991), but testing one language at a time is likely to produce a clearer picture of the student's language performance in each. Research is limited on which language to test first in bilingual assessment, however. Experience suggests that it is best to begin the testing with the language that is the most familiar to the student, based on (1) a review of the cumulative record, (2) results of preliminary proficiency tests, and (3) reports from teachers, parents, and caregivers. Although it is important to acknowledge every student response, even if it is not in the language being tested, the student should be encouraged to re-spond in the target language as much as possible.

There is little information on how much time should elapse between testing in one language and testing in the other. The guidelines of a few tests that include versions in two languages recommend that one language be tested in the morning and the other in the afternoon. Testing the student on different days may be a better procedure, however. If students are assessed on the same day, there may be carry-over from one language to the other. For example, Pollack (1980) found that young bilingual children performed better than expected in English because they had been tested in Spanish earlier that same day.

How Should the Assessment Be Conducted?

Because testing and assessment of educational achievement is much more fre-quently practiced in countries of the Western hemisphere than in other countries, some immigrant children may lack experience in being tested. Yet, as the Ameri-can Educational Research Association (1985) noted, "For a non-native English-speaker, and for a speaker of some dialects of English, every test given in English becomes, in part, a language or literacy test" (Chapter 13). In addition, the success of testing may depend partly on the interaction between the clinician and the stu-dent. Data on communication between clinicians of varying ethnicity and His-panic children are still scant, but Kayser (1989a) found indications that Hispanic and Anglo clinicians may use slightly different strategies. For example, Kayser found a 10% fail rate by Hispanic clinicians, contrasted with a 60% fail by Anglo clinicians, for her sample in which all subjects had normal language development. When administering tests, the Hispanic clinicians did not change the test items; instead, they repeated the items as they felt the children needed encouragement. Both groups of clinicians used expressions of encouragement; however, Anglo clinicians used comments to tease, whereas the Hispanic ones used comments to console. These interactional findings are preliminary, but they deserve further in-vestigation.

To obtain important information while administering test items, the clinician should first administer the items according to the guidelines of the test manuals. After completing the test, the clinician may readminister those items on which the student responded incorrectly by using one or several of the following strategies, depending on the type of task: (1) rewording the instructions, (2) offering further explanations of what the student should pay attention to, (3) providing more ex-amples of the same type of items that are being tested, (4) providing more time for the student to respond, and (5) explaining to the student how to maximize recall for certain information presented either orally or in writing. Strategies may also include visualization techniques or finding key words in a text to aid comprehension. Some of these techniques have been suggested by Erickson and Iglesias (1986), Kayser (1989b), and Weddington (1987).

INTERPRETATION OF TEST RESULTS

The administration of "standardized" measures alone is not an adequate basis for the conclusion that a mainstreamed student, much less a student with a different linguistic and cultural background, has a language-learning disability. The process may be helpful in clarifying the nature and severity of the problem, however, if the test results are interpreted in light of the student's experiences, observations of the student in various contexts with different interactants, analysis of the language sample(s), and input from the family and parents. Classifying all these data as auditory input (i.e., language comprehension) and verbal output (i.e., language expression), although an artificial method of dividing the communicative process, facilitates reporting observations and identifying strengths or areas in need of improvement. Thus, norms can be reported as part of the findings, but with cautionary notations that indicate how the student's background and language experience differ from the norming population for any given test. For example, if using the Spanish version of the Peabody Picture Vocabulary Test, the Test de Vocabulario en Imágenes Peabody (Dunn et al., 1986), the clinician notes that the norms were obtained on Spanish-speaking monolingual children, but the student being tested has been in the United States for a specific number of years. As a result of the lack of exposure to Spanish and the student's difficulty in learning new words, the student's Spanish vocabulary score may be lower than expected for a student of the same age. The test can also be used to identify and classify the types of words that the student can and cannot identify.

Auditory Input (Listening and Oral Language Comprehension)

It is important to evaluate the way in which the student processes oral language in order to identify specific situations in which the student can perform as expected and those in which the student has difficulties. Specific tests that focus on different aspects of language comprehension in Spanish include

- ability to follow oral directions: Subtests of the Brigance Diagnostic Assessment of Basic Skills (Spanish version) (Brigance, 1983), Del Rio Language Screening Test (Toronto et al., 1975), and Preschool Language Scale (Zimmerman, Steiner, & Pond, 1979)
- auditory association: Pruebas de Expresión Oral y Percepción de la Lengua Española (PEOPLE) (Mares, 1980) and the Spanish version of the Illinois Test of Psycholinguistic Abilities (ITPA) (Kirk & van Isser, 1980)

- oral text comprehension: PEOPLE, ITPA, Del Rio, IPT (Ballard & Tighe, 1980, 1982) and LAS (De Avila & Duncan, 1983)
- sentence repetition: PEOPLE, Del Rio, IPT, and LAS

The student's interactions with different persons and in a variety of settings can be observed with the assistance of different staff members who interface with the student, as well as the family and parents. In analyzing the student's responses, the clinician makes notations about those modifications that were helpful in improving performance. In addition, the clinician can make the following observations:

1. Could the student perform better if the input were shorter and/or the sentences less complex?
2. Could the student retain information as stated, but did he or she have difficulty with inferences and hypotheses? Were the responses/comments made during testing and while taking the language sample pragmatically correct?
3. Was the student easily distracted by noise? Was attention better on a one-to-one basis than in a group or classroom situation?
4. How did the observations made in the one-to-one interaction with the clinician compare with those made by other staff members and the family?
5. Was there a difference in any of these areas across languages?

In focusing on the student's ability to comprehend oral language in the various contexts and using the different mediating strategies, the clinician can describe more accurately the response mode and behavior of the student. Thus, scores become more valuable with due interpretation. Also, because the assessment includes tests, observations, and other measures, the clinician is able to identify what the student can or cannot do, and to report conditions that promote better responses.

Verbal Output (Oral Language Expression)

A language sample has traditionally been collected to obtain a measure of sentence length and to determine the use of particular grammatical features (Brown, 1973; Lee, 1974). This technique has been adapted for Spanish by Linares-Orama (1977), who devised a technique to calculate mean length of utterance in Spanish based on Brown's model, and Toronto (1977), who adapted Lee's Developmental Sentence Scoring into Spanish by creating the Developmental Assessment of Spanish Grammar. Although these methods provide a measure of language development, the results must be interpreted with care. Linares-Orama's work was based on a study of Puerto Rican preschoolers, whereas Toronto's subjects were sampled in the Chicago area. The latter test includes norms for Mexican-American and Puerto Rican children aged 3:0 to 6:11. The scoring system for these procedures is not based on Spanish language developmental milestones, however, but rather is a Spanish adaptation of measures initially devised for English-speaking children. Future Spanish language developmental data will make it possible to obtain more accurate measures.

When evaluating a language sample in Spanish, the clinician should consider four aspects.

1. Mechanics of language interaction (discourse): initiating conversation; maintaining topic (e.g., responding to questions by keeping the topic going, following a sequence of ideas, adding information [elaboration], asking for clarification); taking the listener's point of view.

2. Use of language for a variety of purposes: to gather information, to explain, to retell, to inform; to make further abstractions (e.g., thinking beyond current visible referents, integrating old and new experiences).

3. Form and content: use of syntax and grammar, sentence types, and complexity; use of vocabulary; articulation skills; ability to convey intended meaning.

4. Individual communication style: manner of expressing ideas (time delay between comment/question posed by the interlocutor), pauses, hesitations (beginning to say a word but only uttering the initial sound or syllables), word/phrase repetitions, and circumlocutions. Comments should include a notation of the rapport between the clinician and the student, as well as any peer relationships noted during the collection of the language sample.

A list of contexts in which the samples were obtained in both Spanish and English increases the information available on the topics that were covered. The analysis of the sample can be further supplemented with comments based on the criteria developed by Damico (1985) or the description of narrative development by Westby (1989). For example, a student's narrative skills can be evaluated by using a wordless book and determining the schema content of his or her narration (Table 7-4). Final analysis of the language sample should include comments on the effectiveness of the student's communication skills, as well as on the similarities and differences between this sample and those of other students with similar experiences in each one of the languages considered. Therefore, the language sample obtained in the school or clinical setting should be supplemented by feedback from other staff working with the student, family, and parents.

Assessment of Vocabulary

Frequently, the breadth of knowledge of a bilingual student who is experiencing language and learning difficulties is restricted in both languages. Although bilin-

Table 7-4 Progression of Narrative Development

Schema Content	*Text Grammar Structure*
Preschool	
Ability to label.	Isolated description: labels or describes objects, characters, surrounding, and ongoing actions; no interrelationships among the elements mentioned.
Awareness of animate/inanimate distinction, that is, that animate beings act and inanimate objects are acted upon.	Action sequence: a list of actions that are not causally related, but which may be chronologically ordered based on perception; no interrelationships among the characters—characters act independently of each other; centering may be present—story may have a central character or a central theme (actions that each character does).
Awareness of physical cause-effect relationships; beginning of awareness of linear time for familiar sequences.	Reaction sequence: beginning of chaining—a set of actions or events that automatically cause other changes, but with no planning involved (e.g., a rock rolled down the mountain and the people ran).
Early Elementary School	
Awareness of psychological causality for primary emotions (happy, mad, sad, scared, surprised, disgusted); that is, awareness of situations that cause these emotions and what one might do because of these emotions (e.g., brother takes toy—anger—hit brother); theory of mind (awareness that people think and feel, which allows for some perspective taking); ability to conceptualize near future; scriptal knowledge of common characters (e.g., wolves are bad and eat pigs; princes are good and save princesses from dragons).	Abbreviated episode: both centering and chaining present; character(s) engage in cause-effect actions; story describes goals or intentions of characters, but planning must be inferred; story will have at least the components of initiating event, response, and consequence.
Further development of psychological causality (secondary or cognitive emotions; e.g., jealousy, guilt, shame, embarrassment); further perspective taking—awareness of interaction of character attributes with story elements of setting and events	Complete episode: both centering and chaining present; describes the goals and intentions of the characters with some evidence of planning; story has at least an initiating event (problem), internal response (character's reaction to problem), plan,

continues

Table 7-4 continued

Schema Content	Text Grammar Structure
that enable child to comprehend/predict novel behaviors of characters; understanding of longer time frames (days, weeks); meta-awareness of the need to plan and how to plan; understanding of the need to justify plans.	attempt (carrying out of plan), and consequence.

Late Elementary School

Ability to perceive character change/growth (i.e., understand that character attributes change over course of story as result of events); ability to detect deception or trickery and to deceive or trick; awareness of time cycles (seasons, years); beginning awareness of multiple meaning for words and literal versus figurative meanings.	Elaborated stories: Stories may be elaborated in three ways:
	1. Complex episode: A single-episode story that may involve multiple plans, attempts, or consequences.
	2. Interactive episodes: Story is told from the point of view of more than one character—results in parallel episodes.
	3. Multiple episodes: The story has more than one "chapter," with each chapter having the story grammar elements of initiating event, response, plans, attempts, and consequences; in early stages, episodes are sequential, but in later development one episode may be embedded within another episode.

Adolescent/Adult

| Ability to engage in meta-narrative discussion; i.e., discussion of narrative structure and interpretation of characterization, themes, and plots; understanding of abstractions of time and space; ability to understand flashbacks; ability to understand allegories. | Metaphoric stories: the usual structure of stories may be intentionally modified in novel ways for humorous or metaphoric purposes. |

Source: From *Reading Disabilities: A Developmental Language Perspective* (pp. 212–213) by A.G. Kamhi and H.W. Catts (eds.), 1989, Austin, TX: PRO-ED. Copyright 1989 by PRO-ED. Reprinted by permission.

gual individuals may normally have a reduced vocabulary in each of the languages that they speak, language-disordered, learning-disabled students have a significantly lower than expected vocabulary as measured by various test instruments and observation.

Several formal instruments are available to measure this area. For example, the clinician can test recognition of single vocabulary words by using the Spanish equivalent of the Peabody Picture Vocabulary test or Ber-Sil Level I or II; the Dos Amigos and language sections of the Woodcock test, which elicit opposites of words and different concepts; and verbal association tasks, such as the auditory association subtests of the PEOPLE and ITPA. The clinician can also assess expressive vocabulary knowledge by using the Expressive One Word Picture Vocabulary Test (Gardner, 1980, 1983) or one of the language subtests of the Woodcock-Johnson. Asking the student to define different words allows the clinician to evaluate vocabulary knowledge in conjunction with the language sample.

Comments regarding the student's vocabulary knowledge should take into account the properties of the words themselves. It is helpful to analyze the pattern of responses and determine if the student has a repertoire of concrete words, but lacks the more abstract ones, or if the words relate more to home than to learned items. For example, the student may know *cocina* or *estufa* 'stove' in Spanish, but not in English, because there is a stove at home and the word may not be heard as often at school. Thus, measures of vocabulary knowledge without a description are not as accurate and helpful in planning an intervention program for the student as are those with explanatory comments.

Articulation Skills

The Medida Española de Articulación (Mason, Smith, & Hinshaw, 1976), the Austin Articulation Test (Carrow, 1974), and the Melgar Articulation Test (Melgar, 1980) are the principal articulation tests that were available before the advent of more recent approaches, such as assessment of phonological processes (Hodson, 1986a; Mattes, 1987). In all three of the older tests, consonants and vowels are assessed by means of single words in which sounds occur in the different positions. In all instances, the target sound is tested in a single word, and there are no opportunities to consider it in other words or in connected speech. For example, the Medida Española de Articulación uses the word *árbol* 'tree', whereas the Melgar uses the picture of *pastel* 'cake', to test students for the production of final /l/. The clinician notes whether the child articulates the sound correctly.

There are some problems with these more traditional articulation tests. First, the student may not be familiar with the word tested or may not recognize the picture. For example, the word *árbol* may be familiar to a native speaker of Spanish from Mexico, but Mexican-American children may use the word *palo*. These same children may use *quequi* (Americanized word for cake) rather than *pastel*. Thus, the clinician has to resort to imitation and obtains limited data on the student's production of this sound in the final position. Second, the student may not pronounce the sound correctly because of the phonological configuration of the word.

For example, a student may omit the final /l/ because of a difficulty in pronouncing the /l/ in *árbol* but has less difficulty with /l/ in *sol*.

In their tests, Hodson (1986a) and Mattes (1987) focused on phonological processes or error patterns rather than on single errors in phonemes. In Hodson's test, for example, the final /l/ is assessed with the words *árbol* and *azul* 'blue'; in Mattes' test, with the words *mal* 'bad' and others such as *caracol* 'snail', *sol* 'sun', and *árbol*. The student is given more opportunities to produce the phoneme. The Hodson test lists 10 principal processes, such as consonantal omissions, syllable reduction, and strident, labial, velar, glide, and nasal deficiences. The Mattes test not only comprises 7 basic processes, such as initial consonant deletion and final consonant deletion, but also lists 11 additional possible processes. The Hodson test permits only consideration of single words; the Mattes test permits the evaluation of phoneme production in connected speech as well.

The identification of processes facilitates remediation. As Hodson (1986a, 1986b) indicated, it is best to begin with the most stimulable processes. Although this approach has been assessed primarily with English-speaking students, definite suggestions may be made for Spanish-speaking students. For example, some common phonological processes in Spanish-speaking children who may have phonological disorders are (1) syllable reduction, as in /coba/ for *escoba* 'broom'; (2) fronting, as in /ditara/ for *guitarra* 'guitar'; and (3) assimilations, as in /nanis/ for *naríz* 'nose'. It is also important to interview parents and family members to evaluate their intelligibility and phonological patterns. Often, a dialectal variation may be mistaken for a speech disorder.

FINAL DIAGNOSIS AND REPORT WRITING

Arriving at a Final Diagnosis

In analyzing the results of formal and informal discrete-point tests and examining the language sample to arrive at a final diagnosis, the clinician should also consider whether such factors as the student's attendance, school experience, and type of instruction are affecting the student's language performance. By carefully identifying and exploring all the different variables, the clinician can determine if a true problem exists.

A language disorder in an LEP/bilingual child may manifest itself in a variety of areas, just as for a monolingual child. In an LEP/bilingual child, however, certain areas may be affected in one language more than in the other, depending on the exposure to and use of each language. For example, Langdon (1977, 1983) found that bilingual language-disordered children displayed difficulties more evident in Spanish (their first and dominant language) than did bilingual normally developing children because their exposure to English had been brief. The normally developing and language-disordered groups had comparable exposure experience with both Spanish and English. If a problem exists in one language dimension (e.g., syntax, comprehension of complex sentences) in the dominant language, it is very likely that the problem will occur in the less dominant language as well. The fact that such a problem may not be as evident in the initial stages of the second-language acquisition is one important reason for assessing a bilingual student in both languages.

When analyzing the language profile of an LEP/bilingual student who was tested in two languages, it is helpful to consider the BICS and CALP. Thus, four profiles are possible. Within each case, there may be variations in severity (Figure 7-1).

1. The student may have adequate basic communication skills in Spanish, but little abstract language ability and weak academic skills in Spanish. BICS and CALP in English are also very weak. The student needs to acquire more metacognitive-metalinguistic skills to perform better in academic areas.

2. The student may have weak BICS and CALP in both Spanish and English.

3. The student has been able to acquire basic communication skills in both languages, but has problems with CALP in both languages. This may occur when a student has been exposed to English, but has never acquired sufficient metacognitive-metalinguistic skills to enhance his or her performance on academically related tasks in either language.

4. The student may have adequate BICS and CALP in Spanish, but both BICS and CALP are weak in English. Very likely, this student will need more exposure and input in English. This student would not be language-disordered.

Most cases are not as straightforward as these. These sets are helpful in delineating the language profile of an LEP/bilingual child who may have a language disorder, however.

Writing the Report

The clinician should consider nine areas when writing the report.

1. Reason for Referral. List the reason(s) that the student was referred for a bilingual assessment.

2. Background Information. Indicate the sources of information (e.g., cumulative record, other staff's oral or written reports, parent/family personal or telephone interview) used in the report.

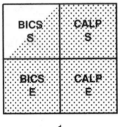

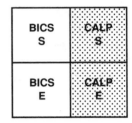

1

BICS S OK
BICS S Abstract No
CALP S Not Developed
CALP E Not Developed

2

BICS S and CALP S
   Weak
BICS E and CALP E
   Not Developed

3

BICS S and E OK
CALP S and E
   Not Developed

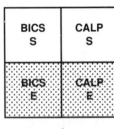

4

BICS S and CALP S OK
BICS E and CALP E
   Not Developed
(4 is not a problem)

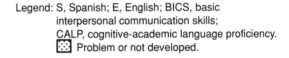

Legend: S, Spanish; E, English; BICS, basic
   interpersonal communication skills;
   CALP, cognitive-academic language proficiency.
   ▦ Problem or not developed.

Figure 7-1 Final Diagnosis of a Language Problem.

- social and family background
   1. place of birth (e.g., home, hospital) and location
   2. sibling position and number of persons living with the student
   3. languages spoken to the student and by the student to different family members
   4. parents' occupation, educational attainment, proficiency in English
   5. language or learning difficulty in any other family member
   6. any trips to the country of origin, including dates and lengths of stay
   7. parents' perception of the student
   8. student's experiences at home with literacy and opportunities for activities outside the home, such as trips to parks, museums, any outings

- health and developmental background
- school background
  1. specific programs that the student has attended
  2. reading programs followed and modifications made to meet the student's needs
  3. school attendance record and any disruptions in education
  4. observations and comments of other staff members
  5. results of other testing

3. Observations. Report observations made during the one-to-one interaction, as well as in the classroom or other settings.

4. Testing Procedures Followed and Materials Used. Indicate if the bilingual assessment was conducted by one clinician, by two clinicians, or with the help of an interpreter. List the materials administered in each language. Make a statement regarding the limitations of the tests and the need to interpret results according to the student's experiences and use of each language. Indicate how testing took place (e.g., different days, weeks, using one language at a time). List the results of the different tests at the end of the report.

5. Verbal Input or Language Comprehension. Describe how the student processes different types of information (e.g., follows directions, responds to different questions based on an orally presented short story, imitates sentences, converses, completes sentences). Indicate if slowing down the pace of item administration, repeating the information, or asking the student to visualize the activity improves the student's performance. Make a notation if noise was interfering with the student's responses. Integrate the information obtained in the one-to-one interaction with observations made by parents and teachers. Note any differences in the student's proficiency in the two languages.

6. Verbal Output or Language Expression. In addition to the results of verbal interactions, report on the student's use of vocabulary and articulation skills. Also report voice quality, fluency, and examination of the oral peripheral mechanism (structure and function of the articulators (e.g., tongue, lips) for adequate speech production).

7. Language Dominance/Preference. Make a statement regarding the student's language dominance and preference for the different tasks. For example, a student may be almost equally proficient in both languages on most comprehension tasks, but perform better on expressive tasks in Spanish. Comment on BICS and CALP in each language.

8. Other Tasks. Not all speech and language assessments permit an evaluation of the reading and writing skills of the student. Where needed, report on what the student can read, the types of words that the student can decode, the level of fluency in reading text, and the level of reading comprehension. Comment on the student's metalinguistic and written skills, if appropriate.

9. Summary and Recommendations. Write a summary of findings. Indicate the nature of any problem, and describe the rationale for the conclusion. If necessary, make suggestions for interventions and recommendations for designated programs, such as speech and language services or resource programs. Include two or three suggestions for parents for follow-up at home.

Assessing an LEP/bilingual student is a lengthy process. In reality, the clinician must carry out two evaluations for each student. Although supervisors and administrators may question the lengthier process necessary to assess an LEP/bilingual student, a survey of expert Spanish-speaking bilingual clinicians indicated that it takes an average of $3^1/_2$ hours to complete and report the assessment for a monolingual student, but almost 6 hours for the LEP/bilingual student (Langdon, 1989b).

CASE STUDIES

Pedro

A Hispanic fifth grader, Pedro is having language and academic difficulties in English. He is attending an English-only program. His teacher is concerned about his lack of progress and is making a referral for possible special education. In deciding if this is an appropriate referral, the team reviewed the cumulative record and conducted a parent interview.

Pedro was born in Arizona, but has been living in the San Francisco Bay area for 8 years. His mother, Mrs. T., is originally from Nicaragua and came to the United States when she was in the third grade. She completed high school in Los Angeles and is a fluent bilingual. Mr. T. is from Guatemala and has been in the United States for only 13 years. He completed elementary school in Guatemala and has not pursued any further education. He can converse in English, but still feels more at ease when communicating in Spanish.

Both Spanish and English are spoken at home. Since Pedro entered school, Mrs. T. has been speaking more English to him, but Mr. T. continues using Spanish when conversing with him. Pedro speaks both English and Spanish with his younger brother. His school attendance has been good, except that he is absent 2 weeks to 1 month at a time when his family goes to visit relatives in Central America. This happens approximately once a year.

Mrs. T. did not suspect that Pedro had a problem with reading comprehension in English until he began to be exposed to more complex material at school. At that time, his difficulties with expressive language also became more apparent. Mrs. T. reported that she needed to "interpret" what Pedro said. For example, one day he said to her in English, "I don't know his house" instead of "I don't know where he lives."

Pedro had been retained in kindergarten because of limited skills in English. His school provided instruction in English as a second language (ESL) but offered no bilingual education. He changed districts when he entered first grade, and he has been attending the same school ever since. The second school did not offer ESL or any other type of bilingual program. His performance was average in first and second grades, but began to decline in third grade. His greatest difficulty was in reading comprehension. Mathematic computational skills were adequate, but Pedro had significant difficulty in solving mathematics-related word problems. His performance was not low enough to warrant a referral, however. When he was in fourth grade, he was given extra tutoring the entire year, but his progress continued to be minimal. Pedro has had difficulty in catching up with his classmates and other students who have received extra help. He is one of few Hispanic students in the school, which has a heavy population of Anglo and Asian students.

Pedro was born in a hospital following an uneventful pregnancy and delivery. He has had repeated ear infections, which have persisted through elementary school. Many notes had been traded between the school nurse and Mrs. T., as Pedro had failed the school hearing screenings several times. Pedro has had a fluctuating conductive bilateral hearing loss that has been frequently aggravated by colds. Mrs. T. could not follow up on referrals for medical assistance because the family had no health insurance.

In this case, several factors signaled the need for a speech and language assessment.

- decline in school performance and lack of language and academic progress observed in the last 2 years, despite extra tutoring
- parent's report that Pedro is having difficulty comprehending material and expressing himself in specific terms
- hearing loss that needs to be treated medically

Because Pedro uses both Spanish and English at home, the clinician should assess his proficiency in both languages. English is his dominant language for academic tasks, but assessing his language skills in English only would not provide a broad picture of his communication abilities.

Assessment Process

A bilingual speech and language consultant was hired to conduct Pedro's assessments. Because no language proficiency test had been administered, the consultant gave Pedro the IPT and a rapid naming task to compare his proficiency in each language. He was also given the Peabody Picture Vocabulary Test in both Spanish and English (Dunn et al., 1986) as well as the Expressive One Word Picture Vocabulary Test (Gardner, 1980). Although Pedro scored as "limited" in both Spanish and English on the IPT (Ballard & Tighe, 1980, 1982), he responded more readily in English. When he spoke in Spanish, there was a greater response delay, and he had more difficulty in expressing his thoughts. To probe Pedro's expressive language skills further, the consultant collected a language sample by asking him to describe his family, talk about his favorite pastimes, and retell a movie seen in each language. In addition, the wordless book *One Frog Too Many* (Mayer, 1976) was used to elicit a narration. Because Pedro had been exposed to English academics only, he was asked to read a story from his reader while the clinician listened. Pedro was also asked to write a letter describing what he would like to do on his next birthday. Pedro was tested separately on each language in two different 90-minute session during the space of a week. His hearing had just been tested by the school nurse prior to the speech-language assessment and was within normal limits.

Language Comprehension

Pedro's language comprehension skills were significantly hampered by a difficulty in processing auditory information. Repetition and rephrasing of questions were necessary before he could give answers to specific questions or perform specific tasks, both for different test items and during conversation. For example, he had difficulty in solving riddles, such as "I am good to drink, I am white, I rhyme with silk. What am I?" This was observed in both languages. Repetition and some rephrasing were helpful in eliciting the correct responses from him. It was also difficult for Pedro to follow directions that included more than two unrelated steps. In conversation, it was necessary to rephrase what had been said, especially when Pedro needed to respond to a hypothetical or inferential question, such as what he would do if he had forgotten his lunch money or what he could do if he felt his grade should have been higher. Response delays were also noted.

Pedro's comprehension skills were generally better in English than in Spanish. Although Pedro was able to read the passage from his textbook in English, his ability to retain the information was very poor. He could not remember who the characters were in the story, what they had done, or when events occurred. He had difficulty even when he was shown strategies that he could use to recall the content, such as finding key words in the text.

Language Expression

Pedro was very willing to communicate in either language, but it was evident that he preferred English. While speaking Spanish, he often had to resort to English words, a common phenomenon in bilinguals. The opposite did not occur when he spoke English, however.

Although Pedro was able to carry on a conversation, there were instances in which he did not interpret the clinician's remarks appropriately, and he had difficulty in expressing his ideas clearly. For example, when the clinician asked,
"What is Guatemala like?" Pedro answered, "Small, I think it is a big city."
"What city did you go to?"
"I don't remember."
"What did you do there?"
(Time delay before he responded.) "I had to go see my . . . my brother and my uncle. That's my dad's father died, so we went there to seen him. We [difficult to understand] flowers, we went back to Guatemala City."

Pedro could convey the general meaning of what he intended to say, but the listener had to interpret what he really meant. His mother's observations were consistent with what the clinician noted during their conversation. In telling the story from the wordless book, he was able to provide references to the story by expressing temporal relationships and some emotional feelings of the characters. The listener needed to make more inferences than would be expected in this situation, however.

Despite these problems, the clinician noted that Pedro's general knowledge was better than his language and academic performance. He was able to identify a map of Florida, the Statue of Liberty, and the Capitol, indicating that he is very capable of comprehending and retaining facts, but needs many opportunities to learn the same information through a multisensory approach. His mother reported that she reads books to her children on different topics and discusses events on TV, including the value of commercials. Pedro's expressive language skills in naming vocabulary was fairly good, considering his auditory and language-processing difficulties. His performance on the Expressive One Word Picture Vocabulary Test was only 1 year below his chronological age in English, and his score was only slightly lower in Spanish.

Pedro's grammatical and syntactical abilities in English varied from context to context. He still made many errors with the use of the past tense in English (e.g., "he paint" instead of "he painted") and the use of the third person singular (e.g., "everything change" for "everything changes"). Also, his verb tense usage was not uniform in his narration. He began using one tense and then switched to another for no apparent reason. Pedro should not have made these types of errors in view of the length of his formal exposure to English (7 years). Similar errors, as well as incorrect use of pronouns and disagreement between nouns and adjectives, were noted in Spanish.

Pedro's articulation skills were adequate in both languages, but his intelligibility sometimes decreased in connected speech. No signs of stuttering were observed. Fluency was disrupted on occasion when Pedro was attempting to express his thoughts. Some pauses, word repetitions, and use of gestures instead of words were noted in both languages, but more in Spanish than in English.

Pedro's receptive and expressive language difficulties had a great impact on his academic performance. Pedro could write only three short sentences (three to four words long) about what he wanted to do for his birthday. Although his spelling was correct, there were errors in punctuation, and his writing was labored.

Discussion

Pedro is an 11:6-year-old bilingual youngster who has had difficulty in progressing in academic subjects. The bilingual speech and language assessment indicates that, although he is English-dominant, his language skills are weak in both Spanish and English. He has some basic communication skills in both Spanish and English, but lacks the ability to use language in a more elaborate fashion. His CALP in English is weak because of language-processing and comprehension difficulties; his CALP in Spanish has not developed at all because he has not been taught academics in that language.

One of Pedro's strengths is his maintenance of the two languages; many individuals who have language/learning problems do not attempt to preserve the language that they do not need for success in school or on the job. Pedro also has an average receptive and expressive single vocabulary (naming, which is better in English), a willingness to try and learn, and parental support. He has problems in the processing of oral language, especially evident when the information requires comprehension of longer and more complex texts; in the expression of specific relationships, such as cause and effect; in the understanding of hypotheses; and in the organization of ideas, in general.

Pedro's academic difficulties stem from a language/learning disability that has been complicated by a long history of fluctuating hearing loss. It is difficult to determine whether the hearing loss is the primary cause for his language problems or whether he also has a difficulty in processing information that is presented orally. Nevertheless, his language disability has had a significant impact on his academic performance. For 2 years of school, he was able to compensate for his hearing problem by learning through visual stimuli. As the content of texts has become more complex, however, he has had more difficulty in achieving in academic areas.

Pedro's primary needs are in the language area. His educational needs must be met in the least restrictive environment possible, and he should receive assistance from both the speech-language clinician and the resource specialist. The consultant made the following recommendations for Pedro:

1. Teaching strategies should be implemented to help Pedro retain and process auditory information more effectively. Ideally, his reading and lan-

guage programs should be integrated; that is, a unit should be discussed orally, then Pedro should read literature based on the unit and also have an opportunity to write a composition on the subject.

2. An ear, nose, and throat specialist should be consulted about Pedro's hearing problem. If this problem is not remediated, it will be difficult for him to make further progress.
3. Pedro's parents should be advised to continue using Spanish at home. It is suggested that Spanish and English be used during separate segments of the day, however, to allow for maximal learning of each language.

Pedro should be encouraged to read and write as much as possible at home in English, as he has been exposed to this language for academic learning. For example, he could practice writing messages, directions from one place to another (what streets to take from the main road to his house), and notes to relatives and friends. Eventually, he may want to write in Spanish. Improving his oral Spanish skills will allow him to communicate more effectively with his father. This, in turn, will enhance his bilingualism and biculturalism, which are assets in today's multicultural and multilingual United States.

Arturo (Sample Report)

Reason for Referral

Arturo has language difficulties in both Spanish and English. In his home, he hears both languages, but his Head Start program is conducted in English only. He is 4:6 years old.

Background Information

Social and Family Background. Arturo was born in San Jose, California. He lives with his parents and 2:6-year-old sister. Mrs. R. is a homemaker, and Mr. R. is a carpenter. Mrs. R. has been in the United States for 9 years, and her husband has been here for approximately 15 years. Both Mr. R. and Mrs. R. are from Mexico (Michoacan and Chihuahua, respectively). Mrs. R. completed seventh grade in Mexico and has taken some English classes since she came to the United States. She is able to understand English quite well, but does not feel very fluent in the language yet; she speaks only Spanish to the children. Mr. R. completed high school in the United States and speaks both English and Spanish to the children. At home, Arturo spends his time watching TV and coloring. He does not have many children to play with, except relatives who visit on the weekends. Arturo speaks Spanish to his sister and the children who visit him. Recently, the entire family went to Chihuahua, Mexico, for 2 weeks. It was the first time that Arturo had traveled abroad.

Mrs. R. has had to adapt English books in order to read to her children in Spanish. Arturo does not enjoy listening to stories, however. His limited attention span in this context has discouraged Mrs. R. from continuing this activity on a steady basis. Arturo attends better if she tells him a story without a book, but this is not a favorite activity for him.

Health and Developmental Background. No complications with pregnancy or delivery were reported. Arturo has been a healthy child. He passed the vision and hearing screenings conducted by the school nurse shortly before the speech and language assessment. He learned to walk at 13 months of age. Mrs. R. reported that Arturo has difficulty following directions in either language at home. Since Arturo has been attending Head Start, his expressive language has improved in both languages. He is still using short sentences, however, and he is difficult to understand in both languages. His younger sister can express herself better than he could at her age.

School Background. Arturo does well in school with most activities that require fine and gross motor coordination. He still lacks some school readiness skills, such as recognizing colors and counting, and prepositional terms seem to confuse him. He does not know his age. His mother has worked on these skills, but Arturo has difficulty retaining the information. Arturo will be going to kindergarten next year.

Observations

Arturo is a very pleasant child whose cooperation and attention were very good. He had difficulty adjusting when his mother left the room, however; he began crying and asking her to stay. He did calm down after being reassured that his mother would come back. In the classroom, he followed directions well because he imitated the other children. When singled out to perform a task or respond to a question, he had more difficulty. He seemed to prefer to play by himself, but if a child approached him, he was willing to share a toy. No verbal interaction was noted between the two children, however.

Testing Procedures Followed and Materials Used

The following formal tests were administered in Spanish by a bilingual speech-language clinician who was hired as a consultant:

1. Preschool Language Scales (PLS), Spanish version, to assess general language comprehension and expression
2. Expressive One Word Picture Vocabulary Test (Spanish version), an expressive vocabulary test

3. Test de Vocabulario en Imágenes Peabody (TVIP), the Spanish equivalent of the Peabody Picture Vocabulary Test (PPVT)

4. Spanish Structured Photographic Expressive Language Test—Preschool (SPELT) to elicit specific grammatical and syntactical forms

5. Assessment of Phonological Processes—Spanish to assess articulation skills

An informal language sample was obtained in conjunction with the tasks administered and conversation.

The equivalent English tests had been administered by Mrs. P. in English. The results of tests in both languages by Arturo's speech and language clinician appear in the Summary and Recommendation section. They must be interpreted with care, as only the Test de Vocabulario en Imágenes Peabody has been normed on Spanish-speaking monolingual children. Although there are norms for the SPELT and the Expressive One Word Picture Vocabulary Test, they are available only in English.

Oral Language Comprehension and Listening Skills

Arturo's comprehension is approximately 1 year below his chronological age in both languages, according to the PLS and observation. His performance on tasks is almost parallel in both languages. He could point to different objects when their use was named, he could differentiate details in pictures, and he could reproduce different block patterns. He could group objects by categories, but repetition and modeling were necessary. Arturo still confuses colors; lacks an understanding of different concepts, such as heavy and light, rough and smooth; and is not sure of terms such as behind, in front of, and beside.

During conversation, he could respond to questions pertaining to his immediate experiences, such as what he does when he bathes, and his comments about pictures were adequate. For example, while looking at a picture of a car, he said, "Tengo un carro" 'I have a car'. With some common pictures, however, Arturo had the concept, but not the word. It was often difficult for him to retrieve the exact words to express his thoughts. At times, he misunderstood what he heard. For example, when he was asked what he uses to dry himself, he said, "Fine" instead of "a towel"; he had confused *con qué* 'what' with *cómo* 'how'. Similar difficulties were noted in English. His receptive vocabulary in both languages was poor. Basals (lowest point from which recording of tests begins) on receptive vocabulary tests could not be established in either language. He could not identify words such as *candle, cage, or furniture* in either Spanish or English. For example, he called a cage a bird and a candle a stick. Lack of exposure to those words could be a factor. Repetition of sentences was difficult as well; he typically repeated only the last two or three words that he heard.

Oral Language Expression

Arturo was very willing to interact with the clinician. Yet, formulation and word-finding difficulties were noted throughout his conversation. Word repetitions and pauses were frequent in both languages. For example, when the clinician asked, ¿Por qué está en la cama el niño? 'Why is the child in bed', Arturo replied, "Porque, porque, porque, no quiere come [comer], tiene . . . tiene frío" 'Because, because, because he does not want to eat, he is . . . he is cold'. Very likely, Arturo meant tired rather than cold. Although Arturo used several tenses correctly in conversation such as the preterite *fué* 'went', he made frequent errors with irregular verbs (e.g., "acuestado" for *acostado* 'lying down'). He also used incorrect gender forms with articles, adjectives, and past participles (e.g., masculine form for most words, regardless of their gender) and either omitted or incorrectly used prepositions (e.g., "yo tengo a la casa" for *yo tengo [eso] en la casa* 'I have some [of that] at home'). Despite his expressive language difficulties, he was able to use language for a number of functions, such as negate, ask, and inquire. His sentence length fluctuated between four and eight words, depending on the context. Some of his sentences seemed to reflect English syntax: "Me stá chiquito baby" 'I am a little baby'. He also mixed the two languages occasionally.

In English, Arturo's expressive language was more limited. He used three- to four-word sentences, and there were also some grammar and syntax errors (e.g., 'He eat hotdog'). Overall, it was estimated that his expressive language in Spanish was more like that of a 3- to 3½-year-old; in English, it was 1 year below that.

Arturo's expressive vocabulary was very limited in both languages. He lacked terms for basic items and often demonstrated the action or used a word association instead of the word. He also showed some preference for the use of some words in one language, but not the other. Most likely, greater frequency in using certain words in English or Spanish was a variable, or some were easier to pronounce in one language than in the other. For example, he said "Halloween" instead of "pumpkin", "bike" instead of *bicicleta* 'bicycle', and "money" instead of *dinero*.

The articulation of sounds in individual words was moderately to severely impaired in Spanish. Most of Arturo's errors were in the production of tap/trill /r/ and lateral /l/. He reduced a number of cluster sounds, saying /kus/ for *cruz* 'cross' and /fo/ for *flor* 'flower'. He also had difficulty sequencing sounds in certain words; he would say "opra" for *ropa* 'clothing', "orido" for *oído* 'ear', and "arlo" for *árbol* 'tree'. Yet, he could pronounce some longer words correctly, such as *manzana* 'apple' and *teléfono* 'telephone'. It could be that the frequency of his use contributed to his ability to pronounce some words better than others. Exhibit 7-6 illustrates the errors that Arturo made in Spanish using the Assessment of Phonological Processes in Spanish. In English, his articulation was more severely impaired because of his unfamiliarity with the language. Examination of the oral peripheral mechanism indicated adequate structures for normal support of speech. Difficulty was noted in his ability to sequence nonsense syllables, however, indicating some weakness in the oral motor musculature.

Summary and Recommendations

Arturo is a predominantly Spanish-speaking 4½-year-old child whose comprehension skills are almost equivalent in both languages, but whose expressive language is much better in Spanish than in English. Processing of oral language is difficult for him in both languages and expressive language skills are limited. He

---

Exhibit 7-6 Phonological Analysis Summary

Client **Arturo**   Date **1-11-90** Examiner **Langdon**

Birthdate **7-11-85**   Age **4: 6**

BASIC PHONOLOGICAL PROCESSES

Phonological Omissions	Number of Occurrences	+	Possible Occurrences	=	Percentage of Occurrence
Syllable Reduction	3		37		8
Consonant Sequence Reduction	26		37		70
Singleton Omissions					
Prevocalic	16		55		29
Postvocalic	8		12		66
Class Deficiencies					
Stridents	1		27		37
Velars	2		22		9
Lateral (l)	8		15		53
Tap/Trill (r)	13		18		55
Glides	5		13		38
Nasals	0		13		0

Total Percentage-of-Occurrence Scores	365
Phonological Process Percentage-of-Occurrence Average	36
Additional Points	5
Phonological Deviancy Score	41
Severity Interval Rating For Phonology	Severe (Low range)

Severe interval: 40 - 59

continues

Exhibit 7-6 Continued

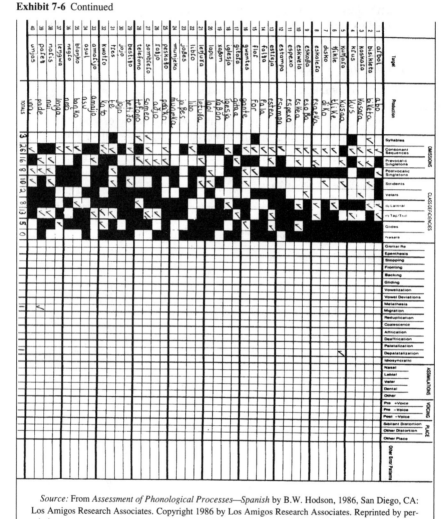

Source: From *Assessment of Phonological Processes—Spanish* by B.W. Hodson, 1986, San Diego, CA: Los Amigos Research Associates. Copyright 1986 by Los Amigos Research Associates. Reprinted by permission.

is performing at a $3^1/_2$-year-level in Spanish and a 2- to $2^1/_2$-year-level in English. Thus, his skills in both languages are weak, as shown by his test results.

	Spanish	English
PLS Receptive	Age 3:6 years	Age 3:6 years
PLS Expressive and observation	Age 3:6 years	Age 2:6 years
Language sample	Refer to the body of the report	

Receptive vocabulary	TVIP	PPVT
	Basal could not be established	
Expressive One Word		
Picture Vocabulary Test	Age 2:7 years	Age 2 years
SPELT	15/25 items correct	8/15 correct

It is recommended that only one language be used at a time while communicating with Arturo (during particular segments of a day or with particular interactants). For example, translating from English to Spanish in the school setting would not be an adequate teaching approach. This is also applicable to the times when Mr. R. converses with him. Mr. R. should speak to Arturo only in one language at a time to offer maximum input in each language. As Arturo develops skills in English, very likely he will be able to transfer them to Spanish.

Arturo qualifies for speech and language services. His problems reflect a language-processing/delay difficulty, compounded by expressive language and phonological problems. Even though his English language skills are more limited than are his Spanish language skills, it is recommended that services be provided in English to allow continuity with his English-only school program.

The goals in developing Arturo's oral language comprehension should include increasing his knowledge of specific concepts and vocabulary, improving his ability to respond to specific questions during play, and reading to him. Expressive language goals should include developing his vocabulary as well as increasing his ability to use more descriptive language, to form sentences, and to describe experiences by using at least two different, but connected, ideas. Other goals should focus on developing sound sequencing skills and stimulation of production of specific phonemes.

His parents can help Arturo at home by working on the following activities:

- When talking to Arturo, his parents could name and describe what is happening. For example, while driving to a supermarket, they could talk about where they are going, what they are going to buy, and what they will do when they get home. If Arturo is with Mr. R., they could use only English most of the time; with Mrs. R., Arturo could use Spanish. When the entire family participates in an activity, they should use Spanish because this is the language in which Mrs. R. feels more comfortable at this time.

- If Arturo uses an incorrect word or grammatical structure, his parents could reword what he said through expansion.

- His parents could read to Arturo, starting with 2 minutes at a time. If he is not interested, they should postpone the activity for later. They should praise him for paying attention and for trying. After reading a page, they should ask him a question to check comprehension. To enhance his interest in printed material, his parents could use pop-up books, and point out signs on roads and stores.

- The family could play games such as Lotto and Twenty Questions. They could work on categories, for example, naming all the vegetables, fruits, domestic animals, zoo animals, and clothing articles that they know.

In the future, Arturo should be placed in a kindergarten program that emphasizes language and school prereadiness skills. Teaching him the alphabet in English may be premature at this time. Rather, efforts should focus on increasing his print awareness and interest in school-related activities. Prereading could be introduced by asking him to identify his name from a choice of two or pointing to some of the words as they are read in the context of a story.

COMMUNICATION WITHIN THE HISPANIC FAMILY

Throughout the assessment process, as these case studies clearly illustrate, it is essential to communicate with the parents regularly. A pleasant initial contact with the family will facilitate the entire process. The clinician should demonstrate a personal as well as a professional concern (Figler, 1979; Fishgrund, Cohen, & Clarkson, 1987; Maestas & Erickson, 1989). Often, explanations may take on a personal note, such as "I have a child your child's age; he is now able to understand me better, and this is what I want to help your child with." Many persons who work with Hispanics in different work settings have suggested that clinicians take this more personal attitude and interest (Figler, 1979; Fishgrund et al., 1987; Meyerson, 1990; Rodríguez, 1983).

In many instances, the initial contact with the home is with the mother. Traditionally, the mother manages the activities in the house and deals with school problems and decisions regarding the children's education (Delgado-Gaitán & Trueba, 1991). Final decisions are often made by the father, however. Thus, the mother should be given the option to discuss the findings and recommendations with the father before she signs a consent form for the program.

It is important to present clear, relevant information. Even though notes and explanations may be written in Spanish, the family should be contacted by telephone or in person to ascertain that the information presented is indeed clear. Too many data may be confusing for any parent. Points should be illustrated with concrete examples that can be applied to everyday life. Thus, instead of saying "your child has an auditory processing difficulty," the clinician should describe what this problem implies, using concrete examples from both school and home situations. The clinician must respect the parents' feelings and beliefs when they attempt to explain the cause of their child's problems for themselves. It may be helpful to consult with other staff members and physicians, if necessary, for specific cases before giving a concrete explanation for the possible causes of a problem.

To avoid missed appointments, Hernández-Grein, who works both in school and hospital settings, calls the parents the night before and explains the urgency and need for the meeting (Personal communication, 1990). When the clinician does not speak Spanish, it is important to have an interpreter. Another family member or a trusted neighbor or friend may also attend meetings to offer support to a parent. More than one family member may be present during the clinician's conversations with a parent at home. If the child or other children are present, it may be wise to ask the parent if they can be excused. If possible, a clinician may ask the parent in advance for a confidential interview.

One of the greatest fears of many Hispanic parents is that their child is *enfermito* 'sick' or *loco* 'insane, crazy' if school personnel suggest placement in a special day class. This is especially true for children with language and learning disabilities where the problem may not be obvious. The clinician must carefully explain the difference between mental retardation and difficulties with language and academically related tasks. Offering the parent an opportunity to visit the class is a very helpful strategy, not only during the assessment process, but also during any necessary interventions.

BIBLIOGRAPHY

Ada, A., & Olave, M. (1986). *Hagamos caminos.* Levels 1–6. Reading, MA: Addison-Wesley.

Amato, D.R., Basque, R., Allen, A., & Kiraithe, J. (1987). *Economy Spanish reading series.* Preprimers through grade 5. Oklahoma City, OK: The Economy Co.

American Educational Research Association, American Psychological Association & National Council on Measurement in Education. (1985). *Standards for educational and psychological testing.* Washington, DC: American Psychological Association.

Ballard, W.S., Tighe, & P.L. (Eds.). (1980, 1982, 1983, 1987). *Idea language proficiency test, Level I, II.* Brea, CA: Ballard & Tighe, Inc.

Barrera, R., & Crawford, A. (1987). *Programa de lectura en español de Houghton Mifflin.* Preprimer to level 6. Boston: Houghton Mifflin Co.

Beringer, M. (1977). *Ber-Sil Level I, Level II.* Ranchos Palos Verdes, CA: Ber-Sil Company.

Board of Education of the City of New York. (1976). *Language assessment battery.* Brooklyn, NY: OREA Scan Center.

Brigance, A. (1977). *Brigance diagnostic assessment of basic skills* (English version). North Billerica, MA: Curriculum Associates.

Brigance, A. (1983). *Brigance diagnostic assessment of basic skills* (Spanish version). North Billerica, MA: Curriculum Associates.

Brown, R. (1973). *A first language.* Cambridge, MA: Harvard University Press.

Note: Multiple dates refer to either different versions, levels, or language versions (English and Spanish).

Burt, M., Dulay, H., & Hernández-Chávez, E. (1975, 1980). *Bilingual syntax measure* (BSM) (Level I, II). San Antonio, TX: The Psychological Corporation.

California Test of Basic Skills (CTBS). Monterey, CA: McGraw-Hill.

Carrow, E. (1973). *Test of auditory comprehension of language (English and Spanish)* (TACL). Allen, TX: DLM Teaching Resources.

Carrow, E. (1974). *Austin Spanish articulation test*. Allen, TX: DLM Teaching Resources.

Chamberlain, P., & Medeiros-Landurand, P. (1991). Practical considerations for the assessment of LEP students with special needs. In E.V. Hamayan & J.S. Damico (Eds.), *Limiting bias in the assessment of bilingual students* (pp. 111–156). Austin, TX: PRO-ED.

Cheng, L., Langdon, H., & Davies, D. (1991). *The art of interpreting: A dynamic process [Videotape]*. San Diego, CA: Department of Communication Disorders, San Diego State University.

Cohen, S., & Cohen, M. (1978). *Prueba de lectura en español*. Berkeley, CA: Bilingual Media Production, Inc.

Critchlow, D.E. (1974). *Dos amigos verbal language scales*. Novato, CA: Academic Therapy Publications.

Cummins, J. (1984). *Bilingualism and special education: Issues in assessment and pedagogy*. Clevedon, England: Multilingual Matters.

Curtis, J.K. (1986). *The development of graphic sense: Preliterate children's knowledge about written language*. Unpublished doctoral dissertation, University of Toronto, Ontario, Canada.

Damico, J.S. (1985). Clinical discourse analysis: A functional language assessment. In C.S. Simon (Ed.), *Communication skills and classroom success: Assessment of language-learning disabled students* (pp. 165–204). San Diego, CA: College Hill Press.

Damico, J.S. (1991). Descriptive assessment of communicative ability in limited English proficient student. In E.V. Hamayan & J.S. Damico (Eds.), *Limiting bias in the assessment of bilingual students* (pp. 157–217). Austin, TX: PRO-ED.

De Avila, E., & Duncan, S.E. (1977, 1979, 1986). *Language assessment scales* (LAS, Includes Pre-LAS). Monterey, CA: McGraw-Hill.

Delgado-Gaitán, C., & Trueba, H. (1991). *Crossing cultural borders*. New York: Palmer Press.

Dunn, L., & Dunn, L. (1981). *Peabody picture vocabulary test—Revised* (PPVT). Circle Pines, MN: American Guidance Service.

Dunn, L.M., Padilla, E.R., Lugo, D.E., & Dunn, L.M. (1986). *Test de vocabulario en Imágenes Peabody* (TVIP). Circle Pines, MN: American Guidance Service.

Erickson, J.G., & Iglesias, A. (1986). Speech and language disorders in Hispanics. In O. Taylor (Ed.), *Nature of communication disorders in culturally and linguistically diverse populations* (pp. 181–217). San Diego, CA: College Hill Press.

Erickson, J.G., & Omark, D.R. (Eds.). (1981). *Communication assessment of the bilingual bicultural child*. Baltimore: University Park Press.

Figler, C. (1979). *A comparative study of Puerto Rican families with and without handicapped children*. Unpublished doctoral dissertation. Amherst, MA: University of Massachusetts.

Fishgrund, J.E., Cohen, O.P., & Clarkson, R.L. (1987). Hearing impaired children in Black and Hispanic Families. *Volta Review, 89*, 59–67.

Fitzgerald, J., & Spiegel, D.L. (1986). Enhancing children's reading comprehension through instruction in narrative structure. *Journal of Reading Behavior, 15*, 1–17.

Gardner, M.F. (1980, 1983). *Expressive one-word picture vocabulary test* (Levels I, II). (Spanish and English versions) (EOWPVT). Novato, CA: Academic Therapy Publications.

Goldman, R.W., & Fristoe, M. (1986). *Goldman-Fristoe test of articulation*. Circle Pines, MN: American Guidance Service, Inc.

Guzmán, A., Long, S., Marías, R., Santiago, R., Somoza, E., & Tinajero, J. (1986). *Mil maravillas*. Preprimer through Grade 5. New York: Macmillan.

Hammill, D.D., Larsen, S.C., Wiederholt, J.E., & Fountain-Chambers, J. (1982). *Prueba de lectura y lenguaje escrito*. Austin, TX: PRO-ED.

Heald-Taylor, G. (1987). Predictable literature selections and activities for language arts instruction. *The Reading Teacher, 17,* 7–12.

Heath, S.B. (1986). Sociocultural contexts of language development. In California State Department of Education, Bilingual Education Office (Ed.), *Beyond language* (pp. 143–186). Los Angeles: Evaluation, Dissemination and Assessment Center, California State University.

Hernández-Grein, A. (1990). Personal communication.

Hodson, B.W. (1986a). *Assessment of phonological processes—Spanish*. San Diego, CA: Los Amigos Research Associates.

Hodson, B.W. (1986b). *Assessment of phonological processes—Revised*. Danville: Interstate.

Hresko, W.P., Reid, D.K., & Hammill, D.D. (1982). *Prueba del desarrollo initial del lenguaje*. Austin, TX: PRO-ED.

Jax, V.A. (1988a). *Narrative construction by children learning English as a second language: A precursor to reading comprehension*. Unpublished doctoral dissertation, University of California at Los Angeles.

Jax, V.A. (1988b). Understanding school language proficiency through the assessment of story construction. In A.A. Ortíz & B.A. Ramírez (Eds.), *Schools and culturally diverse exceptional students: Promising practices and future directions* (pp. 45–50). Reston, VA: Council for Exceptional Children.

Kamhi, A.G., & Catts, H.W. (Eds.) (1989). *Reading disabilities: A developmental language perspective*. Austin, TX: PRO-ED.

Kayser, H. (November 1989a). *Communicative strategies of Anglo and Hispanic clinicians with Hispanic preschoolers*. Paper presented at the American Speech-Language-Hearing Association Convention, St. Louis.

Kayser, H. (1989b). Speech and language assessment of Spanish-English speaking children. *Language, Speech and Hearing Services in Schools, 30,* 226–244.

Kirk, S., & Van Isser, A. (1980). *Prueba Illinois de habilidades psicolinguísticas* (ITPA).Tucson, AZ: University of Arizona, Special Education Department.

Kirk, S.B., McCarthy, J., & Kirk, W. (1968). *The Illinois test of psycholinguistic abilities* (ITPA) (Revised edition). Urbana, IL: University of Illinois Press.

Laesch, K.B., & van Kleeck, A. (1987). The Cloze test as an alternative measure of language proficiency of children considered for exit from bilingual education. *Language Learning, 37,* 171–189.

Lahey, M. (1988). *Language disorders and language development*. New York: Macmillan.

Langdon, H.W. (1977). *Determining a language disorder in a bilingual Spanish-English population*. Unpublished doctoral dissertation, Boston University.

Langdon, H.W. (1983). Assessment and intervention strategies for the bilingual language disordered student. *Exceptional Children, 50,* 37–56.

Langdon, H.W. (1988). Gloria: A case of bilingual learning disabled child. In J.R. Jones (Ed.), *Psychoeducational assessment of minority group children: A casebook* (pp. 257–269). Berkeley, CA: Cobb & Henry.

Langdon, H.W. (1989a). *The interpreter/translator in the school setting: A training module.* Sacramento, CA: California State Department of Education/Special Education.

Langdon, H.W. (1989b). Language disorder or difference? Assessing the language skills of Hispanic students. *Exceptional Children, 56,* 160–167.

Lee, L. (1971). *Northwestern syntax screening test* (NSST). Evanston, IL: Northwestern University Press.

Lee, L. (1974). *Development sentence analysis: A grammatical assessment procedure for speech and language clinicians.* Evanston, IL: Northwestern University Press.

Linares-Orama, N. (1977). Evaluation of syntax in three-year-old Spanish-speaking Puerto Rican children. *Journal of Speech and Hearing Research, 20,* 350–357.

Lomax, R.G., & McGee, L.M. (1987). Young children's concepts about print and reading: Toward a model of word reading acquisition. *Reading Research Quarterly, 12,* 237–256.

Lowe, R.J. (1986). *Assessment link between phonology and articulation* (ALPHA). Moline, IL: LinguiSystems, Inc.

Maestas, A.G., & Erickson, J.E. (November 1989). *Mexican immigrant parents and the education of their handicapped children: Factors that influence parent involvement.* Paper presented at the American Speech-Language-Hearing Association Annual Convention, St. Louis, Missouri.

Mares, S. (1980). *Pruebas de expresión oral y percepción de la lengua española* (PEOPLE). Downey, CA: Los Angeles County Office of Education.

Mason, M.A., Smith, B.F., & Hinshaw, M.M. (1976). *Medida Española de articulación* (MEDA). San Ysidro, CA: San Ysidro School District.

Mattes, L.J. (1987). *Spanish articulation measures.* Oceanside, CA: Academic Communication Associates.

Mattes, L.J., & Omark, D.R. (1984). *Speech and language assessment for the bilingual handicapped.* San Diego, CA: College Hill Press.

Mayer, M & M. (1975). *One frog too many.* New York: Dial Books for Young Readers.

Melgar de González, M. (1980). *Cómo detectar al niño con problemas del habla.* Mexico, D.F.: Trillas.

Merino, B., & Spencer, M. (1983). The comparability of English and Spanish versions of oral language proficiency instruments. *National Association of Bilingual Education Journal, 7,* 1–31.

Meyerson, M.D. (1990). Cultural considerations in the treatment of Latinos with craniofacial anomalies. *The Cleft Palate Journal, 27,* 279–288.

Miller, L. (August 1986). *Language disabilities, organizational strategies, and classroom learning.* Workshop presented at the Language Learning Disabilities Institutes, Emerson College, San Diego, California.

Moreno, S. (1978). *Spanish reading comprehension text.* San Diego, CA: Moreno Educational Company.

Muma, J.R. (1978). *Language handbook: Concepts, assessment, intervention.* Englewood Cliffs, NJ: Prentice-Hall.

Ortíz, A.A., & García, S.B. (1988). A prereferral process for preventing inappropriate referrals of Hispanic students to special education. In A.A. Ortíz & B. Ramírez (Eds.), *Schools and the culturally exceptional student: Promising practices and future directions* (pp. 6–18). Reston, VA: Council for Exceptional Children.

Peterson, C., & McCabe, A. (1983). *Developmental psycholinguistics: Three ways of looking at a child's narrative.* New York: Plenum Press.

Pollack, M.D. (1980). *The effects of testwiseness language of test administration, and language competence on readiness test performance of low socio-economic level, Spanish speaking children.* Ann Arbor: University of Michigan. University Microforms International Microfiche #80-16031.

Prutting, C. (1983). Assessing communicative behavior using a language sample. In D.R. Omark & J.G. Erickson (Eds.), *The bilingual exceptional child* (pp. 89–99). San Diego: College Hill Press.

The Psychological Corporation. (1990). *Aprenda.* San Antonio, TX: The Psychological Corporation.

Ramos, A. (1985). *Lectura en dos idiomas. Readiness through grade 5.* Northvale, NJ: Santillana Publishing Co.

Rodríguez, J. (1983). Mexican Americans: Factors influencing health activities. *The Journal of School Health* (February, Special Issue).

Romero, C., & Miller, P. (1982). *Spanish oral reading test.* Los Gatos, CA: Paradox Press.

Simon, C. (1987). *Evaluating communicative competence: A functional pragmatic procedure.* Tucson, AZ: Communication Skills Builders.

Swanson, E.N., & DeBlassie, R.R. (1979). Interpreter and Spanish administration effects on the WISC-R performance of Mexican-American children. *Journal of School Psychology, 17,* 231–236.

Toronto, A.S. (1973). *Screening test of Spanish grammar* (STSG). Evanston, IL: Northwestern University Press.

Toronto, A.S. (1977). *Toronto test of receptive vocabulary (English/Spanish).* Austin, TX: National Educational Laboratory.

Toronto, A.S., Leverman, D., Hanna, C., Rosenzweig, P., & Maldonado, A. (1975). *Del Rio language screening test.* Austin, TX: National Educational Laboratory.

Toronto, A.S., & Merrill, S.M. (1983). Developing local normed assessment instruments. In D.R. Omark & J.G. Erickson (Eds.), *The bilingual exceptional child* (pp. 105–121). San Diego, CA: College Hill Press.

Tyack, D., & Gottsleben, R. (1974). *Language sampling, analysis and training.* Palo Alto, CA: Consulting Psychologists Press.

Ulibarri, D.M., Spencer, M., & Rivas, G.A. (1981). Language proficiency and academic achievement. *National Association for Bilingual Education Journal, 5,* 47–80.

Wallach, G., & Miller, L. (1988). *Language intervention and academic success.* Boston, MA: College Hill Press.

Wechsler, D. (1974). *Manual for the Wechsler intelligence scale for children—Revised.* New York: Psychological Corporation.

Weddington, G.T. (1987). *The assessment and treatment of communication disorders in culturally diverse populations.* Unpublished manuscript, San Jose State University.

Weddington, T.W., & Meyerson, M.D. (1983). Training paraprofessionals for identification and intervention with communicatively disordered bilinguals. In D.R. Omark & J.G. Erickson (Eds.), *The bilingual exceptional child* (pp. 379–395). San Diego, CA: College Hill Press.

Werner, E.O., & Kresheck, J.D. (1983). *Structural photographic expressive language test, preschool (P) and II.* (SPELT) (English version). Sandwich, IL: Janelle Publications.

Werner, E.O., & Kresheck, J.D. (1989). *Spanish SPELT I and II.* Sandwich, IL: Janelle Publications.

Westby, C. (1989, December). *Clinical evaluation of limited English proficiency children.* Audioteleconference sponsored by the American Speech-Language-Hearing Association (with Aquiles Iglesias), Washington, DC.

Wiig, E.H., & Secord, W. (1985). *Test of language competence.* San Antonio, TX: The Psychological Corporation.

Woodcock, R.W. (1981). *Woodcock language proficiency battery: Spanish form.* Hingham, MA: Teaching Resources Corporation.

Woodcock, R.M., & Johnson, M.B. (1981, 1988). *The Woodcock-Johnson psychoeducational battery.* Allen, TX: DLM Teaching Resources.

Wren, C. (1985). Collecting language samples from children with syntax problems. *Language, Speech and Hearing Services in Schools, 16,* 83–105.

Zachman, L., Jorgensen, C., Huisingh, R., & Barrett, M. (1984). *Test of problem solving* (TOPS). Moline, IL: LinguiSystems.

Zimmerman, I.L., Steiner, V.G., & Pond, R.E. (1979). *Preschool language scale* (PLS). San Antonio, TX: The Psychological Corporation.

Appendix 7-A

Widely Used Language and Language Proficiency Tests Available in Spanish

Test	Ages or Grade	Areas Tested	Scoring Procedure
Assessment of Phonological Processes—Spanish Hodson, 1986 Los Amigos Research Assoc. San Diego, CA 92120	3:0 years and above	Articulation in single words; focus on analyzing phonological processes.	Uses pictures, but preferably toys that the clinician gathers (40 target words).
Austin Spanish Articulation Test Carrow, 1974 DLM Teaching Resources One DLM Park Allen, TX 75002	3:6–12:0 years	Articulation in single words.	Child completes sentences using the target word; test assesses consonants, vowels, and diphthongs.
Ber-Sil I, II Beringer, 1977 Ber-Sil Company 3412 Seaglen Dr Rancho Palos Verdes, CA 90274	4:0–12:0 years	Receptive vocabulary, oral commands, comprehension, and visual motor.	Age levels are given for the receptive vocabulary subtest. Other areas are given age level performance.
	13:0–17:0 years	Receptive vocabulary, dictation of sentences, math, draw a girl or boy.	Age levels are given for the receptive vocabulary and for drawing a boy or girl. Percentile of performance for dictation given.
Bilingual Syntax Measure (BSM) I, II Burt, Dulay, Hernández-Chávez, 1975, 1980 The Psychological Corporation 555 Academic Court San Antonio, TX 78204	K–2nd grade	Ability to use certain grammatical forms correctly.	Classification is according to number of errors. Five possible classifications. 1 (no English or Spanish) to 5 (proficient in English or Spanish).
	3rd grade– high school	Same as above.	Same as above.

Note: N/A, not available

Development and/or Norms	Reliability	Validity	Comments
Field-tested on 3 groups of 20, 4 yr and 4-7 yrs old from Mexicali San Diego, some with/ without problems.	N/A	N/A	Results yield information on 10 basic phonological processes as well as 28 error patterns.
Developed with 20 Mexican-American children in Texas.	N/A	N/A	Test is limited to testing sounds at the word level; does not account for dialectal differences.
Normed on Spanish-speaking children born in Mexico and Los Angeles primarily; some from Central America. Numbers are not specified.	Test-retest reliability only.	Content and construct validity, but information seems incomplete.	Vocabulary testing may be too long. Choice of pictures may not always be adequate: only three choices.
Normed on students from Mexico, El Salvador, and other Spanish-speaking countries. Numbers are not specified.	No specific data offered.	No specific data offered.	Same remarks as for Ber-Sil I. Helpful in describing the student's math skills and screening of spelling.
Normed on 1,572 children from various backgrounds (Mexican, Anglo-American, Puerto Rican, and Cuban).	No internal or alternate form reliability.	No criterion validity offered.	Test is limited to one aspect of language, which is essentially part of grammar. Should be used with other measurements of language.
Normed on 775 students from various backgrounds (Spanish, Korean, Japanese, Chinese . . .).	Internal and test-retest reliability only.	Data presented are not	Topic of the story may be inappropriate for certain youngsters. Same limitations as above.

continues

Test	Ages or Grade	Areas Tested	Scoring Procedure
Del Rio Language Screening Test Toronto, Leverman, Hanna, Rosenzweig, & Maldonado, 1975 National Educational Laboratory P.O. Box 1003 Austin, TX 78767	3:0–6:0 years	Receptive vocabulary, sentence repetition (complexity and length), oral commands, and story comprehension.	Scores are converted into percentiles for any given age; three tables: (1) predominantly Spanish-speaking, (2) predominantly English-speaking, (3) bilingual.
Dos Amigos Verbal Language Scales Critchlow, 1974 Academic Therapy Publications 20 Commercial Blvd Novato, CA 94949	5:0–13:6 years	Verbal opposites in both languages.	Percentiles are given for each age and each language.
Expressive One Word Picture Vocabulary Test—English and Spanish Gardner (EOWPVT) 1980, 1983 Academic Therapy Publications 20 Commercial Blvd Novato, CA 94949	Lower level, 2–11 years; upper level, 12–16 years	Expressive vocabulary, child has to name line drawings, words/concepts are of increasing complexity.	Score derives age level performance and percentiles.
Idea Language Proficiency Test I, II (Spanish and English versions) Ballard & Tighe, 1982, 1987 480 Atlas St Brea, CA 92621	K–8th grade; 9th–12th grade	Vocabulary, syntax, comprehension, and oral expression.	Different levels from A to F, with procedures on when to stop the test. Corresponding to non-Spanish/English-speaking to fluent; Spanish-English proficient.

Development and/or Norms	Reliability	Validity	Comments
Standardized on 384 normal children. Half were Anglo, the other English- or Spanish-speaking Mexican-American children from Del Rio, Texas.	Addressed but incomplete. Internal and test-retest reliability only.	thorough. Mentioned, but arguments are incomplete.	Test should be interpreted cautiously due to small number of subjects and area where developed. Descriptive data can be obtained, especially sentence repetition and story comprehension.
Standardized on 1,224 children from K to 6th grade.	Some description, but incomplete.	N/A	Test has very limited value if used in isolation. Giving opposites may be a learned skill.
Has not been normed on bilingual or Spanish-speaking (dominant) children.	N/A	N/A	Use test to classify type of words child is familiar with (i.e., animals, household items, group words).
Spanish: 654 children from Southern California and Texas; English: 2,061 children from California primarily.	Only internal reliability is described in the two versions.	All data presented for both versions.	As with any proficiency test, results must be interpreted with care. Qualitative data may be helpful: story retelling, naming of objects.

continues

Test	Ages or Grade	Areas Tested	Scoring Procedure
Language Assessment Scales (LAS) I, II Spanish and English versions DeAvila & Duncan, 1983 CTB/McGraw-Hill Book Co 2500 Garden Rd Monterey, CA 93940	K–5th grade; 6–high school	Auditory discrimination, expressive vocabulary, word and sentence repetition, sentence comprehension, story telling.	Yields different levels of language proficiency on a scale of 1 to 5 from totally fluent (5) to nonfluent (1) in Spanish and English.
Medida Española de Articulación (MEDA) Mason, Smith, & Hinshaw, 1976 San Ysidro School District 2250 Smyth Ave San Ysidro, CA 92173	4:0–9:0 years	Articulation in single words.	Errors may be recorded and profile compared to norming sample as reported in the study.
Pre-LAS Spanish and English versions De Avila & Duncan, 1986 McGraw Hill Book Co 2500 Garden Rd Monterey, CA 93940	4:0–6:0 years	Some morphology, syntax, semantics in language comprehension and expression.	Each section has its scoring procedure, yielding a total score from 1 to 5 corresponding to levels of the LAS.
Preschool Language Scale (PLS) Zimmerman, Steiner, & Pond, 1969 Psychological Corp P.O. Box 839954 San Antonio, TX 78283	1:6–7:0 years	Language comprehension and production.	Age score is derived in each area, comprehension as well as expression and a total score. No norms available for Spanish-speaking. Being revised.

Development and/or Norms	Reliability	Validity	Comments
Done over 4 studies with differing numbers of children, but specifics are not given. In one of the studies, the Spanish population is briefly described. Two studies. In the first, 311 English monolingual and 229 Spanish monolingual children were used as norming population; second study used 62 English monolingual.	Some data on interrater reliability.	No data on content; others seem incomplete. Some data on construct, but incomplete.	Test is useful in providing general data on proficiency, but needs to be interpreted with caution. Forms are not equivalent across languages.
Field-tested on 199 boys and 225 girls ages 4–9 in the San Ysidro School District.	N/A	N/A	Exercise caution with how child interprets a picture. No dialectal variations provided. Needs a language sample as with the Austin to ascertain patterns of errors.
No data available yet.	No data available yet.	N/A	Interesting subtests, but again the child's experience has to be taken into account. Interpret with care, as this is a new test.
Not normed per se in English. Based on what children do at different ages from other tests. Spanish version normed on 90 Spanish surnamed children.	Minimal information.	Some data on content and criteria, but incomplete.	Spanish version should be used with care. Universal strategies not reliable. Also, form has many grammar errors. Being revised.

continues

Test	Ages or Grade	Areas Tested	Scoring Procedure
Prueba del Desarrollo Inicial del Lenguaje Hresko, Reid, & Hammill, 1982 PRO-ED 8700 Shoal Creek Blvd Austin, TX 78758	3:0–7:11 years	Comprehension and expression of language in different contexts (describing pictures, answering questions).	Percentiles can be derived for each age level. Separate norms for Mexican and Puerto Rican.
Pruebas de Expresión Oral y Percepcion de la Lengua Española (PEOPLE) Mares, 1980 Los Angeles County Office 9300 E. Imperial Highway Downey, CA 90242	6:0–9:11 years	Five areas tested: memory, auditory association, sentence repetition, story comprehension, and encoding.	Standard scores are derived for each age level. Mean and standard deviation are specified.
Prueba Illinois de Habilidades Psicolingüísticas (ITPA) Kirk & van Isser, 1980 University of Arizona, Special Education Tucson, AZ 85718	3:0–9.9 years	Same areas tested as in the English version of the ITPA. Some tasks are somewhat different.	Scores yield stanines and percentages with interpretation relative to group standing.
Screening Test of Spanish Grammar (STSG) Toronto, 1973 Northwestern University Press 1735 Benson Ave Evanston, IL 60201	3:0–6.6 years	Receptive and expressive measure of specific structures.	Percentiles can be derived based on norms from two different populations: Mexican and Puerto Rican.
Spanish Articulation Measures Mattes, 1987 Academic Comm. Associates P.O. Box 6044 Oceanside, CA 92054	3:0 years and above	Analysis of phonological processes through repetition, stimulability, spontaneous word production task, and production in conversation.	Eighteen processes are identified.

Development and/or Norms	Reliability	Validity	Comments
Approximately 550 children from Mexico, Puerto Rico, and the U.S.	Internal reliability described only.	Incomplete criterion, but data are available for content.	Test should be used with other tests; is difficult to manage due to its design.
Approximately 650 LEP students from primarily the Los Angeles area.	Internal reliability described only.	All described.	Test is helpful tool with children who are LEP. Interpret with caution because the student's experience may be a factor.
Tentative norms based on 436 children from various Spanish-speaking countries.	Internal reliability described only.	Not discussed specifically.	Test should be used with care. Story comprehension (auditory reception) is very poorly worded. Should be used with other language measures.
Normed on 192 children, half from Mexican-American and half from Puerto Rican backgrounds. All were Spanish-dominant and had been in U.S. at least 2 years.	Internal and test-retest reliability only.	Construct described; other is described briefly.	Some pictures may be misleading. Necessary to be aware of dialectal differences.
N/A	N/A	N/A	Test makes it possible to analyze the processes in different contexts.

continues

Test	Ages or Grade	Areas Tested	Scoring Procedure
Structured Photographic Elicitation Language Test (SPELT) (two levels) Spanish version (two levels) Werner & Kresheck, 1989 P.O. Box 12 Sandwich, IL 60548	Pres. 3:0–5:0 + Elem. 5:0–8:0	Elicitation of specific structures using photographs.	25 structures are tested in Level I and 50 structures are tested in Level II.
Test for Auditory Comprehension of Language (TACL), Spanish version Carrow, 1973 DLM Teaching Resources One DLM Park Allen, TX 75002	3:0–6:0 years	Comprehension of concepts and certain sentence structures.	No scoring provided for the Spanish form. In the English version, percentiles can be derived for the different age levels.
Test de Vocabulario en Imágenes Peabody (TVIP) Dunn, Padilla, Lugo, and Dunn, 1986 American Guidance Publishers' Building Circle Pines, MN 55014	2:6–17 years	Receptive vocabulary.	Test yields age level, percentiles, and stanines, as well as standard scores.
Toronto Test of Receptive Vocabulary Toronto, 1977 National Ed. Lab. Publ. P.O. Box 1003 Austin, TX 78767	4:0–10:0 years	Receptive vocabulary in Spanish and English using line drawings; child chooses from a choice of 3 pictures at a time.	Percentiles for different age levels can be derived.

Development and/or Norms	Reliability	Validity	Comments
N/A	N/A	N/A	Great caution is necessary in interpretation; suitable for development of local norms.
Normed on 200 middle-class Black, Anglo-American, and Mexican-American children; normative data provided for the English version only.	Some data on test-retest only.	Discussed, but incomplete.	Test is very restrictive-measure of language comprehension; may yield interesting qualitative data though.
Normed on 1,219 children in Mexico City and vicinity and 148 children from Puerto Rico.	Internal reliability data reported only.	Mainly focuses on content and criterion.	Again, test must be interpreted with care. A vocabulary test is only a small measure of the individual's language skills.
Normed on 1,276 children from three different areas in Texas.	Both test-retest and internal reliability.	Validity studies may be questionable.	Some pictures are ambiguous; caution necessary.

Appendix 7-B

Examples of Achievement Tests in Spanish

Test	Ages or Grade	Areas Tested	Scoring Procedure
Aprenda The Psychological Corporation, 1990 55 Academic Ct San Antonio, TX 78204	K–8th grade	Reading, math, language, study skills, listening.	Grade level performance.
Ber-Sil Secondary Level Beringer, 1976 Ber-Sil Company 3412 Seaglen Drive Rancho Palos Verdes, CA 90274	13:0–17:0 years	Receptive vocabulary, spelling, math, draw-a-person.	Percentiles for age, listing of percentage of errors/age; descriptive test.
Brigance Diagnostic Assessment of Basic Skills Spanish Edition Brigance, 1983 Curriculum Associates 5 Esquire Road North Bellerica, MA 01862	K–6th grade	Readiness; speech, math, reading, listening, language arts.	Criterion-referenced test.
Prueba de Lectura en Español Cohen & Cohen, 1978 Bilingual Media Production, Inc P.O. Box 9337 N. Bethesda Berkeley, CA 94709	Readiness first	Sound/letter associations, word recognition, comprehension of short sentences and paragraphs.	Four levels—excellent, good, satisfactory, and insufficient—according to number of points.
Prueba de Lectura y Lenguaje Escrito (PLLE) Hammill, Larsen, Wiederholt, & Fountain-Chambers, 1982 PRO-ED 5341 Industrial Oaks Blvd Austin, TX 78735	8:0–15:11 years	Words, paragraphs, composition, spelling, style (writing).	Standard scores and percentiles.

Note: N/A, not available.

Development and/or Norms	Reliability	Validity	Comments
Tested on 30,000 students in bilingual programs; standardized in 34 districts across the nation.	Equated to Stanford Achievement Test series.	N/A	One of the newest comprehensive tests.
Tried on students in beginning ESL classes in 2 junior high schools and 1 high school in central Los Angeles.	N/A	N/A	Author does not mention number or more specific background of subjects; restrictive sample, but useful as a screening device.
Educational consultants and experts reviewed the assessment; critiqued by the Board of Bilingual ESL Migrant and Bilingual Special Education Teachers; 150 teachers were asked to administer the test to 2 students each.	N/A	Content validity, 98%.	Selected students can be tested in both Spanish and English. The test "assesses performance to create a specific educational plan for an individual student."
N/A	N/A	N/A	Areas tested in each level vary; it is a descriptive test. Results assist in grouping students according to ability levels.
Items were developed and tried on 250 students in Mexico; discriminant analysis to determine level of difficulty; standardized on 2,372 students in Mexico and Puerto Rico.	Some data; internal consistency.	Construct validity.	Composition subtest seems very difficult (if student has not been exposed to topic of pictures).

continues

Test	Ages or Grade	Areas Tested	Scoring Procedure
Spanish Oral Reading Test Romero & Miller, 1982 Paradox Press 14 Royce Street Los Gatos, CA 95030	1st–6th grades	Word lists, paragraphs, phonics cards.	Necessary to pass a number of questions and make no more than a certain number of errors at a grade level.
Spanish Reading Comprehension Test Moreno, 1978 Moreno Educational Co 7050 Belle Glade Avenue San Diego, CA 92119	1st–6th grades	Reading comprehension (silent); timed 30 min.	Grade equivalents and percentiles according to total score.
Woodcock-Johnson Spanish Edition Woodcock, 1981 Teaching Resources 50 Pond Park Road Hingham, MA 02043	3:0 years and above	Oral language, reading, written language.	Grade and age equivalent, instructional range, percentile ranking, standard scores.

Development and/or Norms	Reliability	Validity	Comments
About 80 students in 4 high schools in Northern California and one elementary school in Southern California.	N/A	N/A	Norming seems incomplete and very "restrictive."
Developed on approximately 5,000 students from different grades and states in Mexico.	Some data; correlation among teachers.	Content.	Valid with students who have completed some education in Mexico. Content extracted from reading books in Mexico and Puerto Rico. English version is a translation.
General Spanish norms (compared to Spanish-speaking world 802 subjects); equivalent English norms on 4,732 subjects aged 3–80 years.	N/A	N/A	Gaps in items tested; seems to work best with children 8 years or older.

Chapter 8

Language Intervention Strategies for Hispanic LLD Students

Carol Beaumont

In planning an intervention program for language/learning-disabled (LLD) students, it is essential not only to focus on the language skills that all students need to succeed in school, but also to acknowledge what each learner brings to the school experience. As Wallach and Miller (1988) stated, "Learning is a constant process of fitting incoming information into what one already knows" (p. xiii). Clinicians can enhance individual students' performance by building on their strengths and targeting areas that need further improvement.

OVERVIEW OF EFFECTIVE TEACHING STRATEGIES

The general trend in shifting paradigms from a reductionistic to a constructivist assessment of students' skills has resulted in teaching strategies that emphasize the whole instead of the parts and focus on language use rather than form alone. Speech-language clinicians who have adopted this approach

1. use authentic, purposeful communication interactions to teach language skills
2. plan activities that use whole texts, themes, events, and experiences
3. incorporate children's home/community communication events into activities
4. connect intervention activities to a larger curriculum context
5. create an environment conducive to a wide range of language uses
6. integrate form, content, and use in activities
7. plan intervention around a vision of effective communication and learning rather than around deficits

Many of the activities used with regular education students in interactive classrooms can be adapted for use with LLD students. Their applicability to special education students is made possible not by breaking the tasks down, but by providing the instructional support necessary for the students' participation.

Scaffolding

Through scaffolding (Wood, Bruner, & Ross, 1976), the clinician provides temporary instructional support until students are able to take over tasks themselves. Consistent with the zone of proximal development described by Vygotsky (1962), this approach is based on the assumption that students have a range of ability that is much wider than that revealed by a static picture of a particular developmental level. New learning does not await a given developmental level; rather, learning moves development forward. Furthermore, students' learning is expanded by interaction with more expert members of society. Greenfield (1984) stated that scaffolding "does not involve simplifying the task during the period of learning. Instead, it holds the task constant while simplifying the learner's role through the graduated intervention of the teacher" (p. 11). Thus, instead of teaching discrete skills, the clinician identifies the larger context and provides the scaffolding that a student needs to participate in authentic communication exchanges. Characteristics of effective scaffolding, which can be applied to any activity, include

- connecting the current task to something the child knows
- directing the child's attention to salient features of the task
- using questioning techniques that lead the child to problem-solving strategies
- demonstrating effective strategies
- modeling mnemonic devices
- following the child's cues to determine when to intervene
- allowing the balance of error and success that allows the child to use errors for growth without becoming discouraged by them
- withdrawing intervention as the child becomes more successful
- transferring control of the task to the child

The framework used in the design of the suggested activities is adapted from a continuum of reductionism-holism developed by Ruíz (1989) from the work done by Poplin (1984, 1988) on holistic constructivism (Figure 8-1). The continuum gives the clinician guidance in creating activities that encourage emphasis on a whole task rather than on its individual parts. Previous practice in special educa-

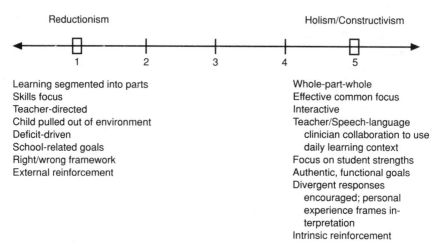

Reductionism   Holism/Constructivism

1   2   3   4   5

Learning segmented into parts   Whole-part-whole
Skills focus   Effective common focus
Teacher-directed   Interactive
Child pulled out of environment   Teacher/Speech-language
Deficit-driven   clinician collaboration to use
School-related goals   daily learning context
Right/wrong framework   Focus on student strengths
External reinforcement   Authentic, functional goals
                                                           Divergent responses
                                                              encouraged; personal
                                                              experience frames in-
                                                              terpretation
                                                           Intrinsic reinforcement

Figure 8-1 Continuum Framework for Activity Design

tion focused on the question, "How can I break this down to make it easier?" Treadway (1987) suggested that teachers and clinicians ask instead, "How can I make this more whole?"

An important feature of this continuum that encourages effective scaffolding is the whole-part-whole framework. For example, the clinician begins with a whole (e.g., a communication event such as conversing, sharing books, writing letters, negotiating task completion), singles out specific skills (the part) for development, and then returns the skills to the whole in their modified (e.g., improved or corrected) form. In order to maintain focus on the whole, activities should be situated in a cultural context, a curriculum context, and/or a communicative context. The following examples contrast reductionistic and holistic activities:

Goal: To improve sequencing skills.

Activity: The clinician asks the student to put sequence cards in order.

How can this activity be made more whole? Situate the activity in a communicative context, and use a whole text that is culturally significant.

Revised activity: Students share a Mexican folktale with a group of younger children, using props, costumes, body language, and vocal inflections in retelling the story.

Goal: To improve the use of regular and irregular verbs in written expression.

Activity: Students practice completing fill-in-the-blank sentences that focus on correct verb tense.

How can this activity be made more whole? Situate the activity in a communicative and a curriculum context (e.g., language arts letter writing unit).

Revised activity: Students write a letter to the school principal, asking for new playground equipment. The letter includes evidence supporting the need. Students work in pairs with an editing checklist.

Goal: To improve auditory memory.

Activity: Students practice recalling items from a shopping list.

How can this activity be made more whole? Situate the activity in a communicative and a curriculum context, and use whole texts.

Revised activity: Students memorize poems about insects and record them on tape for the kindergarten listening center during their science unit on insects.

Goal: To improve understanding of cause-and-effect relationships.

Activity: Students are asked questions from prepared cards that illustrate common situations, such as "The milk is on the floor. How do you think it got there?" and "The little girl is crying. What do you think happened to her?"

How can this activity be made more whole? Situate the activity in a communicative and a curriculum context.

Revised activity: Students work in small groups to make hypotheses about the growth of plants. After several days of observation, they record the plants' response to different environments.

Specific Strategies

Many teaching strategies that benefit all children may be particularly effective with LLD students and second-language learners. Although the effectiveness of such approaches as thematic teaching, sociodramatic play, narratives, predictable texts, visual organizers, and cooperative learning has not been confirmed with LLD students, Weaver (1991) noted that they have been successful with normally developing students. These strategies provide flexible structures that can be adapted to all ages and ability levels. They support a holistic approach and provide many rich possibilities for incorporating students' background and language.

Thematic Teaching

In thematic teaching, the content of all curricular areas revolves around a central theme. Not only do themes provide a supra-organization for experiences and information, but also they emphasize the connections among many facts of a given topic. Thematic teaching can be an antidote to the curricular fragmentation noted by Cazden (1987) and Trueba (1987). Kucer and Silva (1989) suggested that thematic teaching is useful because it encourages two types of learning: "conceptual learning is promoted because students repeatedly encounter a set of interrelated meanings, and language learning is enhanced because students use reading, writing, listening, and speaking to generate meanings related to the theme at hand" (p. 18). Furthermore, with this approach, special education personnel can more easily coordinate their program with the school or district core curriculum to ensure equal access for special education students.

The concept of thematic teaching can be adapted to speech-language services in a number of ways. The special day class teacher can integrate the entire program with themes. The itinerant clinician who has a separate therapy room can organize it around a theme that changes monthly. Small or individual groups of students can work on different themes. Clinicians who work in the classroom or in a collaboration model can design activities to coordinate their services with the classroom theme. Finally, it is even possible to develop themes that allow clinicians who work at different school sites to transport their materials with them (Bush, 1980).

Themes such as sea life, simple machines, or plant life offer many possibilities for interactive language experiences that require negotiation of meaning and the use of many language skills simultaneously. Figure 8-2 illustrates one method of organizing thematic teaching.

Sociodramatic Play

Play corners and dress-up clothes for sociodramatic play are typical of preschool and kindergarten classrooms. For very young children, sociodramatic play is an effective way of developing representational competencies and complex schema for a variety of situations. The benefits of sociodramatic play extend to the later development of oral language and literacy, however (Pellegrini, 1985, 1989).

One connection between symbolic play and literacy lies in the similarity of organizational schema between play episodes and narratives. "By enacting everyday events in a fantasy context, children gain practice in analyzing and reconstructing the temporal and causal structure of these narrative-like events" (Pellegrini & Galda, 1990, p. 81). Harp (1988) suggested that another link between play and reading is "a search for meaning and the development of representation. Just as children manipulate objects to represent ideas, so words are representations of ideas. Both play and reading involve symbols" (p. 244).

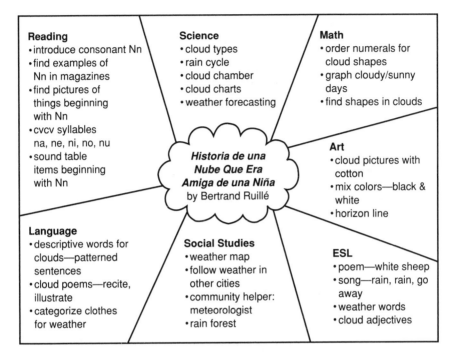

Reading
- introduce consonant Nn
- find examples of Nn in magazines
- find pictures of things beginning with Nn
- cvcv syllables na, ne, ni, no, nu
- sound table items beginning with Nn

Science
- cloud types
- rain cycle
- cloud chamber
- cloud charts
- weather forecasting

Math
- order numerals for cloud shapes
- graph cloudy/sunny days
- find shapes in clouds

Historia de una Nube Que Era Amiga de una Niña by Bertrand Ruillé

Art
- cloud pictures with cotton
- mix colors—black & white
- horizon line

Language
- descriptive words for clouds—patterned sentences
- cloud poems—recite, illustrate
- categorize clothes for weather

Social Studies
- weather map
- follow weather in other cities
- community helper: meteorologist
- rain forest

ESL
- poem—white sheep
- song—rain, rain, go away
- weather words
- cloud adjectives

Figure 8-2 Thematic Teaching Based on *Historia de una Nube Que Era Amiga de una Niña* 'The Story of a Cloud That Befriended a Girl'. ESL, English as a second language.

Sociodramatic play is also helpful for school-aged children who need practice in the pragmatic aspects of language, such as making requests, using an appropriate level of verbal specificity, and repairing communication breakdowns. When Ruíz (1988a) studied the use of sociodramatic play with bilingual special education students, she noted a significant improvement in their oral language skills over their performance in more structured classroom academic tasks. Pellegrini and Galda (1990) indicated that school-aged students benefit from interactive activities that require negotiation of meaning, but are not necessarily tied to "pretend" activities.

In Hispanic homes, children share responsibility for the care of younger siblings, and recreating this familiar communication event offers Hispanic children opportunities for growth in specific language use. Older children adjust their language use when talking to younger children by simplifying vocabulary and providing contextual clues. For this purpose, sociodramatic play may help to recreate events that occur often in the lives of many Hispanic children, such as buying and selling at the *pulga* 'flea market'; celebrating weddings, baptisms, and *quinceañeras* (special celebrations for young girls when they turn 15 years of age); or translating for parents in community agencies. Using these activities and scenarios as basic structures, the teacher or clinician can combine them with the language support that the students need. As children discuss key elements of their play, such as scene, actors, and props, their ability to negotiate meaning improves. In each case, successful negotiation of meaning may require the use of such aspects of communication as particular language structures, turn-taking conventions, and message repair. Parents can be asked to suggest appropriate props for a play center or to participate themselves in the activities.

Narratives

Good stories—real or imagined—are part of everyone's personal, family, community, and national history. Although they may differ in kind and in manner of transmission, stories are part of the communication events of all cultures. According to Lindfors (1987) narratives are universal because they are "a fundamental way of knowing, of making sense of the world" (p. 357). Lindfors further stated that "we want children to be able to tell (or follow the telling of) a story, a series of related events in an orderly time sequence. The child's ability to participate in the lives of others and to share her own life depends in part on the skills of understanding and relating stories" (p. 356).

The narrative form of discourse competence develops through repeated experiences with the patterned organization of stories. Heath (1986b) pointed out that success in communicative exchanges depends on speakers' expressing their experience in predictable ways that will allow the listener to anticipate "the map or plan for stretches of discourse marked orally by prosody and by formulaic phrases (especially as openings) as well as gestures" (p. 86).

The use of narratives can have both communicative and cognitive benefits, as narratives have the power to teach, entertain, amuse, persuade, move, and transform. Language skills that develop through the use of narratives include verbal specificity; sequence; logical verbal formulation; and the ability to repair, clarify, and elaborate a message. The cognitive benefits include the development of schema as a result of repeated experiences with story structure, cause-and-effect relationships, inferencing, and generalization of concepts and experiences to new situations. Other educational benefits of interaction with stories include an enriched vocabulary, increased educational achievement, earlier development of independent reading skills, and a strong sense of story that can serve as the basis for the comprehension and development of rich written language.

In order to use narratives for intervention, the clinician should be familiar with the developmental progression of narrative ability in children. Westby (1984) indicated that children must have certain prerequisite skills before they can understand and create narratives. For example, they must be able to represent knowledge linguistically, and they must understand causal, spatial, temporal, and role relationships (Graesser, 1981). The schema content ranges from a preschool level to an adolescent/adult level. At the preschool level, the child is able to label, has an awareness of an animate/inanimate distinction, and expresses some cause-and-effect relationships. At the other end of the continuum, the adolescent/adult is able to discuss narrative structure, understand abstractions of time and space, and can understand allegories. Descriptions of the various levels appear in Table 7-4. Examples of stories appear below (Westby, 1989). The majority are samples from students that were evaluated by Westby.

Isolated Description—Ask: Is the story limited to isolated descriptions of people, places, or events? There is a ghost and a pumpkin. The witch is a woman. She flies with a broom. The witch is black. The witch chews Skol and makes cigarettes. The witch lives in California and Arizona. She does not come to Alamo.

Action Sequence—Ask: Does the story have a temporally-related sequence of events? Once there was some kids. And they were going to school. A giant bird flew over and landed. Then they got a piece of rope and put it in his mouth. The bird took off. And they had a good, good, good trip. They flew over the ocean, the mountain. Finally they came home.

Reactive Sequence—Ask: Does the story have a causally-related sequence of events? There were two boys who went to China. And they were there. And they made friends with the bird. And so they were flying around China. And they were going over a city where the statue was. And the boys were having a nice time. But then [the eagle's] a storm came. And the eagle's wings [went started to] couldn't flap. [So the] so they crash landed in the trees.

Abbreviated Episode—Ask: Does the story imply goal-directed behavior? One day a little girl went to mail her letter. Suddenly she heard BOooooOH! The letter-stealing, glue-licking monster wanted her letter. He wanted to lick glue from her stamp and envelope. The little girl lost her letter. Beware the letter-stealing, glue-licking monster. He might be waiting for you!

Complete Episode—Ask: Is planning to achieve the goal clear in the story? For a whole month there has been a real big giant that has been throwing things in the houses, and smashing houses and getting people, and throwing them. But one day there was one man that wanted to solve this problem. So he got all the men. And they started up the mountain with torches to see what they can do about it. So they were about 10 feet from him. One of the men threw a torch at him and lit the giant on fire. And the giant fell down the mountain. And they never see him again.

Complex Episode—Ask: Is there an obstacle in the goal path of the story? Once upon a time there was a village in the mountains. And there was a gorilla that escaped from the zoo. And they went hunting for it. And it was on top of a ledge. And they started chasing it with guns and with swords. It ran up the hill. And then it fell over the edge. And then the men tried to get it, but it jumped and it wrecked their house. And then they started chasing it up the mountain again. And he started to ski down cause he found a pair of skis at the top. And then the people got skis too. So they chased him on skis. And they chased him right to the zoo. And he got back. He got caught in the zoo again. And he was there again.

Multiple Episodes—Ask: Is there more than one abbreviated or complete episode in the story? (Sample not included because multiple-episode stories tend to be lengthy.)

Embedded Episode—Ask: Is one episode nested within another episode? A man named Mr. Dirt lived in the country all by himself and own a farm. One calf got away and went to the woods and headed for the mountains. So Mr. Dirt went up the mountain after the calf. On the way a bear came after Mr. Dirt. He ran up a tree and the bear climbed up the tree after him. Mr. Dirt threw his ax at the bear and hit the bear in the head. Blood poured out of his head and the bear fell down and died. A few minutes later the calf ran over to Mr. Dirt and they went back to the farm (Botvin & Sutton-Smith, 1977).

Interactive Episodes—Ask: Does the story describe events from the perspective of more than one character? This big monster came to these people's town. Wrecked up some of their houses. And now the people came to go to try find him. And [he] the big monster's hiding way up in the rocks. And people with lights going into the rocks. And [they're] they want to kill the monster because what it did. And [mo and] the monster doesn't want them to kill him. So he goes way up in the rocks and looks down at them coming and trying to kill him. So he keeps walking up the mountain until he gets to the top. And the people have trouble. They fall and slip trying to get up the mountain, but finally they get up. And they get to the place. And they get to the top of the [moun] mountain. They never get to the top where the monster is. But they went back down and said, "Well, the monster can't get back down, so he'll die up there anyways." So they just leave him alone and go back home.

The clinician should choose appropriate narratives to use in interventions with Hispanic children by determining which types may be most familiar to them. This knowledge will also be helpful in understanding the students' responses to particular narratives and will add depth to evaluations of the stories that the children create and relate to themselves. Heath (1986a) described four universal types of narratives:

1. *recounts.* Adults ask children to relate a shared past experience to another person (e.g., "tell your mom what happened at the park today").
2. *eventcasts.* The individual describes an activity that is occurring at the moment or is planned for the future. Activities accompanied by running narratives ("Let's see, we pour in the milk, then add the honey . . .") or by explanation of what will follow ("Go to recess, then pick up your folders, take them to the library . . .") are eventcasts.
3. *accounts.* The teller provides information that is unknown to the listener or offers further explanations of what the listener already knows.
4. *stories.* The individual describes an animate being who moves through a series of events with goal-directed behavior.

According to Heath (1986a), the most common types of narratives in Mexican-American communities, for example, are accounts and stories. Eventcasts are unusual around daily tasks, but do occur when several family members are planning future events. Recounts are not considered necessary if one person in a communication interaction already knows what happened (see Chapter 4). In her study of four Mexican-American families, Vásquez (1990) found that the retelling of stories was the primary communication event in the home.

> Retellings were formed around oral narratives from the family's depository of *cuentos* (stories). Retellings, in particular, were occasions when family members entertained each other with stories from the native or local community or with experiences the family had shared in the past. The participants listened intently to the story-tellers share their narratives and postponed their reaction until the end of the telling at which time they made linkages to their stories and to their own personal experiences (p. 196).

In discussing cultural differences in narrative style, Cazden (1987) pointed out that Hispanic children's narratives about significant personal events often include both their own reactions and those of the family members to whom the event was recounted. Teachers may find such information superfluous or "off the topic," but this interrelationship helps the child derive meaning. In fact, the responses of Hispanic children to stories that are read or told to them often include inquiries about family members who are not mentioned in the story. In listening to stories of animals or children on adventures of their own, such as *The Three Bears* (Galdone, 1985), they frequently ask, "Where is Goldilocks' mom?" or "Doesn't Goldilocks have a family?" Appendix 8-A lists books in both Spanish and English that have a strong story structure and themes that make them especially effective for reading aloud.

Children with language disorders or learning difficulties often have problems in comprehension and construction of narratives. Comprehension difficulties stem from problems in processing cohesive elements in sentences, in making inferences, in discerning the key features of a story (foregrounding), and in organizing episodes (Crais & Chapman, 1987; Liles, 1987). The impoverished nature of the narratives that these children construct has been attributed to weakness in their understanding of story grammar, failure to use memory or retrieval strategies, linguistic deficits (e.g., vocabulary), and limited background knowledge. In her study of Hispanic students in special day classes for communicatively handicapped students, however, Ruíz (1988a) found that incorporating their personal experiences with stories from their family and community improved their verbal and written performance. The daily reading of well constructed stories, followed by discussion of personal response and work on story structure, has been shown to help LLD students understand and create narratives with confidence. In many cases, their ability has exceeded that of their peers in regular education whose curriculum did not emphasize activities with story structure.

In selecting stories and books to use in an intervention program, the speech-language clinician should consider the guidelines suggested by Huck (1987) for evaluating minority literature.

- *diversity and range of representation.* Stereotyping should be avoided. Books that portray minority groups should cover a wide range of aspects. Black families should not always be depicted living in city housing projects, and Hispanic families should not always be described working in the field. "Only when a collection of books about a particular group offers a wise spectrum of occupations, educational backgrounds, living conditions, and life styles will we offer positive images of minority groups" (Huck, 1987, p. 503). Stereotyping in portrayal of family roles, clothing, or housing should also be avoided.

- *language.* Dialect or foreign words should be used carefully. There should be no translations if the text really represents the language used in authentic communication events.

- *perspective of the book.* The book should be written from the perspective of a member of the minority group being represented. Although not all members of a group share the same perspective, some stories are obviously written from the viewpoint of a non-minority person. For example, "if the major theme of the story is a Latino's desire to master the English language to become 'one of us', we may be certain that that story is being told from a white perspective" (Huck, 1987, p. 503).

Goines (1987) suggested using stories with universal themes and experiences shared by many children. Books about nature bypass race and creed, and those about other common childhood themes (e.g., family relationships, fears of darkness or monsters, and excitement about festival days) are appropriate for multicultural groups of children.

In working on specific language goals, the clinician can incorporate materials that reflect the students' culture. This must be done without stereotyping a particular culture or customs, however, but in a way that accents the value of that culture. Folktales from Mexico, Spain, and Latin America offer rich images, familiar themes, and strong narrative styles—as well as opportunities for vocabulary development, memory enhancement, and problem solving. For example, in *The War between the Lion and the Cricket* (Storm, 1958), the two creatures have a battle of wits as they attempt to outdo each other. In dramatizing or retelling the story, students must recall the names of animals and insects, and they must use vocabulary that describes complex actions.

Brooks (1986) suggested a number of areas for comparisons of cultures. Along with familiar topics, such as festivals and holidays, he advised examining daily living patterns.

- *observance of Sunday.* How do Sunday activities differ from weekday activities?
- *games.* What are the most popular games that are played outdoors and indoors, by children and by adults?
- *errands.* What are typical errands that a young person is likely to be asked to do, either at home or in school?
- *family meals.* What is the special character of each meal, the food eaten, the seating arrangements, the method of serving dishes, the general conversation?
- *personal possessions.* What objects are often found decorating the wall of a young person's bedroom? What objects might be found in someone's pocket or purse?

Brooks noted that these topics and many others have wide possibilities for the classroom teacher and the speech-language clinician who are seeking to create authentic purposes for communication and to develop language skills through narratives. Appendix 8-A lists selected resources on Hispanic folklore.

Predictable Texts

Because they provide patterns and/or repetitions on a variety of levels (e.g., sound, word, phrase, sentence, episode, and theme), predictable texts support children's ability to listen to and comprehend oral language; they provide a dependable structure that children can use to organize what they hear. They also offer students an opportunity to be fluent without taxing the students' memory or verbal formulation skills. The use of rhythm, rhyme, and repetition is an excellent aid for all learners. It is particularly effective for children who have memory difficulties and for second-language learners who need comprehensible input presented in dependable linguistic structures. Appendix 8-A lists predictable books in English and Spanish.

Familiar patterns may recur within a story sequence (e.g., "Run, run as fast as you can, you can't catch me, I'm the Gingerbread Man!"). Repeated episodes provide not only linguistic familiarity, but also conceptual support for developing text comprehension skills. For example, the episode in *The Three Little Pigs* in which the wolf knocks on a pig's door, is turned away, threatens the pig, and attempts to play a trick is repeated three times in most versions of the story.

Children's folklore includes many songs, poems, and chants that are naturally incorporated into children's play and are very useful texts for those needing support in the development of their oral language. Familiar folklore in the Hispanic culture includes *refranes* 'sayings', *proverbios* 'proverbs', *trabalenguas* 'tongue-twisters', *jerigonzas* 'nonsense verse', and *adivinanzas* 'riddles'. Jump rope chants and game songs (e.g., London Bridge, *Amo a To Mata Rile Rile Ron* [no translation equivalent—sung while children play and dance]) are also part of children's folklore.

Visual Organizers

Charts, graphs, rebuses, diagrams, and other visual organizers can provide the support for auditory input that is necessary to make sense of a fast-moving auditory stream. Visual organizers also serve as a reference as students continue to work with concepts, content, and processes. Wallach and Miller (1988) stressed that assisting students in becoming "self-responsible, active learners" should be the first principle of intervention. Furthermore, they stated, "We want to help them recognize and use linguistic and non-linguistic strategies that may be generalizable across contexts" (p. 11). The stability of visual input facilitates processing for some students, including second-language learners. Programs developed for the latter students emphasize the importance of providing visual cues during and after linguistic input (Northcutt & Watson, 1986; Rigg & Allen, 1989).

Cooperative Learning

Cooperative learning activities offer students the opportunity to use a variety of language skills in group interactions. In these situations, students listen, negotiate turn-taking rules, ask questions, clarify information, repair miscommunications, initiate and maintain topics, change roles, plan, explain, persuade, record, summarize, and apply politeness conventions in joining and taking leave of a group.

After working in their small groups, students conduct a debriefing session to evaluate both the product and the process followed. This debriefing session assists them in developing functional communication skills and metalinguistic awareness. The speech-language clinician can collaborate with the classroom teacher in identifying the language skills that individual students need to develop. For example, intervention goals may include helping one or two students develop the ability to ask for clarification questions. The clinician can provide the scaffolding necessary for them to apply the skill in a real situation outside the classroom.

Cooperative learning structures provide a balance of activities that bridge possible discontinuities between home and school learning and communication patterns. The group work provides experience in highly contextualized, here and now activities, more frequently associated with some home cultures. They also enhance practice in school language skills, such as planning and reflecting. For example, a cooking activity is a common home experience that offers many opportunities for purposeful communication. Students can practice using language in more abstract ways by adding a planning component to the activity.

Cooperative learning has been shown to be a particularly effective learning strategy for Hispanic students and second-language learners. In summarizing research on cooperative learning, Cummins (1989) stated, "The achievement gains in cooperative classrooms are particularly dramatic for minority students. Whereas non-minority and high-achieving students generally perform about as well in traditional and cooperative classrooms, low-achieving and minority students appear to be considerably more motivated to learn in cooperative classrooms" (p. 76). Kagan (1986) noted, "In a relatively short time what appears to be a long-term minority student deficiency in basic language skills can be overcome by transforming the social organization of the classroom" (p. 246).

The Finding Out/Descubrimiento science/mathematics program (De Avila & Duncan, 1988), which employs cooperative learning groups, has proved very effective in developing not only content skills, but also language skills. In heterogeneous groups, Spanish-dominant students work with English-dominant students on highly motivating science-related tasks. The materials include illustrated activity cards, objects and equipment to manipulate, as well as worksheets to record observations and results of experiments. Each group member has an assigned role that is essential to the completion of the project.

Young Hispanic LLD students have participated successfully with regular education students in this program, employing high-level language skills that they have not previously demonstrated. While many of the difficulties with form remained, the aspects of content and use were significantly enhanced during the negotiation of meaning involved in these sessions. Similarly, Kessler and Quinn (1987) reported that Hispanic bilingual 11-year-olds from low socioeconomic backgrounds who participated in this program significantly outperformed other students in the quantity and quality of hypotheses generated in science experiments. These investigators suggested that the students' bilingual proficiency facilitated divergent and convergent thinking. The few research studies conducted in bilingual special education classrooms also support these findings (Ruíz, 1988a; Trueba, 1987; Willig & Swedo, 1986). It remains a challenge for systematic research to document the long-term effects and effectiveness of these approaches to Hispanic LLD students, however.

ENHANCING LISTENING AND ORAL LANGUAGE COMPREHENSION

Listening and Oral Language Comprehension in the Classroom Setting

In most school settings, students are required to process a large and continuous stream of linguistic and discoursal information. Because of the transitory nature of the auditory stream, they must process rapidly, accurately, and efficiently in order to derive meaning from what they hear. "They must be able to process the sensory input so that it has logic, regularity, and consistency within itself and with previously stored experience" (Vetter, 1982, p. 15). Most traditional classrooms are still dominated by a number of discourse forms, such as lectures, directions, and demonstrations, that have become ritualized (Bloome & Knott, 1985). As Ripich and Spinelli (1985) indicated, "Getting through the lesson is important because it is an indication of how much was done and allows discretionary time (e.g., recess, relaxation)" (p. 57). Even in those settings, however, it is crucial that students be able to follow verbal exchanges with facility. In more interactive classrooms, the students may have to learn to focus on relevant information and disregard competing auditory signals from the environment. Thus, good listening and comprehension skills are necessary to succeed in any type of classroom setting.

Students with language and learning difficulties whose comprehension strategies are not well developed may struggle with form (e.g., embedded sentences), content (e.g., lexical items), or use (e.g., lecture, story structure, dialogue) for a variety of reasons, including information-processing deficits, memory problems, attentional difficulties, lack of background information, or limited cognitive abilities. As was noted in Chapter 6, second-language learners who have difficulty in remembering auditory information or in recognizing patterns may experience considerably more difficulty in acquiring a second language (Wong Fillmore, 1989a). These students need concentrated support to provide them with focused input, as well as extra nonlinguistic cues. If they miss information during fleeting moments of inattention, it is difficult for them to use inferential strategies to construct meaning. They must determine how the segments of speech relate to the entire content of the speech in addition to "discover how the speech serving as input segments in the first place, finding out where one thing begins and another ends, is critical to the procedure" (Wong Fillmore, 1989a, p. 286).

Krashen (1980, 1981) indicated that comprehensible input is a crucial factor in the rate and quality of second-language acquisition. The input must be slightly above the current level, however, so that it challenges the learner to determine what is being said. Vetter (1982) recommended "that mothers' language should be only slightly longer and more complex than their language-disordered children's. Teachers may find a similar approach to be a good place to start in school" (p. 15).

Intervention to develop listening and oral language comprehension skills is most effective when embedded in the context of meaningful activities that mirror students' daily experiences. Although working on isolated listening skills in a therapy room may improve the student's performance in the specific task at hand, there may be limited transfer to a different context. Rhodes and Dudley-Marling (1988) described the futility of working on memory tasks apart from authentic communication purposes: "Making sense of meaning is one of the factors that significantly affect memory performance" (p. 7). They argued that drilling students on memory tasks or even teaching them strategies to improve memory "begs the more interesting question: memory for what?" (p. 7). Butler (1984) suggested that "simply instructing children to 'listen,' 'remember,' or 'think' may be insufficient. We must take into account the child's own notion of how relevant the chosen memory tasks may be to his or her own memory goals" (p. 76). Intervention targeted to improve organization of auditory input may focus on memory, attention, categorization, evaluation, or analysis. In all cases, the communicative purpose of the tasks must remain central.

Auditory Processing Skills and Strategies

Attention, both sustained and selective, and memory, both short-term and long-term, are skills necessary to sustain the auditory process. Strategies that enhance these skills include

- categorization (i.e., classifying incoming information)
- interpretation (i.e., understanding ambiguous directions and indirect requests)

- evaluation (i.e., foregrounding, which involves selecting the most important information from what is heard, and summarizing, which involves reducing information to key points)
- analysis (i.e., understanding complex information and directions presented in single words, phrases, or embedded sentences)
- synthesis (i.e., relating new information to previous experience)
- adjusting attention to a variety of discourse types

Because of the variety of listening skills and strategies that children must use and the number of contexts in which children must apply them, it is helpful to divide intervention activities into two categories that have broad applications: (1) developing selective attention and (2) listening to remember. All activities can be adapted to various ages and language proficiency levels and can be carried out in Spanish or English, depending on the students' needs.

Developing Selective Attention

Listening for a purpose helps focus and sustain attention. Because most children are able to focus on larger units of speech before smaller ones (Clay, 1979), their attention should be drawn to sentences first, then phrases, then words, and, finally, sounds.

The teacher may begin by having the children listen for a familiar refrain in a predictable text. For example, while listening to the story *I Know an Old Lady Who Swallowed a Fly* (Westcott, 1980), the children may be asked to stand up every time they hear the phrase, "I guess she'll die." This is especially helpful for second-language learners who are still trying to determine the boundary markers of their new language. The same activity could be adapted to Spanish by reading a book such as *El Oso Más Elegante 'The Best Dressed Bear'* (Blocksma, 1984; translated by Ada, 1986) and asking the children to look at their clothes or those of a dressed-up teddy bear each time they hear *"Y el más elegante voy a ser"* "And I will be the best dressed one."

A special "word of the day" can be introduced during class. Children add a mark on a large tally sheet every time they hear it. This strategy can be used to extend the students' vocabulary by substituting synonyms for words used in phrases repeated many times a day. For example, *siéntense en el tapete, por favor* 'everybody on the rug, please' could be replaced by *siéntense en la alfombra* 'everybody on the carpet'. Words used in idiomatic expressions, such as *up* in warm *up*, clean *up*, finish *up*, think *up*, and look *up*, can help draw attention to the variety of uses that some English words have. Although there is no equivalent of such a paradigm in Spanish, a similar activity could be adapted to reinforce prepositions as in *pongan las manos arriba (sobre* or *encima) de la mesa*, then *abajo* or *debajo de la mesa* 'put your hands on top of the table', then 'under the table', thus teaching different words for the same prepositions in Spanish.

In a bilingual classroom students can listen for code-switching to improve their awareness of foreign language. During the English language portion of the day, the teacher can occasionally use a Spanish word and have students respond by raising their hands or marking a tally sheet.

Preview-review is a strategy commonly used in bilingual classrooms when instruction takes place in the students' nondominant language. The key concepts and vocabulary that are to be presented in the second language are previewed in the student's dominant language. After the lesson has been presented in the second language, the concepts are reviewed in the dominant language. When instruction in their primary language is not available, this strategy can be adapted to meet the needs of LLD students. It is an effective method of scaffolding a lesson for students who need support in selective attention. It provides assistance in both foregrounding and summarizing. The clinician can preview a lesson using visual organizers to highlight key concepts and vocabulary that will be heard during the lesson. After the student participates in the classroom lesson, the clinician can use the same visual organizers to help the student with a review.

Listening to Remember

Often, LLD students have difficulty in recalling information that is presented orally. Not only do these students need to have many opportunities for authentic listening in context, but also they may need to learn specific strategies that have broad applicability. Strategies that have been helpful for improving memory include rehearsing; using rhythm, rhyme, and repetition; making logical connections; chunking (a form of categorization into units); and categorizing (Blachman, 1984; Israel, 1984; Rubin, 1986; Schuele & van Kleeck, 1987). The following activities offer practice in these skills:

- In trying to recall a series of specific objects, for example, students can be taught to rehearse, cluster, or tally. In *Mr. Rabbit and the Lovely Present* (Zolotow, 1962), the little girl models a rehearsal process as she prepares a fruit basket for her mother: "Let's see, I have an apple, a banana, grapes, so far. What else can I put in the basket?"
- Repetitive, cumulative stories, such as *I Know an Old Lady Who Swallowed a Fly* (Westcott, 1980) and *The House That Jack Built* (Galdone, 1971)/*La Casa Que Juan Construyó* (Celorio, n.d.), use the predictability of rhythm, rhyme, and repetition to aid recall. Older students may enjoy more elaborate versions, such as *Bringing the Rain to Kapiti Plain: Anandi tale* (Aardema, 1981) or *The Rose in My Garden* (Lobel, 1984).

- Cumulative stories such as *If You Give a Mouse a Cookie* (Numeroff, 1985) use the strategy of logical connections to aid recall.
- Weber's (1971) "The Ten Best List" from *Nobody is Perfekt* offers practice in recalling items that are clustered by category. It can also be an introduction to the strategy of making lists as an aid to memory. *Frog and Toad Together* (Lobel, 1979)/*Sapo y Sepo Inseparables* (Lizcano, 1980) also provides story structures that include lists.

Cooperative learning structures appear to be successful strategies in developing oral language skills, especially for Hispanic students. Cooperative learning uses peer-oriented structures for learning that are culturally congruent with students' interaction patterns (Delgado-Gaitán, 1987; Kagan, 1986; Ruíz, 1988a). In addition, these types of activities often incorporate problem-solving tasks that increase the English proficiency of second-language learners (Cathcart, 1986; Doughty & Pica, 1986; Duff, 1986).

In addition to the Finding Out/Descrubrimiento program that was discussed earlier (De Avila & Duncan, 1988), Science Activities for the Visually Impaired and Science Enrichment for Learners with Physical Handicaps (De Lucchi & Malone, 1981) also provide motivating interactive activities. This program was specifically designed to meet the needs of a variety of special education students and has been translated into Spanish.

DEVELOPING ORAL LANGUAGE COMMUNICATION EFFECTIVENESS

Students organize their verbal language on many levels that integrate the parameters of form, content, and use. They are expected to (1) develop a large, effective vocabulary for full participation in all aspects of language, including listening, speaking, reading, and writing; (2) produce complete and complex sentences with acceptable levels of intelligibility (language form); and (3) use their language for an increasingly wide range of purposes for communication and for learning at increasingly high levels of abstraction.

Increasing Vocabulary

Cambourne (1987) noted that children are immersed in language from their first hours, an observation borne out by the astonishing number of words that they acquire at a very early age. Hillerich (1987) commented that, with very limited direct teaching of vocabulary, children have a minimum of 6,000 active vocabulary words as they begin kindergarten, and beginning basal readers assume this minimum level of vocabulary. Furthermore, these young children understand many more words than they can use. As they continue through school, students are exposed to 16,000 to 24,000 words a year. Simply counting words does not accurately indicate how children use their vocabulary for different communicative purposes, however. They use words for concrete purposes, such as understanding labels, directions, and explanations; they learn that words have abstract referents, such as concepts and ideas. Children must also discern word relationships (e.g., synonyms, antonyms) and infer the meaning of words that they have never before encountered. To use words for a large variety of oral and written communicative purposes, students must be able to select them with appropriate specificity; have ready access to them; learn new ones at a rapid rate; and define, categorize, and associate them with previous knowledge. They also need to develop their metalinguistic awareness.

Although LLD students frequently obtain low scores on formal vocabulary tests, even those students whose scores are within the normal range may not always have the richness of word meanings necessary for some communication situations or for reading comprehension. Understanding the variation and nuances of word meanings provides a greater access to the depth and subtleties of communicative language interaction as in person-to-person or author-to-reader communication, however. As a matter of fact, oral and written communication share a similar process. As Nystrand (1987) indicated, "When writers do certain things and readers do certain other things, the result is the unique interaction of lucid, comprehensible text. This is why writing is no less interactive in either principle or practice than speech" (p. 206). A child may be able to identify pictures of *delgado* 'slender' and *flaco* 'skinny', and may understand that they can be used as synonyms. An awareness that the former is usually a more complimentary way of describing a person's size requires more in-depth word knowledge.

The multiple meanings and nuances of a word can be a source of confusion for second-language learners. Students who have learned the word *under* in the context of hiding games with objects and people, for example, may be puzzled by phrases such as *under* the circumstances, *under* the gun, *under* the weather, and *under* the wire. Also, the use of idioms, metaphors, and irony are particularly difficult for LLD children (Kamhi, 1987; Nippold, 1985; van Kleeck, 1984a, 1984b). Clinicians may be able to assist classroom teachers in monitoring their word use to minimize confusion.

Vocabulary instruction seems a daunting task, given the volume and complexity of words that children encounter and must learn to use. Hillerich (1987) suggested that

> most vocabulary effort ought to be devoted to helping youngsters become avid accumulators of vocabulary on their own since it is humanly

> impossible to teach all of the words they must and will learn . . . general
> expansion of vocabulary ought to be every teacher's goal. . . . The best
> way to develop vocabulary is through repeated exposure to words in a
> variety of meaningful contexts, with an interest in language. (p. 26)

Research on vocabulary acquisition has indicated that students learn approximately 1 of 20 words to which they are exposed in context alone (Nagy, 1988). Over time, this results in a sizable increase in vocabulary. General vocabulary development enhances all levels of communicative competence. In a social context, for example, competence involves selecting appropriate words for different situations (e.g., *belongings* in a formal situation and *stuff* in an informal situation). Clarifying a message may involve simplifying vocabulary (e.g., *tired* for *fatigued*).

Direct instruction in specific vocabulary may be warranted when students lack labels for people, things, and experiences that are a regular part of their environment. Lahey (1988) suggested that those who teach vocabulary to young children should consider (1) the phonological preferences of the child, (2) the range of applications that a word will have in the child's environment, and (3) the child's need for labels to fulfill particular referents. Within these broad categories, further decisions must be made about the level of abstraction and appropriate specificity. For example, does the child need to know items by their individual names or by their class? Individual names such as *manzana* 'apple', *plátano* 'banana', and *durazno* or *melocotón* 'peach' may be more useful than the general word *fruta* 'fruit', since children are often asked to make such choices in daily situations. In contrast, the general word *árboles* 'trees' may be sufficiently specific to allow a child to participate in conversation about them; specific names of trees such as *pino* 'pine', *secoya* 'redwood', or *olmo* 'elm' are generally not important to young children. Israel (1984) suggested that words be taught in groups to take advantage of the process of chunking, which "provides ease of storage and retrieval" (p. 247). A categorization system assists children who have difficulty in organizing the input that they receive. For example, Israel suggests that a teacher review words such as *cows*, *horses*, and *goats* as animals and then work on associations such as "a penguin is a ──" (*fish* or *bird*).

Students in the upper elementary or higher grades may need specific vocabulary instruction to understand texts and content area lessons. Nagy (1988) suggested that words be selected for instruction according to the following criteria: (1) they are conceptually difficult; (2) they can be grouped in some related way; (3) they are important to the understanding of a reading selection; or (4) they have wide applicability in general language use. It is not necessary to teach every unfamiliar word. The meaning of many words can be derived from the context of a reading selection, as in the following passage: "The villagers made their home from snow and large blocks of ice. These igloos provided shelter from the fierce cold and served as meeting places for village leaders."

Vocabulary instruction for second-language learners follows similar principles. Teaching relevant, widely functional, interrelated vocabulary in the context of communication events expands vocabulary much more rapidly than does drilling on word lists. For young second-language learners, however, the process of acquiring vocabulary often has two very different dimensions. They may encounter new vocabulary for concepts that they already have, and the similarities and differences in words in the first and second languages may either aid or confuse them. For example, cognates such as *metamórfosis*/metamorphosis or *crisalida*/chrysalis have the same meaning, but false cognates such as *asistir* 'attend'/assist or *arena* 'sand'/arena have different meanings. At other times, students may be acquiring concepts and vocabulary simultaneously. As they acquire new concepts and new labels in a second language, they may require more exposure, more review, and more practice before they really have an in-depth knowledge of the vocabulary.

Selecting Words That Reflect the Child's Interests

Observing children as they interact within an enriched environment provides many opportunities to identify their interests. A child who returns again and again to the same toy or looks high and low for a favorite book is demonstrating a need for specific vocabulary words. Older students who make requests using vague referents, such as "that thing we used to build a house," must acquire more specific vocabulary. Research on vocabulary development indicates that children need to hear a word several times in appropriate situations before they incorporate it into their lexicon; estimates range from 10 to 100 times, depending on the child's ability (Treadway, 1987). Repetition should not be achieved through rote instruction, however, but through interaction in a contextualized environment.

Teaching Words That Are Related to One Another

Semantic Mapping. Most researchers and speech-language clinicians are familiar with semantic mapping as an effective strategy for vocabulary development with school-aged children. In the following example, the teacher uses semantic mapping with a small group of children before reading a literature selection, in this case, *Swimmy* (Lionni, 1963), a story about a fish who learns about loneliness, courage, and leadership. A similar strategy may be used with the Spanish *Bolitas, el Pececito Rojo 'Beady, the Little Red Fish'* (Da Passano, 1989).

1. The teacher chooses a topic central to the book and writes it in the middle of a large piece of chart paper. In this case, the word *fish* or *ocean* may be

appropriate (Figure 8-3). The teacher then asks the children to provide as many words as they can that they associate with the word.

2. The teacher writes their suggestions in a vertical column on the left side of the paper.

3. After writing category titles on the chart paper, the teacher asks the children to decide where each word belongs. In this example, the categories are about fish—how they feel, how they look, what they do, and what names they have.

4. Older children can work in cooperative learning groups to make categories and discuss where to list the words.

5. The teacher should add one or two words from the text that are probably new to the children.

6. After the words have been organized into groups, the teacher can work on word relationships to provide more in-depth knowledge. The teacher may ask, "Which word means the opposite of long?" "Which word means the same as dangerous?" "Which word begins the same way as 'big'?"

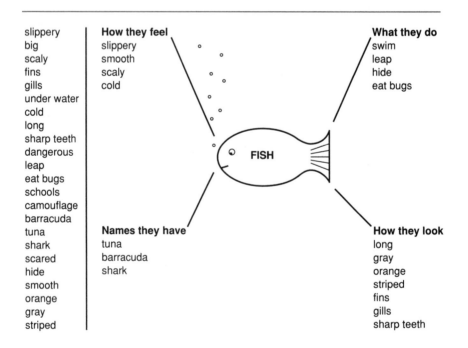

Figure 8-3 Semantic Mapping: *Swimmy* (Lionni, 1963)

7. The teacher can then ask about the words that were embedded in the text. For example, "Which word that you heard means to be afraid?"
8. When the students have all these words in front of them, they will be able to pay better attention to the occurrence of the words in the text.
9. Following an initial reading of the story for pleasure and personal response, a second reading may focus on vocabulary words. For example, the teacher might ask the students to raise their hands when they hear one of the vocabulary words.

For young children who may not benefit from the printed words, pictures can be used to teach words related to each other. For example, before reading *There's a Nightmare in My Closet* (Mayer, 1968), the teacher may engage children in a discussion of things that frighten them (Figure 8-4). (Diéguez [1989] has translated this book into Spanish as *Una Pesadilla en Mi Armario*.)

Word Substitution Activities. Adaptations of predictable books are helpful in teaching new words that can be related to each other in a number of ways. The strategy can be adapted for all ages and ability levels in the oral and written mo-

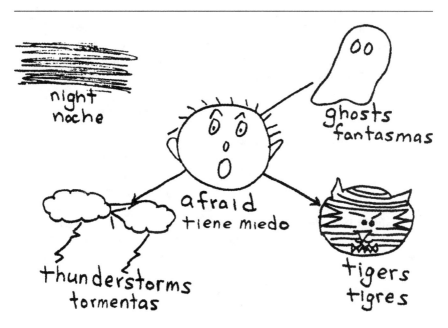

Figure 8-4 Semantic Mapping with Pictures: *There's a Nightmare in My Closet* (Mayer, 1968)

dalities. Appendix 8-A includes a more detailed list of predictable books. For example, *Brown Bear, Brown Bear* (Martin, 1983) can accommodate adjectives other than color and nouns other than animals, as well as a variety of action words. The original text

> Brown Bear, Brown Bear,
> What do you see?
> I see a red bird
> Looking at me.

can be changed by substituting adjectives of size instead of color, resulting in

> Brown Bear, Brown Bear,
> What do you see?
> I see a big (tiny, giant, little, etc.) bird
> Looking at me.

Substituting adjectives of feeling results in a text such as

> Brown Bear, Brown Bear,
> What do you see?
> I see an angry bird
> Looking at me.

The clinician can improve the students' metalinguistic ability and related vocabulary by drawing their attention to the class of words that will be substituted. Word categorization activities, such as brainstorming, should precede substitution activities. For example, vocabulary charts displayed around the room can be used for many activities that focus on word meaning.

Color Words	Feeling Words	Size Words
red	angry	giant
blue	scared	enormous
green	worried	huge
purple	lonely	immense
beige	sad	miniature

In a similar activity, the children may read a number of books on the same topic and categorize some of the vocabulary. For example, reading Carle's *The Very Busy Spider* (1984), *The Grouchy Ladybug* (1986), and *The Very Hungry Caterpillar* (1979) exposes children to many words and concepts related to insects. They may enjoy using the words to adapt the poem "Bugs" from *The Fish with the Deep-See Smile* (Brown, 1939).

> I like bugs.
> Black bugs.
> Green bugs.
> Bad bugs.
> Mean bugs.

> I like bugs.
> A bug on the rug.
> A bug in a glass.
> A bug in the grass.
> I like bugs.

For a more advanced discussion of word choice, students may study a particular author, focus on that author's words, and examine their meaning in context. DeGroff (1989) provided helpful examples of word study based on literature. In discussing *The Snowy Day* (Keats, 1962) she suggested drawing students' attention to the author's description of the protagonist's actions. For example,

> teacher and students might speculate on Keats' use of "smacking" to describe what Peter did with the stick to the tree. What other words could Keats have chosen? "Tapping" implies a light touch. Maybe the snow wouldn't have fallen "plop" on Peter's head if he had only "tapped." "Hitting" works also, but seems to lack the strength of swing and sense of sound that "smacking" conveys. (DeGroff, 1989, p. 119)

Discussion of word choice can not only enhance the music, meaning, and pleasure of what students read, but also model a process that can render their own oral and written narratives much richer. (Refer to Appendix 8-A for a list of English and Spanish books appropriate for this activity.)

Teaching Children to Become Avid Accumulators of Words

Young children can use predictable books to develop vocabulary and learn research skills at the same time. For example, to write their own version of *El Oso Más Elegante 'Best Dressed Bear'* (Blocksma, 1984; translated by Ada, 1986), children can identify the items of clothing mentioned in the story and substitute different clothing words taken from picture dictionaries, such as *My First Thousand Words in Spanish* (Amery, 1979), or Scary's picture books, such as *Best Word Book Ever* (1967), *Cars and Trucks and Things That Go* (1974), or *My First Word Book* (1986). This activity lends itself to cross-age tutoring in which older, more advanced students help younger, less advanced students in acquiring basic lexicon words in either English or Spanish.

Rockwell's stories, such as *The Toolbox* (1971), *Nice and Clean* (Rockwell & Rockwell, 1984), *Things That Go* (1986), or *Things to Play With* (1988), or Crews' stories, such as *Truck* (1980), *Harbor* (1982), or *Parade* (1983), illustrate vocabulary related to specific themes and are very helpful in increasing both oral and written language. These books can serve as references for children in their own construction of texts.

A bulletin board of "interesting words" can be a central focus in the classroom. The clinician can assist students by setting up "word hunts" as part of the therapy.

Students may be asked to look for such words as homonyms, rhyming words, difficult to pronounce words, long words, funny words, or multiple-meaning words. All these categories of words are known to be difficult for LLD students and second-language learners, and this activity provides excellent ongoing practice (Schuele & van Kleeck, 1987; van Kleeck, 1984a, 1984b). Older elementary and junior high school students may do the same type of exercises, using newspapers and magazines.

Developing Language Form

As Bloom and Lahey (1978) indicated, form, content, and use are interacting components of language. Lahey (1988) defined syntax as "the arrangement of words according to the meaning of the relations among them" (p. 14). Yet, she cautioned that "the combination of forms depends only in part upon the meaning relations we express; the purpose of the utterance and the context of the utterance—language use—will also help to determine the form of the utterance" (p. 15). Halliday (1973) argued that the functions of language give rise to complexity and flexibility of form: the greater the range of purposes, the more complex and flexible the forms for communicating them.

The syntactical structures that young children use reflect their cognitive development. For example, the child who says *no more* and *all gone bottle* demonstrates the concepts of nonexistence or disappearance. Saying *hot stove* reflects the child's understanding that objects are separate from their properties. Utterances such as *more cookie* demonstrate the concepts of recurrence, and *daddy car* expresses possession. Older children understand temporal, causal, and conditional relationships by responding to and using expressions such as *when . . . , because . . . , if . . . then*. An understanding of subtle syntactical relationships is important to students' success in listening and reading. For example, a student may be able to understand sequentially related utterances such as *There was a man, He had a hat, It was black*, and *He hit the car*, but still have difficulty processing an embedded sentence such as *The man with the black hat hit the car*. Sentences with multiple referents that require active manipulation of semantic-syntactical relations, such as *After we went to the movie, he told her that she should get him some popcorn*, may cause problems to the LLD student.

In their review of several studies on the use of cohesive elements, Wallach and Miller (1988) noted the complexity and subtlety of meaning relationships. For example, although coherence renders a discourse meaningful, it need not be in what is written or said directly (Blank & Marquis, 1987). Often, the application of some inferential strategies makes it possible to understand a poorly structured oral or written message. Second-language learners may have difficulties with the application of such strategies, however. The meaning relationships in a sentence may be expressed in an unfamiliar word order; verb inflections may be confusing;

and morphological changes, which affect meaning, may go unnoticed. Thus, LLD children who are acquiring a second language need concrete demonstrations of meaning relationships. Activities that highlight inflections and morphological changes are also useful.

Enhancing Syntactical Development

Efforts to increase grammatical competence may focus initially on discerning the key meaning elements in sentences. Gaining meaning from connected discourse requires foregrounding—identifying the main message of a sentence when listening, reading, or writing. Working with kernel sentences (i.e., two-word combinations that convey a complete thought) is helpful to both LLD students and second-language learners, because it provides them with a basic structure around which to build meaning. The notion of kernel sentences can be introduced with a simple poem, such as the following from *Another Here and Now Storybook* (Mitchell, 1948):

> Frogs jump
> Caterpillars hump
> Worms wiggle
> Bugs jiggle
> Rabbits hop
> Horses clop
> Snakes slide
> Seagulls glide
> Mice creep
> Deer leap
> Puppies bounce
> Kittens pounce
> Lions stalk
> But . . . I walk

The power of a simple sentence becomes evident when vocabulary and story structure are combined as they are here.

In order to practice with kernel sentences, students may work in small groups or pairs to determine how many sentences they can generate in a given time period, usually 2 to 3 minutes (Treadway, 1987). If they race the teacher to see who can generate the greatest number of sentences, they will discover that kernel sentences are most efficient. Subsequently, students may combine their kernel sentences to create their own poem. Writing headlines, advertisements, posters, or want ads where students are restricted to a given number of words can also highlight the importance of kernel sentences.

Once students understand the concept of kernel sentences and have seen it demonstrated in poems, stories, and environmental print, they may begin to alter these basic structures by manipulating sentences through word substitution, sentence expansion, or sentence reduction. In word substitution activities, students change specific words in a sentence while maintaining the basic sentence structure. They may choose from a suggested list or generate their words. In this excerpt from the *Three Billy Goats Gruff* (Galdone, 1973b, p.1), for example, students have substituted the following words:

Under the bridge lived a <u>great</u>   <u>ugly</u>   troll
                 big   hideous
                 huge   mean
                 gigantic   scary
                 enormous frightening

with eyes as big as <u>saucers</u>   and a nose as long as a <u>poker</u>
              suns   fishing pole
              dishes   telephone wire
              plates   cane

In sentence expansion activities (Cloze sentence procedures), students are given a basic sentence and asked to add words to it.

The _____ cat _____ caught the _____ rat.
    fat   quickly   poor
    clever   suddenly   surprised
    sneaky   easily   clumsy

Older elementary, middle-school, and high-school students can be asked to add words from specific categories, such as adjectives or adverbs.

Conversely, in sentence reduction activities, students try to eliminate words while maintaining the meaning of the sentence. An excerpt from *Millions of Cats* (Gag, 1928, p.1), "Once upon a time there was a very old man and a very old woman. They lived in a nice clean house which had flowers all around it," can be reduced to "A man and a woman lived in a house," for example. The use of literature to demonstrate the ways in which authors manipulate sentences is an effective way of introducing the concept to students.

Working with More Complex Sentences

LLD students and second-language learners benefit from practice in unraveling complex sentences. Westby (1989a) noted that structures such as relative clauses, conjunctions, and inverted sentences are present in familiar stories. LLD students can profit from practice with this type of discourse because it supplies a variety of structures as well as specific vocabulary, carefully identified referents, and cohesive elements—qualities often missing from their language. Rigg and Allen (1989) suggested that second-language learners need to hear literature read aloud "because this is one of the easiest ways to discover the sorts of English we call 'literary.' This is how they learn 'once upon a time,' 'happily ever after,' and many other phrases. They learn the sorts of English that are found only in the literature, and their reading, writing, and conversation are all enriched by this" (p. xiii).

Sentence-combining activities, such as those suggested by the California Writing Project (California State Department of Education, 1987), can be particularly useful when applied to student-generated writing. For example, students in the third grade may practice inserting adjectives and adverbs, thus transforming *I ate a hamburger; the hamburger was soggy* into *I ate a soggy hamburger*. In fourth grade, activities can center on producing parallel sequences, such as *Maria wanted a bike*, *Maria wanted a doll*, and *Maria wanted a baseball bat*, and transforming them into *Mary wanted a bike, a doll, and a baseball bat*. Numerous other examples are provided for each grade through elementary school.

Students involved in writing programs that include feedback from peers might be asked to listen for other possible sentence combinations. Their editing checklists can include some of the choices listed in the California Writing Project (California State Department of Education, 1987).

Books that contain syntactical patterns embedded in a strong story structure help students understand and eventually use more complex language structures. *The Runaway Bunny* (Brown, 1942) includes the conditional structure in repeated episodes.

> "I will become a little sailboat,
> and I will sail away from you."
> "If you become a sailboat and sail away from me,"
> said his mother, " I will become the wind
> and blow you where I want you to go."

The Carrot Seed (Krause, 1945)/(translated by Palacios, *La Semilla de Zanahoria*) uses a number of syntactical structures that express feelings in an exquisitely simple story about faith. As the little boy plants a carrot seed, the family warns:

> Father: "I'm afraid it won't come up."
> Mother: "I'm afraid it won't come up."
> Brother: "It won't come up."
> Everyone kept saying it
> wouldn't come up.

When the seed finally emerges, the authors say,

> "Then, one day, a carrot came up.
> Just as the little boy had known
> it would."

Students can produce pieces of writing that are adaptations of original texts, using the same syntactical structures, but varying the setting, characters, and events. As these structures begin to emerge in the students' own writing on self-selected topics, the teacher or clinician can draw attention to them.

While it is essential to acknowledge and support the similarities between oral and written language, it is also important to note the differences (Purcell-Gates,

1989; Table 8-1). Both are interactive processes through which a certain message is conveyed, but they vary in stream of speech, nonverbal communication, type of message, accuracy, vocabulary, and syntactical use. For example, gestures and facial expression, as well as intonation and rhythm, supplement oral language; in print, however, these representations are not always possible. Drawing attention to some of these differences can support the development of oral and written grammatical competence.

Planning for Use of Specific Sentence Structures

Wong Fillmore (1989b) proposed that grammar be developed through thematic units of interesting content. "The most effective instances of language oriented instruction involve the teaching of whatever structures are needed to talk about the content at hand" (p. 135). Furthermore, she indicated that second-language learners acquire language more readily when language interaction draws attention to

---

Table 8-1 Differences between Oral and Written Language

Oral Language	Written Language
The stream of speech is transient and cannot be captured unless the speaker agrees to repeat.	Print is permanent and can be easily referenced for clarification of meaning.
Gestures, facial expressions, intonations, and rhythm give richness to oral language.	Gestures, facial expressions, intonation, and rhythm have few representations in print.
Messages are often delivered in incomplete sentences.	Sentences are generally required for clear communication.
Shared knowledge allows for more vagueness of referents and omission of information.	Print requires very specific word use and word order to make messages clear.
Vocabulary is simple, direct, consisting largely of verbs, nouns, and adjectives.	Print contains many words that would sound inappropriate in speech: participles, adverbs (the singing bird or quickly he ran to the gate).
Word order is efficient and predictable: noun + verb + object.	Literary studies make use of various syntactical structures (off the fence they jumped) to add interest and voice to a passage.

Source: From "What Oral/Written Language Differences Can Tell Us about Beginning Instruction" by V. Purcell-Gates, 1989, *The Reading Teacher, 42*, pp. 290–294. Copyright 1989 by the International Reading Association.

form as well as meaning. Thus, planning language intervention within meaningful content instruction requires

1. *attention to language form.* Drawing attention to form does not imply a return to grammar drills; instead, the teacher allows students to listen to particular patterns that occur naturally in talking about a given topic. Over the length of a theme, students will hear the structures many times in meaningful context and will use them when they are ready to do so.

2. *specific elicitation techniques.* The variety of elicitation techniques available allows the teacher or clinician to focus on form at the students' level of proficiency. Single-word responses can be elicited by such questions as What do you need? More complex responses result from open-ended questions, such as Tell me about . . . .

3. *corrective feedback.* Learners use corrective feedback to construct meaning in the new language. They need good modeling in order to determine which forms are correct, particularly when the only fluent speakers in a classroom are the teacher and the aide. Although greater emphasis should be on communication of meaning, the teacher should model, extend, and expand the students' utterances.

The integration of form and function can occur in many authentic communication activities. For example, students who are preparing a booth for an all-school carnival must determine the game that the booth will offer, the equipment needed, the cost of the tickets, the prizes to be awarded, and a method of marketing their booth. All these activities involve a wide variety of language structures and lexical items. Collaboration between the classroom teacher and the speech-language clinician is especially appropriate in such a situation. The clinician can target specific structures by scaffolding the students' participation in planning this complex classroom event. A planning chart is an effective way to organize both content and structure after the students have brainstormed ideas for various components of the carnival task (Figure 8-5). The clinician can use the chart as a reference for work on language structures (e.g., "We will need . . . for the donkey game," "Let's help David write a newspaper ad," "How can Janet get her piñata?"). Over the course of the days or weeks needed to complete the task, language patterns will be recycled many times. Written work associated with the planning, such as posters, flyers, and newspaper ads, can draw particular attention to language form.

Developing Speech Intelligibility

Caution is necessary in planning an intervention program for a phonological disorder. Before determining that the student has a problem in pronouncing a particular sound or sound combination, the clinician should interview the parents and significant others to determine if the pattern is deviant or reflects a dialectal differ-

Planning for the Carnival

Students	Game Ideas	Prizes	Equipment	Marketing	Ticket Price
Juan	Pin the Tail on the Donkey	Stickers	Donkey picture Straight pins Blindfold Tails	Posters	25¢
Maria	Drop the Clothespin in the bottle	Candy	Narrow-neck bottle Clothespins	Announcement on P.A. system	5¢ for each pin
David	Darts	Peanuts	Velcro darts Bullseye	Newspaper ad	10¢ for each throw
Janet	Piñata	Pennies	Piñata Candy Blindfold Rope Stick	Flyers	$1.00
Jessica	Bowling	Ribbons	Ball Pins Tape	Class announcements	50¢ for each ball

Figure 8-5 Planning Chart to Develop Specific Grammatical Structures

ence (Eblen, 1982a, 1982b). When intervention for phonological disorders is necessary, it should include language activities. As Fey (1986) reported, there seems to be a high correlation between phonological disorders, limited vocabulary, and semantic-syntactical abilities. Strategies for remediation of phonological disorders in Spanish are similar to those used in English.

Auditory training has been found to be a helpful approach in some students with phonological problems in English (Hodson, 1983, 1986). It is important to initiate therapy with patterns that are familiar to the student to ensure that the child experience some success. Working with true words rather than nonsense words ensures that the activity is meaningful (Hodson, 1986). Langdon (personal communication, 1990) found the use of both nonsense and true Spanish words effective with 3- to 4-year-old Spanish-speaking preschoolers who had phonological problems, but the number of children who have been followed is still too small to permit definitive conclusions on the effectiveness of this approach. It is possible that a variety of approaches can be successfully used to remediate a set of phonological deviances in Spanish-speaking children as in English-speaking children (Ingram,

1983). However, a limited number of materials are specifically available to remediate phonological problems in Spanish. They are listed in Appendix 8-B.

Increasing the Range of Language Use

Language should be used and enjoyed for its music and rhythm, for interaction, and for learning. Wong Fillmore (1991) has encouraged teachers to help their language minority students use their language as fully and richly as possible. The speech-language clinician should observe the students' learning environment to determine if it is conducive to language learning. Whether direct service to students is on a pull-out basis or within the classroom, the speech-language clinician can offer valuable assistance to the classroom teacher (Schory, 1990). Simple modifications to the environment can often enhance language learning in children of all ages. Questions such as the following should be considered:

- Are there materials that enhance communication?
- Are materials for creative expression, such as paint, clay, paper, glue, and puppets, readily accessible?
- Do new materials appear and old ones disappear to foster inquiry and exploration?
- Are activity centers set up with sufficient materials for each student, or are there only a few so that the children will have to negotiate their use?
- Are there places to listen to a variety of materials?
- Is the classroom routine occasionally changed so the students will have to reorganize their thinking?

Even in a small therapy room, an interesting pop-up book, a mobile, a bookshelf, or a bottle of bubbles encourages comments, questions, comparisons, and sharing of personal experiences.

In addition to an interesting environment of ongoing projects, specific activities can be designed to foster authentic use of language for a variety of purposes. For example, a jigsaw activity is a cooperative learning strategy that requires students to work in groups to become "experts" on a given topic or activity. When they have mastered the material, they disperse themselves throughout the class to teach that material to a new group. This is an ideal activity for heterogeneous language groups. The *Come with Me Science Series* (different dates) provides many activities for students in kindergarten to sixth grade that are ideal for oral language development using the jigsaw format. Each science unit contains directions for several different activities related to the theme—a song, an art project, drawing lessons, pictures, and interesting facts. The clinician can teach these activities to a small group of students, who then move to different groups to teach their peers.

Paper folding and assembly tasks are useful activities that require students to attend to specific directions. (See *Fun Folds* [1984] or *A Paper Menagerie* [Brown, 1984].) All these activities are most effective when they occur in the context of a larger theme so that language is used for broader goals. This technique provides excellent opportunities for including parents or community members who have a specific skill that they can teach to the students.

Information gap activities, often known as "barrier games," require students to use precise language to answer questions, clarify their remarks, or repair their language in response to another's needs. One student may have some information to communicate to another. A physical barrier is placed between students so that the speaker must use oral language only to communicate the information. While watching the listener attempt to follow directions, the speaker can revise the directions (e.g., using different vocabulary, shortening phrases) to aid understanding. Students enjoy this activity as a game, and it can also be used when the listener is not present (e.g., using the telephone or writing a note or letter). Wong Fillmore (1989b) indicated that the skill of letting interlocutors know whether a message has been understood is crucial. With this information, they can make necessary adjustments so that input remains comprehensible.

Pairing activities encourage students to ask questions, organize information, revise hypotheses, and assist others in completing a task. They require students to find one or more persons that fit a given criterion. For example, young students may be asked to (1) find the partner who has a card to match theirs so that they can play Old Maid, (2) find the other half of a geometric shape so that they can make a bulletin board for the mathematics center, or (3) find animals that go with their picture of a zoo, farm, or forest so that they can begin working on a diorama. Older students may be asked to (1) find the person who has a picture to match their newspaper headline so that they can prepare a current events display, (2) match a famous quotation with its author as a way to review for a test, (3) match characters with book titles as an alternative to book reports, and (4) fill in an interview form that requires the student to find someone who has done something unusual that can be the focus of an article for the class newspaper.

INTERACTING SUCCESSFULLY WITH PRINT

The traditional view that listening precedes speaking and speaking precedes reading and writing does not accurately describe children's experience in becoming competent communicators. From a very young age, children are asked to respond to, manipulate, evaluate, and create both oral and written language. Although other literacy-related behaviors do not develop with the amazing speed with which children's oral language develops, they do develop in tandem. The compelling nature of writing is apparent to anyone who has watched a 2-year-old sit with rapt attention, felt marker in hand, making marks on any surface available. In their overview of emergent literacy, Teale and Sulzby (1989) concluded that "reading and writing develop concurrently and interrelatedly in young children" (p. 3). Oral language acts as a base for literacy development, but in recursive fashion, reading experiences influence oral language. Literacy skills develop during meaningful and authentic interactions, just as oral language does. As Teale and Sulzby (1989) noted, "Children may see adults reading newspapers or greeting cards, writing checks, completing crossword puzzles, or using the TV guide. Children are ushered into the world of literacy viewing reading and writing as aspects of a much larger system of accomplishing goals" (p. 3).

Supporting Emergent Literacy

As Ruíz (1988a, 1989) noted, print awareness plays a critical sociocultural role in the process by which language minority children learn to read and write. There is great variation in children's print awareness as they enter school for the first time. Some can recognize signs in familiar context, name letters, know what a "word" is, and understand why people read and write. Others have very limited exposure to print and little knowledge of its functions.

Awareness of print has been shown to correlate highly with measures of reading ability (Curtis, 1986; Lomax & McGee, 1987; Ruíz, 1988a, 1989).

Although well developed print awareness has been often associated with socio-economic status, several studies contradict this viewpoint (e.g., Harste, Woodward, & Burke, 1984; Wells, 1986). The homes of successful readers generally provide ready access to print and consistent interaction in events, independent of socioeconomic status (Adams, 1990). Print awareness does not necessarily imply exposure to written language only, however. For example, Vásquez (1990) identified literacy skills that were developed through the rich oral language of the home. She indicated that " 'Literate' behavior may occur during a verbal interaction" and she described a critical literate behavior that develops from oral interaction as "the ability to respond to extended pieces of text, to hold them in memory and then to objectify them by making linkages from them to other texts and to one's own personal experience" (p. 198).

Most studies have indicated that children, regardless of their backgrounds, benefit from an environment that is rich in print (Adams, 1990). This type of environment provides many opportunities for integrating all language systems: listening, speaking, reading, and writing. "Children must be immersed in a print environment equivalent in intensity to the oral language environment from which speech emerged" (McCracken & McCracken, 1986b, p. 1). This immersion draws attention to specific features of print in an authentic way. Repeated opportunities to interact with print in a functional way should precede direct instruction in letter names and sounds (Ferreiro & Teberosky, 1982).

It is quite common for LLD students to have significant difficulties interacting with print. Early language disorders may seem to "disappear" until students are exposed to reading and writing, but their previous language difficulties resurface in the form of "learning disabilities" (Bashir, Kuban, Kleinman, & Scavuzzo, 1983; Sawyer, 1985; Wallach & Miller, 1988; Westby, 1985). The difficulties may be related to one or several of the following factors: a poorly developed oral language base, problems with the abstraction required in using print, problems internalizing metacognitive and metalinguistic awareness, inefficient strategies for memory retrieval and access, inability to organize new information, or weakness in connecting previous information with new learning. Still, some children have difficulty because they were introduced to print as an abstract system of isolated skills that were never part of a meaningful context.

Second-language learners who do not have the benefit of primary language instruction should be immersed in the functions of print before reading English in a more formalized fashion. Hudelson (1984) presented strong evidence of the positive impact of environmental print on students who are acquiring English; "even children who speak very little English are reading some of the print in their environment and are using that reading to increase their English" (p. 222).

Enriching Interaction with Print

Environmental Print

Signs, symbols, packages, charts, lists, enlarged dictionaries—in short, any print that a child sees in the home, school, or community is environmental print. A variety of activities can be designed around such print material. For example, young children can bring everyday items, such as cereal boxes, soup can labels, or toothpaste tubes, from home to create a three-dimensional bulletin board of real-life print. Attention can be drawn to many features of print, such as letter names, size, style, words, word-picture matches, likenesses, and differences.

Older children can bring in newspapers or TV listings to look for specific words, letters from their names, or other key words in their personal and/or school vocabulary. Store receipts, bills, grocery lists, and letters from relatives can all be used to foster communication about print. Because the use of environmental print enables the teacher to adjust the level of difficulty to match any child's need, it is particularly suited to classrooms with heterogeneous populations.

The environmental print in the classroom is also an important source of meaning for students. Labels for children's belongings, daily schedules, lists of helpers and their jobs, as well as displays of rules and procedures are valuable for making connections between everyday life and print.

A "felt pen table" can be extremely helpful in creating a print-rich environment. It requires only a long table covered with paper and a box of felt-tipped pens. Students of all ages enjoy creating pictures, stories, and murals that can be captioned or used as teacher-student or student-student interactive "journals."

Appropriate print materials can be added to the sociodramatic play center to help students make natural associations between the daily activities that they are dramatizing and the importance of print. For example, a notepad and pencil can be placed next to the telephone; paper for making shopping lists, near the play store; stationery and envelopes, next to the play post office; and prescription pads, near the doctor's office. If students are not using these items naturally, the teacher may join the play one day and model their use.

Functional Uses of Print in the Classroom

Curtis (1986) suggested offering students several opportunities to engage in the procedural, correspondence, and record-keeping uses of print.

- Students may take attendance or a lunch count. Recognition of each other's names is often one of the first reading skills.
- Students can prepare activity centers by following instructions left by the teacher as to what materials must be gathered: crayons, paste, rulers, scissors, stapler, felt markers. At first, these instructions may be accompanied by rebuses, but with daily practice, they should become "sight words" for the students.
- Individual student mail boxes foster letter writing and are a "legitimate" form of note passing that is popular with students.
- Forms for charting patterns of changes in weather, growth of animals, or days for watering plants help students begin to associate print with learning.
- During the school day, an agenda form may be prepared for conducting class meetings at the end of the day. On a large piece of chart paper that is divided into sections, one for compliments and one for conflict, the students list their names and, in parentheses, the name of the person whose behavior they want to discuss during the meeting. This chart may be one of the first things that the students set up when they enter the classroom every morning. After the day is over, the children make comments.
- A sign requesting "Please don't break it" may be placed next to a laboriously completed puzzle or by a precious Lego construction that represented the joint efforts of two or three students.
- Students may use drawings, place markers, letters, syllables, or words when first using print and gradually develop more conventional spelling as their literacy skills increase.

These functions of print are also adaptable to small therapy rooms. Smith (1983) offered the following poetic view of the various functions of print, providing clinicians with many ideas for incorporating print into authentic activities during the school day:

What Written Language Is For

Stories to be read
Books to be published
Poems to be recited
Plays to be acted
Songs to be sung
Newspapers to be browsed through
Letters to be mailed
Jokes to be told
Notes to be passed
Greeting cards to be sent
Cartons to be labeled
Instructions to be followed
Recipes to be cooked
Designs to be made
Programs to be organized
Excursions to be planned
Messages to be exchanged
Entertainment guides to be consulted
Reviews to be considered
Catalogs to be compared
Memoranda to be circulated
Announcements to be posted
Bills to be collected
Posters to be displayed
Diaries to be hidden
Cribs to be concealed . . .

"Written language is for ideas, action, reflection, and experience. It is not to have your ignorance exposed, your sensitivity destroyed, or your ability assessed."*

Reading Aloud

The value of reading aloud for the development of oral language and literacy skills has been documented in many studies (Adams, 1990; Strickland & Morrow,

*Source: From *Joining the Literacy Club: Essays into Literacy*, by F. Smith (ed.), 1983, Victoria, Canada: Frank Smith Educational Associates, Inc. Copyright 1983 by Frank Smith Educational Associates, Inc.

1989). Most students enjoy a story time in their classroom on a daily basis. The speech-language clinician can support this activity by helping readers select books with strong story lines, vivid vocabulary, and language structures that need to be emphasized. The clinician can also work with individual students to ensure that they have adequate background knowledge to benefit from the reading selection.

Reading aloud by the clinician in a pull-out program can be an effective way to approach many language skills if it is coordinated with the classroom teacher's activities. Beginning each session with a few minutes of oral reading elicits natural language interactions; students ask questions, express personal feelings or experiences, and develop listening skills. In the therapy setting, the clinician can model these skills for the LLD students' benefit. Picture books with short, simple stories can be read in a very short time. Books with several chapters may also be used to assist students who are ready for more complex discourse. (See Appendix 8-A for a list of books that serve as excellent openers for a therapy session.)

Many studies with both monolingual and bilingual children have supported the importance of background knowledge in reading comprehension (Au, 1979; Pearson, 1982; Ruíz, 1989). The clinician can help students in developing the necessary background and in organizing, retrieving, and applying that knowledge to new information. Lindfors (1987) suggested that "language can provide a means by which we 'represent' past experience—present it again, isolate it, consider it, reinterpret it in light of our ever changing and growing 'theory of the world in the head' " (p. 269). Background knowledge allows a student to interact with a text in all these ways. The clinician's role in developing background knowledge may be to scaffold this retrieval process by a series of questions or to help the classroom teacher use appropriate questions to improve the student's understanding of a given topic (Blank & White, 1986).

Children from non–English-speaking homes and non-mainstream cultures are often assumed to be lacking in background knowledge. Maria (1989) cautioned teachers not to make premature judgments, however. Children may have the necessary background knowledge, but may fail to retrieve it and use it as an aid to comprehending a text. Even in groups of mainstream children with very similar backgrounds, variation in knowledge is to be expected. As students become immersed in reading, the worlds that open up to them will shape and reshape their thinking, expanding what they already know, have experienced, and have organized as their reality. By teaching students ways to retrieve what they know, the clinician can enrich a reading experience.

At the present time, most classrooms have a time devoted to silent reading during which students select books and have uninterrupted time to explore them. These Drop Everything and Read (DEAR) or Sustained Silent Reading (SSR) times offer many opportunities for the clinician to help students in the classroom benefit from an authentic literacy event. Emerging readers often spend DEAR time going back and forth to the bookshelf, choosing books that they look at for only a few seconds. The clinician can help these students develop sustained attention by asking them to

- look at the cover and note the title, author, and illustrations.
- see if there are many words or letters that they recognize.
- open the back of the book and see if there is a picture of the author and illustrator.
- see if one page has a dedication.
- see if they can guess what the story will be about.
- think about other stories on this topic. Will this story be the same or different?
- follow the story by looking at the pictures. Are there any words or letters that they know on each page?
- think about how the illustrator made these pictures. Did he or she use paint, crayons, or water colors?
- look for pages that they think their friends would like to see or hear about.
- close the book when they are finished and see if they can remember what happened in the story. Then open the book and see if they were right.
- think about how they will share this book with the class.

Retelling Stories

After DEAR or SSR time, students may enjoy sharing what they have read with each other. Working in pairs, they can show their partners the title of the book and offer a summary in some form, for example, by showing a favorite page or telling how the book made them feel. Although this may be a very brief exchange, the language skills involved are difficult and must be modeled many times and then scaffolded as students begin to take on the sharing task themselves.

Children delight in hearing their favorite stories read over and over. After hearing stories many times, they will be able to take over the role of rereading. A scrapbook of "Old Favorites" can be made by photocopying the cover of the book and putting it into an album. Each day a different student is chosen to make a selection from the album and read the old favorite. This provides excellent practice in sequencing stories correctly, as the listeners will complain if something is missed; in practicing and rehearsing effective expression (e.g., in *The Three Little Pigs*, "Then I'll huff, and I'll puff and I'll blow your house down!" or, in *Little Red Riding Hood*, "Grandma, why do you have such . . .?"); and in internalizing story structure.

A small group can work on retelling stories by reconstructing a book that has been cut apart. The clinician can make a collection of these by buying two copies of a paperback version, mounting the pages on cardboard, and laminating them so that the students can put the pages in order without concern for running them from front to back. Galdone's versions of folk and fairy tales, such as *The House That Jack Built* (1971), *Little Red Hen* (1973a), *Little Red Riding Hood* (1974), and *The Gingerbread Boy* (1975), are excellent resources for this activity. Children never seem to tire of sequencing the pages, for example, where the Gingerbread Boy is first on the fox's tail, then on his back, then on his nose, and then . . . . An unfamiliar wordless book can provide an extra challenge as the child tries to order the story by determining the logical sequence of events.

Students in fourth grade and above can practice a more challenging retelling task by simplifying a familiar story, such as a fairy tale, and reading it to younger children. They can compare several versions of a fairy tale and note how the different authors have told the stories. Modifying vocabulary or eliminating episodes are effective ways of simplifying. In the tale of *The Three Little Pigs* (Galdone, 1970), for example, some authors omit the series of tricks the wolf plays on the pigs, and the story still retains its essential elements.

Student-Generated Stories

Students should be encouraged not only to enjoy good literature, but also to generate their own stories to practice and develop their own language structures. In the traditional language experience approach (LEA), students dictate a story based on an experience. The resultant text is used to promote such language skills as word recognition and fluency. As noted earlier, however, many LLD children have difficulty with recall and often struggle to remember sentences, even if they themselves generated the sentences. Trying to teach them the decoding of words by asking them to associate the word with its printed representation becomes a frustrating experience that serves neither communicative nor cognitive purposes. Requesting that students create a mini-episode or chapter books alleviates this difficulty with recall while retaining the benefits of the LEA.

- Using a Polaroid camera, the teacher can take photographs of the student's daily activities (a real-life version of the familiar sequence cards published by many companies), and the student can dictate one sentence describing the action. This is transcribed on one page and then used in a variety of ways.
- Special events can be displayed on the bulletin board as "Headline News," with the child's sentence written in large letters for everyone to see. These are especially effective if they can be gathered into a life milestones book, a record of such events as birthdays, lost teeth, and First Communion. This gives a sense of long-term as well as short-term sequence. These events can

be kept in monthly books, each of which becomes a "chapter" in a big book assembled at the end of the year.

- The teacher may read aloud a book that describes an experience common to all children, such as *Let's Be Enemies* (Udry, 1961) or *No Good in Art* (Cohen, 1980), and have the students write extra episodes of the story. This provides them with a structure without overloading their auditory memory.

- Wordless books make it possible to combine the child's own language with a dependable story structure that can provide cues to help the child in later readings. The clinician can put the pages of the book on an overhead, and students dictate a sentence describing what is happening in the story. These pages can be duplicated for each child, becoming the students' reader for the week or for the duration of time that the topic is to be studied in the classroom. The advantage of wordless books is that students can generate stories in either English or Spanish. These books are listed in Appendix 8-A.

Prediction Strategies

Comprehension of connected discourse is strongly related to a student's predictive ability. Skillful readers make predictions constantly as they read or are read to. Among the organizing schemes that help children develop these skills are (1) rhythm, rhyme, and repetition; (2) building up the board; and (3) directed reading/ thinking activity.

Rhythm, Rhyme, and Repetition. Having heard many language patterns, children develop a sense of rhythm that helps them anticipate text. Using this internalized awareness of the music of language, they can respond to pattern books that use familiar language structures. For example, the teacher can use the following passage from *The Magic Fish* (Littledale, 1986) to establish a pattern:

> Oh fish in the sea
> Come listen to me!
> My wife begs a wish
> From the magic fish.

After several episodes in which the man returns to call on the fish, the children can fill in the blanks left when the teacher reads:

> Oh fish in the _____
> Come listen to me!
> My wife begs a _____
> From _____

Pattern books are excellent resources for second-language learners and LLD students because of their predictability and the opportunity for language use that does not tax verbal formulation skills. (See Appendix 8-A for a list of additional titles in English and Spanish.)

Building up the Board. Bassano (1987) developed a technique called "building up the board" that helps second-language learners and LLD students develop prediction strategies. The teacher asks questions about a story to be read and records possible answers on a large piece of chart paper. Figure 8-6 is an example from *Frederick* (Lionni, 1967). As the students make their predictions, the teacher

1. Do you think the mice are preparing for:

    a new home   winter   hiding from
                                                  the owl

2. What do you think Frederick will collect while they are preparing?

    nuts   corn   the sun

3. Where do you think the mice will wait?

    in the stones   in the barn   among the
                                              corn stalks

4. What will keep the mice warm?

    leaves   the sun   snow

Figure 8-6 Example of Building up the Board, Using *Frederick* (Lionni, 1967).

circles the pictures and/or words that indicate their ideas. Then the teacher reads the story aloud in its entirety while the students note whether their predictions were confirmed or rejected. (This strategy also helps to develop selective attention.) After reading the story, the teacher reviews the students' predictions and records the outcome. The students should refer to the text when validating their predictions. For example, the teacher may ask, "When did we learn that the mice were worried about winter?" "How did the author show us the mice were impatient with Frederick?" "Why did the mice stop chatting in their winter home?" Students can show the pages on which their predictions were confirmed or rejected. Emphasis should be placed on the process of referring to the text and determining the accuracy of the prediction rather than on the correctness of the prediction.

Directed Reading/Thinking Activity. Students who have some independent reading skills benefit from a prediction strategy that requires more attention to the text and the context cues available. To aid students in reading comprehension, the speech-language clinician may point out the cohesion elements used by authors to hold their stories together and to make transitions from one idea to another. For example, in a directed reading/thinking activity (Nessel, 1989; Nessel, Jones, & Dixon, 1989), students are given a small piece of information about a book or story—perhaps something as limited as a title or cover illustration. The teacher asks what the students think the story will be about or what will happen. Most important, students are asked to explain why they are making a certain prediction and what evidence supports their thinking. Although divergent responses are encouraged, they must be supported by logical explanations. Next, a portion of the text is read aloud. When they hear information that relates to the predictions, students stop and use the text to determine whether their prediction was confirmed or rejected. Even when the predictions are rejected on the basis of text information, the students should be complimented for gaining skills in using the text appropriately. After the first predictions have been confirmed or rejected, the remaining predictions are revised to be consistent with the new information presented. The clinician can work closely with students to help them make the logical connections necessary in revising their predictions. This strategy complements the focus on narratives, because good stories have logical stopping points where new predictions can be made.

A modification of the directed reading/thinking activity focuses on the question-answer-relationships technique (Raphael, 1982, 1986). This approach helps students examine their own comprehension process and develop metacomprehension skills. After reading a passage, students look in the text for answers to questions. Like the directed reading/thinking activity, this technique relies on the students' use of the text itself to support their responses. Students identify their answers as Type 1, 2, or 3, depending on the way in which they arrived at the answers. Type 1 is a "right there," which means that the words to make the question and the answer are right there in the same sentence. Type 2 is a "think and search" answer, which is in the story, but is a bit more difficult to find. Type 3 is an "on my own" answer, which means that the student must infer the answer.

The following summary of the comprehension process can be shared with students to enable them to develop metacomprehension skills:

> Reading is comprehending. When we comprehend, we use *prior knowledge* to make accurate *predictions* that are *confirmed.* Comprehension means *confirmed prediction,* surprise means *prediction not confirmed,* and confusion means *no prediction to confirm.*

Literature Studies

The study of literature is a social event that engages students in sharing a reading experience as they collaborate to make a personal response. Beyond the personal response, students begin to study the elements that support the piece of literature (García, 1990). This reading comprehension strategy, perhaps more than any other, allows students to use their language "richly and fully." It taps the upper range of students' abilities by providing high-interest, meaningful subject matter related to personal experience. It "has the potential to awaken the joy of reading and literature, a joy often suppressed among students with a record of school failure" (Ruíz, 1988b). It can be done in collaboration with the classroom teacher, but it has also been effective in small group language therapy settings with students from second grade and up. The procedure is as follows:

1. Multiple copies of several titles are purchased.
2. Students select the book they would like to read based on "book talks" given by the teacher (later by the students themselves). These book talks consist of a synopsis of the book and a tantalizing piece of information that might persuade students to choose that book.
3. Students reading the same text agree on a time to discuss its content. At their meeting, the teacher begins the discussion by asking open-ended questions about personal opinions. Based on the ensuing discussion, the teacher suggests further questions for the students to consider in a second reading.
4. The students record their responses in a literature log that they share with the teacher or, if agreed upon, with other students.

5. After recording their personal responses, the students are ready to study the story structure elements of literature (e.g., characterization, personification).

The clinician can assist students in this literacy event by scaffolding their reading with some of the comprehension activities that have been described. Once the students understand the text well, the teacher can focus on the language demands of the literature discussion. The students need to (1) express personal opinions, (2) listen to others' opinions, (3) clarify their thoughts, (4) organize thoughts logically and clearly, (5) use vocabulary that is sufficiently specific, and (6) record their personal responses.

Working on Story Structure

As a follow-up to reading a text, many aspects of literature can be studied. One of the most helpful activities for second-language learners and LLD students is working on story structure. This activity helps students to organize their own understanding and expression of meaning, and it prepares them to make appropriate predictions for future texts. Even very young children can benefit from having story structure brought to a conscious level. Figure 8-7 illustrates two ways to represent story structure visually. This type of activity should be carried out only after the student has heard a large number of well developed stories and has begun to internalize story structure. For example, after a story is read, the teacher may fill in the chart with information from the text that highlights different features of the story such as the characters, the sequence, the plot, and the resolution.

Content Area Reading Skills

In helping those students who are having difficulty with academic discourse problems, the speech-language clinician should use materials from the classroom curriculum. As in all other activities, the clinician takes on the role of guide or facilitator. In the context of these activities, students may take on the role of teacher and generate questions about a passage. This type of interaction is based on the principle of reciprocal teaching in which spoken and written discourse are interwoven. Thus, oral discussions take place in the context of reading (Hoskins, 1990). Three text comprehension strategies are particularly helpful to both second-language learners and LLD students: (1) the survey text method, (2) metacognitive strategies, and (3) modification of expository text. The first two strategies are implemented by the student; the third, by the teacher or clinician.

In the survey text method, students can use the following strategies:

1. Analyze features of the chapter such as title, subtitles, illustrations, and graphic information.
2. Devise a question to be answered by reading each subsection.

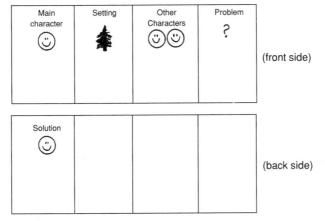

Main character	Setting	Other Characters	Problem	
☺	🌲	☺☺	?	(front side)

Solution				
☺				(back side)

Figure 8-7A Example of a Story Planning Chart

El Cuento (The Story)	Problema (Problem)	Respuesta (Answer)	Acción (Action)	Resolución (Resolution)
Los Tres Osos (The Three Bears)	La niña quebrando cosas (The girl breaking things)	Oso enojado (Angry bear)	Buscar a la niña (Look for the girl)	La niña se escapó (The girl ran away)
La Caperucita Roja (Little Red Riding Hood)	El lobo tomó el lugar de la abuelita (The wolf took the grandmother's place)	La Caperucita lloró (Little Red Riding Hood cried)	El cazador metió piedras (The hunter stuffed in stones)	La abuela se escapó (The grandmother escaped)
Los Tres Cochinitos (The Three Little Pigs)	El lobo quiere comerse a los cochinitos (The wolf wants to eat the little pigs)	Los cochinitos tenían miedo (The pigs were scared)	Se metieron en la casa de ladrillos (They went inside the brick house)	El lobo se quemó (The wolf got burned)

Figure 8-7B Beaumont's Adaptation for Fairy Tales. *Source:* From "First and Fifth Graders Coauthor Books" by D. J. Davis, 1989, *The Reading Teacher, 42,* p. 653, Copyright 1989 by the International Reading Association. Reprinted by permission.

3. Read the introductory and concluding paragraphs and the post-reading questions provided at the end of the chapter.
4. List ideas to be covered in the chapter. From this list, the teacher and students generate a statement about the main idea or theme of the chapter.
5. Read the chapter to evaluate predictions made.

In developing the cognitive and metacognitive strategies for text comprehension used in their cognitive academic language learning approach for second-language students, Chamot and O'Malley (1989, 1990) expanded on the concept of the survey method. Palincsar and Brown (1984), as well as Deshler and Schumaker (1986), have also applied this approach to teaching. For metacognitive strategies, they begin by examining the advanced organization of the text, which includes previewing the main ideas and concepts of the material by skimming the text. Intermediate steps include activities on organizational planning, selective attention, and self-monitoring. They end with a self-evaluation, which includes judging how well learning has taken place. Among the cognitive strategies used are reference to resource materials, such as dictionaries, encyclopedias, or textbooks; grouping; note taking; summaries; deduction/induction; imagery; and auditory representation. Diagramming a story is also helpful. For example, for *The Three Little Pigs*, the characters, then the different events and settings (houses), can be listed.

Students who have difficulty with expository text may benefit from the same material presented in story form. Working in collaboration with the teacher, the clinician can identify content area materials that are difficult for the student and modify them by creating a narrative structure that contains the essential information. An example is provided below.

Expository Text

Small fish face many dangers in the ocean environment. Larger fish who are their predators are constantly searching for food. The big fish are faster, stronger, and have larger teeth and jaws. If small fish spend all their time hiding under rocks or among seaweed, they will not be able to hunt for food themselves. Small fish must develop strategies to protect themselves while they hunt for food.

One defense mechanism is called camouflage. The fish may change color to look like their surroundings. Fish may hide in plants that have a similar texture. Another defense mechanism is to swim close together in large groups called schools. When many small fish swim together, they appear to be one large fish. In this way, they can discourage their predators from attacking.

Narrative Text (Based on *Swimmy* [Lionni, 1963])

A school of little red fish were swimming in the ocean one day. While they were playing they forgot to stay close together like their mother had shown them. They suddenly saw a huge fish with sharp, jagged teeth swimming toward them. He was swimming so fast that the little fish could not escape. The big fish ate them all—all but one who managed to escape.

Now that the little fish didn't have playmates to protect him, he went in search of a place to hide. He searched the ocean floor for some red plants so he could hide among them. He saw some red coral and tucked himself between the branches. Now he was well camouflaged. No one could tell a fish was hiding there. But he was getting hungry. How would he find food without being caught by another big, hungry fish? He waited and waited until a school of little red fish swam by. He darted out from the coral and joined the school. All the little red fish swimming close together looked like a big, strong fish. Now he could find food, protected by his new friends.

DEVELOPING METALINGUISTIC AWARENESS

Background Information

As mentioned earlier, part of academic performance and school success is an ability to reflect consciously on the nature of language, that is, metalinguistic awareness. Many LLD students have difficulty in this area (van Kleeck, 1984a, 1984b; van Kleeck & Schuele, 1987). As they interact with oral and written language, however, children need to be aware of the following language features:

- *Language is symbolic.* Words stand for something else.
- *Language is arbitrary.* The same thing can have different names in various languages. The same sound sequence can have different meanings (e.g., *bark* meaning a dog's sound or *bark* meaning the covering of a tree).
- *Language is segmented.* Words have boundaries both aurally and in print. Because the acoustic stream is not naturally segmented, it is sometimes difficult for children to get the idea of "words." Phonological awareness is part of understanding segmentation.
- *Language is combined by grammar.* Meaning relationships change as word order changes.
- *Language is related to logical thinking.* Grammar must precede logical-verbal reasoning, and language is necessary for planning, predicting, and reflecting.

Although most studies indicate that metalinguistic awareness does not develop until ages 4 to 5 years, this awareness has been observed in younger children (van Kleeck & Schuele, 1987). Two- and three-year-olds observe and reflect on language by making conscious word substitutions, playing with sounds by making rhymes and changing initial consonants, and by noticing different language systems (e.g., Spanish vs. English). Some researchers have concluded that bilingual children have better developed metalinguistic skills than do monolingual children (Díaz, 1983; Hakuta, 1986; McLaughlin, 1987). Their experience in negotiating two languages has heightened their awareness of language features, particularly their knowledge of the arbitrary nature of language.

Skills that are associated with reading appear at a more mature level of development. The ability to segment the spoken word into its sounds is a difficult, late-developing skill for most children, but students are frequently asked to apply a knowledge of language in reading tasks that require them to identify words with a given beginning sound, make up sentences with specific words, or compare phonological patterns. Often these "prereading" skills are presented before the larger concepts involved in reading have been addressed: print awareness, sense of story, and integration of new knowledge with previous experience. As van Kleeck and Schuele (1987) indicated, academic difficulties in children may result from assuming that children "have a rudimentary awareness of phonemic units and basing instruction on that assumption" (p. 28).

Observation of students also provides some insight into the level of their metalinguistic awareness. The following examples are indicative of poorly developed metalinguistic awareness:

- A student writing his last name, Cervantes, spells it Cervante5. To him, the visual similarity of the lower case *s* and the number *5* obscures the fact that one is a letter representing the final sound in his name, while the other is a number not at all related to sound/symbol relationships. If he had simply commented that the *s* and the *5* look alike, it would have indicated a better developed metalinguistic awareness.

- Another child writing his last name, Padilla, calls the teacher with great enthusiasm and, pointing to the *ll*, says, "Look, my name has an eleven in it!" Providing the student with both symbols and explaining the difference should help him understand the distinction between the sound and the number.

- The same child learning to write the word *amarillo* 'yellow', referring to *ll* asks the teacher, "Do I put another stick?" To him, the *ll* is a symbol with one or two "sticks" rather than a sound that appears at this point in the phonological sequence that makes up the word *amarillo*. To make him aware of the difference, the teacher can explain that the *l* looks like a stick, but is really a letter.

- A child is asked to copy the sentence *La casa es roja* 'The house is red'. The teacher provides lines for each word to guide the child ____ ____ ____ ____ The child copies *Lacasaesroja*, leaving the lines unused. To assist the student in recognizing word boundaries, the clinician or teacher may provide cards that the student can manipulate and then copy on to her paper.

These patterns frequently appear in the work of kindergarten and first-grade children who are just beginning to negotiate the complex world of print. If the patterns persist, however, further in-depth assessment of metalinguistic development may be warranted. In collaborating with teachers on reading instruction, the clinician must consider metalinguistic development and suggest alternative methods of instruction for those students whose skills in that area are not yet well developed.

Activities for Metalinguistic Awareness

Drawing students' attention to words and their features and uses is an effective way to increase the students' metalinguistic awareness. A particularly successful manner of incorporating word consciousness is to prepare a display center that has as its heading the following portion of a poem from *Squeeze a Sneeze* (Morrison, 1977):

> You're using words
> And words, as you know,
> Will help you out wherever you go.

On this bulletin board or table, a frequently changing display can highlight words in a variety of ways.

To increase the students' foreign language awareness, common objects may be displayed with color-coded word cards that identify each object in several languages. The foreign language series by Dunham (1987a, 1987b, 1987c, 1987d) provides illustrations of common objects creatively surrounded by the object name in four languages. In a similar technique, small flags from various Spanish-speaking countries may be displayed across the top of a chart. A familiar object is also displayed, and the common word used in the various countries for that object is listed. This is especially helpful for students from Mexico, who may be unfamiliar with the vocabulary used in literature books printed in other Central or South American countries. Finally, newspapers, magazines, posters, and other environmental print from different countries can be displayed, and the children can be asked to find which words they think mean the same thing.

Books that depict sign language and Braille, such as *Hand Talk: An ABC of Finger Spelling and Sign Language* (Remy, 1974), *The Whatchamacalit Book* (Hunt, 1976), *Sesame Street Sign Language ABC with Linda Bové* (Bové, 1985), and *Handtalk Zoo* (Ancona, 1989), can be used to emphasize the arbitrary and symbolic nature of language. Activities in which students have to make up words for objects can deepen their understanding of the functions of language. Words can come alive even more by illustrating their meaning or using sound/meaning relationships (onomatopoeia).

Arabella and Mr. Crack: An Old English Tale (Grachenback, 1982), like *The Whatchamacalit Book*, plays with names for objects. Arabella goes to work for a gentleman and explains to him that she has different names for everything. As they go through the house, the confusion that results as she uses her words and he uses his delightfully emphasizes the arbitrary nature of labels. *The Whatchamacalit Book* reminds the reader that everything has a name, some of them so difficult and obscure that it is easier to say the "thingamajig" or "whatchamacalit." This is an effective way to work with students who use such vague labels and who need to develop more specific vocabulary.

Discerning word boundaries in a second language can be a very difficult task. It may also be a difficult task for many LLD students, particularly in written work. Adapting patterned texts by substituting words is a simple way to identify and respond to word boundaries. In working with word cards and a pocket chart or a word slotting device, students receive additional visual and tactile reinforcement by actually seeing words moved around. For example, after buying, washing, and eating strawberries, the students can learn the following poem:

> Strawberries are ripe!
> Strawberries are ripe!
> I hear the children say.
> Strawberries are ripe!
> Strawberries are ripe!
> Let's all have some today. (Anonymous)

In a follow-up activity, students can provide substitute words for ripe, such as red, juicy, or sweet, to create another poem.

> Strawberries are juicy!
> Strawberries are juicy!
> I hear the children say.
> Strawberries are juicy!
> Strawberries are juicy!
> Let's all have some today.

Students who need additional practice with English phonology can apply their emerging sound to alliterative or repetitive sounds and poems in the context of a whole text during classroom oral language development. Books and games that emphasize alliteration are an enjoyable way for students to make both auditory and visual associations with letters. *My Name is Alice* (Bayer, 1985), *Faint Frogs Feeling Feverish* (Obligado, 1983), and *Zoophabets* (Tallon, 1971) make clever use of illustrations, rhythm, rhyme, and repetition in playing with sounds. *Zoophabets* can be easily adapted for use with speakers of other languages, because the author uses nonsense names for his imaginary animals. The large number of alphabet books available offer the clinician and classroom teacher many creative avenues to follow in teaching letter-sound relationships. Those books that emphasize connections between letter form and sound, such as *Alphabatics* (McDonald, 1986) and *Action Alphabet* (Neumeier, 1985), are excellent resources to teach sounds. A future effort should be made to adapt such books for Spanish-speaking children.

Songs and poems that play with sounds are of great interest to children and employ the powerful extralinguistic cues of rhythm and rhyme to emphasize connections between sounds and symbols. Some Spanish songs such as "Una Mosca" 'A Fly' (de La Paz, no date) or other folk songs in which vowel sounds are switched create delightful nonsense songs that are enjoyed by children over and over.

> *Una mosca parada en la pared, en la pared, en la pared*
> 'A fly standing on the wall, on the wall, on the wall'
> Substitution with *a*: *Ana masca parada an la parad, an la parad, an la parad . . .*
> Substitution with *e*: *Ene mesque perede en le pered, en le pered, en le pered . . .*

A similar song in English is "Apples and Bananas" (Cassidy & Cassidy, 1986), which switches vowel sounds.

> I like to eat, eat, eat apples and bananas
> I like to ate, ate, ate appl*a*s and bananas
> I like to ote, ote, ote *o*ppl*o*s and bonon*o*s (etc.)

Syllable awareness, so important to Spanish readers, can be developed and reinforced with the use of songs such as "La Pulga de San José" 'At the Flea Market of San Jose' (Orozco, 1988).

> *En la pulga de San José, yo compré una guitarra, tarra, tarra, tarra, la guitarra*
> 'At the flea Market of San Jose, I bought a guitar, tar, tar, tar, the guitar'
> *En la pulga de San José, yo compré un clarinete, nete, nete, nete, el clarinete*
> 'At the flea market of San Jose, I bought a clarinet, net, net, net, the clarinet'

The use of these activities appears to be extremely effective in helping young bilingual LLD students comprehend and use sound segmentation as well as establish sound-symbol relationships. As indicated earlier, however, the long-term effectiveness has yet to be thoroughly studied.

CONCLUSION

Clearly, there is a broad range of techniques available to enable second-language learners and LLD students to become more competent in linguistic and academically related tasks. In addition, there are several types of materials available. (See Appendix 8-C for a list of distributors.) Although today, the trend is to teach holistically, speech-language clinicians should remember that there may be "holes" that need to be filled with more traditional approaches, such as repeated practice on patterns or phonics.

REFERENCES

*Aardema, V. (1981). *Bringing the rain to Kapiti Plain: Anandi tale*. New York: Dial Press.

*Ada, A. (1986). *El oso más elegante*. Chicago: Children's Press.

Adams, M. (1990). *Beginning to read: Thinking and learning about print*. Urbana, IL: The Reading Research and Education Center.

*Amery, H. (1979). *My first thousand words in Spanish*. London: Osborne.

*Ancona, G. (1989). *Handtalk zoo*. New York: Four Winds Press.

Au, K. (1979). Using the experience-text-relationship method with minority children. *The Reading Teacher, 32,* 677–679.

Bashir, A., Kuban, K., Kleinman, S., & Scavuzzo, S. (1983). Issues in language disorders: Considerations of cause, maintenance, and change. In J. Miller, D. Yoder, & R. Schiefelbush (Eds.), *Contemporary issues in language intervention: Report No. 12* (pp. 92–106). Rockville, MD: American Speech-Language-Hearing Association.

Bassano, S. (1987). *Second language acquisition activities*. Presentation to multidepartmental training of trainers program. San Jose, CA: San Jose Unified School District.

*Bayer, J. (1985). *My name is Alice*. New York: Dial Press.

Blachman, B. (1984). Language analysis skills and early reading acquisition. In G. Wallach & K. Butler (Eds.), *Language learning disabilities in school-age children* (pp. 271–287). Baltimore: Williams & Wilkins.

Blank, M., & Marquis, A. (1987). *Teaching discourse*. Tucson, AZ: Communication Skills Builders.

Blank, M., & White, S. (1986). Questions: A powerful but misused form of classroom exchange. *Topics in Language Disorders, 6*(2), 1–12.

Bloom, L., & Lahey, M. (1978). *Language development and language disorders*. New York: Macmillan.

Bloome, D., & Knott, G. (1985). Teacher-student discourse. In D.N. Ripich & F.M. Spinelli (Eds.), *School discourse problems* (pp. 53–76). San Diego: College Hill Press.

*Blocksma, M. (1984). *The best dressed bear*. Chicago: Children's Press.

Botvin, G.J., & Sutton-Smith, B. (1977). The development of structural complexity in children's fantasy narratives. *Developmental Psychology, 13,* 377–388.

*Bové, L. (1985). *Sesame street sign language ABC with Linda Bové*. New York: Random House.

Brooks, N. (1986). Culture in the classroom. In J. Valdes (Ed.), *Culture bound* (pp. 123–129). New York: Cambridge University Press.

*Brown, M. (1939). *The fish with the deep-sea smile*. Hamden, CT: Shoe String Press.

*Brown, M.W. (1942). *The runaway bunny*. New York: Harper & Row.

*Brown, W. (1984). *Paper menagerie*. Belmont, CA: Pitman Learning Co.

Bush, C. (1980). *Language remediation and expansion: School and home program*. Tucson, AZ: Communication Skills Builders.

Butler, K. (1984). Language processing: Halfway up the down stair case. In G. Wallach & K. Butler (Eds.), *Language disabilities in school-age children* (pp. 60–81). Baltimore: Williams & Wilkins.

Note: * indicates books or activity materials mentioned in chapter.

California State Department of Education. (Ed.). (1987). *Practical ideas for teaching writing as a process.* Sacramento, CA: State Department of Education.

Cambourne, B. (1987). *Coping with chaos.* Portsmouth, NH: Heinemann.

*Carle, E. (1979). *The very hungry caterpillar. (La oruga hambrienta.)* New York: Philomel.

*Carle, E. (1984). *The very busy spider.* New York: Philomel.

*Carle, E. (1986). *The grouchy ladybug.* New York: T.Y. Crowley Co.

*Cassidy, J., & Cassidy, N. (1986). (song) *Apples and bananas.* "Kids' songs". Palo Alto, CA: Klutz Press.

Cathcart, R. (1986). Situational differences in the sampling of young L2 children's school language. In R.R. Day (Ed.), *Talking to learn: Conversation in second language acquisition.* Rowley, MA: Newbury House.

Cazden, C. (1987). Teachers as language advocates for children. In P. Rigg & D.S. Enright (Eds.), *Children and ESL: Integrating perspectives.* Washington, DC: TESOL.

*Celorio, M. (no date). *La casa que Juan construyó.* Arranged and recorded by Gabriela de la Paz on Lectura con Gabriela. Los Angeles: Pan American Publ. Co.

Chamot, A., & O'Malley, J. (1989). The cognitive academic language learning approach. In P. Riggs & V.A. Allen (Eds.), *When they don't all speak English.* Urbana, IL: National Council of Teachers of English.

Chamot, A., & O'Malley, J. (1990). Adaptation of the Cognitive Academic Language Learning Approach (CALLA) to special education. In A.L. Carrasquillo & R.E. Baecher (Eds.), *Teaching the bilingual special education student* (pp. 218–223). Norwood, NJ: Ablex.

Clay, M. (1979). *Reading: The patterning of complex behavior.* Portsmouth, NH: Frank Smith Educational Associates.

*Cohen, M. (1980). *No good in art.* New York: Greenwillow.

Come with me science series: Single Springs, CA: Science Series Publishing Co. (Many different dates for their materials.)

Crais, E., & Chapman, R. (1987). Story recall and inferencing skills in language/learning disabled and non-disabled children. *Journal of Speech and Hearing Disorders, 52,* 50–55.

*Crews, D. (1980). *Truck.* New York: Greenwillow.

*Crews, D. (1982). *Harbor.* New York: Greenwillow.

*Crews, D. (1983). *Parade.* New York: Greenwillow.

Cummins, J. (1989). *Empowering minority students.* San Francisco: California Association for Bilingual Education.

Curtis, J.K. (1986). *The development of graphic sense: Preliterate children's knowledge about written language.* Unpublished doctoral dissertation, University of Toronto, Ontario, Canada.

*DaPassano, A. (1989). *Bolitas, el pececito rojo.* Mexico, D.F.: Trillas.

De Avila, E., & Duncan, L. (1988). *Finding out/Descubrimiento.* Northvale, NJ: Santillana.

DeGroff, J. (1989). Developing writing processes with children's literature. *The New Advocate, 2*(2), 115–123.

Delgado-Gaitán, C. (1987). Traditions and transitions in the teaching process of Mexican children: An ethnographic view. In G. Spindler (Ed.), *Interpretive ethnography of education: At home and abroad* (pp. 333–359). Hillsdale, NJ: Earlbaum.

De Lucchi, L., & Malone, L. (Eds.). (1981). *Science activities for the visually impaired and science enrichment for learners with physical handicaps (SAVI/SELPH).* Berkeley, CA: Center for Multi-Sensory Learning, Lawrence Hall of Science.

Deshler, D.D., & Schumaker, J.B. (1986). Learning strategies: An alternative to low achieving adolescents. *Exceptional Children, 52*, 583–590.

Díaz, R. (1983). Thought in two languages: Impact of bilingualism. *Review of Research in Education, 10*, 23–54.

Diéguez, M. (1989). *Una pesadilla en mi armario*. Madrid: Ediciones Altea.

Doughty, C., & Pica, T. (1986). Information gap tasks: Do they facilitate second language acquisition? *TESOL Quarterly, 20*, 305–325.

Duff, P. (1986). Another look at interlanguage talk: Taking task to task. In R.R. Day (Ed.), *Talking to learn : Conversation in second language acquisition*. Rowley, MA: Newbury House.

*Dunham, M. (1987a). *Colors: How do you say it?* New York: Lathrop, Lee & Sheppard Books.

*Dunham, M. (1987b). *Numbers: How do you say it?* New York: Lathrop, Lee & Sheppard Books.

*Dunham, M. (1987c). *Picnic: How do you say it?* New York: Lathrop, Lee & Sheppard Books.

*Dunham, M. (1987d). *Shapes: How do you say it?* New York: Lathrop, Lee & Sheppard Books.

Eblen, R. (1982a). Some observations on the phonological assessment of Hispanic-American children. *Journal of the National Student Speech, Language, Hearing Association, 10*, 44–54.

Eblen, R. (1982b). A study of the acquisition of fricatives by three-year-old children learning Mexican Spanish. *Language and Speech, 25*, 201–220.

Ferreiro, E., & Teberosky, A. (1982). *Literacy before schooling*. Portsmouth, NH: Heinemann.

Fey, M. (1986). *Language intervention with young children*. Austin, TX: PRO-ED.

Fun folds. (1984). Tucson, AZ: Communication Skills Builders.

*Gag, W. (1929). *Millions of cats*. New York: Coward, McCann & Georhegan. Now available from Scholastic.

*Galdone, P. (1970). *Three little pigs*. New York: Clarion Books.

*Galdone, P. (1971). *The house that Jack built*. New York: McGraw Hill.

*Galdone, P. (1973a). *Little red hen*. New York: Seabury Press.

*Galdone, P. (1973b). *Three billy goats gruff*. New York: Clarion Books.

*Galdone, P. (1974). *Little red riding hood*. New York: McGraw Hill.

*Galdone, P. (1975). *The gingerbread boy*. New York: Houghton Mifflin.

*Galdone, P. (1985). *The three little bears*. New York: Clarion Books.

García, E. (1990, March). *Literature study*. Presentation to the Optimum Learning Environment (OLE) Special Education Demonstration Project, Watsonville, CA.

Goines, K. (1987). *Oral language development*. Presentation at San Jose County Office of Education, San Jose, Santa Clara County, CA.

*Grachenback, D. (1982). *Arabella & Mr. Crack: An old English tale*. New York: Macmillan.

Graesser, A.C. (1981). *Prose comprehension beyond the word*. New York: Springer Verlag.

Greenfield, P. (1984). A theory of the teacher in the learning activities of everyday life. In B. Rogott & J. Lave (Eds.), *Everyday cognition: Its development in social context*. Cambridge, MA: Harvard University Press.

Hakuta, K. (1986). *Mirror of language: The debate on bilingualism*. New York: Basic Books.

Halliday, M.A. (1973). *Explorations in the functions of language*. London: Edward Arnold.

Harp, B. (1988). Doesn't play steal time from reading? *Reading Teacher, 42*, 244–245.

Harste, J., Woodward, V., & Burke, C. (1984). *Language stories and literacy lessons*. Portsmouth, NH: Heinemann.

Heath, S.B. (1986a). Sociocultural contexts of language development. In Bilingual Education Office, California Department of Education (Eds.), *Beyond language: Social and cultural factors in schooling language minority students*. Los Angeles: Evaluation, Dissemination and Assessment Center, California State University.

Heath, S.B. (1986b). Taking a cross-cultural look at narrative. *Topics in Language Disorders, 7*(1), 84–94.

Hillerich, R. (1987). Developing vocabulary. *Teaching K–8*, March, pp. 25–27.

Hodson, B. (1983). A facilitative approach for remediation of a child's profoundly unintelligible phonological system. *Topics in Language Disorders, 3*(2), 24–34.

Hodson, B. (1986). *Assessment of phonological processes—Revised*. Danville, IL: Interstate.

Hoskins, B. (1990). Language and literacy: Participating in the conversation. *Topics in Language Disorders, 10*(2), 46–62.

Huck, C. (1987). *Children's literature in the elementary school*. New York: Holt, Rinehart & Winston.

Hudelson, S. (1984). Kan yu ret an rayt en ingles: Children become literate in English as a second language. *TESOL Quarterly, 18*, 221–235.

*Hunt, B.K. (1976). *The whatchamacalit book*. New York: GP Putnam's Sons.

Ingram, D. (1983). Foreword. *Topics in Language Disorders, 3*(2), vii–viii.

Israel, L. (1984). Word knowledge and word retrieval: Phonological and semantic strategies. In G. Wallach & K. Butler (Eds.), *Language learning disabilities in school-age children* (pp. 230–250). Baltimore: Williams & Wilkins.

Kagan, S. (1986). Cooperative learning and sociocultural factors in schooling. In California State University (Ed.), *Beyond language: Social and cultural factors in schooling language minority students* (pp. 231–298). Los Angeles: Evaluation, Dissemination and Assessment Center, California State University.

Kamhi, A.G. (1987). Metalinguistic abilities in language-impaired children. *Topics in Language Disorders, 7*(2), 1–12.

*Keats, E.J. (1962). *The snowy day*. New York: Viking Press.

Kessler, C., & Quinn, M.E. (1989). Language minority children's linguistic and cognitive creativity. *Journal of Multilingual and Multicultural Development, 8*, 173–186.

Krashen, S. (1980). The input hypothesis. In J.R. Alatis (Ed.), *Current issues in bilingual education* (pp. 168–180). Washington, DC: Georgetown University Press.

Krashen, S. (1981). *Second language acquisition and second language learning*. Oxford: Pergamon Press.

*Krause, R. (1945). *The carrot seed*. New York: Harper & Row.

Kucer, S., & Silva, C. (1989). The new California English language arts framework: A step in the right direction. *California Association of Supervisors of Curriculum Development Journal*, Winter, pp. 14–25.

Lahey, M. (1988). *Language disorders and language development*. New York: Macmillan.

Liles, B.Z. (1987). Episode organization and cohesive conjunction in narratives of children with and without language disorders. *Journal of Speech and Hearing Research, 30*, 185–196.

Lindfors, J. (1987). *Children's language and learning*. Englewood Cliffs, NJ: Prentice-Hall.

*Lionni, L. (1963). *Swimmy*. New York: Pantheon.

*Lionni, L. (1967). *Frederick*. New York: Pantheon

*Littledale, F. (1986). *Magic fish*. New York: Scholastic.

Lizcano, P. (1980). *Sapo y sepo inseparables.* Madrid: Alfaguara Publ.

*Lobel, A. (1979). *Frog and toad together.* New York: Harper & Row.

*Lobel, A. (1984). *The rose in my garden.* New York: Greenwillow.

Lomax, R.G., & McGee, L.M. (1987). Young children's concepts about print and reading: Toward a model of word reading acquisition. *Reading Research Quarterly, 12,* 237–256.

*Macdonald, S. (1986). *Alphabatics.* New York: Bradbury Press.

Maria, K. (1989). Developing disadvantaged children's background knowledge interactively. *Reading Teacher, 42,* 296–300.

*Martin, B. (1983). *Brown bear, brown bear, what do you see?* New York: Holt, Rinehart, & Winston.

*Mayer, M. (1968). *There's a nightmare in my closet.* New York: Dial Books.

McCracken, B., & McCracken M. (1986a). *Stories, songs, and poetry to teach reading and writing.* Winnipeg, Canada: Penguin Publs.

*McCracken, B., & McCracken, M. (1986b). *Tiger cub readers.* Winnipeg, Canada: Penguin Publ.

McLaughlin, B. (1987, December). *The development of bilingualism.* Paper presented at the Institute on Bilingual Education: Research to Policy to Practice, Harvard University, Cambridge, MA.

*Mitchell, L. (1948). *Another here and now story book.* New York: Dutton.

*Morrison, B. (1977). *Squeeze a sneeze.* Boston: Houghton Mifflin.

Nagy, W. (1988). *Teaching vocabulary to improve reading comprehension.* Urbana, IL: National Council of Teachers of English.

Nessel, D. (1989). Do your students think when they read? *Learning, 89,* 55–58.

Nessel, D., Jones, M., & Dixon, D. (1989). *Thinking through the language arts.* New York: Macmillan.

*Neumeier, M. (1985). *Action alphabet.* New York: Greenwillow.

*Numeroff, L. (1985). *If you give a mouse a cookie.* New York: Harper & Row.

Nippold, M.A. (1985). Comprehension of figurative language in youth. *Topics in Language Disorders, 5*(3), 1–20.

Northcutt, L., & Watson, D. (1986). *Sheltered English teaching handbook.* Carlsbad, CA: Northcutt, Watson, Gonzales.

Nystrand, M. (1987). The role of context in written communication. In R. Horowitz & J.S. Samuels (Eds.), *Comprehending oral and written language.* San Diego: College Hill Press.

*Obligado, L. (1983). *Faint frogs feeling feverish.* New York: Viking Press.

*Orozco, J.L. (1988). (song) *La pulga de San José (San Jose's Flea Market).* Recorded on La Lírica Infantil, Vol. 1. Berkeley, CA: Arcoiris Records.

Palacios, A. (n.d.). *La semilla de Zanahoria.* New York: Scholastic.

Palincsar, A., & Brown, A. (1984). Reciprocal teaching of comprehension fostering and monitoring activities. *Cognition and Instruction, 1,* 117–175.

Pearson, P.D. (1982). A primer for schema theory. *Volta Review, 84,* 25–34.

Pellegrini, A.D. (1985). Relations between symbolic play and literate behavior. In L. Galda & A. Pellegrini (Eds.), *Play, language and story: The development of children's literate behavior.* Norwood, NJ: Ablex.

Pellegrini, A.D. (1989). Classroom contextual effects on children's play. *Developmental Psychology, 25*(2), 289–296.

Pellegrini, A.D., & Galda, L. (1990). Children's play, language, and early literacy. *Topics in Language Disorders, 10*(3), 77–88.

Poplin, M.S. (1984). Towards a holistic view of persons with learning disabilities. *Learning Disability Quarterly, 7,* 290–294.

Poplin, M.S. (1988). Holistic/constructivist principles of the teaching learning process: Implications for the field of learning disabilities. *Journal of Learning Disabilities, 21,* 401–416.

Purcell-Gates, V. (1989). What oral/written language differences can tell us about beginning instruction. *Reading Teacher, 42,* 290–294.

Raphael, T.E. (1982). Question-answering strategies for children. *Reading Teacher, 36,* 186–191.

Raphael, T.E. (1986). Teaching question-answer-relationship revisited. *Reading Teacher, 39,* 516–522.

*Remy, C. (1974). *Handtalk: An ABC of finger spelling and sign language.* New York: Parents' Magazine Press.

Rhodes, L., & Dudley-Marling, C. (1988). *Readers and writers with a difference: A holistic approach to teaching learning disabled and remedial students.* Portsmouth, NH: Heinemann.

Rigg, P., & Allen, V. (1989). *When they don't all speak English.* Urbana, IL: National Council of Teachers of English.

*Rockwell, A. (1971). *The toolbox.* New York: Macmillan.

*Rockwell, A. (1986). *Things that go.* New York: Dutton.

*Rockwell, A. (1988). *Things to play with.* New York: Dutton.

*Rockwell, A., & Rockwell, H. (1984). *Nice and clean.* New York: Macmillan.

Rubin, H. (1986). *Linguistic awareness in relation to reading and spelling abilities.* Workshop presented at the Language Learning Disabilities Institute, Emerson College, Boston and San Diego State University, San Diego.

Ruíz, N. (1988a). *Language for learning in a bilingual special education classroom.* Unpublished doctoral dissertation, Stanford University.

Ruíz, N. (1988b). *The optimum learning environment guide: A resource for teachers of Spanish-speaking students in learning handicapped programs.* Unpublished manuscript, University of California at Davis.

Ruíz, N. (1989). An optimal learning environment for Rosemary. *Exceptional Children, 56*(2), 130–144.

Sawyer, D.J. (1985). Language problems observed in poor readers. In C.S. Simon (Ed.), *Communication skills and classroom success.* Austin, TX: PRO-ED.

*Scary, R. (1967). *Best word book ever.* New York: Golden Press.

*Scary, R. (1974). *Cars and trucks and things that go.* New York: Golden Press.

*Scary, R. (1986). *My first word book.* New York: Random House.

Schory, M.E. (1990). Whole language and speech-language pathologist. *Language, Speech, and Hearing Services in Schools, 21,* 206–211.

Schuele, C.M., & van Kleeck, A. (1987). Precursors to literacy: Assessment and intervention. *Topics in Language Disorders, 7*(2), 32–44.

Smith, F. (Ed.). (1983). Joining the literacy club. In *Essays into literacy.* Victoria, B.C.: Frank Smith Educational Associates.

Storm, D. (1958). The war between the lion and the cricket. In E. Ross (Ed.), *The buried treasure and other tales.* New York: Lippincott.

Strickland, D., & Morrow, L. (1989). *Emerging literacy: Young children learn to read and write.* Newark, DE: International Reading Association.

*Tallon, R. (1971). *Zoophabets.* New York: Bobbs-Merrill.

Teale, W., & Sulzby, E. (1989). Emergent literacy: New perspectives. In D. Strickland & L. Morrow (Eds.), *Emerging literacy: Young children learn to read.* Newark, DE: International Reading Association.

Treadway, G. (1987). *Language experience approach to reading.* Presentation to multidepartmental training of trainers program. San Jose, CA: San Jose Unified School District.

Trueba, H. (1987). Cultural differences or learning handicaps: Towards an understanding of adjustment process. In S. Goldman & H. Trueba (Eds.), *Schooling language minority youth: Proceedings of the University of California linguistic minority research project conference* (Vol. II). Los Angeles: University of California.

*Udry, J. (1961). *Let's be enemies.* New York: Harper & Row.

*Una Mosca. (song) (unknown composer). Recorded by Gabriela de la Paz on Lectura con Gabriela (no date given). Los Angeles: Pan American Publ. Co. Inc.

van Kleeck, A. (1984a). Assessment and intervention: Does "meta" matter? In G.P. Wallach & K. Butler (Eds.), *Language learning disabilities in school-age children* (pp. 179–198). Baltimore: Williams & Wilkins.

van Kleeck, A. (1984b). Metalinguistic skills: Cutting across spoken and written language and problem solving abilities. In G.P. Wallach & K. Butler (Eds.), *Language learning disabilities in school-age children* (pp. 128–153). Baltimore: Williams & Wilkins.

van Kleeck, A., & Schuele, C.M. (1987). Precursors to literacy: Normal development. *Topics in Language Disorders, 7*(2), 13–31.

Vásquez, O. (1990). *Connecting oral language strategies to literacy: An ethnographic study among four Mexican-American families.* Unpublished doctoral dissertation, Stanford University.

Vetter, D. (1982). Language disorders and schooling. *Topics in Language Disorders, 2*(3), 13–19.

Vygotsky, L.S. (1962). *Thought and language.* Cambridge, MA: MIT Press.

Wallach, G., & Miller, L. (1988). *Language intervention and academic success.* Boston: College Hill Press.

Weaver, C. (1991). Whole language and its potential for developing readers. *Topics in Language Disorders, 11*(3), 28–44.

*Weber, B. (1971). *The ten best list in nobody is perfekt.* Boston: Houghton Mifflin.

Wells, C.G. (1986). *The meaning makers.* Portsmouth, NH: Heinemann.

*Wescott, N. (1980). *I know an old lady who swallowed a fly.* Boston: Little Brown.

Westby, C. (1984). Development of narrative language abilities. In G. Wallach & K. Butler (Eds.), *Language learning disabilities in school-age children.* Baltimore: Williams & Wilkins.

Westby, C. (1985). Learning to talk—Talking to learn: Oral literate language differences. In C.S. Simon (Ed.), *Communication skills and classroom success: Therapy methodologies for language-learning disabled students.* San Diego: College Hill Press.

Westby, C. (1989a). Assessing and remediating text comprehension problems. In A. Kamhi & H. Catts (Eds.), *Reading disabilities: A developmental language perspective.* Boston: College Hill Press.

Westby, C. (December 1989b). Clinical evaluation of limited English proficient children. American Speech-Language-Hearing Association. Audioteleconference seminar, Washington, DC.

Willig, A., & Swedo, J. (1986, April). *Improving teaching strategies for exceptional Hispanic limited English proficiency students: An exploratory study of task engagement and teaching strategies.* Paper presented at the annual meeting of the American Education Research Association, Washington, DC.

Wong Fillmore, L. (1989a). Language learning in social context: The view from research in second language learning. In R. Dietrick & C.F. Graumann (Eds.), *Language processing in social context.* Holland: Elsevier Science Publishers.

Wong Fillmore, L. (1989b). Second language learning in children: A model of language learning in social context. In E. Bialystok (Ed.), *Language processing in bilingual children* (pp. 49–69). New York: Cambridge University Press.

Wong Fillmore, L. (1991). Language and cultural issues in early education. In S.L. Kagan (Ed.), *The care and education of America's young children: Obstacles and opportunities* (pp. 30–49). Chicago: Chicago University Press.

Wood, D., Bruner, J., & Ross, G. (1976). The role of tutoring in problem solving. *Journal of Child Psychology and Psychiatry, 17,* 89–100.

*Zolotow, C. (1962). *Mr. rabbit and the lovely present.* New York: Harper & Row.

Appendix 8-A

Books and Activity Materials

RECOMMENDED NARRATIVES

English

Berger, B. (1984). *Grandfather Twilight*. New York: Philomel.

Cooney, B. (1982). *Miss Rumphius*. New York: Viking Penguin.

De Paola, T. (1979). *Oliver Button Is a Sissy*. New York: Harcourt Brace Jovanovich.

De Paola, T. (1981). *Now One Foot, Now the Other*. New York: G.P. Putnam's Sons.

Ets, M. (1963). *Gilberto and the Wind*. New York: Viking Penguin.

Hall, D. (1979). *Ox Car Man*. New York: Viking Penguin.

Johnson, T. (1985). *The Quilt Story*. New York: G.P. Putnam's Sons.

Lionni, L. (1970). *Fish Is Fish*. New York: Pantheon.

Lionni, L. (1986). *It's Mine*. New York: Knopf.

Rylant, C. (1982). *When I Was Young in the Mountains*. New York: Dutton.

Steptoe, J. (1987). *Mufaro's Beautiful Daughters*. New York: Lathrop, Lee & Shepard Books.

Van Allsburg, D. (1985). *The Polar Express*. Boston: Houghton Mifflin.

Wilhelm, H. (1985). *I'll Always Love You*. New York: Crown Publishers.

Spanish

Ada, F. (No date). *Amigos*. Compton, CA: Santillana.

Alonso, F. (1978). *El Hombrecillo de Papel*. Valladolid: Editorial Minon.

Alonso, F. (No date). *El Árbol Que No Tenía Hojas* (abridged version by A. Ada). Compton, CA: Santillana.

Armijo, C. (1981). *Mone*. Valladolid: Editorial Minon.

Balzola, A. (1978). *El Erizo*. Valladolid: Editorial Minon.

Baumann, K., & McKee, D. (1981). *Joaquín el Barrendero*. Barcelona: Editorial Juventud.

Broger, A., & Kalow, G. (1978). *Buenos Días, Querida Ballena*. Barcelona: Editorial Juventud.

Claret, M. (1983). *La Ratita Blasa*. Barcelona: Editorial Juventud.

Gerson, S. (1986). *La Noche Más Oscura del Mundo*. Mexico, D.F.: Trillas.

Kurusa (1981). *La Calle Es Libre*. Caracas: Ekare.

Lang, A. (1982). *Aladino y la Lámpara Maravillosa*. Mexico, D.F.: Promexa.

Martínez i Vendrell, M., & Vendrell, C.S. (1983). *Yo Las Quería*. Barcelona: Ediciones Destino

Munter, A. (1975). *Las Gafas Maravillosas*. Valladolid: Editorial Minon.

Osorio, M. (1978). *La Mariposa Dorada*. Valladolid: Editorial Minon.

Ruillé, B. (No date). *Historia de Una Nube Que Era Amiga de Una Niña*. Valladolid: Editorial Minon.

Sendak, M. (1984). *Donde Viven Los Monstruos ('Where the Wild Things Are'*; translated by Agustin Gervas). Madrid: Ediciones Alfaguara.

Sonneborn, R.A. (1978). *Alguien Se Está Comiendo al Sol* (translated by M.L. Serrano). Buenos Aires: Sigmar.

Steadman, R. (1972). *El Puente*. Valladolid: Editorial Minon.

Turin, A. (1976). *Rosa Caramelo*. Barcelona: Editorial Lumen.

Turin, A. (1976). *Una Felíz Catástrofe*. Barcelona: Editorial Lumen.

SELECTED RESOURCES ON HISPANIC FOLKLORE

Ada, A.F. (Ed.). (1990). *Días y Días de Poesía*. Carmel, CA: Hampton Brown. A collection of poems written by parents and children.

Alatorre, M.F., Alatorre, A., & Merlin, S. (1973). *Lírica Infantil Mexicana*. Ilustrado por niños de los talleres infantiles de Artes Plásticas. Mexico: Artes de México #162. Thirty-five nursery rhymes and singing games collected from different parts of Mexico (identified as to source and location), with an introduction by Margit Frenk Alatorre on Mexican children's folklore. The book contains a chapter in which the original nursery rhymes from Spain are compared with the collected Mexican versions and an essay on children's folklore by Antonio Alatorre that includes the history of Spanish language nursery rhymes and examples with music for songs. There is also a section of children's art.

Antología de la Literatura Infantíl Española Vol 3: Folklore. (1973). Madrid: Doncel, Libro Joven de Bolsillo. Paperback volume extracted from the hardback two-volume version. The book contains Spanish language children's nursery rhymes, finger plays, counting rhymes, singing games, lullabies and 25 folk tales from Spain. The rhymes are grouped by type, but there is no index by title or subject—only a table of contents by type. This is an invaluable resource for Spanish nursery rhymes.

Jacob, E. (1987). *Cómo Leer un Códice*. Ilustrado por Bruno López. Mexico, D.F.: Trillas. Story on the significance of prehispanic codex. Grade level comprehension is approximately third grade, but a clinician or teacher could adapt it for younger students. Illustrations are beautiful.

Que Será, Qué No Será? Adivinanzas, Rimas y Retahilas Populares. (1978). Ilustrado by A. Padrón. Caracas: Colección rimas y adivinanzas. Banco del Libro: Ediciones Ekaré. A small book with black and white, cartoon-style illustrations of many different types of jokes, riddles, and rhymes in use by Venezuelan children. It is very useful for any Spanish-speaking juvenile population, as most of the items (or variations of them) are in use all over the Spanish-speaking world. It contains tongue-twisters, questions and answers, and finger plays also. No index or table of contents. An afterword notes that the contents were collected from juvenile library patrons in several of the Venezuelan libraries.

Salgado, T. (1989). *Lana Sube la Navaja: Las Mejores Adivinanzas Modernas de Mexico*. Mexico, D.F.: Editorial Selector. A series of riddles arranged in alphabetical order.

PREDICTABLE BOOKS

English

Brown, R. (1984). *A Dark, Dark Tale*. New York: Dial Books for Young Readers.
Carle, E. (1984). *The Very Busy Spider*. New York: Philomel.
Charlip, R. (1964). *Fortunately*. New York: Four Winds Press.
Cook, B. (1976). *The Little Fish That Got Away*. Reading, MA: Addison-Wesley.
Keats, E.J. (1971). *Over in the Meadow*. New York: Scholastic.
Galdone, P. (1984). *Henny Penny*. Boston: Houghton Mifflin.
Ginsburg, M. (1981). *Where Does the Sun Go at Night?* New York: Greenwillow.
Hutchins, P. (1982). *Goodnight, Owl!* New York: Macmillan Penguin.
Hutchins, P. (1987). *The Doorbell Rang*. New York: Scholastic.
Littledale, F. (1985). *The Magic Fish*. New York: Scholastic.
McGovern, A. (1984). *Too Much Noise*. New York: Scholastic.
Shaw, C.B. (1947). *It Looked Like Spilt Milk*. New York: Harper & Row.
Storm, D. (1958). The War between the Lion and the Cricket. In E. Ross (Ed.), *The Buried Treasure and Other Tales*. New York: Lippincott.
Zolotow, C. (1958). *Do You Know What I'll Do?* New York: Harper & Row.

Spanish

Ada, A.F. (1988). *Los Seis Deseos de la Jirafa*. Carmel, CA: Hampton-Brown.
Ada, A.F. (1988). *Sale el Oso*. Carmel, CA: Hampton-Brown.
Ada, A.F. (1988). *Una Semilla Nada Más*. Carmel, CA: Hampton-Brown.
Blocksma, M. (1984). *Apple Tree! Apple Tree!* (translated by Alma Flor Ada). Carmel, CA: Hampton-Brown.
Blocksma, M. (1984). *The Best Dressed Bear* (translated by Alma Flor Ada, 1986). Chicago: Children's Press.
Blocksma, M. (1986). *Little Koala Looking for a Home* (translated by Lada Kratky). Carmel, CA: Hampton-Brown.
Blocksma, M. (1988). *What's in the Tub?* (translated by Lada Kratky). Carmel, CA: Hampton-Brown.
Cumpiano, I. (1988). *Pan, Pan, Gran Gran*. Carmel, CA: Hampton-Brown.
Kratky, L. (1988). *Pina, Pinta, Gregoria*. Carmel, CA: Hampton-Brown.
Kratky, L. (1988). *Veo, Veo, Qué Veo?* Carmel, CA: Hampton-Brown.

Repetitive, Cumulative Predictable Books

Aardema, V. (1981). *Bringing the Rain to Kapiti Plain: Anandi Tale*. New York: Dial Books for Young Readers.
Bonne, R., & Mills, A. (1961). *I Know an Old Lady Who Swallowed a Fly*. Chicago: Rand-McNally.
Emberley, E. (1967). *Drummer Hoff*. Englewood Cliffs, NJ: Prentice-Hall.
Kent, J. (1971). *The Fat Cat*. New York: Parents' Magazine Press.
Lobel, A. (1984). *The Rose in My Garden*. New York: Greenwillow.
Sutton, E. (1973). *My Cat Likes to Hide in Boxes*. New York: Scholastic.
Wood, A. (1984). *The Napping House*. New York: Harcourt Brace Jovanovich.

BOOKS FOR BEGINNING THERAPY SESSIONS

These books are appropriate for beginning therapy sessions because they are short and effectively illustrate concepts; strong, simple narratives; or interesting language patterns.

English

Barton, B. (1973). *Buzz, Buzz, Buzz*. New York: Macmillan.
Brown, M.W. (1947). *Goodnight Moon*. New York: Harper & Row.
Crews, D. (1978). *Freight Train*. New York: Greenwillow.

Fox, M. (1987). *Hattie and the Fox*. New York: Bradbury Press.

Ginsburg, M. (1980). *Good Morning, Chick!* New York: Greenwillow.

Ginsburg, M. (1982). *Across the Stream*. New York: Greenwillow.

Hill, E. (1980). *Where's Spot?* New York: G.P. Putnam's Sons.

Hoban, T. (1984). *Is It Rough? Is It Smooth? Is It Shiny?* New York: Greenwillow.

Hoban, T. (1987). *Dots, Spots, Speckles, and Stripes*. New York: Greenwillow.

Jonas, A. (1985). *The Trek*. New York: Greenwillow.

Krauss, R. (1945). *The Carrot Seed* (translated by Argentina Palacios). New York: Greenwillow.

Tafuri, N. (1984). *Have You Seen My Duckling?* New York: Greenwillow.

Spanish

Krauss, R. (1977). *Leo el Capullo Tardío* (translated by R. Guibert). New York: Windmill Books.

Rothman, J. (English words) & Palacios, A. (Spanish words). (1979). *This Can Lick a Lollipop: Body Riddles for Kids. Esto Goza Chupando un Caramelo: Las Partes del Cuerpo en Adivinanzas Infantiles*. Garden City, NJ: Doubleday.

Stinson, K. (1985). *El Rojo Es el Mejor* (translated by Kiki & Clarisa de la Rosa). Caracas: Ediciones Ekaré-Banco del Libro.

Tison, A., & Taylor, T. (1973). *Barbapapa*. Barcelona: Editorial Juventud.

Wylie, J., & Wylie, D. (1984). *El Cuento Curioso de Colores* (translated by Lada Kratky). Chicago: Children's Press.

Wylie, J., & Wylie, D. (1984). *Un Cuento de un Pez Grande* (translated by Lada Kratky). Chicago: Children's Press.

WORDLESS BOOKS

English

Anno, M. (1983). *Anno's USA*. New York: Philomel.

Anno, M. (1986). *All in a Day*. New York: Philomel.

Briggs, R. (1978). *The Snowman*. New York: Random House.

Carle, E. (1971). *Do You Want to Be My Friend?* New York: Harper & Row.

De Paola, T. (1978). *Pancakes for Breakfast*. San Diego: Harcourt Brace Jovanovich.

Goodall, J. (1968). *The Adventures of Paddy Pork*. San Diego: Harcourt Brace Jovanovich.

Goodall, J. (1986). *The Story of a Castle*. New York: McElderry/Macmillan.

Goodall, J. (1986). *The Story of a Farm*. New York: McElderry/Macmillan.

Hutchins, P. (1968). *Rosie's Walk*. New York: Macmillan.

Mayer, M. (1974). *Frog Goes to Dinner*. New York: Dial Books for Young Readers.
McCully, E.A. (1985). *First Snow*. New York: Harper & Row.
McCully, E.A. (1988). *The Christmas Gift*. New York: Harper Junior Books.
Omerod, J. (1982). *Moonlight*. New York: Lothrop.
Speir, P. (1977). *Noah's Ark*. New York: Doubleday.
Speir, P. (1982). *Rain*. New York: Doubleday.
Turkle, B. (1976). *Deep in the Forest*. New York: Dutton.
Ward, L. (1973). *The Silver Pony*. Boston: Houghton Mifflin.

Spanish

Baum, W. (1977). *La Expedición*. Caracas: Ediciones Ekaré-Banco del Libro.
Felix, M. (1981). *Historia de la Ratita Encerrada en un Libro*. Caracas: Ediciones Ekaré-Banco del Libro.
Franco, M., & Franco, E. (1981). *Rabo de Gato*. Caracas: Ediciones Ekaré-Banco del Libro.
Mitgutsch, A. (1973). *Vamos al Agua*. Barcelona: Editorial Juventud.
Mitgutsch, A. (1979). *Paseando por Mi Ciudad*. Barcelona: Editorial Juventud.
Villarrubias, P. (1977). *Collección Tina Ton*. Barcelona: Editorial Juventud.

Appendix 8-B

Remedial Materials Available in Spanish

Name	Description	Publisher
Hecho a la Medida (Made to Order) McFarlane, C. Presnell, C. Walters, S.	Activities for Spanish language intervention. Topics center on the body, school, animals, food, people and the class-room.	Los Amigos Research Associates 705 Galewood, Suite D San Diego, CA 92120
Initial Sounds in Spanish	Series of 352 cards to reinforce initial sounds in Spanish. Backs of the cards have the Spanish and English words.	Ideal School Supply 11000 S. Lavergne Oak Lawn, IL 60453
Multiple Skills Series	Level 1 to Level 3 to develop reading skills in Spanish.	Barnell Loft, Inc. 958 Church St. Baldwin, NY 11510
Sequencing stories In Spanish and English Meza Steckbeck, P.	Series pictures to develop narrative skills in both languages.	Communication Skills Builders 3830 E. Bellevue Tucson, AZ 85733
Teaching Spanish Speech Sounds: Drills for Articulation Therapy Mattes, L.J. Santiago, G.	Practice drills for phonemes in Spanish. Strategies for providing individualized programs are offered.	Academic Communica-tion Associates P.O. Box 586249 Oceanside, CA 92058
Una Programa de Articulación: El sonido/s/	Criterion-based program to remediate /s/ from the phoneme to sentence level.	Los Amigos Research Associates 705 Galewood, Suite D San Diego, CA 92120

340

Appendix 8-C

Selected Companies That Supply Books and Materials in Spanish

Basics Plus
The Spanish Big Book Company
97 Cresta Verde
Rolling Hill Estates, CA 90274

Bilingual Educational Services, Inc.
2514 South Grand Ave.
Los Angeles, CA 90007

Bilingual Publications Co.
1966 Broadway
New York, NY 10023

Children's Press
1224 West Van Buren St.
Chicago, IL 60607

Claudia's Caravan
P.O. Box 1582
Alameda, CA 94501

Edumate Educational Materials
P.O. Box 2467
Del Mar, CA 92014

El Correo de Cuentos
P.O. Box 6652
Pico Rivera, CA 90681-6852

Hispanic American Publications, Inc.
  (East Coast)
257 Union St.
Northvale, NJ 07647

Hispanic American Publications, Inc.
  (West Coast)
942 South Gerhart Ave.
Los Angeles, CA 90022

Lectorum Publications, Inc.
137 West 14th St.
New York, NY 10011

Mariuccia Iaconi Book Imports—
  Children's Spanish Language
  Literature
1110 Mariposa
San Francisco, CA 94107

Pan American Book Co.
4362 Melrose Ave.
Los Angeles, CA 90029

Perma-Bound
Vandalia Road
Jacksonville, IL 62650

Santillana Publishing Co.
942 South Gerhart Ave.
Los Angeles, CA 90022

Scholastic/Macmillan
866 Third Ave.
New York, NY 10003

Silver Burdett & Ginn
250 James St.
Morristown, NJ 07960

The Economy Company
1200 Northwest 63rd St.
Oklahoma City, OK 73125

Chapter 9

Service Delivery Issues

Carol Beaumont

To ensure the successful implementation of any program to enhance oral language and literacy skills for Hispanic limited-English–proficient (LEP) students who are also experiencing language development problems and academically related difficulties, it is important to consider the students' background and experience. Several related issues affect the implementation of the intervention strategies, including (1) influence of the second language, (2) selection of the language of instruction, (3) delivery models, and (4) individualized education programs (IEPs) for those students.

INFLUENCE OF A SECOND LANGUAGE

Application of Cummins' Framework

The framework of cognitive development proposed by Cummins (1981) is a helpful guide for planning intervention with language/learning-disabled (LLD) students who are acquiring a second language. Cummins indicates that it is possible to manipulate contextual features to increase these students' abilities to perform cognitively and linguistically demanding activities. Providing highly contextualized environments allows students with only emerging language skills to engage in higher level thinking skills, such as comparing and contrasting, classifying, sequencing, interpreting, inferring, and generalizing.

Use of Daily Classroom Activities

Teachers and clinicians can use daily classroom routines successfully to foster higher level thinking skills. By highlighting certain features of familiar activities, a teacher or clinician can take advantage of the natural contextualization and authenticity that occurs during these times. Snack time, for example, offers an authentic opportunity for comparing and contrasting size, shape, color, and quantity.

- Offering cookies that are small, large, round, rectangular, full of chocolate chips, or with only a few chips gives students a chance to consider these features and apply knowledge of them to a real situation.
- Glasses can contain different colored juice poured to different levels for comparison of volume as well as experience in observing conservation of quantity.
- Student choices can be graphed to give the class a visual representation of more and less.

Providing a play area with props for familiar activities makes it possible for second-language learners to use nonlinguistic understanding to make sense of the language that they hear. Offering them props for universal activities, such as cooking, caring for babies, or going to the doctor, gives them a common center around which to communicate. Adding cross-cultural props, such as a *comal* (flat surface used to cook tortillas) for cooking or sashes used to strap babies to their mothers' backs, makes the exchange richer for all students. Those students who are at more advanced language levels can describe the similarities and differences between objects and, using that information, persuade a peer that one particular prop is better than another. This can take place in the context of constructing a space machine or setting up the doctor's office in the sociodramatic play area.

Sustained Silent Reading and Story Time

The daily sustained silent reading period can become an opportunity for classifying, comparing, and contrasting. For example, young LLD students may classify books according to type (e.g., pop-up books vs. flat books, water color illustrations vs. pencil drawing, big books vs. small books) or according to genre (e.g., fairy tales, fiction, nonfiction, poetry). During shared reading, students may explain why they chose a particular book, or the teacher may provide some modeling by saying, "I notice Eduardo chooses pop-up books for his reading time instead of flat books." Having a corner set aside for an "Author of the Week" display encourages students to identify authors' and illustrators' different styles, themes, and language by comparing and contrasting books over time. Keeping a scrapbook with information about these authors and examples of their work enables students to review their observations frequently. A useful resource for information about authors is *Something about the Author*, an encyclopedia of biographies of children's authors that includes pictures and references on each author's work (Commire, 1971–ongoing). These activities address similar cognitive processes but vary in the level of contextualization provided, in the level of linguistic input given, and in the expectations for verbal output in either a first or second language.

Second-Language Acquisition Strategies

Children who are learning a second language appear to use distinct strategies, some of which were discussed in Chapters 5 and 6. Although the research on the acquisition of language has been conducted primarily with normally developing children, some studies have shown that cognitively and linguistically handicapped children acquire a second language with levels of proficiency comparable to those in their first language (Greenlee, 1981). In addition, despite limited research on the strategies that these students use to acquire a second language, years of daily observations in the classroom suggest that Hispanic LLD students use strategies very similar to those described by Wong Fillmore (1976, 1983). This information can serve as a guideline for continued observation of LLD second-language learners. It can also be used in developing intervention programs that are useful for both monolingual and bilingual LLD students.

Lindfors (1987) identified strategies that children use in acquiring a first language and compared them with the strategies that Wong Fillmore (1976, 1983) observed in second-language learners. Lindfors (1987) concluded that "the second-language learner, like the first-language learner, is a child creatively constructing language in a social world" (p. 470). Three of the language acquisition strategies that Lindfors identified are (1) use of nonlinguistic understanding (p. 448); (2) use of whatever is salient and interesting to the student (p. 450); and (3) use of others' responses to production and observation of others' expression (p. 455).

Use of Nonlinguistic Understanding

Children make sense of particular situations by assuming that what people say is relevant to the situation at hand. They may lack complete linguistic knowledge about the adult's talk, but they have nonlinguistic knowledge that "enables them . . . to make connections between situational meanings and language forms" (Lindfors, 1987, p. 178). Wong Fillmore (1976) identified a similar cognitive strategy used by second-language learners; that is, the child assumes that what people are saying is directly relevant to the situation or to what they or the listeners are experiencing. To encourage the use of this strategy, the clinician needs to ensure that there is a close match between linguistic and nonlinguistic information. Several suggestions for intervention originate in this principle: providing opportunities for play experiences (e.g., the sociodramatic play discussed earlier), reading books with universal themes, and establishing a daily routine.

The use of wordless books with strong story lines that depict universal themes and experiences supports students' understanding of linguistic structures, because they can be "read" with simple vocabulary and sentence structure to make the connection between meaning and linguistic form. These may be the first books that students "read" to themselves and others as they begin to code the understanding of concepts and ideas in English. (See Appendix 8-A for a list of wordless books.)

Daily routines can be highlighted in the type of narrative that Heath (1986) described as an "eventcast"—in this case, a description of the sequence of daily events. Recurring routines become paired with recurring linguistic structures. Each morning, the schedule for the day is displayed on a large piece of chart paper on the chalkboard or easel near which the day's opening activities take place. An illustration of the activities accompanied by a printed word remains available for the children to see all day.

The day is previewed in the morning. After each activity has been completed, a student puts an X through the numeral that represents the activity. At the end of the day, the activities are reviewed, and a variety of responses can be made. For example, the children may write their names next to their favorite activity. The name of a particular activity may be written on a large piece of paper, and the students write yes or no under it to indicate whether they enjoyed it. Students may be given an individual copy of the schedule, on which they respond to each activity with yes/no or happy/sad faces; then they take the schedule home to describe their activities to their parents. (See Cheng [1989] for another type of eventcast—the multicultural calendar.)

Use of Material That Is Salient and Interesting to the Student

Children employ selective attention to focus on certain features of a situation. According to studies of early language acquisition (e.g., Clark, 1974; Nelson, 1973), students focus primarily on objects that they can act on and those that move and/or change form. Individual children may focus either on nonlinguistic attributes, such as color, shape, or texture, or on linguistic features, such as words, sentences, or certain sound sequences. As explained by Lindfors (1987), "Children notice the objects that embody these salient properties, and they notice how these objects are named in the language community" (p. 179). Wong Fillmore (1976) also identified this strategy in her observations of successful second-language learners. Children tended to engage in the preferred activities repeatedly, and these formed the foundation of their first English uses.

In order to support the use of this strategy for LLD students who are first- or second-language learners, the clinician should structure the environment so that they can build their selective attention skills, which are very often poorly developed in these students (Carrow-Woolfolk & Lynch, 1982; Lahey, 1988; Wiig & Semel, 1980). They may be unable to focus, may have diffuse or rapidly shifting attention, or may focus so intently on one aspect of a situation that they miss the large picture. The use of space, color, sound, and print in the classroom environment can support the development of selective attention by providing boundaries for activities; for example, areas may be designated for specific activities with visual aids, and only those students whose names are selected for a given activity may play, read a book, or work on a particular task in those designated areas. The classroom or therapy room should provide opportunities for both verbal and nonverbal activities; for both those that require movement and those that require stillness; and for auditory, visual, and tactile activities. In addition, the environment should contain objects and offer experiences that have cultural salience for Hispanic students.

In attempting to organize their curriculum around activities that prove salient and interesting to most children, Higginson and Falbel (1985) sought the types of activities and topics that engage children not only emotionally and intellectually, but also linguistically in lively and authentic communicative exchanges. They found that children enjoy

- *testing their physical capabilities.* Children are interested in their bodies, especially their strengths and limitations. They enjoy devising tests to measure how fast they can run and how much weight they can lift, for example.

- *interacting with different animals.* Children enjoy watching animals, petting them, playing with them, and caring for them.

- *trying a variety of games.* Children learn much from games that are not specifically designed around educational content, such as team sports, card games, puzzles, and magic.

- *tasting different foods.* Children like to eat. The chemistry of cooking is a fascinating subject. What makes bread rise? How does a tiny hard kernel of popcorn turn into a big, fluffy grain?

- *looking at colors.* Children are attracted to colorful items. They enjoy spectacular displays of light and gazing at colorful objects.

- *experiencing motion.* Children are interested in active, dynamic, visual things that move. They like to construct objects and "give life" to an inanimate object.

- *engaging in communication.* Most children like to talk.

- *listening to music.* Children love making noises of all kinds. They enjoy singing and playing musical instruments.

- *completing crafts projects.* Children enjoy working on crafts and are especially attracted to people who are skillful in this area.

- *participating in drama activities.* Children enjoy putting on a play, acting foolish, or even, at times, acting serious. They learn much from assuming the role of a character and putting on a production, especially from the teamwork involved.

- *manipulating money.* Children enjoy taking on adult roles and dealing in the earning, exchanging, and spending of money.

These activities may motivate parents and community members to contribute to the class by creating some of these activities themselves, by demonstrating their jobs, or by explaining cultural celebrations.

Use of Others' Responses to Production and Observation of Others' Expression

Another strategy in language acquisition involves production and comprehension strategies (Nelson, 1973). Although there seems to be considerable cultural variance in the way that different societies encourage or accept these strategies and the extent to which children prefer them, both are effective for language acquisition. Production strategies have the advantage of eliciting feedback from others so that children are surrounded by more expressive language. On the other hand, children who attend to others and to the interactions in their environment are also active cognitively. They may talk less, but they are developing an equally strong language ability.

Wong Fillmore (1976) found evidence that production and comprehension strategies helped in identifying successful second-language learners, although neither pattern consistently emerged as critical for success. Both "talkers" and "listeners" acquired a second language with comparable degrees of proficiency in roughly equivalent time periods. Those children who used a production strategy relied on substrategies, such as "get some expressions you understand, and start talking" (Wong Fillmore, 1976, p. 639); "look for recurring parts in the formats you know" (p. 644); "join a group and act as if you understand what's going on" (p. 667). Intervention activities that may enable students to employ these production strategies include (1) teaching survival phrases that double as politeness conventions and (2) teaching pragmatic skills, such as taking turns in conversation, getting and holding attention, and asking questions. In addition to sociodramatic play, the use of predictable texts is helpful.

Predictable texts that construct dialogue patterns or simple stories by means of question-answer exchanges are useful tools to encourage second-language learners to begin asking questions. McCracken and McCracken (1986) publish *Tiger Cub Readers*, which use repetitive question-answer exchanges in conjunction with pictures. For example, the text that accompanies a picture of a little boy hanging from a tail asks, "Do you swing by your tail?" "No, no, no, a monkey swings by his tail." The predictable text allows students to practice these exchanges with a friend or take them home to share with family members who may also be learning English. (A list of predictable books can be found in Appendix 8-A.)

Students who seem to prefer a comprehension strategy may benefit from listening to predictable books on tape, records and cassettes of favorite songs, or filmstrips accompanied by voice.

Another important variable in the successful development of the second language is effective use of English as a second language (ESL) instruction techniques. The following suggestions may allow second-language learners to benefit from English instruction:

1. Create a need to communicate some message (e.g., set up a "real life" situation or as close as possible) that is interesting to the students.
2. Focus on the message that is communicated rather than on the form. In order to modify or simplify their speech, teachers or clinicians should

   - speak more slowly
   - use clear articulation (e.g., Do you want to? rather than D'ya wanna?)
   - increase volume on key words, exaggerate intonation somewhat, and use body language to help students understand better
   - use students' names rather than pronouns
   - clarify the meaning of possibly unfamiliar words
   - use visuals to increase comprehension of vocabulary (e.g., pictures, objects and/or gestures)
   - repeat and elaborate on key topics (e.g., Did you have a good weekend . . . you know, Friday, Saturday?)
   - begin by speaking about "here and now" topics, such as the students' lives and interests, before introducing more abstract subjects

It is not necessary to follow a grammatical protocol. Comprehensible vocabulary, not grammar, enhances understanding. Error correction should be limited to modeling the correct form for the student. Finally, it is important not to force students to speak before they are ready.

SELECTION OF THE LANGUAGE OF INSTRUCTION

Determining the language to be used for intervention is one of the most important and most difficult decisions that the speech-language clinician must make. Many variables must be taken into account to arrive at a decision that best suits the needs of the student and the availability of school resources. For example, intervention in the first language (in this case, Spanish) may be indicated in the following circumstances:

1. The first language continues to be the child's dominant language for several aspects of communication. In addition, the student is familiar with more concepts in the first language.
2. The student's background knowledge and prior experiences have been developed and coded linguistically in the first language.
3. The first language reflects the cultural environment in which the student was raised.
4. The student may potentially lose the ability to communicate with family members who speak only in that language if the first language is not enhanced (Wong Fillmore, 1991).

Other factors must also be considered. For example, the student's language preference and proficiency levels in each language should be thoroughly assessed, both by means of general language proficiency tests and by more in-depth testing. According to Terrell and Krashen (1983), four levels can be identified.

1. pre-production (the silent period)
2. early production
3. speech emergence (telegraphic speech)
4. intermediate fluency (see Chapter 7)

Often, Spanish-speaking LLD students have had inconsistent school experiences because of frequent moves, erratic attendance, or changes in the language of instruction from one year to another. The clinician should determine the languages in which the student has received instruction and the length of time that the student received instruction in each language. Students with "checkered" school histories need special attention to ensure that their programs are integrated appropriately.

The language of instruction to be used in the student's classroom should also be carefully analyzed. An English-only classroom is not necessarily detrimental to an LEP student. It could provide rich nonlinguistic cues and consistent comprehensible input that is potentially of benefit to language acquisition. Conversely, a bilingual classroom does not guarantee that the student will be receiving the comprehensible input needed. Thus, the type of classroom and the type of "language" discourse in the classroom must be determined.

The clinician should determine whether the student will have formal and informal opportunities for peer interaction in both languages by observing the student in a number of situations and consulting the classroom teacher. As previously discussed, learning strategies of second-language students differ (Wong Fillmore, 1976, 1983). Some children look to peers for help. They may be concerned primarily with belonging to a social group and may be highly motivated to acquire the second language. Children who adopt observer strategies may not participate actively in verbal exchanges for some time; it is important to observe the type of input that they are receiving as they go through this learning process, however.

The attitude of school personnel toward the student's primary language is very important. If they ignore or merely tolerate the first language, it will be difficult for the student to sustain the motivation to use that language. If they are bilingual or demonstrate respect and encouragement for the primary language, they will support bilingual students in their efforts to learn in their native language. Similarly, the attitudes of parents and other family members, as well as their proficiency in each language, are important.

Minimal competence in the language can enable a speech-language clinician to support the child's first language and carry on basic conversations. To instruct the student adequately in Spanish or any other foreign language, however, the clinician should be at least a strong intermediate speaker of the language and have near-fluent pronunciation. A level 3 on the scale of 5 levels possible on the Foreign Service Institute examination (Lowe, 1983) has been designated by the Institute as the minimum level at which an individual has the skills necessary to carry out a job competently in a second language. At this level, a person can converse in formal and informal situations, resolve problems, discuss unfamiliar topics, provide explanations, and offer supported opinions; the person can converse about practical, social, professional, and abstract topics as well. The pronunciation may be "foreign," but it should not interfere with intelligibility.

Although no research on the minimal second-language competence necessary for speech-language clinicians serving clients who speak languages other than English has been conducted to date, the level required for Foreign Service personnel should also be considered minimal competence for bilingual clinicians. Merino and Langdon (1986) used these criteria in their development of the Bilingual Cross-cultural Certificate of Assessment Competence Examination (BCACE) to certify Spanish-speaking bilingual speech-language clinicians and psychologists. Informal feedback from clinicians and assessors has indicated that this level is a fair measure of the minimal competence necessary to serve a Spanish-speaking student or client adequately in Spanish.

The decision about the language of instruction is inevitably tied to decisions about service delivery models. The clinician's proficiency in the student's primary language may determine whether the clinician will serve the student directly in that language or will function within the consultation model (see Appendix 9-A).

DELIVERY MODELS

The principal delivery models that Miller (1989) described to serve students with various speech and language problems within the school setting are applicable to LEP students.

1. The language specialist teaches in a self-contained classroom.
2. The specialist teaches with the regular classroom teacher, special education teacher, or resource teacher.
3. The specialist provides one-on-one classroom-based intervention with selected students.
4. The specialist consults with the classroom teachers or special education providers.
5. The language specialist provides staff development, curriculum development, or program development to the school or district.

School-Based Programs

When a bilingual speech-language clinician is available, instruction in the primary language may take place during the specific intervention time—even if there is no bilingual language instruction in the regular classroom—to facilitate the development of concepts and to communicate with the student's family. Non–Spanish-speaking clinicians can follow up some of the strategies by providing either direct services to the students in English or consultation services to the teachers.

Only those students who have an identified language disorder in Spanish should be included in a speech-language clinician's caseload. Instruction may be provided in either a self-contained classroom or on a pull-out basis. Under the specialist's supervision, a bilingual aide may supplement instruction to increase the student's skills in Spanish in specific areas. If the student's language difficulty is primarily the result of a second-language acquisition process rather than a disorder, however, the student should receive services from other resource personnel, such as an ESL specialist, language development specialist, or the classroom teacher.

In providing consultation services to the regular or special education teacher, the clinician often observes the student and offers suggestions to the teacher about the type of scaffolding necessary to enhance the student's understanding and expression of language (see Appendix 9-A). The clinician can also provide suggestions on the appropriate materials to use to enhance certain areas in the student's native language. Because the number of remedial materials available in Spanish is very scarce, the preferred materials are literature-based. Books can be used to develop many language-based skills, depending on the student's needs.

Family Support

Working with parents and significant others should be an important goal for both bilingual and non–Spanish-speaking clinicians who work with LEP/LLD students. Parents need to know that they, too, are teachers of their children. Showing Hispanic parents the videotape in Spanish produced by Biddick (1987) is an effective way to convey the importance of parent participation in the educational and remedial process.

Parents need to know that using Spanish at home is not detrimental to their children's educational success. Rather than focus on the language itself, they need to assist their children in expanding their variety of language uses, depending on the students' needs to succeed in school. To develop accounts and sense of stories, parents can watch TV with their children and discuss what they see; they can comment on the positive or negative aspects of commercials for a given product or program. Another approach is to discuss activities that they do together, such as shopping, visiting the post office or bank, or going to the park. In fact, parents should expose their children to as many activities as possible to familiarize them with different types of discourse exchanges.

Reading books and magazines expands the children's exposure to written language. If the parents' literacy is limited in Spanish, the clinician may recommend the use of wordless books and magazines at first. If students are older and have some reading ability, they can read to their parents. In turn, the parents can participate by asking questions about the text. The participation of other family members, such as older siblings or extended family, is also very helpful.

Parents should show an interest in what their children have done at school by asking questions about their activities. A set time should be allocated for the children to complete their homework or for a parent and siblings to complete a joint project or to play a game. For example, the family can make special decorations for the home for the different holidays, or the family can play games such as lotto or checkers that are essentially universal. Parents can also help other parents by creating networks, facilitated by bilingual school personnel or an interpreter.

The role of the clinician is more difficult when the student has a phonological disorder. Even the clinician who does not speak Spanish can carry out direct intervention, however; for example, the clinician may work on exercises to strengthen the student's oral peripheral musculature in case of apraxia or a phonological disorder. It may be necessary to seek the assistance of an aide, community member, or relative to engage the student in production of target sounds and practice in Spanish, but such a step requires a great deal of caution. Under no circumstances should that person be asked to work with a student without adequate training. It is important to remember that "the aide's main responsibility is to implement instructional programs, not to take on the responsibility for planning instructional programs or writing educational objectives" (Mattes & Omark, 1984, p. 109).

In summary, clinicians and school staff should recommend strategies that will empower the parents and family of LEP/LLD students. Appendix 9-B lists some resources printed in Spanish for parents and families of Hispanic children who have various speech and language disabilities.

Holistic Approach in the Bilingual Education Classroom

Westby and Rouse (1985) described a bilingual special education classroom that provided activities to bridge the differences between home and school. One of the basic principles of the program was to reverse the activities of each setting. High context activities, such as cooking and shopping, were provided in the classroom, while low context activities, such as reading, were to be conducted at home. The reading program provided books for the students to take home and discuss with their parents. During meetings with the family, the clinician offered the parents suggestions on how to read to their children and how to encourage their involvement in the stories, characters, and themes of the books. Follow-up activities included both written reports and oral discussions. Parents who were unable to read were encouraged to call on a member of the extended family to participate in the home reading program, although these parents could also participate by using wordless books that spanned a wide range of more complex content and story structure. These activities took place in either Spanish or English, depending on the parents' proficiency in the languages. (See Appendix 8-A for a list of wordless books.)

Seawell (1985) used literature and puppet activities in a language development program to support a home reading program for families in which the parents cannot read. In this program, children practice listening to and retelling a variety of stories in books that are accompanied by a cassette tape and a set of puppets. They are encouraged to check out the packets to take home and share with their families. The increasing availability of books on tapes and videos provides a helpful resource for students of all ages and parents of varying literacy levels. For example, the PBS series, "Reading Rainbow" (Great Plains, no date), broadcasts narrations and enrichment activities related to the theme of each featured book.

INDIVIDUALIZED EDUCATION PROGRAMS

An IEP is the special educator's primary tool for organizing and focusing instruction. It is also a vehicle for communicating with parents about their child's program. The IEP reflects the specialist's underlying beliefs regarding a number of central issues: the nature of successful instruction, the critical components of the language processes, and the relationship of expectation to performance. Any shifts of focus that occur in theory and practice should be reflected in the IEP plan.

Present Levels of Performance

The description of a student's present levels of performance contained in the IEP is often the introduction of the teacher or clinician to the student. The following guidelines for writing these descriptions reflect the belief that language cannot be discussed out of its context in the student's life:

- Orient the description of the child to strengths and needs rather than deficits; indicate how the student's strengths can be used to support new learning.

  Juan is a friendly, affectionate child who is eager to learn and takes responsibility for his own learning. He works well independently and organizes his time and materials well. He is effective in teaching younger children by using modeling strategies and genuine positive reinforcement. He is creative in applying prior learning to new situations. His creativity is appropriately channeled into music, drama, and art, which are excellent activities to use for the introduction of new concepts. Juan's primary needs lie in the areas of verbal organization and vocabulary development.

- Describe conditions under which the student performs optimally.
  1. Although standardized tests indicated delayed vocabulary and syntax, José takes on a variety of character roles when engaged in sociodramatic play, using precise vocabulary, correct syntax, and appropriate changes in vocal inflections.
  2. José is most engaged and effective in his work when involved in cooperative learning groups.
- Describe oral and written language in terms of the range of purposes for which it is used.
  1. María shows turn-taking behavior in conversation and is able to maintain the topic and encourage her conversation partner to continue the exchange.
  2. María uses language well in content areas to hypothesize, analyze, compare, and categorize information.
  3. Among her peers, María uses language to tease, argue, and joke.
  4. María needs to develop the ability to follow academic discourse, such as lectures, explanations, and discussions.
  5. María needs to develop the ability to persuade and persist in requests.
- Describe the student's proficiency in both languages, again in terms of range of uses.

1. Although fluent in English, Luis uses Spanish with his peers on the playground to express frustration about broken rules, to give directions, or to cheer his team.

2. Luis switches from English to Spanish when explaining an idea from content area lessons.

3. When working on math problems, Luis talks to himself in Spanish as he goes through the problem-solving steps.

- Give basic information on the student's cultural context.

  Raúl is a Mexican-American child whose parents have recently moved to the United States. He is the third of five siblings who all attend Washington school. Both parents work, and his aunt and cousin care for Raúl after school.

- Situate the student in a curricular context.
  1. Pilar's classroom is organized around the fifth-grade curriculum, as outlined in the district curriculum. State-adopted textbooks are the primary source of reading/writing assignments.
  2. Pilar's classroom is organized around thematic units. Literature selections, newspapers, and magazines provide the content for reading/writing activities. The student spends two-thirds of the day in the regular classroom and is pulled out for ESL instruction during mathematics and social studies every other day.

Objectives

Writing effective IEP goals can be a difficult task. The nature of the process often encourages a reductionistic approach, because language skills must be broken into small, observable, measurable behaviors. Rhodes and Dudley-Marling (1988) observed that "it's easy enough to state that some isolated skill will be learned by such and such a date, . . . but meaningful types of learning just don't work this way. It's not possible to predict the rate or precise course of higher forms of learning including oral or written language" (p. 73).

Nelson (1989) acknowledged this dilemma, but offered seven guiding principles to assist the clinician in writing goals which include:

1. Programs should be tailored to meet students' individual needs, because LLD students vary with respect to the difficulty that they have with form, content, or use of language.

2. Integration of content, form, and use of language is important.

3. The language intervention program should include a combination of structured and naturalistic activities that mirror the student's communicative needs.
4. Language should be integrated throughout the curriculum.
5. The goals of the program should include practice in context.
6. The goals should have developmental validity.
7. The goals should not focus on content only, but should stress the teaching of strategies.

The following goals are consistent with Nelson's (1989) guidelines:

- The learner will summarize main points from a content area lesson by recording information in written, oral, or pictorial form (e.g., constructing a semantic map, sequencing pictures, or illustrating concepts) and sharing that information with a peer.
- The learner will make requests in an interactive language experience in which necessary equipment is missing (e.g., brushes are missing from the easel, dolls are missing from the doll house), using two-word utterances (noun + verb, locative + noun, adjective + noun).
- The learner will demonstrate knowledge of print functions by incorporating writing into dramatic play sessions (e.g., writing telephone messages, making shopping lists).
- The learner will summarize information in kernel sentence structures in print media (e.g., designing signs, posters, flyers) for authentic communicative purposes.
- The learner will retell a favorite story to a peer or group of peers, using correct sequence and key phrases in appropriate context (e.g., "Run, run as fast as you can," while showing a picture of the Gingerbread Man).

Writing goals in this format allows clinicians and teachers to focus on the process of language learning rather than on its form. The language of instruction should also be specified.

FUTURE RESEARCH NEEDS

Data are not yet available to determine conclusively what, when, and how certain strategies work best with LEP/LLD Hispanic children. Further efforts should be concentrated on documenting the effectiveness of the programs offered to these students. Figueroa, Ruíz, and Rueda (1988), and Ortíz (1988), are currently performing some research in this area. In the meantime, however, it is practical to consider Cummins' remarks:

> Research is unlikely to provide answers to these questions for a considerable period; thus, it is crucial for teachers and resource personnel in schools to become their own researchers by systematically observing the effects of assessment and placement decisions on students' development over time and by sharing these observations with other professionals in order to provide a coherent experiential basis for future decisions. Essentially, this suggestion represents an extension and systematization of longitudinal monitoring techniques. (1984, pp. 268–269)

Thus, clinicians and universities should collaborate on projects to document the success of various intervention strategies. For example, one or two classes within a district could be designated as models for the implementation of specific programs. Sufficient time and funds must be allocated for these programs, however. There should be a commitment from school administrators, staff, parents, community, and university to carry out such projects.

REFERENCES

Biddick, M. (1987). *Los padres son maestros: An educational videotape for Spanish-speaking parents.* Watsonville, CA: Department of Special Services, Pajaro Valley Unified School District.

Carrow-Woolfolk, E., & Lynch, J.I. (1982). *An integrative approach to language disorders in children.* San Francisco: Grune & Stratton.

Cheng, L. (1989). Intervention strategies: A multicultural approach. *Topics in Language Disorders, 9*(3), 84–91.

Clark, E. (1974). Some aspects of the conceptual basis for first language acquisition. In R. Schiefelbush & L. Lloyd (Eds.), *Language perspectives: Acquisition, retardation and intervention* (pp. 105–128). Baltimore: University Park Press.

Commire, A. (1971–ongoing). *Something about the author.* Detroit: Gale Resources (updated yearly).

Cummins, J. (1981). The role of primary language development in promoting educational success for language minority students. In Office of Bilingual Cultural Education, California State Department of Education (Ed.), *Schooling and language minority students: A theoretical framework* (pp. 3–49). Los Angeles: Evaluation, Dissemination and Assessment Center, California State University.

Cummins, J. (1984). *Bilingualism and special education: Issues in assessment and pedagogy.* Clevedon, England: Multilingual Matters.

Figueroa, R., Ruíz, N., & Rueda, R. (1988). *Special education research project for Hispanic students: The OLE model.* Research proposal, University of California, Davis.

Great Plains/Nebraska Educational Television Network. (no date). *Reading Rainbow.* Lincoln, NE: Lancit Media Productions.

Greenlee, M. (1981, February). *Communicative competence in Spanish/English developmentally disabled persons.* Paper presented at the Council for Exceptional Children Convention, New Orleans.

Heath, S.B. (1986). Sociocultural contexts of language development. In California State Department of Education (Ed.), *Beyond language: Social and cultural factors in schooling language minority students* (pp. 143–186). Los Angeles: Evaluation, Dissemination, and Assessment Center, California State University.

Higginson, W., & Falbel, A. (1985). *Hoopla about curriculum.* Unpublished working paper, Project Headlight Committee Meeting, Boston.

Lahey, M. (1988). *Language disorders and language development.* New York: Macmillan.

Lindfors, J. (1987). *Children's language and learning.* Englewood Cliffs, NJ: Prentice-Hall.

Lowe, P. (1983). *Manual for LS oral interview workshops: The Defense Language Institute and Foreign Service Institute oral proficiency examination.* Monterey, CA: Defense Language Institute.

Mattes, L., & Omark, D. (1984). *Speech and language assessment for the bilingual handicapped.* San Diego: College Hill Press.

McCracken, B., & McCracken, M. (1986). *Tiger cub readers.* Winnipeg, Manitoba, Canada: Peguins Pub.

Merino, B., & Langdon, H. (1986). *Bilingual cross-cultural certificate assessment examination. Technical manual.* Sacramento, CA: The Cross-Cultural Resource Center.

Miller, L. (1989). Classroom based language intervention. *Language, Speech and Hearing Services in Schools, 20,* 153–169.

Nelson, K. (1973). Structure and strategy in learning to talk. *Monograph of the Society for Research in Child Development, Serial No. 149.* Chicago: The University of Chicago Press.

Nelson, N.W. (1989). Language intervention in school settings. In D.K. Bernstein & E. Tiegerman (Eds.), *Language and communication disorders in children,* 2nd ed. (pp. 417–468). Columbus, OH: Charles E. Merrill.

Ortíz, A. (1988). *Effective practices in assessment and instruction for language minority students: An intervention model.* Arlington, VA: Innovative Approaches Research Project, Office of Bilingual Education and Minority Language Affairs, U.S. Department of Education.

Rhodes, L., & Dudley-Marling, C. (1988). *Readers and writers with a difference: A holistic approach to teaching learning disabled and remedial students.* Portsmouth, NH: Heinemann.

Seawell, R.P.M. (1985). *A microethnographic study of a Spanish/English bilingual kindergarten in which literature and puppet play were used as a method of enhancing language growth.* Unpublished doctoral dissertation, University of Texas, Austin.

Terrell, T., & Krashen, S. (1983). *The natural approach.* Oxford, England: Pergamon Press.

Westby, C., & Rouse, C. (1985). Culture in education and the instruction of language learning-disabled students. *Topics in Language Disorders, 5*(4), 19–29.

Wiig, E., & Semel, E. (1980). *Language assessment and intervention for the learning disabled.* Columbus, OH: Charles E. Merrill.

Wong Fillmore, L. (1976). *The second time around: Cognitive and social strategies in second-language acquisition.* Unpublished doctoral dissertation, Stanford University.

Wong Fillmore, L. (1983). The language learner as an individual: Implications of research on individual differences for the ESL teacher. In M.A. Clark & J. Handscombe (Eds.), *On TESOL '82: Pacific perspectives on language, learning and teaching* (pp. 157–173). Washington, DC: Teachers of English to Speakers of Other Languages.

Wong Fillmore, L. (1991). Language and cultural issues in early education. In S.L. Kagan (Ed.), *The care and education of America's young children: Obstacles and opportunities* (pp. 30–49). Chicago: University of Chicago.

Appendix 9-A

Student Profiles[*]

*Underscores indicate differences due to clinician's language proficiency in Spanish.

361

STUDENT 1

Spanish-speaking kindergarten student identified through bilingual assessment as delayed in language development. The student is in a bilingual classroom that provides strong nonlinguistic cues, interactive pedagogy, and many opportunities for hands-on activities. This is her first school experience. She is at Stage 1 of English acquisition. She interacts with peers in both English and Spanish. In English, she uses familiar phrases that she has learned to imitate. Spanish is spoken at home by all family members. The school has a high percentage of Hispanic students and offers bilingual education. The assessment report suggests the following goals:

- Develop concepts and vocabulary.
- Increase selective attention and auditory memory skills.
- Increase pragmatic skills, including turn-taking and topic maintenance.

Clinician: English only

Language of Instruction	Service Delivery	Focus of Intervention	Coordination with Regular Curriculum	Home Support
Spanish	Consultation with teacher/ aide	Encourage sociodramatic play for concept schema development. Use repetitive, cumulative books and songs for selective attention and auditory memory (books on tape). Read aloud for concept/vocabulary development.	Identify kindergarten social skills for pragmatic development. Choose books to complement class theme.	Send home wordless books to read together with family.

Comments: Clinician should participate in classroom language activity to determine what type of scaffolding is necessary.

Clinician: Bilingual

Language of Instruction	Service Delivery	Focus of Intervention	Coordination with Regular Curriculum	Home Support
Spanish	Small group therapy 2x weekly for 25–30 min	Encourage sociodramatic play for concept/schema development, pragmatic skills. Use repetitive, cumulative books for selective attention and memory. Read aloud for concept/vocabulary development.	Identify kindergarten social skills for pragmatic development. Choose books to complement class theme. Student invites Spanish-speaking peer to session.	Invite parent to observe/participate in therapy session. Send home wordless books to read together with family. Visit home to observe verbal interaction.

Comments: Clinician should participate in classroom language activity to determine what type of scaffolding is necessary.

STUDENT 2

First-grade Spanish-speaking student identified through bilingual assessment as having a severe oral language disorder. Student was retained in kindergarten and then referred to a special education day class for communicatively handicapped students, where she is now. The class provides instruction in English only, but has a Spanish-speaking aide. The classroom is organized in a traditional special education model, with small group instruction around carefully sequenced skill development. The student is at Stage 1 of English acquisition. She interacts with the other girls in her class in play activities. The school has primarily English-speaking monolingual students. Her parents speak only Spanish and have three younger children at home who also speak Spanish. The IEP goals include

- Develop comprehension of English and Spanish.
- Increase ability to express needs.

Clinician: English only

Language of Instruction	Service Delivery	Focus of Intervention	Coordination with Regular Curriculum	Home Support
Spanish English	Consultation with teacher/ aide. Individual or small group for English language development, beginning with social skills	Assist aide in providing experiences with wordless books and predictable books in Spanish. Provide opportunities for sociodramatic play. Promote English social language for turn-taking.	Provide Spanish reading materials for aide. Assist aide in providing preview-review for group lessons. Suggest ways for teacher to provide integrated instruction in both languages.	Meet with parents and aide to encourage shared reading. Encourage parents to include student in planning outings, celebrations, etc., and encourage use of eventcasts.

Comments: Bilingual classrooms are not available for all special education students who would benefit from them. It may be possible to provide primary language support by incorporating community members or older students.

Clinician: Bilingual

Language of Instruction	Service Delivery	Focus of Intervention	Coordination with Regular Curriculum	Home Support
Spanish English	<u>Small group in classroom or pull-out for language arts period</u> <u>Consultation with aide for follow-through of activities</u> Individual or small group for English language development, beginning with social skills	Provide experiences with wordless books and predictable books in Spanish. Encourage sociodramatic play around specific schema (e.g., doctor, train station). Promote English social language for turn-taking, games. Expose student to children's folklore.	Provide Spanish reading materials. Demonstrate preview-review for group lessons for aide to do. Suggest ways teacher can provide integrated instruction in both languages.	<u>Encourage parents to join therapy session from time to time.</u> Encourage parents to include student in planning outings, celebrations, etc., and in using more eventcasts.

Comments: Bilingual classrooms are not available for all special education students who would benefit from them. It may be possible to provide primary language support by incorporating community members or older students.
<u>If no first-language instruction is available, provide English language development via natural approach.</u>

STUDENT 3

Third-grade Spanish-dominant student identified through bilingual assessment as LLD. He is at the intermediate fluency stage of English development. He is in an English-only classroom and receives resource specialist services 1 hour each day for reading. The classroom is organized around thematic units and literature-based reading, but the resource specialist uses basal readers with a strong phonics approach. The student goes to Mexico for an extended period of time each year, usually missing 2–3 months of school. He interacts with students in both Spanish and English, but prefers to be spoken to and taught in English. The school has a large percentage of Hispanic students, but few bilingual classrooms. The parents speak only Spanish, but three siblings are also intermediate speakers of English. The assessment report suggested the following goals:

- Improve reading comprehension.
- Develop vocabulary.
- Improve verbal organization.

Clinician: English only

Language of Instruction	Service Delivery	Focus of Intervention	Coordination with Regular Curriculum	Home Support
English	Consultation with classroom teacher and resource specialist	Prepare student for reading selections in classroom with small group of students. Consult with teacher on vocabulary activities appropriate for whole class. Facilitate literature studies group in classroom to scaffold verbal organization.	Work in classroom. Suggest use of basal readers that support text comprehension strategies.	Encourage parents to engage student in discussions about social and political events. Send home complex wordless books that provide opportunity for prediction, and "text" analysis. Recruit interpreter to discuss program goals.

Comments: Students at the intermediate stage of English acquisition need special attention because their oral fluency can mask difficulties in academic language.

Extra caution should be taken with students who already have one pull-out session. Fragmenting their programs may complicate rather than facilitate their progress.

Suggest inexpensive materials that students can take with them when absent from school.

Clinician: **Bilingual**

Language of Instruction	Service Delivery	Focus of Intervention	Coordination with Regular Curriculum	Home Support
English	Consultation with classroom teacher and resource specialist <u>Direct intervention in Spanish where appropriate to develop expressive language skills</u>	Prepare student for reading selections in classroom with small group of students. Consult with teacher on vocabulary activities appropriate for whole class. Facilitate literature studies group in classroom to scaffold verbal organization.	Work in classroom. Suggest uses of basal texts that support text comprehension strategies.	Encourage parents to engage student in discussions about social and political events. Send home complex wordless books that provide opportunity for prediction, and "text" analysis. If student can read Spanish, encourage sharing/reading with family.

Comments: Students at the intermediate stage of English acquisition need special attention because their oral fluency can mask difficulties in academic language.

Extra caution should be taken with students who already have one pull-out session. Fragmenting their programs may complicate rather than facilitate their progress.

STUDENT 4

First-grade Spanish-dominant student identified through bilingual assessment as delayed in language skills that affect literacy development. He is in Stage 2 of English acquisition. He is in a bilingual classroom, where instruction is based on the use of a basal reader, traditional ability grouping, and teacher-directed activities. He was considered for retention in kindergarten, but was promoted for social reasons. He interacts with peers primarily in Spanish and does not seek contact with English-speaking peers. The school has a high percentage of Hispanic students. The parents speak Spanish at home. Three older siblings are bilingual; they speak English among themselves and Spanish with their parents and grandparents. The assessment report suggested the following goals:

- Develop concepts and vocabulary.
- Develop metalinguistic awareness.
- Increase understanding of narrative structure.

Clinician: English only

Language of Instruction	Service Delivery	Focus of Intervention	Coordination with Regular Curriculum	Home Support
English	Consultation with teacher Small group with bilingual student who can provide scaffolding	Work at Stage 2 of English acquisition: • sequencing wordless books • environmental print awareness • children's folklore to encourage interaction • predictable books • eventcast of high-interest	Choose stories, activities related to classroom science or social studies.	Ask interpreter to explain use of predictable books. Encourage parents to share folk tales or stories about their own childhood and experiences.

Comments: Model to develop varying uses of Spanish (e.g., expand on what the child says when reading, make comments about the content of the book).
Comment about ongoing activities.

Clinician: **Bilingual**

Language of Instruction	Service Delivery	Focus of Intervention	Coordination with Regular Curriculum	Home Support
Spanish	Small group 2x a week	Work on story structure through dramatization. Read aloud predictable books; student will learn to share with peers, parents. Encourage word play with 2 languages. Promote social exchanges in 2 languages. Use children's folklore in English to encourage interaction.	Choose stories related to classroom science or social studies texts. Use characters from basal reader to create stories.	Send home predictable books to read with parents. Encourage parents to share folk tales and have student share with clinician.

Comments: Same as above.

STUDENT 5

Fifth-grade student who is 2–3 years behind grade level in all curriculum areas. Previous referrals for a speech-language evaluation have not been carried through. The student was retained in kindergarten. He received Spanish instruction in Grades 1 and 2, but has received English-only instruction since Grade 3. He has experienced significant Spanish loss and now scores at level 3 in both English and Spanish. He speaks to peers and adults in English, but speaks Spanish with his parents at home. He is in a bilingual classroom that follows a traditional fifth-grade curriculum based on state-adopted texts. The current assessment suggested the following goals:

- Improve ability to organize verbal information.
- Improve reading comprehension.
- Improve written expression.

Clinician: English only

Language of Instruction	Service Delivery	Focus of Intervention	Coordination with Regular Curriculum	Home Support
English Spanish	Individual or small group In classroom literature studies or writer's workshop response or editing groups	Use text comprehension strategies, metacognitive strategies. Prepare student to read stories to kindergarten students. Use correspondence for authentic purposes. Establish silent dialogue practice among group members. Simplify text material to enhance comprehension.	Use grade-level texts. Encourage cross-age tutoring to give practice in math/reading.	Request interpreter to encourage parents to include student in discussion. Encourage parents to share folk tales and own experiences.

Comments: Establish a dialogue journal between parents, teacher, and pupil (if parents are literate). Foster use of Spanish or English consistently in each context (oral and written language). Expose student to age-appropriate materials.

Clinician: Bilingual

Language of Instruction	Service Delivery	Focus of Intervention	Coordination with Regular Curriculum	Home Support
English Spanish	Individual or small group	Use text comprehension strategies, metacognitive strategies. Prepare student to read stories to kindergarten students. Use correspondence for authentic purposes. Establish silent dialogue practice among group members. Simplify text material to enhance comprehension.	Use grade-level texts. Preview content area lessons in Spanish. Encourage cross-age tutoring to give practice in math/reading.	Encourage parents to include student in discussions. Encourage parents to share folk tales, experiences.

Comments: Same as above.

Appendix 9-B

Materials for Parents on Various Speech and Language Problems

Consejos: Lo Que Deben y No Deben Hacer los Padres de Niños con Problemas de Oído 'Some Advice about Do's and Don'ts for Parents of Children with Hearing Problems' (Leaflet)
National Easter Seal Society
2023 West Ogden Ave.
Chicago, IL 60612

¡Escuchen, Oigan! Para Padres de Niños con Deficiencia de Audición 'Listen, Hear, For Parents of Children with Hearing Impairments' (Brochure)
Alexander Graham Bell
3417 Volta Place, N.W.
Washington, DC 20007

Un Futuro Prometedor: Para Su Niño con Labio Hendido y Paladar Hendido 'Bright Promises For Your Children with Cleft Lip and Cleft Palate' (Booklet)
National Easter Seal Society
2023 West Ogden Ave.
Chicago, IL 60612

Lista de Actividades Auditivas y del Lenguaje 'Speech and Hearing Checklist' (Leaflet)
Alexander Graham Bell
3417 Volta Place, N.W.
Washington, DC 20007

Partners in Language: A Guide for Parents (The Baby, The Toddler, The Young Child) (Three sets of books)
American Speech-Language-Hearing Association
10801 Rockville Pike
Rockville, MD 20852

¿Qué Tal Habla y Oye Su Niño? 'How Does Your Child Talk and Hear?' (Brochure)
American Speech-Language-Hearing Association
10801 Rockville Pike
Rockville, MD 20852

Si Su Hijo Tartamudea: Una Guía Para los Padres 'If Your Child Stutters: A Guide for Parents' (Booklet)
Speech Foundation of America
P.O. Box 11749
Memphis, TN 38111

Chapter 10

Acquired Neurological Disabilities in Hispanic Adults

Gustavo Arámbula

As stated in Chapter 2, an estimated 2.3 million Hispanic persons are in need of speech, language, and hearing services, with approximately 69 percent or 1.5 million being adults (18 years or older). Between the mid 1980s and the year 2000, it is estimated that the aged minority population will nearly double (Manuel & Reid, 1982). The trend has already begun. During the years from 1970 to 1980 alone, the Hispanic elderly population grew from 382,000 to 709,000, a 98% increase (U.S. Bureau of the Census, 1989).

A recent survey of 1 million Hispanics who are 65 years old and over, conducted by the Commonwealth Commission on Elderly People Living Alone, indicated that the typical Hispanic elderly person's weekly income is $104 or less (Select Committee on Aging, 1989). The study also showed that 22% of elderly Hispanics live in poverty, compared with 12% of all the elderly in the United States. Only 29% receive a pension, compared with 45% of the general retired population. In addition, 54% reported fair to poor health, compared with 35% of the general elderly population. These difficult conditions were attributed to "cumulative deficits throughout life," such as lack of education (75% of the elderly Hispanics had an eighth-grade education or less) and a language barrier (40% did not speak English). Very likely, these conditions will not improve in the near future, and they considerably affect Hispanic patients' access to rehabilitation services, their use of these services, and, thus, the benefits that they obtain from them.

The heterogeneous nature of Hispanics as a group also affects their utilization of health care services. For example, Puerto Ricans are twice as likely than are other Hispanics to use hospital outpatient programs or emergency rooms (Schur, Bernstein, & Berk, 1987). Keefe and Casas (1980) suggested that the underutilization of mental health and rehabilitative services by Mexican-Americans is largely due to their perception of mental illness and its treatment. For example, it is still uncommon for some Hispanic families to seek the assistance of a psychologist or a psychiatrist for feelings of distress, depression, or anxiety. The counsel of a priest, a trusted friend, or a teacher is a more accepted practice. Furthermore, medical services are underutilized because many Hispanics are "undocumented" persons who are apprehensive about seeking out services for fear of being reported to the Immigration and Naturalization Service. Finally, those in the lower socioeconomic classes may not seek services simply because they cannot pay for such services.

ACQUIRED NEUROLOGICAL DISABILITIES

Stroke, head trauma, various infections, and/or chemical toxicity may result in acquired neurological disabilities. The incidence of stroke in the United States is between 400,000 and 500,000 cases per year. As many as 200,000 people may acquire a neurological disability as a result of head trauma, which is the third leading cause of death, following coronary heart disease and cancer, in the U.S. population (Trunkey, 1983). Possibly 300,000 more acquired neurological disabilities are due to various infections and chemical toxicity (U.S. Department of Health, Education, and Welfare, 1980). Exact figures for Hispanics are not available. Based on the proportion of Hispanics to the entire population (8% to 9%), however, it is reasonable to forecast 32,000 to 35,000 stroke cases per year, with an additional 16,000 cases due to head trauma and 18,000 due to infections and chemical toxicity.

Classification of Cerebral Vascular Accidents

The anatomical and physiological causes of cerebral vascular accidents (CVAs) determine their classification (Chusid, 1982; Stein, 1986). They can be classified as ischemic or hemorrhagic. Ischemic CVAs, which are the most common, can be further classified as thrombotic or embolic. These CVAs result from partial or complete occlusion of a cerebral vessel. The most common ischemic CVA is thrombotic in nature and occurs when a blood clot is localized within a blood vessel feeding into the brain. The clot may result from atherosclerotic plaques (cholesterol and calcium deposits), inflammation of the vessel walls, or damage following a head injury. In an ischemic CVA that is embolic in nature, a fragment of clot or plaque travels from its site of origin to the brain, where it occludes the vessel.

There are two general types of hemorrhagic CVAs, depending on their location in the brain. Intracerebral hemorrhagic CVAs originate from a vessel within the brain and are caused by excessive blood pressure, weakening of the vessel wall, injury, inflammation, or congenital defects. The subarachnoid type results from an aneurysm or malformation of the arterial walls that leads to bleeding in the subarachnoid space surrounding the brain.

All these CVAs have one feature in common—they interrupt the blood supply to the brain, leading to damage to the nervous tissue. The damage can involve cortical and subcortical areas, the lower brain stem, cerebellar areas, and peripheral nerve areas (Chusid, 1982; Kety, 1979). Numerous types of speech and language disorders can result. In general, the more severe the interruption of the blood supply, the more significant the resultant deficits.

Behaviors Associated with Acquired Neurological Disabilities

Recent technological advances, such as the increased use and improvement of computed tomography (CT) and magnetic resonance imaging (MRI), have been helpful in localizing the site of different lesions in the brain. Localization of a lesion alone does not necessarily make it possible to determine the appropriate assessment or treatment of a patient, however (McNeil, 1983). It is best if the results are supplemented by a description of behaviors associated with the stroke, head trauma, or any acquired neurological deficit. A localizationalist model often lends itself to a better association between clinical findings and neurology, especially with the accessibility of imaging techniques to establish this connection in cases of CVA.

Schwartz-Cowley and Stepanik (1989) commented on the great difficulty of classifying the symptoms associated with head trauma. One of the problems is that symptoms vary from moment to moment. Even so, a classification system is helpful in the selection of appropriate interventions. For example, Hagen (1984) developed a classification system that delineates three different phases of neurological communicative-cognitive dysfunction. First, there is a global suppression of all communicative and cognitive functions. This is followed by a phase in which there are persisting symptoms with some impairments. Finally, a permanent and irreversible neurological impairment is noted, along with an associated neurobehavioral and communicative impairment. The majority of patients will go through these three phases, although not all of them do. As a result, patients may have different cognitive impairments, along with secondary language problems; have minimal cognitive impairments, but have a specific language impairment; or have attentional, retentional problems, but have no problems with short-term memory and no specific language problem (Schwartz-Cowley & Stepanik, 1989, p. 4).

The prevalence of gradual neurogenic damage and dementia, such as that associated with Alzheimer's, Huntington's, or Parkinson's disease, increases with age. Some families adjust rather well—perhaps too well—to the gradual onset of a neurological illness such as Alzheimer's; the onset may be so gradual that there is no sense of urgency to seek out professional help. Often, this disease is not diagnosed or treated until the psychosocial problems are great enough to influence family life. In the case of Hispanic patients, the cross-cultural barriers and attitudes about the disease may cause a further delay in a family's seeking appropriate care. All too often families interpret a possible neurogenic disorder as the result of "old age," just as if old age made mental deterioration inevitable. Although there has been an extensive review of such cases in the mainstream population (e.g., Cummings & Benson, 1983), there has been little attention given to the treatment of these disorders among cultural or language minority groups.

Clinical Management

In planning an intervention program for a patient who has an acquired neurological disability, particularly a Hispanic patient, it is important to consider the patient's environment, diet, and life style, as well as cultural, economic, and educational background. Many of these patients still believe in the effectiveness of healers and, therefore, do not comply with treatment suggested by physicians. They do not recognize the benefits of a balanced healthy diet and exercise as preventive measures for age-related problems as readily as do members of the mainstream group (Pérez-Stable, 1987). A large number of Hispanics tend to live in poorer neighborhoods, with a lesser quantity and quality of services from medical, public, and educational institutions. In this situation, deficiencies tend to perpetuate themselves.

The attitudes that the patient and family have and their perception of the illness are sometimes as important as the actual recognition and diagnosis of the disease. Lefly (1985) and Valle (1989a, 1989b) found that proper access to services depended not only on ethnicity, but also on socioeconomic status. They noted that people from the same economic background, but of different ethnic groups, responded in different ways to the onset of a neurological disease in a family member; thus, the "cultural definition" of an impairment is critically dependent on a group's values. The anticipated reaction varies considerably, even within a homogeneous group, however. Yet, many generalizations can and have been made regarding the attitudes of the Hispanic community toward medical treatment.

Speech-language clinicians who work with the Hispanic population must be aware that the success of their interventions depends to a significant extent on their understanding of differences in attitudes among different ethnic groups. For example, many patients and families have had only limited exposure to "technical medicine" that requires a high degree of technology, specialization, and ancillary services. Many first-generation Hispanics and, for that matter, many of those in the mainstream population who live in isolated or rural areas may not have had any exposure to hospitals and have difficulty communicating their concerns in those circumstances. They may not comprehend the extent of the disability or its immediate and future implications for the patient and family. Also, they may not know where and how to seek technical, emotional, or economic assistance.

Any prescribed treatment plan is put in jeopardy without a thorough appraisal of the family's dynamics. The speech-language clinician and the other members of the team must understand the family's views of the illness, as well as their beliefs concerning their own roles and those of medical personnel. Also, the team must consider the family's ability to cope with the illness and the family's resources; the latter includes not only economic resources, but also the time necessary to cover patient management in the home and the willingness to accept possible changes in family members' roles. The clinician must also be aware of the family's support network outside of the home (e.g., friends, religious faith, activities) that existed prior to the onset of the illness. The family's acceptance of the illness as a long-term process should be considered as well.

In a hospital setting, the medical system has primary control over the outcome of the patient up to the point of discharge. Continued care is primarily dependent on the family, and follow-up cannot always be adequately provided because of linguistic or economic barriers. The management of an illness of this nature and its impact on all family members are difficult, regardless of ethnic background. The mismatch between an established medical system and a population for which the system was not designed, however, contributes to unpredictable treatment outcomes.

Under these circumstances, it is not uncommon for bilingual speech-language clinicians who work in close contact with physicians and rehabilitation specialists to be called upon at times to perform duties that may be considered beyond the scope of their professional responsibility. This may be a necessary effort, however, if treatment is to be economically efficient, if the family is to follow a prescribed medical plan, and if the patient is to regain a life style as normal as possible. Bilingual clinicians must view their role as providing assistance to the family and patient both in implementing the team plan and in facilitating the patient's speech, communication, and psycholinguistic abilities. For example, in the absence of a social service program, the bilingual clinician may function as a liaison between the hospital staff and the family in (1) planning the patient's discharge; (2) arranging the details of transfer from the hospital to the home or another institution; (3) translating documents, as well as facilitating the family's need for financial arrangements; and (4) providing teaching and directions for the patient at home.

IMPACT OF ACQUIRED NEUROLOGICAL DISABILITY ON THE BILINGUAL INDIVIDUAL

Since the initial experimental research during the 1960s, traditional aphasiology has focused on the salient linguistic aspects that are governed primarily by the left hemisphere. A review of the literature supports the theory that the left cerebral hemisphere is more involved in language processes such as analysis, synthesis, and formulation than is the right hemisphere (Damasio, 1984). In the last decade, however, there have been sporadic neurological reports of right hemispheric mediation of language (Gazzaniga, Naas, Reeves, & Roberts, 1984). Sustained CVAs in the right hemisphere also affect communication skills; for example, personality changes, alteration of melody and cadence of voice, visual-perceptual deficits, and difficulty in socializing or participating in conversation have been noted. In a critical review of research, Bryden (1982) demonstrated the importance of the involvement of the right hemisphere in neuropsychological processing. These findings have affected the assessment and treatment of patients who have sustained right hemispheric damage (Burns, Halper, & Mogil, 1983). Thus, patients affected by right hemispheric CVAs need assistance in improving communication, as well as in regaining the social skills that are often affected by this type of neurological insult.

The speech and language deficits following stroke can be described neuropsychologically with a good deal of consistency. For example, the Boston Veterans Administration Hospital uses a neuropsychological classification system based on knowledge that certain areas of the brain are primarily responsible for certain language functions. Focal damage to those areas results in specific diagnostic categories that are essentially invariant, except in cases where the damage is widespread or affects multiple areas of the brain.

In the last decade, research on the differential impairment of languages in some bilingual or multilingual patients who have sustained injury to cerebral nervous tissue has been reported in isolated chapters of books or journal articles (e.g., Lecours, L'Hermitte, & Bryans, 1983; Soares, 1984; Vaid, 1986). The summaries prepared by Albert and Obler (1978), and Paradis (1977, 1983), show that many studies have focused on stroke patients because neurological damage in these patients tends to be more focal in nature. In this instance, the neurological assessment seems "cleaner." The damaged nervous tissue is often relatively easy to detect through radiological imaging. Although it may appear that differential language impairment is the norm, only a few studies have been conducted on the differential impairment in the general multilingual stroke population. Furthermore, the vast majority of cases show impairment of both or all languages to the same relative degree.

As was discussed in Chapter 5, there are various degrees of bilingualism. A *balanced* bilingual has equal or native proficiency in both languages. A *dominant* bilingual is one whose proficiency is greater in one language than in the other, although the degree of proficiency in each language may not be specified. The lack of adequate assessment materials often makes it difficult to determine language dominance in adults, but the concepts of compound, coordinate, and subordinate bilingualism are often used to differentiate among types of bilingualism for this population age (Albert & Obler, 1978). *Compound* bilingualism is a system in which the languages act like a single unit. Theoretically, sudden neural damage would impair both languages in this case. *Coordinate* bilingualism, on the other hand, is a system in which the languages are maintained separately, but are interconnected by subconscious, possibly subcortical, switching mechanisms. In this instance, focal damage would affect one language more than it would affect the other; the idea of a separate neural representation of each language is difficult to accept, however, for it contradicts the view that people have focal localization of neurolinguistic processes. *Subordinate* bilingualism is a system in which one language mediates the other. Neurologically, the two languages are related, but damage would affect some areas in one language more than in the other.

Many other factors should be considered in describing bilingualism in adult language functioning. These factors include the manner in which the second language was acquired, the individual's age at the time of acquisition, the specific use of each language, social and emotional factors, the structure of the languages, and the linguistic relationship between the two languages. For example, bilingualism with the combination of Spanish and French, which are both Romance languages, may differ from that with Spanish and Japanese, which are Romance and Altaic (also polysyllabic and ideographic) languages, respectively. The recovery of two languages that have common roots, such as Spanish and French, may occur more rapidly than the recovery of two languages that have different roots, such as Spanish and Japanese. On the other hand, the opposite may also be true. Because two languages have common roots, there may be interference that will slow the pace of recovery. Studies on the nature and relationship of two languages and the way in which these factors affect the process of recovery have not yet taken place. Language loss, frequency of use, and aging also must be considered.

RECOVERY PATTERNS FOR BILINGUALS

It is important to understand the possible recovery mechanisms that a bilingual person may experience in order to implement effective remedial techniques. Researchers have provided various insights into the possible underlying mechanisms for language recovery following strokes or traumatic head injury. Some of these theories were developed as far back as the late 1800s, prior to the advent of modern technology, such as CT and MRI. They still have considerable applicability for categorizing many stages of recovery, however, although they are based on single case histories and it may be difficult to derive generalizations.

Early Theories

In 1882, Ribot hypothesized that a bilingual with an acquired language deficit recovers the first language first because it is more resistant to damage. To illustrate this case, Dreifuss (1961) reported the case of a 34-year-old bilingual poet who had emigrated from Germany to the United States at the age of 10 years and had had no exposure to German since then. Migraine headaches resulted in the loss of his second language (English), while his first language (German) remained intact. Eventually, English was recovered, but not to the same level of proficiency as German.

Pitres (1895) proposed that the most familiar or most recently learned language returns first. Consistent with this theory, Halpern (1941) reported the case of a 24-year-old German who had gone to Israel at age 20 years and had been hit by a bullet. It damaged his left temporal region, resulting in sensory aphasia. In recovering, his comprehension and expression in Hebrew preceded his comprehension and expression in German in both the oral and written modalities. Both languages gradually recovered, but he regained Hebrew at a faster rate than he regained German.

A theory proposed by Minkowski (1963) was based on the premise that the emotional importance of a language may influence its recovery. In his review of the Russian literature, he presented cases where multilingual aphasics from central Asia who spoke Turkmenian, Kazakh, or Georgian were inducted into the army, where they learned to speak Russian. After suffering brain injury, the patients were admitted to hospitals at which there were only Russian speakers. Their Russian skills recovered first. In this case, Russian, rather than the soldiers' native language, became the "emotionally charged" language. It is possible that for these soldiers Russian symbolized the primary communication vehicle to plan the country's defense as well as the protection of their own lives. Although these earlier studies were clearly not stringent in their methodologies, they are useful in illustrating the complexity of bilingual aphasic syndromes.

Some early researchers proposed still other theoretical neurological mechanisms of language recovery. Goldstein (1948), for example, suggested that the recovery of only one language results from an inhibition of the switching mechanism; he hypothesized that, under certain conditions, the recovery of one language may inhibit the recovery of the other. He reported the case of an English-Swedish bilingual woman who switched from English to Swedish when she was making emotional statements. She could not translate from either language on command, however, and she could not perform all language functions voluntarily. Thus, the "switching ability" could operate only under certain conditions. Cases such as this one are relatively rare.

Minkowski (1963) proposed a model that involved two switches. According to this theory, an "output" switch that operates under voluntary control inhibits one language, while allowing the production of the other. An "input" switch alerts or sets the language-processing system to filter in or out the different incoming languages.

More Recent Theories

When Paradis (1977) did a retrospective analysis of recovery in 138 multilingual aphasics, he organized the paths of recovery into five general patterns. The first three refer to the recovery patterns in bilingual patients, while the last two refer to the recovery patterns in trilingual or multilingual patients.

Synergistic and Differential Recovery. In a synergistic recovery, both languages are impaired, and they eventually recover—although not necessarily at the same rate. If the languages are not equally impaired or if they recover at different rates, the recovery is referred to as differential. The synergistic and differential recovery is by far the most common type, as 95% to 98% of bilingual aphasic patients follow this course of language restitution. Of the 138 cases reviewed by Paradis, 67 were synergistic and 56 were differential. Of those 138, only 6 were speakers of Spanish and another language. This recovery pattern may be different for bilingual patients from different countries, however, where the combined influences of culture and individual history are vastly different.

Antagonistic Recovery. Also referred to as regressive recovery, an antagonistic recovery involves the return of one language at the apparent expense of a previously recovered language. One language may gradually improve, but begin to fade upon the emergence of the second language.

Successive Recovery. When one language returns only after another has been completely restored, the recovery is successive. The second language does not reemerge until the patient has achieved relative fluency in the first one.

Mixed Recovery. In one type of mixed recovery, the languages are intermingled in all four processes (i.e., comprehension, expression, reading, and writing). A person may be able to read better in one language and speak better in another. In another variety of mixed recovery, also referred to as reciprocal antagonism, successive restitution is followed by antagonistic recovery. For a person speaking three languages, for example, two of them recover successively to a relatively fluent degree. After a few months, the patient's third language emerges, detrimentally affecting the most dominant, fluently recovered language thus far.

Selective Recovery. When one of the languages never recovers and remains impaired, even when the other language(s) have returned, the recovery is selective.

CLINICAL EVALUATION PROTOCOL

Although many advances in technology have facilitated the detection of lesions caused by CVAs and other traumas that affect the neurological system, the role of the clinician is still paramount. Assessment and intervention are most successful when the clinician understands the medical aspects of the disease and is familiar with the patient's cultural and social background. Ideally, an evaluation of the language ability of a bilingual with a neurological impairment should include three components: (1) sociocultural appraisal, (2) assessment of communication, and (3) evaluation of results of technological tests. All three are essential in planning an appropriate treatment plan. The following areas should be considered (Lecours, L'Hermitte, & Bryans, 1983):

- Case history
  1. date of birth
  2. language(s) spoken at home
  3. language spoken by both parents at home (specify)
  4. age of acquisition of first and second languages
  5. age of acquisition of reading and writing skills in first and second languages
  6. handedness
  7. educational background
  8. occupational history
  9. medical history (e.g., CT scans, MRI)
- Linguistic evaluation
  1. orientation to time and space
  2. memory (i.e., immediate, delayed, and remote)
  3. fluency
  4. auditory comprehension (e.g., pointing, identification, directions)
  5. naming (e.g., response to questions, direct confrontation naming)
  6. repetition (words and sentences)
  7. paraphasias (phonemic vs. verbal)
  8. automatic speech (series)
  9. oral reading (words and sentences)
  10. reading comprehension (letters, words, and sentences)
  11. writing (copying, dictation, spontaneous writing)
  12. numerical calculation
  13. translation between the two languages
- Cognitive evaluation
  1. low-level selective attention
     (a) tracking, visual and auditory

  (b) sound recognition

  (c) shape recognition

  (d) word recognition

  (e) word recognition in noise

2. discrimination

  (a) visual (color, shape, size, color shape and size)

  (b) auditory (words)

  (c) pictures/objects

  (d) sentences

3. orientation

  (a) time

  (b) place

  (c) biographical history

  (d) awareness of impairment

4. organization

  (a) categorization

  (b) closure

  (c) sequencing

5. recall

  (a) immediate

  (b) delayed

  (c) remote

  (d) with interference

  (e) cued recall

  (f) word fluency

  (g) auditorally presented directions

  (h) visually presented material

6. high-level thought process

  (a) ability to understand main idea

  (b) ability to understand cause-effect

  (c) ability to make inferences

  (d) ability to generalize

7. reading skills

  (a) word level/sentence level

  (b) paragraph comprehension

  (c) following directions

8. written language
   (a) mechanics
   (b) recall of written symbols
   (c) written formation
9. pragmatic/social language
   (a) nonverbal communication
   (b) conversation skills
   (c) use of linguistic context
   (d) organization of narrative
   (e) appreciation of metaphorical language
10. voice
    (a) pitch
    (b) quality
    (c) intensity
11. oral agility/intelligibility
    (a) muscular weakness
    (b) production of syllables

Clinicians must have a theoretical model on which they can base their evaluation of patients' strengths and weaknesses. A neuropsychological model such as this one assumes a close and direct connection between neurology and the psycholinguistic process of language and cognition. Not all patients need assessment in all of these areas, however; the content of the evaluation will vary from case to case. Some patients will respond well to some of the low-level tasks, but not the higher ones. In addition, the patient's premorbid skills affect the content of the evaluation. For example, reading assessment is unnecessary if the patient's literacy ability was minimal prior to injury. For another patient, reading may constitute an important area for assessment and intervention.

Sociocultural Appraisal

The contact between clinician and patient constitutes a locally-based communicative event. The interaction is bound to the cultural background of the clinician and patient (American Speech-Language-Hearing Association, 1989). For example, many minority patients have difficulty relating to their clinicians. Some Hispanic patients feel alienated by the clinician-patient situation, and the language barrier further complicates this feeling. Thus, the clinician must be aware of possible conflicts that may arise from the patients' cultural and communicative norms prior to the onset of their trauma or illness. The expectations of the family, as well as their trust in the delivery of services, must be considered. Their educational background, degree of acculturation and closeness, and bonding to the ill family member are important variables as well. Some families have great respect for therapists, clinicians, and physicians as individuals, yet they do not adhere to a prescribed treatment plan. They feel that the elderly family member has "had a difficult life" and that it is the family's turn to take care of the patient. The philosophy of "helping patients help themselves" on which rehabilitation professionals base their efforts to instill a sense of independence in the patient often conflicts with what the Hispanic family and patient desire. Nevertheless, out of respect for the medical professionals, the family may not clearly communicate their desires. The rehabilitation team may find out too late that their efforts were essentially in vain.

The culture, religion, and traditional beliefs of Hispanics may also affect treatment. For example, the church in Mexico continues to influence various facets of life, particularly in the rural areas of the country. The belief in "higher" forces that intervene in the cause and healing of a disease is quite prevalent. Most U.S. citizens rely on medical technology to define the causes of illness and to treat medical problems. In Third World countries, the lack of public services and medical technologies can result in very different attitudes. Therefore, clinicians must acknowledge those differences in belief and attitudes by suggesting a service delivery model from a mutually beneficial standpoint.

> At age 68 years, a second-generation Mexican-American who had gone to school all his life in the United States and was equally fluent in both Spanish and English sustained a dense right cerebral hemispheric stroke with accompanying left hemiparesis and left visual field difficulties. On numerous occasions, he asked about the cause of his stroke and received a detailed explanation with a scientific basis. Four months after his stroke, he inquired whether the clinician thought a folkhealer in Mexico could help ameliorate his left hemiparesis. It became clear that all along the patient had wanted approval to justify his belief in an alternative method of dealing with his illness.

The role of the clinician should be to listen to the patient and offer possible explanations, which have been confirmed by physicians and other specialists, while respecting the beliefs of the patient.

Assessment of Communication

It is important to question the spouse, a relative, friends, or the patient, when possible, to obtain a careful language history of the patient prior to the neurological insult. Educational and occupational histories are also helpful. A language barrier may prevent the clinician from obtaining this information personally, however.

The ratio of clients who are non-native speakers of English to bilingual speech-language clinicians is high. Yet, the likelihood that the number of bilingual clinicians will increase significantly in the foreseeable future is slim. Alternative strategies, such as the use of a bilingual consulting clinician or an interpreter/translator, must be adopted. Ideally, a monolingual or partially bilingual clinician should never work with a Spanish-speaking patient alone. It may be a disservice to the patient, and, at times, may even be detrimental to treatment. It is imperative that clinicians objectively recognize their own linguistic capabilities and limitations.

Although there are no generally accepted standards for evaluation or treatment of patients using an interpreter/translator, a certain level of competence must be established. In Chapter 7, Langdon outlined some procedures for the use of an interpreter/translator in the schools that can also be followed in the clinical and hospital settings. As in the schools, for example, the clinician and the interpreter/translator should have a briefing conference before the assessment. During that time, details about the accident and evaluation procedures can be discussed. Also, information about the patient's language history, skills, and job responsibilities can be evaluated with the assistance of the family or co-workers. Following the evaluation, the observations and results of testing can be analyzed with the input of the interpreter/translator.

In order to provide ready access to an interpreter/translator, the hospital may form interdisciplinary teams on which one member of the team is Spanish-speaking. This is generally preferred to an outside contact, as the general treatment plans among disciplines developed in the acute care setting often overlap. It may be advantageous for all therapists involved to do co-evaluations on bilingual patients; this process lends itself to the development of consistent and cohesive treatment plans.

In the absence of cooperatives, networks, or contacts with universities who have Spanish-speaking students, a family member may serve as an interpreter/translator. The clinician must be cautious, however, in selecting the appropriate family member to accomplish an objective evaluation. Family members may be biased and inclined to give the patient the benefit of the doubt during an evaluation. Unconsciously, this relative may give verbal or gestural cues to the patient. Despite this disadvantage, there is a value in using a family member, especially if this person will carry over the treatment plan once the patient is dismissed.

The formal diagnosis of a problem in an adult patient who has sustained a stroke or traumatic head injury, or is suffering from a progressive neurological illness should include an assessment of phonological, linguistic, suprasegmental, and cognitive skills. Some areas can be assessed even when the clinician is not familiar with the primary language of the patient, such as pure-tone testing and the physical parameters of the oral peripheral mechanism, including swallowing.

To assess language areas, the clinician can choose from a number of aphasia tests. In the case of a bilingual stroke patient, it is suggested that the cognitive-linguistic areas be assessed in each one of the two languages within a short time. The assessment of the two languages needs to be immediate, as spontaneous recovery can affect the determination of the relative fluency between the two languages. The evaluation should focus initially on the language that is suspected to be the most dominant. In this manner, a clearer picture of language proficiency in general can be obtained.

Tests that are translated and adapted in Spanish, but are not yet published are The Boston Diagnostic Aphasia Examination (Goodglass & Kaplan, 1983), the Token Test (De Renzi & Vignolo, 1977), the Porch Index of Communicative Abilities (Porch, 1981b), and the Differential Diagnosis of Aphasia (Schuell, 1972). Only the manual of the Bilingual Aphasia Test (Paradis, 1987) has been translated into Spanish and other languages—not the test protocols. The Exámenes para Diagnosticar Impedimentos de Afasia (Marshall & Rojas, 1982) is a Spanish version of the Keenan and Brassell (1974) Aphasia Performance Scale. Most of these tests focus on language form or content. Assessment instruments that focus more on language use and communication are the Communicative Abilities in Daily Living (Holland, 1980) and the Functional Communication Profile (Sarno, 1969), but neither translations nor adaptations of these tests into Spanish are available. Together, the Boston Diagnostic Aphasia Examination and the Token Test provide relatively complete information on strong and weak modality areas, however.

No formal assessment instrument for written language for patients who have sustained neurological damage is presently available in Spanish in the United States. Future efforts should be made to investigate materials that are used in Spanish-speaking countries to assess these areas. In those countries, however, many available formal tests are translations of existing English tests.

Basic medical information written in Spanish for the Hispanic population is limited. Some dictionaries and glossaries that contain medical terminology may be helpful, for example, the *Bilingual Special Education Dictionary* (Figueroa & Ruíz, 1983) and the *Bilingual Language, Speech, and Hearing Dictionary* (Mattes, 1986). In addition, some tapes and courses designed for doctors and nurses who work with Spanish-speaking patients may be very useful to bilingual speech-language clinicians. Some examples are *Medical Spanish*, a series of cassettes (Audio-Forum, 1991); *Medical Spanish*, a textbook (DiLorenzo-Kearon & Kearon, 1981); and a videotape to teach "survival" Spanish to health care personnel (Savariego, 1985).

The clinician should have a list of available resources for the patient and the family on different matters, including health, medical, educational, and legal matters. The American Heart Association distributes materials in Spanish on aphasia that emphasize the role of the family in the intervention process. Also, there are guides (e.g., Schorr, 1989) that provide different resources for the Spanish-speaking. Additionally, the clinician may contact the patient's community services office for information on different agencies or programs available in that particular community.

Results of Technological Tests

The information obtained by CT and MRI is valuable in clarifying the reasons that bilingual patients sometimes present such peculiar linguistic profiles. Computed tomography scans are radiological techniques in which sections or "slices" of a patient's cerebral tissue are irradiated with a beam. A computer calculates average differences in density as the beam moves through the tissue, and these density differences are then plotted on a screen or photographic plates to show the intracerebral structures, including damaged tissue.

Magnetic resonance imaging, a more sophisticated procedure, involves the use of a large electromagnet that induces a magnetic field throughout the tissue in the brain. All atoms in the body have nuclei that react as if they were spinning. They possess some physical characteristics, such as a magnetic movement of their own. The magnetism in the atomic nuclei is random, however, because the atoms and molecules are mostly randomly oriented in bodily tissue. The powerful electromagnet of the MRI forces the atoms (hydrogen for the most part) to align themselves with the magnetic field that it induces. In the process, they absorb energy and are excited. Through this rapid oscillating absorption and release of energy from the hydrogen atoms, as well as the water content in all body tissue, it is possible to detect small differences in intracerebral density. Lesions can be identified more accurately with this method than with the CT scanner. These technological advances provide clinicians unprecedented and exciting tools to conduct research and often do clarify the differential recovery of bilingual patients.

INTERVENTION

Most clinicians agree that the success of therapeutic intervention with patients suffering from acquired neurological problems depends on three primary factors: (1) the quality of service being delivered, (2) the patient's neurological deficits, and (3) the patient's support network (e.g., family and friends). As Bollinger (1983) stated, however, "There are few areas of communicative intervention in which the clinician's personal feelings influence treatment as much as they do in the management of the aphasic individual . . . . [The] intervention process is closely related to the clinician's philosophy of aphasia treatment, the amount and type of clinical experience, and ability to observe and modify behavior in various contexts" (p. ix). Because of the lack of bilingual personnel, the Spanish-speaking staff member or consultant to the case may function as the spokesperson for the entire treatment team.

The bilingual speech-language clinician can apply the same treatment principles to bilingual patients as are applied to English-speaking monolingual patients, provided that sociocultural and sociolinguistic factors are taken into account. Including family members in the intervention is crucial. In this manner, the clinician can be more certain that a planned program will be followed once the patient is dismissed from the hospital.

The process of rehabilitation should include strategies both to teach and to facilitate processes to reestablish communicative competence. As for children and adolescents, the focus of intervention strategies for adults with acquired neurological disorders has shifted from form to the functional aspects of communication. Thus, for example, Ulatowska and Bond (1983) suggested that "traditional sentence level activities be incorporated along with discourse level tasks" (p. 33). Furthermore, it is necessary to consider pragmatic factors, such as (1) initiating and sustaining a conversation, (2) using contextual information to understand and produce messages as a situation may require, and (3) clarifying or asking for clarification (Davis, 1986; Wilcox, 1983). Although pragmatic competence may be relatively intact in certain aphasic patients, therapy may be required to develop communicative rather than purely linguistic competence. For example, using the model for promoting aphasic communicative effectiveness developed by Davis and Wilcox (1981), which focuses on aspects of communication such as the exchange of new information, equal participation by the clinician and patient, and free choice in selecting a channel to convey a specific piece of information rather than on linguistic accuracy, has assisted patients in achieving higher degrees of linguistic competence and is helpful in delineating paths for intervention. Other models to foster communication, such as the functional communication treatment (Aten, 1986), can be applied. Aten (1986) contrasted traditional and functional communication strategies, as shown in Table 10-1.

Other intervention approaches that can be very successful include the cognitive model, which focuses on increasing vocabulary retrieval and retention span, enhancing skills attributed to the right hemisphere function, and providing highly redundant conversational settings that allow the patient to retrieve as much as possible from the nonlinguistic aspects of the situation (Fitch-West, 1983). Overall, Fitch-West suggested a combination of approaches to enhance both right and left hemisphere processing strategies "with an emphasis on intact functioning rather than an emphasis on impairment" (p. 63). When therapy stresses very specific

Table 10-1 Comparison of Traditional Treatment and Functional Communication Treatment

Traditional Treatment	Functional Communication Treatment
1. Major focus on language	1. Major focus on communication
2. Clinician is more often in the role of stimulator/facilitator and initiates and directs linguistic based exchanges (Schuell et al., 1964; Sarno et al., 1970)	2. Clinician is more often in the role of an alternating listener-speaker (dyadic) and creates situations requiring equal participation from patient (Davis and Wilcox, 1981)
3. Goal is to improve comprehension of language (spoken, written) via stimulation of input modalities to successful criterion level (Marshall, 1981)	3. Goal is to maximize comprehension of informational exchanges by enriching context of natural conversation accompanied by writing and gesture (Fitch-West, 1983; Wilcox, 1983)
4. Goal is to improve spoken and written language by improving propositional word retrieval and increasing length/completeness of utterance (Schuell et al., 1964; Duffy, 1981)	4. Goal is to improve effectiveness of patient's getting message across and language is only one of several possible communicative channels (Davis, 1983; Holland, 1977, 1983)
5. Frequently uses Cloze and other convergent/confrontative approaches to increase available vocabulary	5. Encourages divergent utterances or circumlocutions stimulated by general situational cues and interrogative probes, accepting related, holophrastic, and prosodic productions (Beyn and Shokhor-Trotskaya, 1966; Chapey, 1981; Martin, 1981)
6. Most treatment conducted in individual, clinical settings using pictorial and/or printed stimuli; reduced emphasis on personal relevancy of lexicon or grammar	6. Treatment conducted in settings as natural as possible including groups and when contrived situations are employed, they simulate real-life scenes/content and stress functional communicative content (Holland, 1980, 1983; Ulatowska and Bond, 1983)
7. Treatment based upon analysis of individual patient's profiles of language strengths and deficits from results of formal language tests; selects preferred input/output modalities for language reception/production (Porch, 1981)	7. Treatment based upon formal language test results but also stresses use of functional measures of communicative ability (CADL, FCP, discourse analysis, observation of patient's communicative performance in real-life settings) (Lubinski, 1981; Holland, 1982; Davis, 1983; Ulatowska and Bond, 1983)

Source: From *Language Intervention Strategies in Adult Aphasia,* 2nd ed., (p. 268) by R. Chapey (ed.), 1986, Baltimore, MD: Williams & Wilkins. Copyright 1986 by Williams & Wilkins. Reprinted by permission.

aspects of communication, such as comprehension skills, the patient should be asked to recall main ideas rather than details. Materials with high imagery and personal relevance are also useful (Brookshire, 1987).

With the ever advancing field of technology, computers are becoming important tools in the intervention process. Although the availability of software in Spanish is very limited, several software packages allow the clinician to create a file to meet the unique needs of a patient. Some programs are difficult to adapt because of the different language, but software in Spanish used for school-aged children may be useful. Computerized material enables the patient to practice certain skills that otherwise would be difficult to access. It is still the clinician's role to develop and plan this program carefully, however.

There is an extreme scarcity of published materials that are designed specifically for Hispanic adults with communicative disorders, but a few resources are available (Table 10-2). Some of the materials, such as the *Manual Terapéutico para el Adulto con Dificultades del Habla y Lenguaje* (Kilpatrick, Jones, & Reller, 1982), are written in Spanish and have no English translations in the same volume. This material is useful for fully bilingual clinicians who have a thorough command of Spanish. Other resources are translated and adapted for the Hispanic population, while still others provide texts in both Spanish and English, such as *El Habla después de una Embolia* (Stryker, 1985). The latter are useful for clinicians who may have a partial command of Spanish and can refer to the English text to follow along as an interpreter/translator or family member assists the patient.

Texts that have English and Spanish versions come in two different formats. Some present the material in both languages with one language following the other on the same page. This may be advantageous for patients who can rely on one language to mediate the other in the earlier stage of recovery by referring visually to the written material or for patients who were equally fluent in both languages prior to their injury. It is also useful to clinicians who feel more comfortable with the English material, but want to enhance their own knowledge of Spanish. In the other format, the English and Spanish materials are on opposite pages. This is helpful when the clinician wants to control the modality of the language in the course of therapy.

The majority of these materials focus on the form of language. There is a critical need for materials in Spanish that emphasize the functional use of language, such as programs that would assist patients to gain as much independence as possible (e.g., asking for help to have access to their wheelchair, requesting specific food items both at home and at a restaurant, or describing their health status). It is crucial that the clinician adopt a pragmatic-functional approach to therapy that will best meet the needs of the client.

One major difference between the treatment of adults with communication difficulties and the treatment of children is in the use of languages in the intervention process. With younger children, it is recommended that only one language be used at a time to develop one language system maximally. With adults who had command of both languages prior to their injury, using the languages alternatively is

Table 10-2 Intervention Materials Available in Spanish

Publications	Publishers	Comments
Ejercicios de Lenguaje para Adultos	Chason Publishers 3410 Purdue St. Hyattsville, MD 20783	Manual designed for use with language-impaired Spanish-speaking adolescents and adults. The manual includes exercises for receptive, expressive, reading, and writing skills.
Ejercicios para las Destrezas de Comunicación (EDC)	P and R Publications P.O. Box 3127 Escondido, CA 92025	Manual with exercises in five language areas, including, among others, vocabulary, reading, and writing. The first half of the book is exclusively in Spanish; the second, in English.
El Habla después de una Embolia	Stryker Illustrations 1688 Meridian Ave., Suite 307 Miami Beach, FL 33139	Manual for the rehabilitation of the stroke patient, Spanish and English versions. The manual includes material to improve comprehension articulation, vocabulary, reading, and writing
Illustrated Vocabulary Levels 1 and 2	The National Hispanic University 255 East 14th St. Oakland, CA 94606	Illustrations and terminology related to concepts such as human body, family, home, people, school, transportation, numbers. Level 1 is useful for beginners at any age. Levels 2 and 3 contain key words and survival language.
Initial Sounds in Spanish	Ideal School Supply Company 11000 S. Lavergne Ave. Oak Lawn, IL 60453	Word/picture series of 352 cards to reinforce pronunciation of Spanish words. The written words are on the back in both languages. Spanish dialectal words are included as well.
Janus Survival Vocabulary Series	Janus Book Publishers 2501 Industrial Parkway West Hayward, CA 94545	Ten workbooks to teach vocabulary and phrases for specific situations, such as supermarket, job application, restaurant, bank, driver's license, medical facility, and drugstore.
Language Rehabilitation Program	DLM Teaching Resources One DLM Park Allen, TX 75002	Two-level program for mildly impaired adult aphasics that assists in retrieval of specific sentence structures.

continues

Publications	Publishers	Comments
Manual Terapéutico para el Adulto con Dificultades del Habla y Lenguaje	Visiting Nurses Service, Inc. 1200 McArthur Drive Akron, OH 44320	Spanish version of the therapy guide for English-speaking adults. The manual includes same sections, such as expressive, receptive, reading, and writing exercises.
Picture Communication Symbols Spanish translation	Mayer-Johnson Company P.O. Box AD Solana Beach, CA 92130	A reusable set of picture symbols specifically for nonverbal communication. The words above the symbols are in Spanish, and the guide is only in English.
Places and Things: Household Items	Modern Education Corporation P.O. Box 721 Tulsa, OK 74101	In Spanish and English. Pictures of common items from the kitchen, bathroom; men's and women's personal effects are included.

frequently very useful to trigger the recall of words and to facilitate language processing as well as expression. The sequential use of two languages may not always be appropriate for adults, however. The language that is appropriate for intervention depends on three components: (1) premorbid language history, (2) relative strengths and weaknesses in each language, and (3) environmental factors at the time of discharge (e.g., the family constellation, ability to sustain a job). Language of intervention for adults is an important area to consider for further systematic research.

CASE STUDIES

Case of J.C.

J.C. was a 58-year-old Mexican-American man whose Spanish and English were equally impaired. He regained the languages in a synergistic recovery pattern; he was able to express some of his needs in Spanish, but not in English following his stroke.

J.C. was born, raised, and married in Mexico. He emigrated to the United States when he was 32 years old. Prior to that time, he had never been exposed to English. After moving to the United States, he worked as a foreman for a construction company and learned English to a functional level that allowed him to converse freely on everyday topics. Spanish continued to be the language that he used in his home and with his children. J.C. had completed fifth grade in Mexico, but never had an opportunity to further his formal education. Prior to his stroke, however, he had enjoyed reading in Spanish and was interested in reading about and freely conversing on diverse subjects.

J.C. sustained a lesion of 3 x 2 cm over the left midtemporal lobe, as was evident on his CT scans. Yet, his language deficits involved receptive and expressive areas, with English, his second language, being more severely impaired than Spanish. J.C.'s test results are presented in Table 10-3. As can be noted, J.C. initially was moderately to severely impaired receptively and expressively in English, but relatively less impaired in Spanish. His recovery was characteristic of synergistic improvement in which both languages return at the same time, but the originally dominant language (Spanish) maintains its dominance over the second (English).

Because J.C.'s language skills in Spanish were not as affected as his skills in English were, all initial intervention took place in Spanish. A home program was developed in Spanish to allow maximal communication with family members. At first, activities centered on everyday events, including routines such as getting dressed, having meals, and getting in and out of his wheelchair. Many visual cues and repetitions were provided as well. The complexity of output gradually increased until J.C. could describe pictures in books and magazines and could read

Table 10-3 J.C.'s Linguistic Profile

Area	Percentiles	
	Spanish	English
Auditory comprehension		
Word discrimination	70	30
Body part identification	60	30
Commands	60	20
Paragraph level	40	10
Naming		
Responsive naming	70	40
Confrontation	50	20
Animal naming	70	40
Oral reading		
Word reading	80	40
Sentence reading	30	0
Repetition		
Words	60	20
High-probability sentences	70	30
Low-probability sentences	90	50
Automatic speech		
Sequences	70	60

headlines, titles, and short sentences. Material was taken from books brought from his home on topics of interest to him, such as hunting, mechanics, building, and construction design. Eventually, when J.C. was able to communicate his basic needs and feelings in Spanish, the clinician began to introduce English so that he could communicate with his grandchildren, who did not understand or speak Spanish. The therapy was designed to increase J.C.'s functional communication so that he would feel at ease with his family and in his immediate surroundings. Also, efforts were made to teach him to follow written directions so that he could complete some of his manual projects. Eventually, therapy centered on higher level language skills, such as associations and specific word recall.

As can be noted in the language profile, J.C. had impaired skills in all areas of oral and written communication in spite of the fact that the preliminary CT scan showed a temporal lobe infarction that would be expected to cause primarily auditory-receptive deficits. Intervention centered on a multimodality approach. Fortunately, J.C. was able to recover his language sufficiently to communicate satisfactorily with the members of his family, but he continued to have considerable difficulty in English. He was never able to return to his same level of employment because of a residual weakness in the upper and lower extremities. His family was supportive and assisted him in gaining as much independence as was possible, however.

Case of Sister C.R.

Sister C.R. was a bilingual woman who, following a stroke, was unable to express herself at first in English, but could comprehend conversational Spanish and English.

Sister C.R. was born in Central Mexico and lived in a remote town most of her life. She had never been exposed to English before her arrival in the United States at the age of 20 years. Sister C.R. settled in a suburb of San Francisco where she stayed in a convent for the remainder of her life. Because the other sisters at the convent did not speak Spanish, Sister C.R. lost total contact with the language. On the day that she sustained her stroke, Sister C.R. was visiting friends. She was immediately transferred to the nearby hospital.

The clinical examination of Sister C.R. showed that she had sustained a left hemispheric CVA, resulting in right-sided weakness, aphasia, right homonymous hemianopsia, and a right sensory deficit. She appeared lethargic. A neurodiagnostic assessment indicated that there was damage in the reception, processing, and association pathways. Her tongue was deviated to the right, and she had right central weakness. Although a CT scan done on the day of the admission showed no cerebral anomalies, a subsequent MRI scan revealed an area of infarction in the left basal ganglia that included the caudate nucleus, internal capsule, putamen, and possibly a portion of the dorsomedial nucleus of the thalamus. The MRI revealed that the anterior corpus callosum and, possibly, the hypothalamus were involved, as shown in the left midsaggital sections circled on the second and third frames of Figure 10-1.

Sister C.R. was extremely cooperative during the diagnostic evaluation. English and Spanish versions of the Boston Diagnostic Aphasia Examination were used, in addition to some informal assessments. Language samples were also obtained in both languages. Sister C.R. presented a rare and peculiar form of aphasia, as the impairment was different in both languages. English, which had been acquired more recently, was more impaired in verbal expression; Spanish, which was her first language and rarely used, was relatively intact.

A very tranquil person, Sister C.R. tried her best to communicate. At first, her Spanish was labored, and her English was almost nonexistent. She tried to be as independent as possible by moving from one location to another in her wheelchair. She had many daily visitors and also attempted to communicate with them. Her recovery pattern conformed to Ribot's (1882) early theory to some extent. She appeared aware of her difficulties and could describe them with some detail in Spanish, as indicated in the following language sample:

Clinician: Sister C.R., I want you to tell me what the convent is like. How many different people are there?

Sister C.R.: *** *hablan español, muy bien. Pero el español quere* *** *todo en inglés* '*** They speak Spanish, very well. But the Spanish want *** everything in English'.

Clinician: How many sisters are there?

Sister C.R.: *** Well, *yo* *** *son treinta y dos* 'Well, I *** there are thirty-two'.

Clinician: Treinta y dos? Thirty-two?

Sister C.R.: Thirty-two, *me parece . . . Pode son treinta y tres, treinta y cuatro . . .yo la verdad no sé ahorita* 'Thirty-two, I think . . . Perhaps thirty-three, thirty-four . . . to tell the truth I don't know right now'.

Clinician: Where is it located?

Sister C.R.: En . . . en Menlo Park. *Eh, pues yo no sé decirle cómo es, es en español, pero es en* Menlo Park. *Eh para ver si ya viene y es como*

Note: Asterisks (***) are unintelligible words; underlined words are incorrect grammar or word use. Translations are literal.

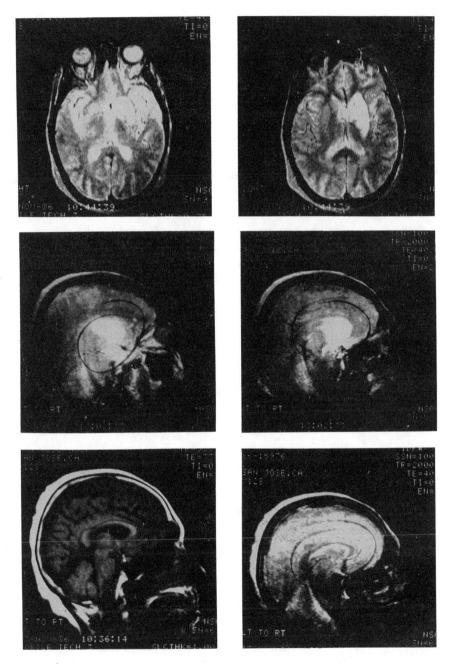

Figure 10-1 MRI scans of patient C.R.

vinieron la primera vez, dieron sus *** 'In Menlo Park. Eh, well, I don't know what to tell you what it's like, it's in Spanish, but it is in Menlo Park. Eh, to see if you come, and that's how they came the first time, they gave ***'.

Clinician: Of the thirty-two or thirty-three people that are there, how many of them speak Spanish?

Sister C.R.: '*Orita todas, todas hablan el español* 'Now all, all speak Spanish' [Sister C.R. really meant to say English].

Clinician: They do?

Sister C.R.: Yeah, *todas hablan el español muy bien mismo que el inglés no lo hablan todas lo mismo porque pues sí comprenden que el español es tan solo, una, una relación para con Dios el español que usa allí y muy pocas veces podemos, podemos enseñar así tenemos que hablar el inglés en español* 'Yeah, all speak Spanish very well, the same as English they do not speak it all of them because they do understand that it is Spanish only, one, one relation with God is Spanish that is used there and very seldom can we, can we teach it so we have to speak English in Spanish.'

Clinician: So you speak English almost all the time? Very few times you speak Spanish? How many years have you been there?

Sister C.R.: Oh, let me see . . . *cincuenta y cuatro* Oh, let me see . . . fifty-four.

Clinician: Fifty-four? You've been at the convent for fifty-four years?

Sister C.R.: Yes.

Clinician: So, where did you come from before. Where were you living?

Sister C.R.: *En* ***, *en . . . cómo se llama el otro lugar yo me vivo . . . en . . . po,* *** 'In ***, in *** . . . what is the name of the other place I live . . . in . . . well, ***'

Clinician: Mexico?

Sister C.R.: *México, sí, México. Por es una, una poblacioncita muy chiquita que no fui por algunos años hasta que nos dieron el permiso del . . . que llegó con el permiso de que no más* *** *sobre* *** *pas, el segundo, el primer año que fue el año del consagra* *** *no el año que, que . . . pues* *** *la existencia de otro camino también había llegado* 'Mexico, yes, Mexico. It is a little town very small that I didn't go to for several years until they gave us permission to . . . that it arrived with the permission that only *** on *** well, the second, the first year that the was the year of consa . . . no, the year that, that *** well the existence of the other route it also had arrived'.

Sister C.R. initiated some of her statements in English, but quickly reverted to Spanish. Also, she showed some confusion and had difficulty expressing her ideas in conversation. There were repetitions and evidence of word finding problems. In addition, she responded in Spanish to questions that the clinician asked in English. The clinician continued to use English in that conversation in order to assess Sister C.R.'s receptive skills in English and encourage her eventually to switch to that language as well. At the time of the evaluation, Sister C.R. did not show left facial weakness as she had during her initial examination at admission. Retraction of her lips was symmetrical, and the rate of repetitive movements, such as /pa-ta-ka/, was adequate. She did complain of reduced sensation on the right side. Results of the communication-based testing appear in Table 10-4.

On numerous occasions, Sister C.R. expressed concern that her comprehension of English conversation was not adequate and that she needed extra time to think about what was said. She also reported that repetition and expansion improved her comprehension. She could express these thoughts, although she used a high pro-

Table 10-4 Sister C.R.'s Linguistic Profile

	Percentiles	
Area	Spanish	English
Auditory comprehension		
Word discrimination	30	30
Body part identification	60	30
Commands	60	50
Paragraph level	60	50
Naming		
Responsive naming	90	55
Confrontation naming	95	20
Oral reading		
Word reading	80	50
Oral sentence reading	50	50
Repetition		
Words	90	90
High-probability sentences	90	70
Low-probability sentences	100	70
Automatic speech		
Sequences	90	90

portion of jargon language while she conversed. Long-term memory was not formally assessed, but she had no difficulty recalling long-term biographical information (e.g., historical events, family). Tasks that required short-term memory were apparently not difficult for her either. She was able to recognize therapists and recalled newly learned tasks fairly quickly.

The test results clearly indicated that Sister C.R.'s Spanish language skills were better in all processes than were her English language skills. In some language areas, such as oral sentence reading, repetition tasks, and sequences in automatic speech, her skills were equivalent in both languages, however. Her expressive language in English was characterized by so many paraphasias that it interfered with intelligibility, but she could repeat model sentences quite well, even in English. Her naming skills in Spanish were increased by the use of Spanish as the language of intervention. Her auditory comprehension was low in both languages, but she performed better when more context was provided and also during conversation.

The two languages were used sequentially in the therapy sessions. In working on auditory sequencing, for example, numbers were rehearsed in one language and then immediately in the second. A similar technique was used to work on sentence completion and association-type tasks. The emphasis was on functional communication in order to ease her into her daily living activities. Sister C.R. continued to enjoy reading the *Bible* and worked on memorizing and recalling passages that she already knew; she did this latter activity in English only, because English had been the language that she had used most recently in that context. The use of both languages during therapy enabled her to have maximal language input and, in her case, did not confuse her. The use of visual cues and language expansion techniques assisted her in regaining both receptive and expressive skills in both languages.

Eventually, Sister C.R. regained her ability to communicate in both languages at a conversational level, but her proficiency was never as high as before the onset of her CVA. Her speech continued to be characterized by the hesitations and transpositions of words that were apparent in both languages at the time of her dismissal from the hospital. One advantage that bilingual persons have is that working in the more dominant language can mediate learning of the other language, however.

Case of D.S.

A 56-year-old Hispanic man, D.S. sustained a left hemispheric CVA that involved an infarction of approximately 3 to 4 cm in the left posterior temporal lobe.

D.S. had been born in Arizona, but had learned and spoken Spanish in the home until he enrolled in an elementary school in New Mexico at age 6 years. Instruction was conducted entirely in English. He completed eighth grade. As an adult, he married an English-speaking monolingual woman, and his children were raised speaking only English in the home. In fact, as adults they did not understand conversational Spanish. Thus, as an adult D.S. had spoken only English and had not spoken Spanish a great deal. Following his stroke, his family could not communicate with him at all, as Spanish was the only language that returned initially. D.S. stated numerous times with considerable difficulty and paraphasias, *"Pero no me sale nada en inglés. ¿Cómo puede ser?"* 'But I can't get anything out in English. How can this be?'

D.S.'s communication skills are listed in Table 10-5. His profile is that of a patient severely involved across most modalities. He lost all skills in English. His speech was fluently articulated, but contained many paraphasias and neologisms. His intelligibility was very low.

Because D.S.'s language skills were so depressed in English, it was virtually impossible to use English in the initial stages of his therapeutic program. Most of the sessions were conducted in Spanish. Subsequently, the English counterparts were used in conjunction with the Spanish terms or phrases. Over the following 2 months, English began to reemerge. As D.S. began to regain his skills in English,

Table 10-5 D.S.'s Linguistic Profile

	Percentiles	
Area	Spanish	English
Auditory comprehension		
Word discrimination	30	0
Body part identification	30	0
Commands	20	0
Paragraph level	0	0
Naming		
Responsive naming	30	0
Confrontation naming	20	0
Animal naming	30	0
Oral reading		
Word reading	40	0
Oral sentence reading	0	0
Repetition		
Words	20	0
High-probability sentences	30	0
Low-probability sentences	50	0
Automatic speech		
Sequences	30	20

his family could participate directly in the therapy sessions. Prior to that time, his communication with his family was almost nonexistent because of the loss of English. D.S. gradually recovered his command of expressive English over the following 2 months, conforming to a successive recovery pattern. His residual impairments 6 months after the CVA were essentially equal in both languages. The two languages had recovered to a relatively equal level of functioning after approximately 12 weeks.

Like Sister C.R., D.S. had been able to read books and magazines before the CVA. Both also had at least average narrative writing skills. This is not always true with the geriatric Hispanic population, particularly with those who are first-generation immigrants. In these cases, however, it was possible to use not only auditory and visual cues during the treatment sessions, but also written language cues for recall of words. When the patient's education is limited, most if not all treatment must be done auditorally.

Case of J.P.

When a patient has a neurologically progressive disease, which slowly affects the patient, the family must adjust to changes in a different manner than in cases of CVA.

J.P. was referred to a rehabilitation center because both her primary physician and her family had noted increasing signs of apathy in her. She was no longer interested in visiting with friends, eating, or even watching TV, which she had previously enjoyed. In the past, J.P. and her husband had been very active in their community, had many friends, and had participated in many social events. As time went on, family and friends observed that J.P. was often "daydreaming."

The findings obtained from CT scans, blood tests, and tests of body fluids were unremarkable. Antidepressants were administered to improve her mood, but their effectiveness proved to be limited. A progressive degenerative disease was suspected. Testing of communication skills indicated low performance across all modalities. At the onset of her disease, J.P. had been more fluent in Spanish, but ultimately Spanish and English were equally affected. In fact, the gradual impairment resembled that of a reverse synergetic recovery. J.P.'s primary characteristics were her loss of cognitive functioning and her failure to initiate activity, both of which are often observed in patients with frontal lobe deficits. In these cases, patients lose their ability to stay on task, lack motivation to participate in any activity, and become passive altogether.

In a case such as J.P.'s, family members must be involved and support the patient as much as possible. Great emphasis was placed on maintaining J.P.'s memory skills for biographical information, describing her immediate environment in the home and the hospital, and exposing her to activities that she had previously enjoyed. J.P.'s mental functioning continued to decrease over the following 5 years, and it was ultimately necessary for her family to place her in a residential treatment center for the elderly. This decision was complicated by her family's protectiveness and desire to take care of her. She came from a background where elderly persons were never placed outside their homes. This required an extra adjustment on the part of her children and family. Their Hispanic background, which strongly emphasized family ties, very likely rendered this type of decision even more difficult.

FUTURE TRENDS

The research on the assessment and intervention process for Hispanic adults who suffer from a variety of acquired neurological disabilities is almost nonexistent. A seminal article with remarks that the author has humbly referred to as "more common-sense oriented and experiential than scholarly" (Holland, 1983, p. 69) still applies today when working with the older population, particularly with older members of different cultural or linguistic groups.

- "In the absence of corroborating evidence, make the fewest possible assumptions" (Holland, 1983, p. 70). For example, not all Hispanics come from Mexico, are poor, and have a low level of formal education.
- Take into account the patient's linguistic history. Gather information regarding the use and proficiency of each language prior to the accident.
- "Be sensitive to cultural differences in response to the elderly in regard to disability and in response to fear and anxiety" (Holland, 1983, p. 72). For example, respect the wishes and requests of the patient. Some may not acquire independence and may prefer to spend time on activities different from those planned by the clinician or the family.
- Consider that some of what the patient may say "reflects earlier styles of communication or has occurred as a result of aging" (Holland, 1983, p. 73).

Clearly, speaking the language of patients is not as important as understanding the culture, beliefs, and attitudes of their ethnic group and the possible individual variations.

Further research needs to be conducted regarding assessment practices with this population, the course and the best language(s) of intervention, and the design of materials that focus on functional language development and can be used in the home by the patient's family. Also, further information on the treatment of Hispanic head-injured patients, as well as those suffering from different types of dementia, is needed. The relatively few clinicians who are involved in working with this segment of the population have the opportunity to do significant and important research and to develop useful diagnostic and treatment materials.

As the "graying" of America continues in the years to come, there will be a greater demand for speech-language clinicians who can work with the adult population. These professionals must be prepared to work with a multicultural and multilingual population as well. By the year 2000, 13% of the population will be 65 years old or older; the number of those 80 years old and older will be increased by 400% by the year 2025. Life expectancy will increase as well. Predictions are that at least 72% of patients will be cared for by their spouses or families. The health care process and provision of services will be greatly changed (Shadden et al., 1990).

REFERENCES

Albert, M., & Obler, L. (1978). *The bilingual brain.* New York: Academic Press.

American Speech-Language-Hearing Association. (1989). Office of minority concerns newsletter, 10(1). Rockville, MD: American Speech-Language-Hearing Association.

Aten, J.L. (1986). Functional communication treatment. In R. Chapey (Ed.), *Language intervention strategies in adult aphasia* (2nd ed.). Baltimore: Williams & Wilkins.

Audio-Forum. (Ed.). (1991). *Medical Spanish* [Cassettes, listener's guide and text]. Guilford, CT: Audio-Forum.

Beyn, E.S., & Shokhor-Trotskaya, M.K. (1966). Preventive method of speech rehabilitation in aphasia. *Cortex, 2,* 96–108.

Bollinger, R.L. (1983). Foreword. *Topics in Language Disorders, 3,* ix–xi.

Brookshire, R.H. (1987). Auditory language comprehension disorders in aphasia. *Topics in Language Disorders, 8*(1), 11–23.

Bryden, M.P. (1982). *Laterality: Functional asymmetry in the intact brain.* New York: Academic Press.

Burns, M., Halper, A., & Mogil, S. (1983). *Communication problems in the right hemispheric brain damage: Diagnostic treatment approaches.* Chicago: Education and Training Center, Rehabilitation Institute of Chicago.

Chapey, R. (1986). *Language intervention strategies in adult aphasia* (2nd ed.). Baltimore, MD: Williams & Wilkins.

Chusid, J.G. (1982). *Correlative neuroanatomy and functional neurology.* Los Altos, CA: Lange Medical Publications.

Cummings, J.L., & Benson, D.F. (1983). *Dementia: A clinical approach.* Boston: Butterworth.

Damasio, A.R. (1984). Behavioral neurology: Research and practice. *Seminars in Neurology, 4,* 117–119.

Davis, G.A. (1983). *A survey of adult aphasia.* Englewood Cliffs, NJ: Prentice Hall.

Davis, G.A. (1986). Pragmatics and treatment. In R. Chapey (Ed.), *Language intervention strategies in adult aphasia* (2nd ed.). Baltimore: Williams & Wilkins.

Davis, G., & Wilcox, M. (1981). Incorporating parameters of natural conversation in aphasia treatment. In R. Chapey (Ed.), *Language intervention strategies in adult aphasia*. Baltimore: Williams & Wilkins.

De Renzi, E., & Vignolo, L.A. (1977). The Token Test (revised): A sensitive test to detect receptive disturbances in aphasia. *Brain, 85,* 665–672.

DiLorenzo-Kearon, M.A., & Kearon, T.P. (1981). *Medical Spanish: A conversational approach.* New York: Harcourt Brace Jovanovich.

Dreifuss, F. (1961). Observations on aphasia in a polyglot poet. *Acta Psychiatrica Scandinavia, 36,* 91–97.

Duffy, J. (1986). Schuell's stimulation approach to rehabilitation. In R. Chapey (Ed.), *Language intervention strategies in adult aphasia* (2nd ed.). Baltimore, MD: Williams & Wilkins.

Figueroa, R.A., & Ruíz, N.T. (1983). *The bilingual special education dictionary: A resource for special educators and parents.* Oakland, CA: The National Hispanic University.

Fitch-West, J. (1983). Aphasia: Cognitive considerations. *Topics in Language Disorders, 3*(4), 49–66.

Gazzaniga, M.S., Nass, R., Reeves, A., & Roberts, D. (1984). Neurologic perspectives on right hemisphere language following surgical section of the corpus callosum. *Seminars in Neurology, 4,* 126–135.

Goldstein, K. (1948). Disturbances of language in polyglot individuals with aphasia. In K. Goldstein (Ed.), *Language and language disturbances.* New York: Grune & Stratton.

Goodglass, H., & Kaplan, E. (1983). *Boston Diagnostic Aphasia Examination.* Philadelphia: Lea & Febiger.

Hagen, C. (1984). Language disorders in head trauma. In Holland, A. (Ed.), *Language disorders in adults* (pp. 247–281). San Diego, CA: College Hill Press.

Halpern, L. (1941). Beitrag zur Restitution der Aphasie bei Polyglotten im Hinblick auf das Hebraeische. *Schweizer Archiv fuer Neurologie und Psychiatrie, 47,* 150–154.

Holland, A. (1977). Some practical considerations in aphasia rehabilitation. In M. Sullivan & M. Kommers (Eds.), *Rationale for adult aphasia therapy.* Omaha, NE: University of Nebraska Medical Center Print Shop.

Holland, A. (1980). *Communicative abilities in daily living (CADL).* Baltimore: University Park Press.

Holland, A. (1983). Language intervention in adults: What is it? In J. Miller, D. Yoder, & R. Schiefelbusch (Eds.), *Contemporary issues in language intervention* (Report No. 12). Rockville, MD: American Speech-Language-Hearing Association.

Holland, A. (1983). Nonbiased assessment and treatment of adults who have neurologic speech and language problems. *Topics in Language Disorders, 3*(3), 67–75.

Keefe, S., & Casas, M. (1980). Mexican-Americans and mental health: A select review and recommendations for mental health service delivery. *American Journal of Community Psychology, 8,* 303–326.

Keenan, J.S., & Brassell, E.G. (1974). A study of factors related to prognosis for individual aphasic patients. *Journal of Speech and Hearing Disorders, 39,* 257–269.

Kety, S. (1979). Disorders of the human brain. *Scientific American, 241,* 120–127.

Kilpatrick, K., Jones, C.L., & Reller, J. (1982). *Manual terapéutico para el adulto con dificultades del habla y lenguaje—Tomo 1* (translated by I. Bahler & G.K. Gatto). Akron, OH: Visiting Nurse Service.

Lecours, A.R., L'Hermitte, S., & Bryans, L. (1983). Aphasia in bilinguals and polyglots. In M. Paradis (Ed.), *Readings on aphasia in bilinguals and polyglots.* Montreal: Marcel Didier.

Lefly, H.P. (1985). Families of the mentally ill in cross-cultural perspective. *Psychosocial Rehabilitation Journal, 8,* 57–75.

Lubinski, R. (1981). Environmental language intervention. In R. Chapey (Ed.), *Language intervention strategies in adult aphasia.* Baltimore, MD: Williams & Wilkins.

Manuel, R.C., & Reid, J. (1982). A comparative demographic profile of the minority and non-minority aged. In R. Manuel (Ed.), *Minority aging: Sociological and social psychological perspectives.* Westport, CT: Greenwood Press.

Marshall, M.H., & Rojas, L. (1982). *Exámenes para diagnosticar impedimentos de afasia* (Adaptation from Aphasia Performance by S. Keenan and E. Brassell). Murfreesboro, TN: Pinnacle Press.

Marshall, R. (1981). Heightening auditory comprehension for aphasic patients. In R. Chapey (Ed.), *Language intervention strategies in adult aphasia.* Baltimore, MD: Williams & Wilkins.

Martin, A.D. (1981). An examination of Wepman's thought centered therapy. In R. Chapey (Ed.), *Language intervention strategies in adult aphasia.* Baltimore, MD: Williams & Wilkins.

Mattes, L. (1986). *Bilingual language, speech, and hearing dictionary.* Oceanside, CA: Academic Communication Associates.

McNeil, M. (1983). Aphasia: Neurological considerations. *Topics in Language Disorders, 3*(4), 1–20.

Minkowski, M. (1963). *On aphasia in polyglots: Problems of dynamic neurology.* Jerusalem: Hebrew University.

Paradis, M. (1977). Bilingualism and aphasia. In H. Whitaker & H.A. Whitacker (Eds.), *Studies in neurolinguistics,* vol. 3. New York: Academic Press.

Paradis, M. (1983). *Readings on aphasia in bilinguals and polyglots.* Montreal: Didier.

Paradis, M. (1987). *Bilingual aphasia test.* Hillsdale, NJ: Lawrence Erlbaum Associates.

Pérez-Stable, E.J. (1987). Issues in latino health care: Medical staff conference, University of California, San Francisco. *Western Journal of Medicine, 2,* 213–218.

Pitres, A. (1895). Etude sur l'aphasie chez les polyglottes. *Revue Médicale, 15,* 873.

Porch, B.E. (1981a). Therapy subsequent to the PICA. In R. Chapey (Ed.), *Language intervention strategies in adult aphasia.* Baltimore, MD: Williams & Wilkins.

Porch, B.E. (1981b). *Porch index of communicative ability (PICA).* Palo Alto, CA: Consulting Psychologists Press.

Ribot, T. (1882). *Diseases of memory: An essay in the positive psychology.* London: Paul.

Sarno, M.T. (1969). *The functional communication profile: Manual of direction (FCT).* New York: Institute of Rehabilitative Medicine, New York University Medical Center.

Sarno, M.T., Silverman, M., & Sands, E. (1970). Speech therapy and language recovery in severe aphasia. *Journal of Speech and Hearing Disorders, 13,* 607–623.

Savariego, B. (1985). *Spanish for health professionals* [Videotape]. Dallas, TX: University of Texas Health Science Center.

Schorr, A.E. (1989). *Hispanic resource directory.* Juneau, AK: Delani Press.

Schuell, H. (1972). *The Minnesota test for differential diagnosis of aphasia (MTDDA).* Minneapolis: University of Minnesota Press.

Schuell, H., Jenkins, K., & Jiménez-Pabón, E. (1964). *Aphasia in adults.* New York: Harper & Row.

Schur, C., Bernstein, A., & Berk, M. (1987). The importance of distinguishing Hispanic subpopulations in the use of medical care. *Medical Care, 25,* 627–641.

Schwartz-Cowley, R., & Stepanik, J.J. (1989). Communication disorders and treatment in the acute trauma center setting. *Topics in Language Disorders, 9*(2), 1–14.

Select Committee on Aging, House of Representatives, 100th Congress. (1989). *Demographic charac- teristics of the older Hispanic population*. Washington, DC: U.S. Government Printing Office.

Shadden, B., Herer, G., Kemper, S., Holland, A., Obler, L., Au, R., & Chapman, S. (November 1990). *Advances in language and communication research with older adults*. Miniseminar presented at the ASHA Convention in Seattle.

Soares, C. (1984). Left-hemisphere language lateralization in bilinguals: Use of the activities para- digm. *Brain and Language, 23*, 86–96.

Stein, S. (1986). Medical management of cerebrovascular accidents. In R. Chapey (Ed.), *Language intervention strategies in adult aphasia* (2nd ed.). Baltimore: Williams & Wilkins.

Stryker, S. (1985). *El habla después de una embolia*. Miami, FL: Stryker Illustrations.

Trunkey, D.D. (1983). Trauma. *Scientific American, 249*, 28–35.

Ulatowska, H., & Bond, S.A. (1983). Aphasia: Discourse considerations. *Topics in Language Disor- ders, 3*(4), 21–34.

U.S. Bureau of the Census. (1989). *Statistical abstract of the U.S.* (109th ed.). Washington, DC: U.S. Government Printing Office.

U.S. Department of Health, Education and Welfare. (1980). *National survey of stroke* (NIH Publica- tion No. 80-2069). Washington, DC: U.S. Government Printing Office.

Vaid, J. (Ed.). (1986). *Language processing in bilinguals: Psycholinguistic and psychological per- spectives*. Hillsdale, NJ: Lawrence Erlbaum Associates.

Valle, R. (1989a). *Culture and ethnic issues in Alzheimer's disease family research. Alzheimer's dis- ease treatment and family stress: Directions for research* (DHHS Publication No. 89-1569). Washington, DC: U.S. Government Printing Office.

Valle, R. (1989b). U.S. ethnic minority group access to long-term care. In T. Schwab (Ed.), *Caring for an aging world: International models for long-term care, financing and delivery*. New York: McGraw-Hill.

Wilcox, M.J. (1983). Aphasia: Pragmatic considerations. *Topics in Language Disorders, 3*(4), 35–48.

Index